Commercial Transactions in the Virtual World

T0350627

New technology has challenged commercial law to adapt its traditional principles or create new solutions. These challenges are at their most extreme in the virtual world where even the very concept of property is uncertain. In this stimulating collection, Dr. Avnita Lakhani has brought together a team of commentators who skilfully blend knowledge of the virtual world realities with legal expertise to illuminate a broad range of issues. Their analysis often has a comparative flavour and, whilst invaluable for Hong Kong, it also has much to add to debates in the wider region and internationally. It deserves a wide audience of scholars and policy-makers.

Geraint HOWELLS
Professor of Commercial Law and Head of the School of Law
Manchester University

Dr. Lakhani has completed an enviable edited volume on a highly topical and unexplored topic, that of commercial transactions conducted in a virtual world environment. The contributors are well known experts in this field and I highly commend the coherent outcome that Dr. Lakhani ensured. I strongly recommend this book.

Ioannis KOKKORIS
Professor, Chair in Law and Economics
University of Reading

This is a timely work. Dr. Lakhani has harnessed a panel of expert contributors to produce a wide ranging book which explores the multifarious dimensions of virtual worlds and the implications of this fast developing phenomenon for commercial law. When I was Roy Goode's student, no one could have anticipated this brave new world and the challenges its poses not only for legal systems, honed in a different age, but also for contemporary policy makers and regulators. The editor and the contributors have admirably risen to the challenge in addressing the pressing issues which the virtual world generates. The book deserves a place in every commercial law library.

John LOWRY
Chair Professor of Commercial Law, The University of Hong Kong;
and Professor Emeritus, University College London, Faculty of Laws

The virtual world presents a series of complex challenges to traditional forms of contracting. This truly international collection of essays examines the topic from every perspective, including the making of contracts, the taking of security and dispute resolution. Dr. Lakhani is to be congratulated on her vision and thoroughness in producing this work.

Rob MERKIN
Lloyd's Professor of Commercial Law
University of Exeter

Commercial Transactions in the Virtual World

Issues and Opportunities

Avnita LAKHANI

City University of Hong Kong Press

ISBN: 978-962-937-229-3

Published by
          City University of Hong Kong Press
          Tat Chee Avenue
          Kowloon, Hong Kong
          Website: www.cityu.edu.hk/upress
          E-mail: upress@cityu.edu.hk

Printed in Hong Kong

Table of Contents

Part IX   Money Lending and Banking Virtual World

Part X   Consumer Protection
in Virtual World Transactions

Part XI   Dispute Resolution/ADR in the Virtual World

Detailed Chapter Contents

Part IX Money Lending and Banking Virtual World

Part XI   Dispute Resolution/ADR in the Virtual World

Foreword

I am pleased to be invited to provide some context for Commercial Opportunities in the Virtual World, Issues and Opportunities, edited by Prof. Avnita Lakhani of the School of Law of City University of Hong Kong (CityU). In the 2012-13 academic year, all publicly funded Hong Kong universities, including CityU, underwent an historic transition from a 3-year to a 4-year undergraduate curriculum. CityU boldly used this opportunity to create a unique Discovery-enriched Curriculum (DEC). The simple goal of the DEC is for all students to have the opportunity to make a discovery/invention/creative project in their discipline. By learning what it means to create new knowledge in their field and then by communicating, curating and cultivating that knowledge to benefit society, students experiencing the DEC have the chance to explore the unknown and to take measured risks under the guidance of their staff mentors. These characteristics of the DEC should better prepare our students for the extraordinarily dynamic world they will enter as professionals.

Prof. Lakhani's edited volume exemplifies the spirit and objectives of the DEC. Prof. Lakhani and her students have explored in detail an exciting new area of scholarship that lies at the intersection of IT law, business law and commercial law. They have examined a wide range of issues that will shape how this emerging field of virtual commercial transactions develops. By publishing their findings in this book and presenting some of this work at various international conferences, our students have also had a chance to learn how to communicate, curate, and cultivate their new-found knowledge so that others may build upon it. This blending of teaching, learning and research in which students are partners in the discovery process has broad applicability, as illustrated by the interdisciplinary nature of this topic. We hope that readers will benefit both from the content of this volume as well as from an understanding of the DEC that helped shape it. I wish all who contributed to this book continued success in exploring new frontiers of knowledge.

Arthur B. ELLIS
Provost, City University of Hong Kong
May, 2014

Acknowledgments

I would like to extend a warm and generous gratitude to several individuals and groups for their support and contribution to this project.

First and foremost, the contributing authors to this book deserve recognition and praise for pursuing an attitude of discovery and innovation in analyzing and investigating the various aspects of the commercial issues and opportunities arising in the virtual world from a local, national, and international perspective.

Second, I would like to thank Professor Arthur Ellis, Provost of City University of Hong Kong in particular and City University of Hong Kong in general, for setting the foundation of discovery and innovation through CityU's Discovery-enriched Curriculum®, a foundation which encouraged a positive, discovery-based attitude towards the investigation of the issues and opportunities arising out of commercial transactions in the virtual world.

Third, I would like to express my sincere gratitude to the distinguished and accomplished professors and practitioners who, based on their expertise, took the time to provide review comments on and endorsements for this book. Their insights and support for this project are immeasurable and a testament to the importance of advancing the fields of commercial law, information technology, and business practice as expressed through the contents of this interdisciplinary book.

Finally, I would like to extend my appreciation to the City University of Hong Kong Press (CityU Press) for their immeasurable support and enthusiasm in publishing and promoting the book to the greater local and international community.

About the Author

Dr. Lakhani has a BA (Canada), JD/MSEL cum laude (USA), LLM (USA) and PhD (Australia). She is admitted to the Bar of the State of New York and the Bar of the Supreme Court of the United States. She is an accredited mediator with HKIAC and HKMAAL and holds member status with the Chartered Institute of Arbitrators (MCIArb). Dr. Lakhani has over 20 years of international professional working experience. She has published a variety of articles dealing with critical international issues in both law and conflict resolution journals.

In addition to numerous professional and academic awards as well as several academic appointments at City University of Hong Kong (CityU), Dr. Lakhani is the Associate Program Leader of the Master of Laws in Arbitration and Dispute Resolution (LLMArbDR) Program at City University of Hong Kong School of Law. Most recently, she is also the Editor-in-Chief of the *Journal of Law, Technology and Public Policy*^{TM}, an important initiative of the Law and Technology Solutions Center, a project funded through the Office of the Provost's Idea Incubator Scheme under CityU's Discovery-Enriched Curriculum$^{®}$.

Commercial Transactions in the Virtual World

Issues and Opportunities

PART I
INTRODUCTION

1

Commercial Transactions in the Virtual World: Introduction

Avnita LAKHANI*

1. Background and Definitions

This book is about the impact of virtual world activities and transactions on commercial law. It is also an interdisciplinary look at issues arising out of the intersection of technology or IT law, commercial law, and business law as evidenced by the growing trend in virtual commercial transactions.

Virtual worlds may be defined as "digitally constructed 3D environments where users can interact with each other through a virtual user, called avatar."[1] An avatar is an online persona

---

* Assistant Professor, School of Law, City University of Hong Kong. Among other duties, Dr. Lakhani is the course leader and course examiner for the commercial law course and the principal investigator of the Law and Technology Solutions Centre project under the Idea Incubator Scheme of the Office of the Provost, City University of Hong Kong.

1 Dominik Schrank, 'A Trustful Payment System for Virtual Worlds: Design and Implementation of a Payment System for Virtual Worlds' (Master's Thesis, Graz University of Technology September 2009) 5 (citing Yesha Sivan, 'Real Virtual Worlds SOS (State of Standards) Q3–2008' (2008) 1(2) *Journal of Virtual Worlds Research*: Consumer Behavior in Virtual Worlds 11 <http://journals.tdl.org/jvwr/index.php/jvwr/article/view/359/271> accessed December 3, 2013; See also Adam Chodorow, 'Tracing Basis through Virtual Spaces' (2010) 95 Cornell L. Rev. 283, 288 (defining virtual worlds as "online spaces that permit people to interact with one another through characters they create, often called avatars.").

that represents the real person and, in the context of a game environment, plays the online game from within that role.[2] Within non-scripted virtual worlds such as Second Life®, the avatar is an artificial 3D construction of the real person who may not look like the real person at all but whose actions in the virtual world are controlled by the real person. Virtual worlds have three primary characteristics. First, virtual worlds are interactive, meaning that while the virtual world may exist on one computer or one server, it can be accessed remotely, by a large number of people, with "command inputs from one person affecting the command results of other people."[3] Second, virtual worlds provide a level of physicality that simulates the real world. In other words, people in the real world can access a virtual world program through an interface which provides a "first-person physical environment on their computer screen... [an] environment [that] is generally ruled by the natural laws of Earth and is characterized by scarcity of resources."[4] The third important feature of virtual worlds is persistence, the ability for the virtual world program to continue running regardless of whether anyone is using it at any given point in time.[5] The programme recalls the location of people and ownership of objects as well as the actions of the avatars.

---

2 Bryan T. Camp, 'Play's the Thing: A Theory of Taxing Virtual Worlds' (2008) *59 Hastings L.J.* 1, 3.

3 Edward Castronova, 'Virtual Worlds: A First-Hand Account of Market and Society in the Cyberian Frontier' (CESifo Working Paper Series No. 618, December 2001) 12 <http://papers.ssrn.com/sol3/papers.cfm?abstract_id=294828> accessed December 3, 2013; See also Edward Castronova, 'On Virtual Economies' (CESifo Working Paper Series No. 752, July 2002) 7 <http://papers.ssrn.com/sol3/papers.cfm?abstract_id=338500> accessed December 3, 2013; Edward Castronova, 'Theory of the Avatar' (CESifo Working Paper Series No. 863, February 2003) 2 <http://papers.ssrn.com/sol3/papers.cfm?abstract_id=385103> accessed December 3, 2013; Edward Castronova, *Synthetic Worlds: The Business and Culture of Online Games* (University of Chicago Press 2006) 11.

4 Castronova, 'Virtual Worlds: A First-Hand Account of Market and Society in the Cyberian Frontier' (n 3) 12.

5 *ibid.*

Virtual worlds are generally categorized as scripted and unscripted.[6] A scripted virtual world, represented by the well-known massively multi-player online role playing games (MMORPGs) such as World of Warcraft, Everquest, City of Heroes, The Sims Online, and Dark Age of Camelot, is "any virtual environment where a user customizes and creates an avatar for participation inside a computer game,"[7] with the eventual goal of character advancement.[8] In scripted virtual worlds, the game developers and creators provide a pre-scripted environment including scenery, plotlines, preset roles, rules for interaction, and rewards.[9] The defining characteristic of scripted game worlds is that "players must feel that they are advancing, that the advancement is worthwhile, and that there are some definite goals that indicate they have 'won'."[10] Players in MMORPGs are simply navigating the virtual world using the tools provided by the game developers. Players then make decisions on the paths the avatar will take within the confines of the game's pre-designed restrictions and rewards.

In contrast, an unscripted virtual world, most notably represented by Linden Lab Inc.'s 2003 creation called Second Life®,[11] is an environment where not only do users create their own avatars, the avatars' activities greatly simulate real world activities and thus have unprecedented real world commercial

6 See e.g., Leandra Lederman, ' "Stranger than Fiction": Taxing Virtual Worlds' (20007) 82 N.Y.U. L. Rev. 1620, 1628–1631 (using the terms "game world" and "unscripted world"); cf Camp (n 2) 4–8 (using the terms "structured" and "unstructured" for virtual world categories). In this article, I use the terms "scripted" (game world) and "unscripted" (unstructured world).

7 William E. Arnold IV, 'Tax Enforcement in Virtual Worlds — Virtually Impossible?'(2012) *40 Syracuse J. Int'l. L. & Com.* 187, 190–191.

8 Richard A. Bartle, 'Virtual Worldliness: What the Imaginary Asks of the Real' (20005) *49 N.Y.L. Sch. L. Rev.* 19, 30.

9 Chodorow (n 1) 288.

10 Bartle (n 8) 30–31.

11 The Sims™ also falls under the category of an unscripted virtual world.

implications.[12] Unscripted virtual worlds do not contain pre-set storylines or activities. Users of unscripted virtual worlds create their own story lines and activities which simulate real world activities such as creating, selling, and buying virtual products for their avatars,[13] engaging in real estate and property acquisition (virtual land acquisition),[14] "invite[ing] others to their virtual homes, embark[ing] on career paths, attend[ing] concerts, or go[ing] to parties."[15] Most notably, in Second Life®, these transactions are facilitated through purchases using real money through Second Life's exchange system, which converts real money into Second Life's own currency, called Linden Dollars.[16] In addition, players using Linden Dollars "can convert or cash out their Linden Dollars for US dollars, similar to the way a casino works."[17]

The result of the advancements in the design and use of unscripted virtual worlds represents a significant blurring of the lines between the real world and virtual worlds such that the overall transaction values of virtual world activities are generating a new virtual economy,[18] complete with real currency exchange

---

12   Arnold IV (n 7) 192–193

13   Arnold IV (n 7) 195; See also Chodorow (n 1) 288–289 (describing unscripted virtual worlds and their virtual economies).

14   Arnold IV (n 7) 195–196

15   Arnold IV (n 7) 192 (referring to activities that are possible in The Sims™).

16   Arnold IV (n 7) 195

17   Arnold IV (n 7) 195

18   Arnold IV (n 7) 193; See also Chodorow (n 1) 288; Castronova, 'Virtual Worlds: A First-Hand Account of Market and Society in the Cyberian Frontier' (n 3); Vili Lehdonvirta, 'Real-Money Trade of Virtual Assets: New Strategies for Virtual World Operators' in Mary Ipe, Virtual Worlds (Icfai University Press, Hyderabad, India 2008) 113–137 <http://ssrn.com/abstract=1351782> accessed December 3, 2013; David A Bray and Benn Konsynski, 'Virtual Worlds, Virtual Economies, Virtual Institutions' (Virtual Worlds and New Realities Conference, Emory University February 2008) <http://papers.ssrn.com/sol3/papers.cfm?abstract_id=962501> accessed December 3, 2013.

rates, online financial services providers, and real millionaires.[19] Despite the fact that there may be some key differences between real world and virtual economies,[20] these virtual economies[21] have proven to be very profitable for real world persons and have significant real world implications for commercial transactions and commercial law.[22] Therefore, the investigation into the issues and opportunities presented by commercial transactions in the virtual world remains an area ripe for research and legal reform.

2. Real World Implications to Commercial Transactions in the Virtual World

One must appreciate and understand the commercial implications of virtual world economies in order to determine to what extent

---

19 Rob Hof, 'Second Life's First Millionaire' (*Bloomberg Businessweek*, November 26, 2006) <www.businessweek.com/the_thread/techbeat/archives/2006/11/second_lifes_fi.html> accessed December 3, 2013; 'Anshe Chung Becomes First Virtual World Millionaire' <www.anshechung.com/include/press/press_release251106.html> accessed December 3, 2013.

20 Schrank (n 1) 24 (discussing the difference between real world and virtual economies as articulated by Castronova (2001) and Lehdonvirta (2005) as having the following attributes: "[1] No basic needs exist in virtual worlds; [2] Scarcity of goods; [3] No marginal costs of production in virtual worlds; [4] Negative effect of economic growth in virtual worlds; [5] No unemployment in virtual worlds.")

21 Schrank (n 1) 23–24 (describing virtual economies as economies based on the trading of virtual goods and objects, which may be categorized as: a) collectible objects; b) consumable objects; and c) customizable objects).

22 United States Congress Joint Economic Committee, 'Press Release # 109–98: Virtual Economies Need Clarification, Not More Taxation (October 17, 2006) <www.jec.senate.gov/republicans/public/?a=Files.Serve&File_id=08e6fa84-ee4f-4267-9f47-ad0ad33a072d> accessed December 3, 2013 (stating, inter alia, that "The population of these online worlds has been estimated to exceed 10 million people worldwide....Clearly, virtual economies represent an area where technology has outpaced the law."); See also Robert Bond, 'Business Trends in Virtual Worlds and Social Networks—An Overview of the Legal and Regulatory Issues Relating to Intellectual Property and Money Transactions' (2009) 20(4) *Entertainment Law Review 121* (discussing how Facebook, MySpace, and Second Life, etc. bring new legal challenges and relationships).

existing laws in business, technology, and commercial transactions are deficient or effective.

In a 2001 article, Professor Edward Castranova described the economy of Norrath, a scripted virtual world in the online game called Everquest, as one that "...produce[s] a GNP per capita somewhere between that of Russia and Bulgaria... virtual worlds are making money—with annual revenues expected to top USD 1.5 billion by 2004."[23] Gartner Research, Inc.'s 2009 report and analysis showed that in 2006, nearly 30 million people regularly participated in online virtual world and that by 2011, nearly 80% of online users would be active participants in virtual worlds.[24] In the first quarter of 2009, Second Life®, users spent more than 120 million dollars on virtual goods and services.[25] In 2011, the *World Bank Virtual Economy Report* stated that the virtual economy was valued at an estimated three billion dollars.[26]

In addition to the trading of virtual goods and services, virtual worlds also account for a significant trend in real money trading (RMT), defined as "the sale of virtual property or virtual currency for real world currency, such as World of Warcraft gold for US dollars."[27] While such cross-border RMT transactions may have significant implications for international tax systems, RMT

---

23 Castronova, 'Virtual Worlds: A First-Hand Account of Market and Society in the Cyberian Frontier' (n 3) 1.

24 Schrank (n 1) 7 (citing Gartner, Inc., 'Gartner Says 80% of Active Internet Users Will Have A "Second Life" in the Virtual World by the End of 2011' (Gartner.com April 24 2007) <www.gartner.com/newsroom/id/503861> accessed December 3, 2013; See also Gartner, Inc., 'Gartner Says 90% of Corporate Virtual World Projects Fail within 18 Months" (Gartner.com May 15 2008) <www.gartner.com/newsroom/id/670507> accessed December 3, 2013.

25 Schrank (n 1) 29.

26 Dr. Vili Lehdonvirta, 'World Bank Virtual Economy Report: Secondary Markets Worth $3 Billion,' (Virtual Econ. Res. Network [VERN] April 7, 2011) <http://virtual-economy.org/2011/04/07/world_bank_virtual_economy_rep/> accessed December 3, 2013.

27 Michael Druckman-Church, Taxing a Galaxy Far, Far Away: How Virtual Property Challenges International Tax Systems, *51 Colum. J. Transnat'l L.* 479, 485 (2013).

transactions also result in "annual trade estimates valued in billions of dollars."[28]

In addition to RMT transactions, gold farming is another phenomenon or cottage industry emerging out of virtual worlds. Gold farmers meet the demand for rare items and other valuable goods of MMORPGs by providing such items and services on the virtual market.[29] Gold farming is particularly prevalent in developing worlds, such as China.[30] In 2008, it was estimated that the annual revenues from gold farming were between USD200 million and 1 billion.[31]

Finally, it is reasonable to conclude that the virtual economy is the future of e-commerce and transcends Web 2.0 to create a new, sophisticated Web 3.0 environment[32] that has tremendous potential and implications for commercial transactions and the development of commercial law. In addition to everyday people engaging in the virtual world, businesses and organizations are reaping the benefits of the virtual world. Today, over 200 real

---

28 See e.g., Vili Lehdonvirta and Mirko Ernkvist, Converting the Virtual Economy into Development Potential: Knowledge Map of the Virtual Economy 11–15 (2011), available at <www.infodev.org/en/Document.1056.pdf.> accessed at December 3, 2013; Maggie Shiels, 'The US Virtual Economy is Set to Make Billions' (BBC News, December 29 2009), <http://news.bbc.co.uk/2/hi/technology/8425623.stm> accessed December 3, 2013; Joshua Fairfield, 'Virtual Property' (2005) *85 B.U. L. Rev.* 1047, 1050.

29 Arnold IV (n 7) 197–198.

30 Richard Heeks, 'Current Analysis and Future Research Agenda on "Gold Farming": Real-World Production in Developing Countries for the Virtual Economics of Online Games' 6–7 (University of Manchester, Institute for Development Policy and Management, IDPM Working Paper No. 32, 2008) <www.sed.manchester.ac.uk/idpm/research/publications/wp/di/documents/di_wp32.pdf> accessed December 3, 2013.

31 Heeks (n 30) 10.

32 Schrank (n 1) 16 (citing Gary Hayes, 'The Virtual Worlds Hype Cycle for 2009' (2009) <www.muvedesign.com/the-virtual-worlds-hype-cycle-for-2009/> accessed December 3 2013). Hayes analyses and articulates the three developmental stages of the Internet, with Web 3.0 representing a real-time, co-creative web environment with 3D portals and avatars.

world brands, such as Sun, IBM, Dell, Adidas, Nissan, Coca Cola, and some law firms,[33] have created a presence in Second Life®. The aim of these virtual companies is to provide goods and services through in-world transactions as well as translate these in-world sales and the virtual world experience into the virtual world avatar making real purchases from the same company, thus increasing brand impact and brand recognition. Combined together, these virtual companies "employ over 3,000 people globally with estimated annual sales of $60 million according to Linden Lab."[34] In addition to well-known brands, politicians,[35] educational institutions,[36] and governments[37] have entered the virtual world, more specifically Second Life®, for brand reinforcement, business development, and as a way to connect with the greater public.

The opportunities present in unscripted virtual worlds, in particular, also give rise to both legal and business challenges

---

33 Bond, 'Business Trends in Virtual Worlds and Social Networks—An Overview of the Legal and Regulatory Issues Relating to Intellectual Property and Money Transactions' (n 22) 124.

34 ibid.

35 Bond, 'Business Trends in Virtual Worlds and Social Networks—An Overview of the Legal and Regulatory Issues Relating to Intellectual Property and Money Transactions' (n 22) 122–123 (discussing the use of Second Life by politicians such as France's former president Nicolas Sarkozy and U.S. President Barack Obama).

36 Bond, 'Business Trends in Virtual Worlds and Social Networks—An Overview of the Legal and Regulatory Issues Relating to Intellectual Property and Money Transactions' (n 22) 123.

37 Arnold IV (n 7) 192–193 (discussion how several governments have opened embassies in the virtual world); 'Maldives Unveils World's First Virtual Embassy' (The Sunday Times Online, May 27, 2007) <www.sundaytimes.lk/070527/FinancialTimes/ft328.html> accessed December 3, 2013; Cari Simmons, 'Sweden Opens Virtual Embassy 3D-Style' (Sweden.se, May 30 2007) <www.sweden.se/eng/Home/Lifestyle/Reading/Second-Life/> accessed December 3 2013; 'Estonia launches embassy in virtual world Second Life' (The Sydney Morning Herald smh.com.au, December 5, 2007) <www.smh.com.au/news/Technology/Estonia-launches-embassy-in-virtual-world-Second-Life/2007/12/05/1196530704693.html> accessed December 3, 2013.

which have yet to be mastered by practitioners and academics. These challenges include, but are not limited to, issues of taxation,[38] property recognition and rights,[39] money laundering,[40] terrorism financing,[41] online and virtual financial services providers,[42] cross-border virtual exchange rates and virtual currencies,[43] virtual banking and money lending,[44] and resolution of virtual disputes.

This book aims at providing a more detailed analysis and investigation of the issues and topics most directly attributed to and impacting the field of commercial law as articulated by the texts of eminent scholars such as Goode as well as Sealy and Hooley. Many of these topics eventually overlap with the interdisciplinary challenges discussed above.

---

38 See e.g., Arnold IV (n 7); Eric G. Roscoe, 'Taxing Virtual Worlds: Can the IRS Own You?; (2011) *12 U. Pitt. J. Tech. L. & Pol'y 1.*

39 See e.g., Passman, 'Transactions of Virtual Items in Virtual Worlds' (2008) *18 Alb. L. J. Sci. & Tech.* 259; John William Nelson, 'The Virtual Property Problem: What Property Rights in Virtual Resources Might Look Like, How They Might Work, and Why They are a Bad Idea' (2010) *41 McGeorge L. Rev.* 281.

40 See e.g., Angela S.M. Irwin, Jill Slay, Kim-Kwang Raymond Choo, and Lin Liu, 'Are the financial transactions conducted inside virtual environments truly anonymous? An experimental research from an Australian perspective' (2013) 16(1) *Journal of Money Laundering Control 6–40.*

41 See e.g., Stephen I. Landman, 'Funding Bin Laden's Avatar: A Proposal for the Regulation of Virtual Hawalas' (2009) *35 Wm. Mitchell L. Rev.* 5159; Irwin et al, 'Are the financial transactions conducted inside virtual environments truly anonymous? An experimental research from an Australian perspective' (n 40).

42 See e.g., Schrank (n 1).

43 See e.g., Druckman-Church, 'Taxing a Galaxy Far, Far Away: How Virtual Property Challenges International Tax Systems' (n 27); Takashi Nakazaki, 'Real World Excessive Regulations Might Kill Economic Transactions in Virtual Worlds' (2011) 14(12) *J. Internet* L. 3.

44 See e.g., Andrew Abraham, 'The Regulation of Virtual Banks: A Study of the Hong Kong Perspective' (2007) 10(12) *J. Internet* L. 3.

3.   The Contribution of this Book to Advancing the Field of Commercial Law

Professor Roy Goode, one of the most eminent scholars in the field, has stated that commercial law goes beyond just a collection of the various fields of law and represents the "branch of law which is concerned with the rights and duties arising from the supply of goods and services in the way of trade."[45] Specifically, Goode sees commercial law as encompassing "the totality of the law's response to mercantile disputes...[including] all those principles, rules and statutory provisions, of whatever kind and from whatever source, which bear on the private law rights and obligations of parties to commercial transactions, whether between themselves or in their relationship with others."[46]

This definition encompasses everything from the definition and nature of personal property and property rights all the way to security interests and financial transactions. In this wide continuum that represents commercial law principles and practices, this book makes several contributions to advancing the field of commercial law.

First, Goode recognized as early as 1998 that the evolution of commercial law in the next millennium will depend greatly as much on meeting the legitimate needs of the changing marketplace as the impact of technology on commercial law and

---

45   Roy Goode, *Commercial Law* (3rd edn, LexisNexis Butterworths 2004); See also Bryan A. Garner (ed), *Black's Law Dictionary* (9th edn, Thomas Reuters 2009) 305 (defining commercial law as "The substantive law dealing with the sale and distribution of goods, the financing of credit transactions on the security of goods sold, and negotiable instruments."); Jonathan A. Eddy and Peter Winship, *Commercial Transactions: Text, Cases, and Problems* (1985) 1 ("In American law....synonymous with the legal rules contained in the Uniform Commercial Code.").

46   Roy Goode, *Commercial Law in the Next Millennium* (Sweet & Maxwell, London 1998) 8.

regulation.[47] It is argued that this is all the more applicable in the case of virtual worlds and commercial transactions in the virtual world. While some real world laws may plausibly be applicable to virtual worlds, the very nature of a dynamic, flexible, and new virtual economy means that existing commercial law may not be entirely applicable. This book makes a significant contribution to the advancement of commercial law by addressing the most significant technological change, to date, which will impact the whole of commercial law as well as its discrete bodies of law. To date, while academics and practitioners have begun to analyze issues of taxation, property rights, virtual currency exchanges, and online financial services providers, other important areas such as goods and services contractual relationships, transfer of property and risks, security interests, money lending, alternative dispute resolution processes, and consumer protection within virtual worlds have not been fully explored. In addition, while real world laws may arguably apply to some aspects of virtual world commercial transactions, other laws and regulations will need reform to keep pace with the technological advancements presented by virtual worlds. This book addresses these topics as well as many others from a variety of perspectives.

Second, this book advances the field of commercial law by adopting the spirit of comparative analysis with respect to the issues of virtual commercial transactions. Countries such as the United States, China, Japan, Korea, and Taiwan have begun to generate case law specifically on virtual world issues as well as developed certain laws and regulations governing these transactions. These insights are valuable to other jurisdictions, such as Hong Kong, in developing a more clear and comprehensive jurisprudence surrounding commercial transactions in the virtual world.

---

47 Goode, *Commercial Law in the Next Millennium*, (n 46) 37, 96–98.

Finally, this book advances the field of commercial law by proposing solutions, where possible, to the myriad of issues which are, as yet, unresolved in terms of dealing with commercial transactions in the virtual world. In so doing, this book also raises areas of further research and investigation, thus establishing a rich and complex framework from which future commercial law students, practitioners and academics can draw for inspiration, further study, and research.

4.   Contents of This Book

This book is divided into 11 sections, including this introduction. Each section of the book contains chapters in the form of an article(s) that aims to take an in-depth look at the opportunities, challenges, and solutions presented by virtual worlds as related to the particular area of commercial law. In addition, a comparative analysis of other jurisdictions is advanced in hopes that through this comparative, multi-disciplinary analysis, better and more effective solutions can be found to advance the field of commercial law in these respective areas.

With the introduction presented in section 1 of the book, section 2 of the book analyses virtual worlds from an industry perspective and highlights issues, challenges, and opportunities in greater detail. The chapters in section 2 are important to answering the central question of whether virtual worlds open new marketplaces, the legal and practical implications which arise out of this new marketplace, and what challenges a virtual world industry places on commercial law as well as related areas of law such as intellectual property law.

Section 3 of the book deals with the nature and definition of goods in the virtual world and whether this impacts the validity of virtual world contracts. In general, each jurisdiction has some form of Hong Kong's Sale of Goods Ordinance, which not only defines what trade goods are but also regulates the entire sale of goods contract. Because commercial law would not exist but for trading of goods and services, understanding whether virtual objects and items are considered "goods" or "services" to which law can be applied is extremely important. Nearly all virtual world developers and operators, except for Second Life®, refuse to recognize a user's right to property in the virtual goods they purchase. However, virtual world disputes and related case law in some jurisdictions appear to show a reverse trend in favor of such recognition. The contributing chapters in this section analyze these issues from the perspective of the theories of property rights in goods and services as well as ways in which various jurisdictions have dealt with the nature of property rights in virtual goods.

Section 4 of the book deals with contracts related to the sale of goods and/or services in the virtual world. The central question in this section is to what extent transactions in the virtual world mirror real world contracts for the sale of goods, sale of services, or sale of goods and services. To the extent that these transactions mirror the core elements of contract law, one can argue that real world laws, such as the Hong Kong Sale of Goods Ordinance, may apply. Contracts for the sale of goods or services generally implicate a transfer of rights, benefits, and remedies. However, if virtual goods are not "property" and do not confer property rights in the buyer, are these transactions considered contracts subject to standard contractual rights and remedies? These and other related questions are addressed by the chapters in this section.

Section 5 of the book deals with the transfer of property and risk arising out of contracts for sale of goods or services in the virtual world. The transfer of property and risk is central to the commercial transaction. Once a buyer purchases goods or services from the seller, depending on the nature of the transaction, possession, interest, ownership, or title to the goods transfers to the buyer. Once transfer of goods and services has taken place, certain rights and risks are also conferred along with remedies for the buyer or seller should issues arise with the goods or services. This involves both the intention of the parties as well as explicit contractual provisions. Given that most contractual relations between virtual world developers and users are governed by end-user license agreements (EULAs), the key question in virtual transactions is to what degree there is or should be a transfer of property and how this translates to rights and remedies for the buyer and seller, especially given the industry is now a multi-billion dollar industry.

Section 6 of the book deals with various payment methods and issues arising in virtual world transactions. Payment methods deal with the ways by which a buyer might pay for goods and services under a contract. Traditionally recognized payment methods include cash, cheques, credit cards, bank transfers, debit cards, and some forms of electronic payment. The advent of the virtual world has given rise to new methods of payment, including the use of virtual currencies such as Second Life®'s Linden Dollars, Cyworld's acorns, World of Warcraft's virtual gold, and Cyber Agent's "Ame Gold," and BitCoin. In addition, virtual payment platforms such as PayPal®, PlaySpan, Facebook Credits, and Boku are increasingly playing an important role in facilitating virtual payments. Given the nature of virtual world transactions, payment methods inevitably lead to questions of taxable income and jurisdictional issues.

Section 7 of the book deals with the remedies for buyers and sellers arising out of commercial transactions in the virtual world. In real world commercial transactions, both buyers and sellers may be entitled to remedies in the event of breach of contract. While the debate over whether sale of virtual goods can give rise to property in those goods and thus remedies for breach, an analysis of the need for potential remedies in the event that such a right is recognized is important. Remedies may include action for price, damages for non-delivery or non-acceptance, and specific performance. While the dollar values for a single virtual world purchase may be small, these single purchase values may increase as more and more businesses and organizations enter the virtual world. In addition, these values may be significantly large over time. The chapters in this section deal with the lack of regulations surrounding virtual world remedies and whether real world laws and regulations can serve as a solid foundation for commercial transactions in the virtual world.

Section 8 of the book deals with applicability of the law of security in virtual world transactions, both for real and quasi security. The law of security deals with using real or personal property as an asset against which one can obtain an interest in money or other goods. Security is essential to facilitating large-scale commercial transactions. Specifically, security is "...created where a person (the 'creditor') to whom an obligation is owed by another ('the debtor') by statute or contract, in addition to the personal promise of the debtor to discharge the obligation, obtains rights exercisable against some property in which debtor has an interest in order to enforce the discharge of the debtor's obligation to the creditor."[48] Security can take the form of real security (e.g., pledge, mortgage, lien, or charge) or quasi-security (e.g., guarantee, indemnity, performance bond, or retention of title). The chapters in this section investigate the possibility of applying the law of security to virtual world transactions and whether existing real world laws are sufficient to accommodate the needs of the virtual marketplace.

Section 9 of the book investigates banking and money lending institutions within the context of virtual world transactions. While banks do, in most cases, provide loans and credit, private money lending institutions are subject to strict, separate regulations

---

48 *Bristol Airport plc v Powdrill* [1990] Ch 744 at 760.

than banks. For example, in Hong Kong, private money lending institutions are governed by the Money Lenders Ordinance while banks are governed by the Banking Ordinance. The chapters in this section discuss the nature of virtual world financial transactions, the use of virtual banks, and whether existing banking and money lending laws are sufficiently comprehensive to cover virtual world transactions. Given the rise of virtual banking, which is still in its nascent form, this is an area ripe for further research and reform given the extensive regulations which overshadow the banking industry.

Section 10 of the book looks at the availability and effectiveness of consumer protection laws in virtual world transactions. Virtual worlds, which are generally known to be devoid of extensive rules and regulations, are also potentially an ideal place where unfavorable conduct may occur, especially since most virtual worlds are governed by EULAs and Terms of Service that are seen as one-sided agreements in favor of the virtual world developers and owners. In his 2009 article, Aiken discussed potential cases of assault, harassment, and disruptive or harmful social behavior as reported by some virtual world users.[49] In addition, virtual world users in various jurisdictions around the world have filed cases alleging theft of virtual property. Virtual world transactions may also give rise to misrepresentation, duress, or unconscionable conduct. The chapters in this section look at both in-world and real world ways in which consumers can seek protection and whether existing consumer protection laws are sufficient or deficient in dealing with protection of virtual world

---

49 Claude T. Aiken IV, Sources of Law and Modes of Governance: Ethnography and Theory in Second Life, (2009) *10 Pittsburgh Journal of Technology Law and Policy* 9 <http://ssrn.com/abstract=1148416> accessed December 3, 2013; See also Benjamin Duranske, 'Reader Roundtable: "Virtual Rape" Claim Brings Belgian Police to Second Life' (Virtually Blind, April 24 2007) <http://virtuallyblind. com/2007/04/24/open-roundtable-allegations-of-virtual-rape-bring-belgian-police-to-second-life/> accessed December 3, 2013.

consumers. Given the impending rise in virtual world users and virtual commercial transactions, this is an important area of law which must be solidified and effective if virtual economies are to succeed.

Finally, section 11 of the book explores the mechanisms by which virtual world-related disputes or actual disputes in the virtual world can be resolved. The continuum of dispute resolution includes such well-known processes as negotiation, conciliation, mediation, arbitration, and litigation. Cases involving virtual world creators have, to date, eventually led to litigation although some EULAs contain an arbitration clause compelling the parties to resolve disputes through arbitration. The chapters in this section investigate the extent to which existing dispute resolution process are sufficient to resolve virtual world disputes. In addition, the chapters in this section analyze and explore alternative ways for resolving such disputes, including the integration of online dispute resolution platforms as well as developing new virtual world dispute resolution platforms for resolving disputes within and related to virtual worlds.

5. Conclusion

In conclusion, the rise of commercial transactions in the virtual world means a renewed investigation into the ways in which modern commercial law must evolve to meet the needs of a new marketplace driven by technological advances and real-world, innovative trading demands. The aim of this book is to educate, spark debate, and encourage dialogue about the opportunities, challenges, and solutions that are necessary to support this new, dynamic market.

Students, practitioners, and academics will benefit from the collection of articles in this book. Students will benefit from an introduction to an exciting and emerging new economy that will continue to challenge business practice, technology usage, and legal regulations as the Internet continues to evolve. In turn, students and future graduates must keep abreast and have a working knowledge of these challenges in order to serve clients well. New and existing practitioners in the fields of business, technology, and law will benefit from a comprehensive and interdisciplinary perspective about virtual worlds that will enhance and challenge their respective fields as well as open up opportunities for further brand recognition and business development. Finally, academics will benefit from finding areas of further research and education in hopes of encouraging greater evolution of modern commercial law as it continually strives "... accommodate the legitimate practices and expectations of the business community in relation to their commercial dealings."[50]

---

50 Roy Goode, 'The Codification of Commercial Law' (1988) 14 *Mon L R* 135, 147–155.

PART II
VIRTUAL COMMERCIAL TRANSACTION–INDUSTRY
PERSPECTIVE AND ISSUES

2

The Nature of the Virtual Industry Today: Issues and Recommendations

Jonathan Ying Kit TONG

1. Introduction

Have you ever had times where you found life a bit boring, that the world had lost its color and nothing seems to fit? There are people who choose to start over, to live out a new life in the virtual world.

A virtual world is a place online, where many people can interact with each other and their environment.[1] With the click of a button, users dive into 3D environments with stunning visuals, animations, role playing opportunities and social communities.[2] Users through an avatar can also interact by buying or selling items they make or find in the virtual world.[3]

As these virtual worlds are expanding, along with the increasing amounts of real money involved, cries for regulation of these virtual commercial transactions from users have grown increasingly loud.

---

1 Michael H. Passman, 'Transactions of Virtual Items in Virtual Worlds' (2008) *18 Alb. L.J. Sci. & Tech. 261.*

2 Michael Gannis and David McNeill, 'Commercial and Business Opportunities and Problems of Virtual Worlds' in Mennecke *et al.*, 'Second Life® and other Virtual Worlds: A Roadmap for Research' (2008) 22 (Article 20) Communications of the Association for Information Systems 373.

3 *Ibid.* (n 1) 261.

This chapter seeks to look into the virtual industry of today, discusses the issues it is now facing and provides suggestions to address some of these issues.

2.   Virtual World Industry

As of early 2008, the virtual world *Second Life*® supported almost 12 million unique user accounts, while another massively multiplayer online role-playing game ("MMORPG") called *World of Warcraft* had more than 11 million subscribers.[4] Considering the primary market itself which means the subscription cost for one to participate in game-play is already in itself overwhelming. However, it is the amount of real money involved within these games that makes the industry genuinely intriguing.

In 2001, another fantasy world called *Norrath* was estimated to have a gross national product of $135 million where in each of the 430,000 subscribers theoretically had an average income of $3.42 per hour.[5] These figures translate to a higher per capita income in 2001 for one virtual world than the 2001 reported per capita income of real countries such as Bulgaria, India and China.[6] More recently, in 2009 the *Second Life*® economy grew to $567 million, and this just amounted to 25% of the entire US virtual goods market.

One of the reasons behind the attractiveness of virtual worlds is the real potential which lies in the merging of the possibility for users of virtual worlds to create virtual objects, to sell and

---

4   *Ibid.* (n 1) 373.

5   E. Castronova, 'Virtual Worlds: A First-Hand Account of Market and Society on the Cyberian Frontier', *CESifo Working Paper No. 618*, December, 2001.

6   S. Anil, Angelia K. W. Jie, Jeanne S. H. Min and Queenie C. W. Xiu, 'Virtual Property — A theoretical and empirical analysis' (2012) *European Intellectual Property Review 2*.

buy them and to build a community within a virtual world.[7] Furthermore, conducting commercial transactions in virtual stores as compared to classic web stores has its own attractions. Virtual worlds offer new communication channels like text-based chat or voice chat which offer new ways to interact. This gives a completely new shopping experience and offers a much higher social presence within a virtual shop unlike the classic web shop where you cannot interact with the other customers. Moreover, anonymity is provided where no details or addresses have to be exchanged.[8]

Doing business in the virtual world can also yield financial returns in the real world. Anshe CHUNG, a real estate giant in *Second Life*®, became a real-life millionaire in virtual land assets and, as a virtual avatar, appeared on the cover of *Business Week*.[9] Although she might be only one in tens of thousands of users in the virtual world, there are many others who sustain a living on the virtual economy alone. For example, according to a March 2008 Linden Labs report, there were 156 users who had a monthly cash flow of over USD5, 000 per month.[10]

However, not all businesses are certain to turn out to become great successes in the virtual world. The most prominent of these occurred in *Second Life*® to one Ginko Financial, an in-world bank.

In August 2007, after a ban to in-world casinos, users made a run on the bank, driving it into insolvency. Since the bank was not insured, many residents lost money. This eventually led to a loss

---

7 Dominik Schrank, "A Trustful Payment System for Virtual Worlds", Master's Thesis at Graz University of Technology 23.

8 *Ibid* 30.

9 Claude T Aiken IV, 'Sources of Law and Modes of Governance: Ethnography and Theory in Second Life' (2009) *Journal of Technology Law and Policy* 27.

10 *Ibid.*

of $750,000 in real currency and prompted cries for regulation.[11]

From the abovementioned examples, virtual goods and services are proven to have demonstrable value as indicated by the conceptions of economic value. Virtual properties have also demonstrated utility to the user as the user has willingly spent time, effort and money in exchange for them. It has been shown that labor devoted to games produces durable economic assets with observable market values in the real world.[12]

3.   Issues in the Virtual World Industry — Property Rights of Users

Although virtual items have demonstrated market value, some game developers are determined to keep virtual property completely valueless.

It is most common that a virtual world maker will only allow entry to a virtual world after a user has agreed to an End of License Agreement ("EULA"). A EULA is a contract that generally removes the user's property rights to anything within the virtual world including items the user builds or creates with tools the virtual world maker has provided.[13] For instance, *World of Warcraft* adopts an "exploitation policy" in where if users are found to be in "abuse of the economy" which occurs when one or more characters on the account are identified exchanging or contributing to the exchange of in-game property (items or gold) for "real-world" currency, they will retain the right to suspend

11 Bryan Gardner, 'Bank Failure in Second Life® Leads to Calls for Regulation' (Wired.com, August 15, 2007) <www.wired.com/gaming/virtualworlds/news/2007/08/virtual_bank> accessed April 4, 2013.

12 E. Castronova, 'Virtual Worlds: A First-Hand Account of Market and Society on the Cyberian Frontier', CESifo Working Paper No. 752, July, 2002.

13 *Ibid* (n 1) 263.

the character temporarily from the game or even closure of the account of individuals forever.[14]

However, many game developers market their in-game economies in a way that seems to contradict their EULAs. For instance, *Entropia Universe* extensively advertises its "Real Cash Economy" and the "Entropia Universe Cash Card," which can be used to withdraw in-game currency from real world ATMs, in spite of the fact that players "will not gain any ownership interest whatsoever in any Virtual Item."[15]

In order for us to have an in-depth analysis and better understanding of the issue presented, let us consider the views from different parties concerned.

3.1 *Scholarly View*

Despite the claim from the virtual world makers' to ownership over everything in their virtual worlds, this has attracted a number of voices against this view. There are three main arguments for users' property rights in virtual items namely (a) EULAs are unenforceable, (b) traditional labor-based property theory, and (c) public policy considerations.[16]

First of all, EULA can only remove virtual world users' property rights if they are enforceable. Most of the time, there is no real negotiation involved in drafting EULAs, and the agreements themselves are difficult to access, complex, contained in multiple documents and changeable at will without notice

---

14 Battle.net, 'Exploitation Policy' <https://sea.battle.net/support/en/article/exploitation-policy> accessed April 4, 2013.

15 Entropia Universe, 'Entropia Universe End User License Agreement (EULA), Section 4.1' <http://legal.entropiauniverse.com/legal/eula.xml> accessed April 5, 2013.

16 *Ibid* (n 1) 265.

given by the virtual world maker.[17]

Secondly, virtual world users' property rights are supported by traditional property theory as the earning of virtual money involves expending real world time.[18] Thus if enough users expect that they have a property right, courts may have to protect the users' expectations of obtaining benefits from their time and efforts.[19]

Thirdly, there are favorable public policy arguments for granting user property rights in virtual items. In general, public policy does not tolerate consensual restraints on alienation and in this sense it should not tolerate EULAs which are essentially consensual agreements that prevent the formation of property rights. Furthermore, countries like China, Taiwan and South Korea have, or have attempted to, recognize these rights and in order to compete in the virtual marketplace, it may be favorable for other countries to follow suit.[20]

3.2 User Expectations

According to a survey conducted in Singapore, a majority of the respondents (54% of respondents) indicated that they believed the real life users to be the rightful owners of virtual property in MMORPGs.[21] This is relevant in the sense of forming a contract between the users and the operators, their meeting of the minds are important to forming the intended, thus valid contract.

---

17 *Ibid* 266.
18 *Ibid* 267.
19 *Ibid*.
20 *Ibid*.
21 *Ibid* (n 6) 16.

3.3 Limitations

The arguments above are not without limitations. Due to the dual nature of virtual property, which exists as programming code to developers and, at the same time, is considered a market commodity to users, the question of rights becomes more complex when a dispute arises between a user and the developer of the virtual world. This is partly because there is a clear contribution of expenses on the part of both parties. The developer created the virtual world, its structures and rules as well as the codes that make up the virtual object, while the player obtained possession of the virtual object through time, skill and money invested.[22] In terms of the labor-based property theory, it is unable to answer the basic questions to what is labor and whose labor should be rewarded, as seen in the case of the conflicts between the users and developers.

In addition, this theory is based on the assumption that virtual objects can be owned which fails to understand why and when labor should be rewarded as well as whether virtual property should be recognized.[23]

However, balancing both sides of the arguments, as the nature of technology changes with the rise of user-generated platforms, it seems more likely that the rights of players will take precedence over those of creators.[24]

4.   Practice of Other Countries

In order to better grasp the issues at stake, it is helpful to look at

---

22 Theodore J. Westbrook, Note, 'Owned: Finding a Place for Virtual World Property Rights' (2006) *Michigan State Law Review 779.*

23 *Ibid.*

24 Steven J. Horowitz, 'Competing Lockean Claims to Virtual Property' (2007) *20(2) Harvard Journal of Law and Technology 443.*

the practice of foreign jurisdictions in response to these issues.

4.1 United States

In the United States, the only existing statute that is potentially fit for virtual property protection is the Computer Fraud and Abuse Act.[25] The statute is originally designed to prevent unauthorized breaches of government and financial institution computer systems and networks, however it also safeguards against an intrusion of a computer with the intent to defraud where the perpetrator "obtains anything of value."

There have not been many cases to refer to as most of them were settled out of court. This includes a case in May 2007, where Marc Bragg sued Linden Labs, the creators of *Second Life*® for illegally confiscating his virtual property and locking his account.[26] This case was ultimately settled out of court. More recently, Eros, LLC filed a suit against Linden Labs for allegedly being complicit in the copyright violations of the players of *Second Life*®.[27] However, this case was moved from court to private mediation and appears that a satisfactory solution was reached leading the plaintiffs to end their civil court case.

4.2 China

With a multi-billion dollar annual income and approximately 296 million players, the Chinese online gaming industry has been booming in recent years.[28] However, the protection of virtual property remains untouched territory as there are no regulations

---

25 Nelson S DaCunha, "Virtual Property, Real Concerns" (2010) *4 Akron Intellectual Property Journal* 35.

26 *Bragg v. Linden Research, Inc.*, 487 F. Supp. 2d 593 (E.D.Penn. 2007).

27 *Eros LLC v. Linden Research, Inc.* (N.D. Cal. Case No. 09-CV-4269)

28 *Ibid* (n 6) 17.

and administrative statutes in this regard.[29]

In spite of this, the courts of China have shown willingness towards protecting users' interests in respect of virtual property. This is demonstrated in the case of *Li Hongchen v Beijing Artic Ice Technology Development Co* in 2004,[30] where users have successfully sued providers and users in respect of lost virtual items and have been awarded compensation and reinstatement of their lost items.

Despite this apparent trend, the legal status of virtual items in China is far from clear as decisions in one court are not binding on another.

The willingness of courts to recognize virtual property, as illustrated by various court decisions, may be a step towards substantive recognition of virtual property rights under Chinese law but the conflicting political sentiments may pose difficulties in China's attempt at establishing some guidance regarding virtual property.[31]

4.3 Taiwan

Taiwan is the most active jurisdiction in the regard of seeking measures to protecting virtual property ownership. It was announced in 2001, by the Ministry of Justice in the Taiwanese Criminal Code which explicitly stated that virtual objects are valuable property and should be treated the same as property in the real world, and that the theft of such property is fully punishable under criminal law.[32]

---

29 Stephania Lucchetti and Sherman Lo, 'Virtual Items in a Legal Vacuum: Perspectives on Virtual Property from China' (2009) *54 Inter-Pacific Bar Association Journal 9.*

30 (2004) II No. Min Zhong Zi No. 02877.

31 *Ibid* (n 6) 17.

32 Taiwan Ministry of Justice Official Notation No. 039030 (90).

The Code recognizes that virtual property qualifies as electromagnetic records and should be considered moveable property in cases of fraud and theft and this essentially assigns the right to control the electromagnetic record of the virtual property to the owner of the code object, not the owner of the server on which the code happens to reside.[33]

Taiwan has also advanced a practical and comprehensive body of case law protecting virtual property through the use of such offenses as criminal theft, fraud, and robbery offences.[34]

4.4 Canada

The Canadian Criminal Code does not expressly provide for virtual property; however, it may be contended that some of its provisions are wide enough to protect virtual property from theft and vandalism. This argument is premised upon the notion that virtual property falls within the Criminal Code's definition of data which is defined as "representations of information or of concepts that are being prepared or have been prepared in a form suitable for use in a computer system."[35] The Code provides that any person who destroys, alters, interrupts, or denies access to the legal enjoyment of data is guilty of an offence and can be subject to imprisonment.[36]

Although the Code does not specifically mention virtual property, the provisions protecting computer use and data can potentially cover virtual property that is legally stored in a computer system.[37]

---

33 Fairfield, 'Virtual Property' (2004) *84 Boston University Law Review 1047.*

34 Wayne Rumbles, 'Theft in the Digital: Can You Steal Virtual Property?' (2011) *17(2) Canterbury Law Review 354, 366.*

35 Criminal Code (RSC 1985, c. C-46), s. 342.1(2).

36 Criminal Code (RSC 1985, c. C-46), ss.430(1.1), 430(4).

37 *Ibid* (n 6) 18.

4.5 South Korea

According to DaCunha, in South Korea, it is believed that more than 60% of the population are engaged in virtual worlds.[38] Like its other Asian counterparts Taiwan and China, South Korea has made significant steps towards the protection of virtual property. In the eyes of South Korea, "there is no fundamental difference between virtual property and money deposited in the bank."[39] The law of South Korea instructs that online virtual property holds value independent of the game developer's.[40] Furthermore, in a top court decision in September 2010, it was ruled that unlike online gambling, acquiring game items takes time, effort and skill and thus selling them is legal provided that the money goes through legal channels.[41]

4.6 Hong Kong

Although the scale of online game play is not as comparable to other countries, according to a leading Hong Kong game operator, Gameone Online Entertainment Group Ltd., there are currently approximately 100 to 150 thousand fee-paying online game players and they suspect that this figure will jump to 300 thousand in the next few years.[42]

In Hong Kong, there is currently no law recognizing the virtual property rights of players. However, the interference to the virtual property of a player can arguable fall under the protection of the

---

38 DaCunha (n 25) 35.

39 *Ibid* (n 6) 18.

40 P. Brown and R. Raysman, 'Property Rights in Cyberspace Games and Other Novel Legal Issues in Virtual Property' (2006) 2 *Indian Journal of Law and Technology* 87.

41 *Ibid* (n 6) 18.

42 Stephen Wan, Pauline Chan, Jaffa Lo and Elsa Leung, 'Regulations and Policies on Online Games'<http://newmedia.cityu.edu.hk/cyberlaw/gp21/intro.html> accessed April 5, 2013.

Crimes Ordinance (Cap. 200) under s. 59 and 60 which extends the meaning of criminal damage to property by misuse of a computer program or data. In addition, the Theft Ordinance (Cap. 210) also extends the offence of burglary under section 11 to include unlawfully causing computer to function other than as it has been established and altering, erasing or adding any computer program or data.

5.   Suggestions

Currently in Hong Kong, the amount of money involved in virtual world commercial transactions is not as significant to the real economy as compared to foreign countries such as the United States. In addition, current laws in Hong Kong are broad enough to protect and govern issues that occur out of virtual world transactions. However, in order for Hong Kong to better meet the growing industry and challenges in the future, Hong Kong should take a more proactive stance and pave the way for better regulation of virtual property.

Like its Asian counter-parts, China, South Korea and Taiwan, Hong Kong should recognize virtual property rights in the future. Hong Kong can choose to refer to the model of Taiwan in which virtual property is explicitly recognized as real property on condition that it possesses the three characteristics: rivalrousness, alienability and transferability.[43]

However, due to the complexity and various kinds of virtual worlds in the market, it is still too early for Hong Kong to enact legislature concerning the regulation of virtual property and may cause difficulties towards the legal system. Thus, in order for better preparation, I am of opinion that Hong Kong apart from observing the developments of foreign jurisdictions, it should also

---

43   *Ibid* (n 6) 18.

conduct consultation from the public and users of these virtual worlds to have a better understanding of the situation and its effect in Hong Kong.

6.   Conclusion

The expanding virtual economy demonstrates that its effects are not sustained within the virtual world and calls for a review towards the regulation of virtual property. Through the years, virtual property have not only proved to be desirable utility in the virtual world but are just as valuable in the real world where people spend time and effort in acquiring them. Many jurisdictions have already recognized their existence in the real world and assigned property rights to the owners by enacting legislative protection especially those of South East Asia. Given these legal developments in other economies, Hong Kong, in its capacity as a respected international financial and commercial center, should also become more active in addressing this issue in order to keep up with international developments.

3

Virtual Commercial Transactions: A Multi-Jurisdiction Industry Perspective

Bobo Po Wan CHEUNG

1. Introduction to the Virtual World

A virtual world is defined as a "synchronous, persistent network of people, represented as avatars, facilitated by networked computers."[1] Generally, virtual worlds can be said to divide along a spectrum ranging from massively multiplayer online role-playing games (MMORPGs) and massively multiplayer online real-life games (MMORLGs)[2], allowing users to play specific characters or create their avatars. The distinction between these virtual worlds from previous computer games is that the amount of interaction between users is largely increased.[3] The interaction includes commercial transactions of virtual good in these worlds between users. Some examples of the biggest virtual worlds are *Second Life*, *World of Warcraft*, *There* and *The Sims*. *World of*

---

1 Mark W Bell, 'Toward a Definition of Virtual Worlds' (2008) 1(1) *Journal of Virtual World* <http://jvwresearch.org/index.php/past-issues/volume1issue1> accessed June 27, 2013.

2 Andreas M. Kaplan and Michael Haenlein, 'The Fairyland of Second Life: About Virtual Social Worlds and How to Use Them' (2009) *Business Horizons* 563.

3 Steven Levy, 'Living A Virtual Life; Is World of Warcraft a Game, or Is It a Harbinger of Virtual Realities that We All Might Inhabit? Only a Night Elf Knows for Sure.' (*Newsweek* New York, September 18, 2006) <http://lawley.rit.edu/wordpress/wp-content/uploads/2010/10/Newsweek-Story.pdf> accessed June 27, 2013.

Warcraft has at least eight million players[4] while *Second Life* has approximately two million users.[5] With their tremendous numbers of users, they have created an enormous virtual economy. According to a study from research firm DFC Intelligence, it was estimated that the online game market reached $13 billion and over 40% of the revenues was produced by trading virtual assets in 2012.

The focus of this chapter is on the industry perspective of commercial transactions in virtual worlds. This chapter analyzes different jurisdictions with a focus on the issues arising out of this new industry as well as the ways in which these issues affect commercial transactions and commercial law.

2.   Virtual Commercial Transactions

2.1 Transactions between Users

Some items in the virtual world require a significant investment of in-world time and effort, attracting people who use real money to buy these items.[6] Transactions of virtual goods such as "weapons," "gifts" and "game currency" for real money occur among users. Different providers treat this kind of requests in different ways, including not allowing sales for real-world money at all, allowing sales for real-world money through the system and allowing transfers of specific types of items. There is no

---

4 Julian Dibbell, 'The Life of the Chinese Gold Farmer' (*N.Y. Times Mag.* New York, June 17, 2007) <www.nytimes.com/2007/06/17/magazine/17lootfarmers-t. html?pagewanted=all&_r=0> accessed June 27, 2013.

5 Adam Reuters, 'Europe Takes Lead in Second Life Users' (Reuters Second Life News Centre Feb 9, 2007) <http://secondlife.reuters.com/stories/2007/02/09/europe-takes-lead-in-second-life-users/> accessed June 27, 2013.

6 David P. Sheldon, 'Claiming Ownership, But Getting Owned: Contractual Limitations on Asserting Property Interests in Virtual Goods' (2007) 54 *UCLA L. Rev.* 766.

completely unfettered exchange of virtual items for real-world money allowed.[7] Although it was stated that the majority of the virtual world providers totally restrict real-money transaction,[8] goods created in virtual worlds have undoubtedly been sold for cash in different ways. Besides items in virtual world, avatars and user accounts could also be sold as virtual property.[9] For example, *The Sims* allows users to sell virtual items but not to sell their entire accounts while *The Dark Age of Camelot* does not allow selling items but allow selling entire accounts.[10]

2.2. Transactions between Providers and Users

Commercial transactions of virtual goods occur not only among users, but also between the providers and the users. Some providers such as Entropia Universe allow users to pay cash directly to them in order to obtain virtual currency.[11] The virtual and real-world currency is mutual convertible through real-world automated teller machines,[12] which is in fact one of the features of Entropia Universe where users have a chance to earn real-world money by playing this game.[13] On the other hand, providers have tried to make a profit when users carry out transaction among themselves. For example, in *EverQuest* and *Second Life*, all transactions of virtual items for real-world cash are permitted

---

7   *Ibid*

8   *Ibid*

9   John W. Nelson, 'The Virtual Property Problem: What Property Rights in Virtual Resources Might Look Like, How They Might Work, and Why They Are a Bad Idea' (2010) 41 *McGeorge Law Review* 281, 285–86.

10 Sheldon (n6) 767.

11 'Entropia Universe' <www.mindark.se/mindarks-offer/entropia-universe/> accessed June 27, 2013.

12 Richord Duffek, 'Project Entropia Q&A With Marco Behnnmm' (MMORPG, May 31, 2005) <www.mmorpg.com/gamelist.cfm/setview/features/loadFeature/120/gameID/31/from/features> accessed June 27, 2013.

13 'Virtual Club to Rock Pop Culture' (November 2, 2005) <http://news.bbc.co.uk/2/hi/technology/4385048.stm> accessed June 27, 2013.

provided that they take place through the system run by the providers and a nominal fee is charged for each transaction. In these cases, real money flows from the virtual world users to the providers.

3.   The Industry Perspective

The business of virtual goods transaction could be described as the latest trend. More and more people are using real money to buy virtual goods, which is also called real-money-trade (RMT). In Australia, it is history-breaking that a virtual island is sold for AUS$26,500 real money to a 22-year-old gamer.[14] In the virtual pet-keeping game *FooPets*, the users spent an average of $25 per month for their pets, which approximately equals the amount that people spend on pets in the real world.[15] The commercial world has observed that a new economy has emerged in the virtual world.[16] Not only is money being spent in the virtual world, the public and major companies are also making real money from the virtual world. This section illustrates how virtual transactions would affect real-world commercial markets.

3.1 Virtual World, Real Money

Many people have successfully make real-money profit out of the

---

14 'Gamer Buys $26,500 Virtual Land' BBC News (December 17, 2004) <http://news. bbc.co.uk/2/hi/technology/4104731.stm> accessed June 27, 2013.

15 Michael Fitzgerald, 'Boomtown: The Real Money Behind Virtual Goods' (Fast Company July 2009) <www.fastcompany.com/1298098/boomtown-real-money-behind-virtual-goods> accessed June 27, 2013.

16 B. Ives and G. Piccoli, 'STA Travel Island: Marketing First Life Travel Services in Second Life' (2007) 20(8) *Communications of the Association for Information Systems* 429.

virtual transactions.[17] According to the statistics of Linden Labs, *Second Life's* population has reached 2 million. The commerce is not only limited inside the virtual world, but influencing the real world also. Some people are generating real income from the virtual world. Taking *Second Life* as an example, there were 16,566 users who had a monthly income of US$10 to $50 in March 2008.[18] There are 156 users had a monthly income of over $5,000.[19] Some entrepreneurs have earned in excess of US$1 million annually, including Ansche Chung.[20] Firstly reported by CNN, Ansche Chung has become a millionaire real estate mogul in *Second life* by building an online business that engages in development, brokerage and arbitrage of virtual land. As an avatar of Ailin Graef, she was later put on the covers of a number of prominent magazines such as *Business Week*[21] and *Fortune.*[22] Because the in-game currency is convertible to the US dollar, she has in fact become a millionaire in the real world.

Besides successful stories, there are also great failures. One of the most prominent examples would be the insolvency of virtual bank Ginko Financial in 2007, after the ban of casino in *Second*

---

17 Zhaohui Li, 'Motivation of Virtual Goods Transactions Based on The Theory of Gaming Motivations' (2012) 43(2) <www.jatit.org/volumes/Vol43No2/15Vol43No2.pdf> accessed June 27, 2013.

18 Linden Lab, 'Economic Statistics' <http://secondlife.com/whatis/economy_stats.php> accessed June 27, 2013 .

19 *Ibid.*

20 Paul Sloan, 'The Virtual Rockefeller' (CNN Money, December 1, 2005) <http://money.cnn.com/magazines/business2/business2_archive/2005/12/01/8364581/> accessed June 27, 2013.

21 Robert Hof, 'My Virtual Life' (*Business Week*, April 30, 2006) <www.businessweek.com/stories/2006-04-30/my-virtual-life> accessed June 27, 2013.

22 Roger Parloff, 'From Megs To Riches' (CNN Money, November 28, 2005) <http://money.cnn.com/magazines/fortune/fortune_archive/2005/11/28/8361953/index.htm> accessed June 27, 2013.

life.[23] The bank has created virtual bonds which were tradable on the World Stock Exchange in the world, valued at a pittance of what was originally deposited in the accounts.[24] Roughly $750,000 of real currency was lost due to this operation and many users lost their virtual money, resulting in people urging for more protection on virtual property.[25]

3.2   Commerce of Virtual Goods

There is also a trend that real-world companies increasingly engaged in virtual transactions. Facebook, the world's most populated social gaming platform, is another successful industry generating huge profits from selling virtual goods. Facebook's payments and other fees revenue are generated almost exclusively from games.[26] According to the social networking giant's recent SEC Form 10-Q document, just in the first half of 2012, there were 15 million users on Facebook who purchased virtual goods.[27] The total spending amount was $1.26 billion and the overall average spend per paying gamer is $14 per month.[28]

The popularity of the Internet has attracted different global brands' attention to adjust their business strategies in order to utilize the new market. As the same manner competing in the real

---

23   Bryan Gardiner, 'Bank Failure in Second Life Leads to Calls for Regulation' (Wired, August 15, 2007) <www.wired.com/gaming/virtualworlds/news/2007/08/virtual_bank> accessed June 27, 2013.

24   Claude T. Aiken, 'Sources of Law and Modes of Governance: Ethnography and Theory in Second Life' (2009) 10 *Journal of Technology Law and Policy* 1.

25   Gardiner (n23)

26   Lim Yung-Hui, '1.6% Of Facebook Users Spent Over $1 Billion On Virtual Goods" (Forbes, 8 February 2012) <www.forbes.com/sites/limyunghui/2012/08/02/1-6-of-facebook-users-spent-over-1-billion-on-virtual-goods/> accessed June 27, 2013.

27   United States Securities And Exchange Commission, 'Quarterly Report Pursuant To Section 13 Or 15(D) of The Securities Exchange Act of 1934' <www.sec.gov/Archives/edgar/data/1326801/000119312512325997/d371464d10q.htm> accessed June 27, 2013.

28   *Ibid.*

world, businesses also compete in virtual worlds. As demonstrated by many global brands and organizations, virtual worlds are now regarded as a new platform of advertisement.[29] For instance, Apple has set up online stores in *Second Life*, allowing users to browse the latest products released. In Asia, Coca-Cola offered virtual Coke cars and a Coke racetrack to gamer in the virtual world.[30] There are virtual McDonalds-themed items sold in *Farmville*, for example, flags, tables, houses, farms, etc.[31] Nestlé's Purina brand pet food is the exclusive kibble in *FooPets's* virtual pet world.[32] These companies have discovered that selling virtual goods online helps to market their brands. Although no actual purchase is made, these virtual transactions have given them opportunity to get access to different clienteles and customer demographics.[33]

On the other hand, companies observed that they can benefit from making their virtual goods complimentary to their real products. For example, H&M has set up virtual changing rooms on its website.[34] Companies may also collaborate with a game developer to develop their own games such as MTV and Mall World.[35] The transactions of virtual goods also give companies the opportunity to receive customer's reaction and feedback, which

29   Seung-A Annie Jin and Justin Bolebruch, 'Avatar-Based Advertising in Second Life: The Role of Presence and Attractiveness of Virtual Spokespersons' (2009) 10(1) *Journal of Interactive Advertising* <http://jiad.org/article124.html> accessed June 27, 2013.

30   Fitzgerald (n15).

31   Libe Goad, 'Want Fries with That? FarmVille and McDonalds Team up for Promotion' (Game.com, September 21, 2010) <http://blog.games.com/2010/09/21/farmville-mcdonalds-team-up-for-promot/> accessed June 27, 2013.

32   Fitzgerald (n15).

33   SAA and Bolebruch (n30).

34. H&M, 'Online Dressing Room' <www.hm.com/gb/dressingroom/LADIES> accessed June 27, 2013.

35   Facebook, 'MallWorldGame' <www.facebook.com/MallWorldGame> accessed June 27, 2013.

is crucial to the development of a new product and knowledge of what customers want. In the virtual world *Gaia*, Nike gave away virtual T-shirts which are now a real product in the market.[36]

There are many advantages to using these various types of commercialization tactics.[37] Firstly, cost is lower compared to traditional advertising strategy. Secondly, time and venue is no longer a constraint which exists in the real world.[38] Since these virtual communities have become powerful potential groups of e-commerce, advertisement and marketing communication, it provides a huge commercial opportunity to different companies.[39]

4.   Multi-Jurisdiction Perspective

Due to different technical and social norms, the West and the East tend to have different approaches to virtual life.[40] The unrestricted virtual world allows different jurisdictions to learn from each other, and reshape each other.[41] In this section, situations of virtual commercial transactions of four jurisdictions, namely U.S., Europe, Korea and China, would be briefly discussed.

4.1   United States

According to an online study conducted by Frank N. Magid Associates, Inc., which was discussed by PlaySpan, the Visa-owned Monetization-as-a-service provider, at 2012 Games Developer

---

36 Fitzgerald (n15).

37 *Ibid.*

38 Molly Wasko, Robin Teigland, Dorothy Leidner, Sirkka Jarvenpaa 'Stepping into the Internet: New Ventures in Virtual Worlds' (2011) 35(3) *MIS Quarterly* 645.

39 SAA and Bolebruch (n30).

40 Yesha Y Sivan, 'East vs. West? More like East and West' (2012) 5(2) *Journal of Virtual Worlds Research* 1 <http://journals.tdl.org/jvwr/index.php/jvwr/article/view/6915> accessed June 27, 2013.

41 Ibid.

Conference, the United States spent approximately US$2.3 billion on virtual goods in 2011.[42] In the online study, virtual good was defined as the combination of virtual currency and virtual items. Not only has consumer spending amounts on virtual goods doubled since 2009, but the number of people purchasing virtual goods had also increased by 50% from 2010.

In the study, 70% of Americans who had not purchased virtual goods showed their willingness to purchase in the future.[43] Karl Mehta, the founder of PlaySpan, expressed the view that consumers were becoming comfortable and open to virtual transactions. This provided a huge opportunity not only for gaming industry, but also for the majority of digital content companies which traffic in a variety of goods including music, movies, social gifting, and rewards.[44]

At the same time, the study showed the consumption patterns of virtual goods. For example, the numbers of men purchasing virtual goods were twice as women.[45] Moreover, players typically bought virtual goods because they wanted to advance a level in a game, to have a better in-game experience or create an avatar. Factors affecting whether to purchases or not included price, the genre of the game, friends' recommendations, user reviews and if a game can be played with friends, etc.[46] The study also indicated the consumption habits of virtual goods was changing. For example, although customers still purchased virtual goods in

---

42 PlaySpan, 'Study on Virtual Goods Trends' <www.slideshare.net/robblewis/playspan-magid-virtual-goods-report> accessed November 1, 2013.

43 *Ibid.*

44 Rip Empson, 'Study: U.S. Consumer Spending On Virtual Goods Grew To $2.3 Billion In 2011' (TechCrunch, February, 29, 2012) <http://techcrunch.com/2012/02/29/virtual-good-market-boom/> accessed June 27, 2013.

45 PlaySpan (n 42).

46 Mark Walsh, 'Virtual Goods Sales Hit $2.3 Billion In 2011' (Online Media Daily, February 29, 2012) <www.cmo.com/articles/2012/2/29/virtual-good-sales-hit-23-billion-in-2011.html> accessed June 27, 2013.

connected consoles such as Xbox Live or the PlayStation Store at large, there was a trend showing that more and more users would prefer purchasing goods directly within the game.[47]

4.2 Europe

A research found that the popularity of virtual world such as *Second Life* is higher in Europe than in U.S.[48] According to ComScore research in March 2007, 61% of active *Second Life* users were from Europe while only 16 and 13% were from U.S. and the Asia-Pacific region respectively.[49] The ComScore research found that 61% of the users were male and 39% were female. There were about 1.3 million people ran the official software and logged into *Second Life* and represented an increase of 46% in the number of active users. The result showed that the phenomenal growth of *Second Life* was still continued around the world.

Bob Ivins, Managing Director of ComScore Europe, observed that the number of German users exceeds the number of users in the entire United States. 16% of European users came from Germany, which is the majority number of users across Europe. 8% of users were in France and 6% was in the United Kingdom. The number of users coming from the U.K. grew to 24% within two months while there was a 92% increase in the number of U.S. users and a 70% increase in German users.[50]

As the same result of U.S, it was also observed that bricks and

---

47 PlaySpan (n 42).

48 Steve Ranger, 'Europeans latch on to Second Life' (CNET News, 4 May 2007) <http://news.cnet.com/Europeans-latch-on-to-Second-Life/2100-1043_3-6181431. html> accessed June 27, 2013.

49 Andrew Lipsman, 'ComScore Finds that "Second Life" Has a Rapidly Growing and Global Base of Active Residents' (ComScore, May 4, 2007) <www.comscore. com/Insights/Press_Releases/2007/05/Second_Life_Growth_Worldwide> accessed June 27, 2013.

50 *Ibid.*

mortar businesses in Europe were seeing virtual world as a way of accessing a global, real-world customer base.[51] Continuing and potential future growth of virtual economy in Europe was expected.

4.3 Korea

In South Korea, Nexon's Crazyracing *KartRider* game sold more than 100,000 Mini Coopers which is more than BMW's sales of the actual car.[52] From the statics of the National Internet Development Agency of Korea (NIDA), Korea is one of the leading countries in terms of Internet access in the world.[53] However, virtual goods transactions in Korea still attracted a lot of debates in this stage. In a 2003 survey by the Korea Game Development and Promotion Institute (KGDI),[54] about 20% of companies stated that these transactions should be banned while similar percent of companies said that they were desirable.[55]

Many people believed that there should be regulation and limits on virtual goods transactions. However, at the same time, 27.5% of the companies expressed that virtual items should be freely transacted.[56] Most of the disputes concerned virtual world crimes such as fraud.[57] The public and corporations worried that

51 *Ibid.*

52 Fitzgerald (n 15)

53 National Internet Development Agency of Korea, 'Report of Korea status in 2008' (4 November, 2008) <http://cai.icann.org/files/meetings/cairo2008/ccnso-kr-status-04nov08.pdf > accessed June 27, 2013.

54 Korea Game Development and Promotion Institute, '2004 The Rise of Korean Games: Guide to Korean Game Industry and Culture' (May 2004) <www.kocca.kr/ knowledge/publication/indu/__icsFiles/afieldfile/2010/05/02/70017.pdf> accessed June 27, 2013

55 *Ibid.*

56 *Ibid.*

57 Ian MacInnes, 'Virtual Worlds in Asia: Business Models and Legal Issues' (Paper presented at the Digital Games Research Association Conference, Vancouver, Canada 2005) <http://surface.syr.edu/istpub/113/> accessed November 1, 2013.

hacking would result in loss of other players' items or virtual money. While virtual goods were becoming valuable, hackers were trying to gain access to other players' ID to take their virtual items and currency or gain access to servers of game developers to get illegal virtual money. Some people expressed the concern that the government has not found a suitable method to solve the problem of virtual transaction fraud and one of the reasons might be the lack of applicable laws to regulate virtual transactions.[58]

4.4. China

Tencent, the largest internet portal in China, reported $1.05 billion revenue in 2008, where 88% of revenue came from transactions of virtual goods.[59] Despite of the huge profit earned by Chinese virtual world providers, a study suggested that the industry of virtual world was still in the early stages of the development of business models.[60] In the past, the focus of competition between virtual world providers was on improving distribution channels and operating efficiency. In spite of technology improvement and industry evolution over the past few years, virtual world providers in China were still overcoming some early stage obstacles.[61] Fortunately, the industry was currently moving through the second iteration of the business model stages and adjusting to new technical and environmental issues.[62]

The study stated that, the industry of virtual world in China

---

58 *Ibid.*

59 Fitzgerald (n 15).

60 Ian MacInnes, 'Property Rights, Legal Issues, and Business Models in Virtual World Communities' (2005) 6(1) *Electronic Commerce Research Journal,* 39.

61 David Kurt Herold, 'Escaping the World: A Chinese Perspective on Virtual Worlds' (2012) 5(2) *Journal of Virtual Worlds Research* <http://journals.tdl.org/jvwr/index.php/jvwr/article/view/6206> accessed June 27, 2013.

62 *Ibid.*

had little innovation in terms of business models and technologies in generally speaking.[63] However, it did not mean China had no achievement at all. China had developed some online real-time payment systems for transactions of virtual goods.[64] Consumers could choose to make their purchase of virtual goods by point cards and monthly cards. Compared to other jurisdictions, the payment systems was successful to facilitate users' purchase.[65] Moreover, the virtual world industry in China has a very unique feature called "gold farming," which would be discussed in details in the later part of the essay.

4.5 Implications and Future Development

According to a report from IBISWorld,[66] the US's largest publisher of industry market research, the virtual world industry is likely to continue to grow quickly over the five years to 2016 with a rate slower than the previous five years. Revenue of the Social Network Game industry was expected to increase 24.4% annually to $11.3 billion. Social networking websites were expected to expand their user bases and there will be emergence of new markets in social gaming. Moreover, more smart phones were sold with social gaming options resulting in increasing disposable income. The report also suggested that the fastest growing group of virtual goods consumers is women over 40 years of age, who quickly become consumers through their original participation in online social games.[67]

---

63 MacInnes, 'Property Rights, Legal Issues' (n 60).

64 Herold (n 61).

65 *Ibid.*

66 'Social Network Game Development in the US: Market Research Report' (IBIS World, September 2012) <www.ibisworld.com/industry/social-network-game-development.html> accessed June 27, 2013.

67 *Ibid.*

The development of virtual commercial transactions gives rise to crucial implications to different aspects of commercial industry. The market structure and products available would be affected by rapid development of the virtual world industry. Providers of virtual worlds cover their expenses from labor, electronic resources by placing advertisement and in-game purchases. In latest smart phone technology, it is commonly observed that many games are downloaded for free, however, incorporated in-game purchases of new levels, armor, weapons, extra lives, etc. These virtual goods have created marketplaces everywhere. It is foreseeable that the trend of virtual world provided in future more likely to be free of charge because providers now have increasing opportunities to monetize their free games. This may bring a positive effect to the market that there would be a greater selection and quality of games for users to choose.

5.   Issues Arising out of Virtual Commercial Transactions

The development of virtual world transactions has brought greater business efficiency to society. But this has raised different issues at the same time. The commercial transactions within the virtual world have legal,[68] ethical[69] and security[70] implications to the public.

---

68   Gerald Spindler, Katharina Anton and Jan Wehage, 'Overview of the Legal Issues in Virtual Worlds' (2009) 40 *UCMedia* 189.

69   Orin S. Kerr, 'Criminal Law In Virtual Worlds' (2008) GWU Public Law and Legal Theory Paper No. 391 <http://scholarship.law.gwu.edu/cgi/viewcontent.cgi?article=1714&context=faculty_publications> accessed June 27, 2013.

70   B Mennecke *et al.*, 'Second Life And Other Virtual Worlds: A Roadmap For Research' (2008) 22 (Article 20) Communications of the Association for Information Systems 371 <www.bus.iastate.edu/mennecke/CAIS-Vol22-Article20.pdf> accessed June 27, 2013.

5.1   The Nature of Virtual Goods

One of the most controversial legal issues is the property right of the users to things they created in the virtual world. The first question which has to be answered is whether these virtual items are able to be recognized as "property" by law.

The term "property" was once described as the "relationship of a person to a thing" but in the modern law this concept has been changed.[71] The concept of property is conceived as a bundle of rights, including right to exclude, the right to use, and the right to transfer interest to another.[72] These bundle-of-rights do not necessarily apply on tangible things but also on things which is intangible, such as trademark and copyright.[73] For virtual goods, the property at issue is also not the physical manifestation. In a virtual world, each item is represented by a piece of data. The data stored in the database of the virtual world provider would be regarded as intellectual property by law.[74]

The next question would then be whom the property right belongs to. Data created by the provider would originally owned by it.[75] By entering contract with the users, providers generally transfer some of the right to the users. It grants the users exclusive right to use or, in some case, sell the interest laid in the virtual goods.

---

71   Justin Graham, 'Preserving the Aftermarket in Copyrighted Works: Adapting the First Sale Doctrine to the Emerging Technological Landscape', 2002 *Stan. Tech. L. Rev.* <http://stlr.stanford.edu/pdf/preserving-the-aftermarket> accessed June 27, 2013.

72   John Sprankling, *Understand Property Law* (LexisNexis 1999) 4–6.

73   Adam Mossoff, 'What Is Property? Putting the Pieces Back Together' (2003) 45 *Ariz. L. Rev.* 371, 413–427.

74   David Nelmark, 'Virtual Property: The Challenges of Regulating Intangible, Exclusionary Property Interests Such as Domain Names' (2004) 3 *Nw. J. Tech. & Intell Prop.* 1.

75   Susan Thomas Johnson, 'Note, Internet Domain Name and Trademark Disputes: Shifting Paradigms in Intellectual Property' (2001) 43 *Ariz. L. Rev.* 465.

In some virtual world, the users are allowed to keep the ownership of things which were combined from material given by the provider.[76] According to John Locke, an individual owned his own labor as well as the fruits of that labor. Thus, if an individual's labor created something from the commons, the property right to the creation extended to the individual.[77]

As a result, the users of virtual world would act as if they are the owners of the virtual items. They exercise right to use and right to exclude other participants from the items. The most significant right to commercial transactions is the right to transfer their interests in virtual property.

5.2 Litigation on Virtual Property Rights of Users

The next issue would be the enforcement of these right and the remedies available to the users. The virtual world has bought real disputes which leading to litigation in real courts. Actually, law and virtual world is a hot topic in legal scholarship.[78] There have been users using the courts to enforce their right. In 2003, a gamer successfully sued the provider for the loss his virtual property which was stolen by a hacker.[79] In *Bragg v Linden Research*,[80] Bragg's account was terminated by the virtual world provider, claiming that Bragg acquired virtual land at a lower-than-market

---

76 Linden Lab, 'Corporate Background' (October 2004) <http://s3.amazonaws.com/static-secondlife-com/corporate/LindenLab_Background.pdf> accessed June 27, 2013.

77 See, for example, Book II, Chapter 5 (Of Property), §25 of John Locke, *Two Treatises Of Government (1680–1690)* <http://www.lonang.com/exlibris/locke/loc-205.htm> accessed November 1, 2013.

78 Woodrow Barfield, 'Intellectual Property Rights in Virtual Environments: Considering the Rights of Owners, Programmers and Virtual Avatars' (2006) 39 *Akron L. Rev.* 649.

79 'Online gamer in China wins virtual theft suit' (CNN News, December 20, 2003) <www.cnn.com/2003/TECH/fun.games/12/19/china.gamer.reut/> accessed June 27, 2013

80 (2007) 487 F. Supp. 2d 593.

price. The case was settled before the decision granted but was valuable that the judges have decided on two issues which may be important in future virtual world litigation. Firstly, the court held that the *Second Life* Terms of Service's mandatory arbitration provision was unenforceable. Secondly, interaction with a person in a virtual world can satisfy a state's "minimum contacts" requirement for personal jurisdiction.[81]

More and more people are using litigation as the method to safeguard their property right of virtual goods. Despite of the increasing trend of using litigation as an enforcement of right over virtual property, many pertinent issues are still left for discussion.[82] Whether the users of virtual world can protect their rights from infringement of other people effectively, and whether disputes emanating from virtual worlds could be resolved in the courtroom decisively, is remained to be seen.

5.3 Virtual Goods Farming

The commercial transactions of virtual goods have given rise to a new occupation, namely, the "farmer of virtual goods."[83] These farmers, most of them are in Asia, work full time in real-world companies to play games and earn virtual items. Then the companies sell these virtual items for real money, most likely to Western Countries. These companies are just like real-world factories with the only difference that the products are virtual goods. According to a report prepared by Richard Heeks at

---

81   *Ibid.*

82   Bobby Glushko, 'Note, Tales of the (Virtual) City: Governing Property Disputes In Virtual Worlds' (2007) 22 *Berkeley Tech. L.J.* 507.

83   Richard Heeks, 'Understanding "Gold Farming": Developing-country Production for Virtual Gameworlds' (2009) 3 *Information Technologies and International Development* 5.

Manchester University,[84] there are about 400,000 "gold farmer" in Asia and they produce over £700 million real-world money per year.[85] Although the gold farming industry is about playing games, this is a big business. The industry is now estimated to have a consumer base of over five million people. With increasing users of virtual worlds, the gold farming industry is expected to grow continually.

Companies in the industry are very formal. For example, Wow7gold, one of the companies in the industry, exercised division of labor and divided workers into different departments such as production, sales, advertising and research.[86] Li Hua was one of workers in Wow7gold, which sells *World of Warcraft* in-game items for cash. He made a living by playing computer games, earning about £80 per month.[87] However, given the long hours and night shifts, the hourly salary can amount to as little as 30p.[88] Moreover, the working conditions of these farmers were very harsh. According to Li, workers only have one holiday per month.[89] Interestingly, some traditional concepts of "men's work" and "women's work" were still applicable in this revolutionary industry. Uneducated workers enjoy lower salaries working as

84   Richard Heeks, 'Current Analysis and Future Research Agenda on "Gold Farming": Real-World Production in Developing Countries for the Virtual Economies of Online Games' (2008) Manchester University Development Informatics Working Paper Series No. 32.

85   *Ibid.*

86   Rowenna Davis, 'Welcome to the New Gold Mines' (*The Guardian*, London, 5 March 2009) <www.guardian.co.uk/technology/2009/mar/05/virtual-world-china> accessed June 27, 2013.

87   Richard Heeks 'Understanding "Gold Farming" and Real-money Trading as the Intersection of Real and Virtual Economies' (2010) 2 (4) *Journal of Virtual Worlds Research* <http://journals.tdl.org/jvwr/index.php/jvwr/article/view/868> accessed June 27, 2013.

88   Heeks (n80).

89   Davis (n90).

gold farmer while female graduates enjoy higher salaries working as customer service personnel.[90]

At present, the most of these "farmers" in fact live in developing countries, with four-fifths of them living in China. The Chinese government acknowledged the rising significance of gold farming by introducing a 20% tax on the industry.[91] However, regulations on working hours, salaries, holidays and medical fees are still waiting for development.

5.4 *Virtual Crimes*

With the development of virtual transactions, monetary issues arose in virtual world are similar to those in the real world. In South Korea, as mentioned above, one of the major issues of virtual world is the virtual crimes. Besides fraud and hacking, gangs and mafia have also been reported in the virtual world. Some "powerful" users of virtual worlds demanded other users to give protection fee, which sometimes amounted to threatening and blackmail. Sometimes the users' virtual property is robbed and stolen.[92]

Moreover, the commercial transactions may give rise to inappropriate content such as sex and violent.[93] In *The Sims*, a boy aged 17 once set up a brothel which provided customers cybersex in exchange of sim-money.[94] In July 2007, a virtual

---

90 *Ibid.*

91 *Ibid.*

92 MacInnes (n51).

93 Xeni Jardin, 'Evangeline: Interview with a Child cyber-Prostitute in TSO' (Alphaville Herald, December 8, 2003) <http://alphavilleherald.com/2003/12/evangeline_inte.html> accessed June 27, 2013.

94 Tal Z. Zarsky, 'Information Privacy In Virtual Worlds: Identifying Unique Concerns Beyond the Online and Offline Worlds' (2004) 49 *N.Y. Law School L. Rev.* 231.

crimes offender cracked a stock exchange's computers and stole about US$10,000 and then ran off and disappeared into thin air.[95] The investors in *Second Life* felt so insecure that they have taken actions to ask for more regulations.[96] Comparative speaking, laws regarding virtual world crimes are still immature in the moment. Which jurisdiction should the litigation take place? Which set of laws should be applied? Which countries are the decisions enforceable? In many cases, these questions were left open or answered unsatisfactorily.

6.   Conclusion

Technology and technological advances affecting commercial transactions are evolving. Nowadays, people are not only concerned with purchasing goods online through such sites as e-Bay. They are also intrigued by the ability to purchase virtual goods which have enormous value and influence but which they cannot use, see or touch in the real world. Unconsciously, people are placing more and more reliance on the Internet and virtual worlds. These developments bring great opportunities for the commercial world. At the same time, they raise potential issues. While different jurisdictions are promptly addressing these issues, more work still needs to be done in order to protect people's rights and to perfect the whole system.

---

95   Francesca Di Meglio, 'Virtual Exchanges Get Real' (*Businessweek*, August 13, 2007) <www.businessweek.com/stories/2007-08-10/virtual-exchanges-get-realbusinessweek-business-news-stock-market-and-financial-advice> accessed June 27, 2013.

96   *Ibid.*

Part III
The Nature of "Goods" in the Virtual World

4

The Nature of "Goods" and the Bundle of Property Rights in the Virtual World

Kwan Yee CHEUNG

1. Introduction

In the 21st century, the technology era, our way of life is no longer restricted to traditional definition of it. The line between fantasy and reality, as well as the lines between work, play, data, and property become very confusing.[1] It becomes more and more popular for people to socialize in virtual worlds-three-dimensional online environments with each other and interact with the environment. It is found that there are approximately 12.5 million customers[2] subscribed to one virtual world or another, and at a general access fee of around $15 per month.[3] These players may socialize with other players via their own avatars, collaborate with them in various tasks like "virtual craftsmanship, hunting and warfare, or compete with other

---

1 Edward Castronova, *Synthetic Worlds: The Business and Culture of Online Games* (*University of Chicago Press 2005*) 2

2 Siam Choudhury, 'MMOGData.com, succeeds MMOGCHART.com' (The MMOGAME, June 5, 2007) <www.mmogamer.com/06/05/2007/mmodatacom-succeeds-mmogchartcom> accessed December 3, 2013

3 World of Warcraft Community Site, 'Billing Support' (World of Warcraft, April 5, 2007) <www.blizzard.com/support/wowbilling/?id=ablOl025p> December 3, 2013

players to achieve various goals."[4] This promising industry is making immense profits, over billions of dollars, per year for the providers of virtual worlds.[5] On top of this source of income for providers, these prevalent commercial virtual worlds also give rise to an associated secondary market which circulates "real" currency in exchange for virtual items,[6] generating $3.42 per hour per participant with the unit of currency to have an exchange rate higher than the Japanese Yen or Italian Lira.[7]

As the market of virtual goods grows considerably, it is of paramount importance to understand the extent to which there is real world money being traded for virtual goods, examine feasibility of claiming ownership over virtual goods, and determine the effects of a property right in goods which have no physical manifestation.[8]

Although at first glance, it seems to be impossible for virtual goods to be the subject of any legal property rights, "property" does exist in virtual world and it shares many similarities with the real world personal property. Nevertheless, the differences are unique and distinctive. In virtual communities like the "*World of Warcraft*" (which is an online game), weapons such as "sword" or "armor" can be consumed, transferred, or disposed of within the game just like the same could be done with a pen in the reality. Still, it should be noted that that, at its center, that particular piece

---

4 F. Gregory Lastowka and Dan Hunter, 'The Laws of the Virtual Worlds' *92 Cal. L. Rev.* (2004).

5 Seth Schiesel, 'An Online Game, Made in America, Seizes the Globe' (*N.Y. Times*, September 5, 2006) A1 <www.nytimes.com/2006/09/05/technology/05wow. html?pagewanted=all&_r=0> accessed December 3, 2013

6 Tom Leupold, 'Spot On: Virtual Economies Break Out of Cyberspace' (GAMESPOT, May 6, 2005) <www.gamespot.com/news/2005/05/06/ news_6123701.html> accessed December 3, 2013

7 Edward Castronova, 'Virtual Worlds: A First-Hand Account of Market and Society on the Cyberian Frontier' (December 2001) *CESifo Working Paper Series No. 618* <http://ssrn.com/abstract=294828> accessed December 3, 2013

8 Castronova (n 7); Lastowka and Hunter (n 4).

of virtual property is simply "a bundle of mathematic algorithms run through a computer to simulate the look and utility of a real world good."[9]

The purpose of this chapter is to analyze the nature of the goods and the bundle of property rights contained in the virtual world. It will start with the comparison between virtual property and personal property, and then move on to explain how virtual goods are regulated in reality.

2. The Concept of Virtual Property

In truth, virtual property, such as objects or avatars in virtual worlds, can be considered as non-existent. This is because, when a player acquires money in virtual worlds, it does not mean that there is corporeal object for the participant to claim.[10] Hence, one might ask, "if none of these objects exists, does it even make sense to talk about whether a property interest in them could exist?"[11] This question can be answered in two ways, and in both ways the answer should also be a "yes."

First, logically speaking, property exists due to social construction. Hence, when certain things and ideas are considered to be belonged to certain people who have power over them, then these things and ideas can be regarded as property even though they may not have a corporeal existence.

---

9 Joshua A.T. Fairfield, 'Virtual Property', (2005) *85 B.U. L. Rev.* 1047, 1049.

10 This might not be true in all cases. The game *Magic: The Gathering* exists as both a collectible card game and an online card game. If a player collects a certain number of digital cards in the online game, he may redeem them for physical copies of the cards. See Redemption: Terms and Conditions, <http://wizards.custhelp.com> (search text for "Redemption: Terms and Conditions;" then follow "Redemption: Terms and Conditions" hyperlink) accessed December 3, 2013) (describing the process of redeeming digital cards for physical cards).

11 David P. Sheldon, 'Claiming Ownership, but getting owned: Contractual limitations on asserting property interests in virtual goods' (2007) *54 UCLA Law Review 751*

Second, morally speaking, property interests stem from John Locke's conception of the ability "to enjoy the fruits of one's labor" so that players in the virtual world should enjoy some enforceable interest in virtual items that they have spent considerable time and effort creating or obtaining. This concept will be further elaborated below.

2.1 Traditional Forms of Noncorporeal Property

Before, legal theorists analyzed the term "property" in terms of a person's relation to a thing.[12] Later, starting from the 20th century, legal theorists began to realize this mere term of "property" is insufficient, and tried to incorporate generic concepts into something more descriptive.[13]

Among the legal theorists, Wesley Hohfield can best represent this group of theorists. He redefined "rights" to claims and duties that lie between individuals in society, and suggested that property should be considered as a bundle of these rights.[14] Different from previous theory, which considered that the term "property" was all that was required to define the relationship of a person to a thing, Wesley's approach perceives property as "the relation of people to each other with respect to a thing."[15] It does not define any specific "element" that is necessary to prove in order to be a property of a particular person. Instead, the framework analyzes which of the possible rights and obligations a person has toward other people with respect to the thing.[16] A particular thing will be

---

12 Justin Graham, 'Preserving the Aftermarket in Copyrighted Works: Adapting the First Sale Doctrine to the Emerging Technological Landscape,' *2002 Stan. Tech. L. Rev. 1*

13 Adam Mossoff, 'What Is Property? Putting the Pieces Back Together', (2003) *45 Ariz. L. Rev. 371*

14 *Ibid.*

15 *Ibid.*

16 Susan Thomas Johnson, 'Internet Domain Name and Trademark Disputes: Sifting Paradigms in Intellectual Property' (2003) *43 Ariz. L. Rev. 465*

considered as one's property when a person has certain rights in that particular thing. The usual rights within the bundle are the right to exclude, the right to use, and the right to transfer interest to another.[17]

Under this bundle-of-rights approach, an object can be called as a property even if it is an intangible thing.[18] For instance, an inventor is regarded to have a property right in his invention upon his successful acquirement of a patent.[19] Such property that he obtained is not the physical appearance of his invention, or the official document that he gets from the patent office; the property that he possesses is the ability to practice the idea embodied in the document. The patent grants him "the exclusive right to make, use, or sell the invention, and to transfer or license that right to other people." Hence, although the patent is an intangible object, the idea within the patent is regarded as his property, as he has the rights to exclude, to use, and to transfer.[20]

2.2 Property as the "Fruit" of One's Labor

Among various philosophers, John Locke probably offers the most powerful reasons to support the concept that virtual goods should be regarded as property and those virtual world users should enjoy substantial property interest in their virtual property.[21] The Lockean conception of property contended that property is a natural right and it is derived from labor while each

---

17 William P. Barr *et al.*, 'The Gild That is Killing the Lily: How Confusion over Regulatory Takings Doctrine is Undermining the Core Protections of the Takings Clause' (2004) *73 Geo. Wash. L. Rev. 429.*

18 Wesley M. Oliver, 'A Round Peg in a Square Hole: Federal Forfeiture of State Professional Licenses' (2010) *28 Am. J. Crim. L. 179.*

19 Julian David Forman, 'A Timing Perspective on the Utility Requirement in Biotechnology Patent Applications' (2002) *12 Alb. L. J. Sci. & Tech. 647* (2002).

20 David Nelmark, 'Virtual Property: The Challenges of Regulating Intangible, Exclusionary Property Interests Such as Domain Names (2004) *3 Nw. J. Tech. & Intell. Prop. 1.*

21 Lastowka and Hunter (n 4).

person owned his own labor. Thus, when a person uses the labor he owns to create something, that creation will become property and the creator will own the property right of that creation.[22] In short, a person should be able to enjoy the fruits of his labor. This right is reflected in both "social/creative" virtual worlds and "combat/collection" virtual worlds, even though in a slight different way.

Firstly, "social/creative" virtual world does reflect Lockean concept where property is created by the act of combining labor with material from the commons. Citing "*Second Life*®" as an example, inside the game, it offers players with 3D creation tools, letting them to assemble existing objects and turning them into new forms.[23] Apart from that, it offers a scripting language so that players can make the objects they have created to interact with the environment and react in various fascinating ways inside the virtual world.[24] Such an idea of creating new virtual objects by combining geometric shapes and behaviors is highly similar to Locke's concept of the paradigmatic creation of property.

On the other hand, "combat/collection" virtual worlds do not closely resemble the Lockean ideal as much as creative virtual world do. However, there is an exchange of labor in these virtual worlds. Taking the *World of Warcraft* as an example, the players do not combine various existing objects to create new things, as players do in *Second Life*®. Instead, they are repeatedly carrying out challenging jobs in the game hoping to find certain uncommon items. Such an act of performing arduous task can be considered as doing work or exerting effort. For an avatar to get to the highest level, a normal player has to at least spend over 350 hours in the game, which is equal to nine weeks of work at a

---

22 John Locke, *Two Treatises of Government* (Legal Classics Library 1994).

23 Linden Lab, 'Corporate Background 1' (Oct. 2004), <http://lindenlab.com/LindenLabBackground.pdf> accessed December 3, 2013

24 *Ibid.*

full-time job.[25] After advancing to this highest level, players would then focus more on getting the hidden treasure in the game. Hence, although no invention of new objects are created just like in *Second Life*®, large amount of work and time is invested in obtaining precious objects from the commons and developing high-level avatars in these "combat/collection" virtual worlds.

2.3. Similarities Shared between Virtual Property and Real Property

Virtual property can be defined as "computer code that, when processed, mimics some characteristics of real world property, including exclusivity, persistence and transferability."[26] While a lot of computer code especially for those which is present on the Internet can be used by multiple users at the same time, virtual property cannot. It is this unique feature of exclusivity in virtual property makes it similar to real world personal property.[27] While the objects of intellectual property contain, to a certain extent, concepts that could in theory be used by many people simultaneously, personal and virtual property share the similar attributes in that use and control of the property in question is restricted to a fixed number of people.[28] This makes virtual property to be subjected to the same principle of scarcity that we encounter when dealing with "real" goods in the reality. Therefore, if you own a piece of virtual property, then another person cannot also own it. Same rule applies when you are using, trading, or even throwing it away.

---

25 Nick Yee, 'Distribution of Levelling Times' (PlayOn, September 6, 2005), <http://wow.parc.com/blog/playon/2005/09/distribution_of_leveling_times.html> accessed December 3, 2013.

26 Fairfield (n 9) 1049, 1053–55.

27 Adam Mossoff, 'What Is Property? Putting the Pieces Back Together' *45 Ariz. L. Rev. 371.*

28 Fairfield (n 9).

The second hallmark that both personal property and virtual property share is persistence. This means that a piece of computer code could only be correctly called as virtual property if it will not disappear when the user's computer is turned off. The code must bear the persistence that the user is able to recall it at a later time. This reason should be the similar with the analogy of a piece of furniture, which often does not vanish when one turns away from it. Hence, virtual property must at least have a certain degree of independent existence that its existence does not depend on particular personal computer. As virtual property, in nature, does not has its existence outside the digital world, the persistence criterion can only be satisfied if it exists within at least one computer, and will not be accessible even if that computer is turned off, disabled, or destroyed. The rationale behind this principle is that "an exclusive right to the use of a thing depends on the continued existence of that thing." Hence, the concept of ownership is highly depends upon the concept of persistence.

The third distinctive feature of virtual property is transferability. This feature requires that represented by a string of code, the useful object has to be transferable from a person to another in a meaningful fashion. This is because, it is only if the virtual property is transferrable will the question of property rights be important. Where that object represented by a string of computer code is non-transferrable, it could only be possessed by its creator and first possessor.

The above mentioned characteristics can be further illustrated by the different recognized types of virtual property. For instance, an "Internet Uniform Resource Locator" (URL), such as http:.. cityu.edu.hk, satisfies all the three features of a virtual property.

(a) Firstly, it is comprised of strings of computer code (and hence be considered as "virtual").

(b) Secondly, URL can be exclusively owned by an entity, which remains available by way of networked web servers and does not vanish when the web browser is shut down and hence it is persistent.

(c)   Thirdly, City University of Hong Kong could sell the URL to, for example, the University of Hong Kong, which could use the URL for its own purpose.

Therefore, it is regarded as transferable. Qualifying all these three characteristics, a URL thus is virtual property.

Another separate example of virtual property is that which exist in the "virtual world." These "virtual worlds" are digital representations of a physical space which are often created and maintained as an online game.[29] In essence, they are a host location that imitates various features of our world. When a user of a personal computer logs into a virtual world, a visual depiction will then represent the real user. It will act as his proxy inside that virtual world, following his directions.[30] This representative proxy is known as "avatars." Different from the traditional console-based or non-networked personal computer game environment, virtual worlds offer a connected network platform where countless avatars can flock together, creating a virtual world population that can exceed millions. Representing the users, these avatars carry out many different activities. They can interact with each other through typing, speaking or even pantomiming. They can also move around and manipulate various aspects of the world.

To conclude, virtual property and real world property share many similarities and these unique features are more distinct and more limited virtual worlds. For instance, virtual chattels obviously copy real world goods in terms of the way they are used (as in the limited context of the virtual world), transferable, exclusive, and persistent. Whereas, different from real world

---

29 Lastowka and Hunter (n 4) 5–7.

30 Lastowka and Hunter (n 4) 6.

goods and URLs, they are slightly different from the direct real world goods in terms of usefulness, as they can only be used in one, generally isolated context of virtual world.

3. The Current Relationship between Virtual World Providers and Participants

The participants in the virtual worlds do believe that those virtual items they own are their properties. They will exercise their right of exclusion to prevent other participants from obtaining the items they possess through game mechanics.[31] More surprisingly, some of them may even bring judicial actions against other people so as to enforce their right to exclude who have infringed those rights.[32] But nonetheless, it should bear in mind that these virtual worlds would not even have existed if there were not their respective providers. Participants can enjoy these rights simply because their respective providers write the code, sell the service and have complete control over everything in these virtual worlds at any time. Consequentially, the following part will explore the relationship between virtual world providers and their participants and how these virtual world providers try to limit the property rights of players within the virtual goods.

3.1 Contract

Before the virtual property market gained popularity in the virtual world, virtual world providers, in general, depended on existing intellectual property regimes, such as copyright, in order to protect the content of their worlds. Nevertheless, the

---

31 James Grimmelmann, 'Virtual Worlds as Comparative Law' (2004) *49 N.Y.L. Sch. L. Rev. 147.*

32 CNN.com International, 'Online Gamer in China Wins Virtual Theft Suit' (CNN. com, December 20, 2003), <http://edition.cnn.com/2003/TECH/fun.games/12/19/china.gamer.reut/> accessed December 3, 2013.

growth of virtual item commodification in virtual worlds brought uncertainty as to how intellectual property rights would prevent virtual world participants from freely exchanging virtual items for real world currency. Providers at that time would try to prevent would-be sellers from using copyrighted art in their advertisement in an attempt to make the transaction harder. However, this was not entirely effective.[33] In addition, some critics began to believe that participants might be able to get intellectual property protection because they have spent time and used their creativity when interacting with the virtual world.[34]

Rather than depending wholly on the default protections of intellectual property law, providers started to use contract to allocate the rights to virtual items.[35] Under this new practice, providers will adopt the familiar "end user license agreement" ("EULA"). It was widely adopted where it basically is used in all software transactions.[36] In practice, there are two main differences between using contract rather than intellectual property law to decide the allocation of these rights.

Firstly, the scopes of the rights are more certain under contract. This is because some intellectual property doctrines cover excessive areas of uncertainty. For example, the copyright defense of fair use[37] or the doctrine of equivalents in patent

---

33 Molly Stephens, 'Sales of In-Game Assets: An Illustration of the Continuing Failure of Intellectual Property Law to Protect Digital-Content Creators' (2002) *80 Tex. L. Rev. 1513, 1521–23.*

34 Kelly M. Slavitt, 'Gabby in Wonderland — Through the Internet Looking Glass' (1998) *80 J. Pat. & Trademark Off. Soc'y. 611.*

35 Daniel C. Miller, 'Determining Ownership in Virtual Worlds: Copyright and License Agreements' (2003) *22 Rev. Litig. 435, 460.*

36 *Ibid.*

37 Sarah Deutsch, 'Fair Use in Copyright Law and the Nonprofit Organization: A Proposal for Reform' (1985) *34 Am. U. L. Rev. 1327.*

infringement.[38] These areas of uncertainty would be greatly reduced under the EULAs as they will expressly allocate the rights that may have previously been in doubt.[39]

Secondly, providers can use EULAs to regulate participants' activities in a broader scope than those which intellectual property law seeks to cover. For instance, EULAs can be used to regulate unwanted behaviors by, for example, removing accounts which promote unwanted advertisements or encourage harassment among participants. Therefore, providers can, by adding a term in the contract, have the authority to forbid participants from buying or selling virtual items for real-world currency. This is an ability that is not available to them under intellectual property law.

4.   Analysis of the EULAs

Due to the widespread usage of EULAs in the virtual worlds, it is necessary to understand how the EULAs allocate rights and responsibilities with respect to virtual items. As mentioned above, property is a bundle of rights. Hence, through dissecting the terms of the EULAs, we would be able to know the exact nature of virtual property. In the following passages, three aspects of the EULAs are highly important to understand the nature of virtual property and are discussed in detail in this section, namely: (a) allocation of rights in the form of expressed assignments of the right to use, the right to exclude, and the right to transfer; (b) powers reserved by the provider to alter those arrangements and to strip participants of their virtual items; and (c) remedies

---

38   Christina Y. Lai, 'A Dysfunctional Formalism: How Modem Courts Are Undermining the Doctrine of Equivalents' (1997) *44 UCLA L. Rev. 2031.*

39   Miller (n 36).

granted to participants when they feel their rights under the contract have been violated.

4.1 Allocation of Rights

One important property right is the right to use. In general, all EULAs deal with virtual items and avatars in the same way regarding the right to use. They will explicitly or implicitly grant participants the right to use the avatars in their accounts and the right to use virtual items that are related to those avatars in the game. These rights of usage allow the participants to collect virtual items through controlling an avatar in a virtual world.

Nevertheless, this right to use is in fact very limited when it is compared to the absolute right to use which a person has over tangible properties. Apart from the absolute limitations on use which are enforced by the code,[40] the EULAs further confine the kinds of activities that a participant can participate. If they failed to follow the particular rules of conduct set by providers, their rights to use an avatar and the items associated with an avatar might be taken away.[41] Generally speaking, these rules of conduct usually prevent participants from using his avatar to "harass or offend other participants," "impersonating a staff member of the provider," "defrauding other participants," and "using her avatar

---

40 Lawrence Lessig, *Code and Other Laws of Cyberspace* (Basic Books 1999) 4.

41 These collections of rules are named differently by different virtual-world providers. For example, in *EverQuest* the agreement is called the "Rules of Conduct" and in *World of Warcraft* it is called the "Terms of Use." The general ideas governed by each of these policies are nevertheless the same.

to conduct illegal activity."[42] Sometimes, these rules of conduct might even enforce some restrictions that, in general, would not be considered unlawful or would be directly harmful to the virtual society. Example of this might be a participant leaving his avatar unattended in the virtual world for a certain period of time.[43]

The right to exclude means the right to prevent others from exerting control over the property and is considered one of the most important property rights. Yet, this is the property right which virtual world providers are least concerned with because most virtual world developers and owners do not give this right to the users of virtual worlds. Even though the language used might vary between different agreements, all EULAs reserve the right to exclude to the provider regarding avatars and virtual items. This right usually terms as "a retention of all rights, title,

---

42 If one were to engage in these types of activities in the real world, he may run afoul of the law; however, unlike in the virtual world, complying with the law in the real world is not necessarily a condition of ownership. That is, if a person prints up a newsletter that allegedly defames the company he works for, he may be fired, but his right to possess and use his printer, or the personal items he brought to work, will not necessarily change. Meanwhile, in the virtual world, using an avatar to defame the company providing the world may not lead only to summary exclusion from the world, but may also result in the loss of all associated property. This distinction helps illuminate the dramatic extent to which EULAs regulate activity and ownership in virtual worlds beyond the extent of legal regulation in the real world.

43 Star Wars Galaxies, 'Rules of Conduct Supp. R.3' (Star Wars Galaxies January 26, 2007) <http://starwarsgalaxies.station.sony.coia/enUS/players/content.vm?page=Policies%20Community%20Standards&resurce=policies> accessed December 3, 2013.

and interest in virtual objects and data"[44] and applies to all contents, which are created by the providers or the participants.[45] Among all the providers, *Second Life®* is the only one who gave participants the right to exclude and allows participants to retain the intellectual property rights within the virtual content they created.[46] Nonetheless, even in a virtual world that is as free as *Second Life*, the participants' right to exclude other participants from their creations is not totally absolute.[47]

Different from the right to exclude and the right to use, the right to transfer has been treated in many different ways. In general, these different ways can be categorized as three groups:

(1) Sales for real-world money are not allowed;
(2) Sales for real-world money are allowed if they are done through the system run by the provider, and
(3) Some types of items are allowed to transfer while some are not.

---

44 For example, EA.com, 'Terms of Service' (EA.com January 26, 2007) <www. ea.com/globallegal/tos.jsp> accessed December 3, 2013 ("Once you post or send any Content to EA.com, you expressly grant EA.com Inc. the complete and irrevocable right to quote, re-post, use, reproduce, modify, distribute, transmit, broadcast, and otherwise communicate, and publicly display and perform the Content in any form, anywhere, with or without attribution to your screen name in EA.com's discretion, and without any notice or compensation to you of any kind."); *World of Warcraft* Terms of Use Agreement § 11 (**World of Warcraft**, June 2, 2005) <www.worldofwarcraft.coVlegal/termsofuse.html> accessed December 3, 2013 ("All title, ownership rights and intellectual property rights in and to World of Warcraft (including without limitation any user accounts.... objects, [and] characters...) are owned by Blizzard Entertainment or its licensors.")

45 Miller (n 36) 460

46 Cory Ondrejka, 'Escaping the Gilded Cage: User Created Content and Building the Metaverse' (2004) *49 N. Y. L. Sch. L. Rev. 81* (describing the amount of participant created content in Second Life, and Linden Labs' efforts to allow participants to retain intellectual property rights in their creations).

47 *Ibid.*

These three ways have one common feature. That is, all the analyzed virtual worlds have EULAs that do not allow totally unfettered exchanges of virtual items for real-world money.

Most of the virtual worlds analyzed adopt the first option, which is a total restriction of any sales for real money. This is especially so in the virtual worlds, which have the highest populations.[48] The relevant term of this restriction under these EULAs generally contains language which essentially does not allow a user to buy, sell, or auction any of the game's characters, items, coins or specially copyrighted materials.

A few of providers permit participants to sell only certain items related to the virtual world. For example, the *"Sims Online"* permits participants to trade virtual objects through a third party facilitator, but they cannot use this facilitator to trade the whole of their accounts, whereas the *"Dark Age of Camelot"* is vice versa. It lets the participants to sell the entire accounts, but not virtual items.[49]

Now, recently, more and more virtual worlds adopt the third category of restriction of method. Well-known examples are *"EverQuest 11," "Second Life®"* and *"Entropia Universe."* All of them permit participants to sell their avatars and virtual items in exchange for real world cash, given the transfer takes place through the system run by the provider. The providers seem to want to capture a percentage of the revenue by facilitating transactions between players. However, for *"Entropia Universe,"* the situation is a little bit more complex. Rather than trying to earn money from the transactions made between participants like *"EverQuest II"* and *"Second Life®" "Entropia Universe"* wants

---

48 This list includes *City of Heroes* (and its sequel **City of Villains**), EverQuest, *Lineage* (and its *sequel Lineage II*), *Star Wars Galaxies,* and *World of Warcraft.*

49 *Dark Age of Camelot* has the only EULA of the group analyzed here that chooses to be governed by the law of the State of Virginia, which prevents certain restrictions on the transfer of software licenses.

the players to pay real world money straight to the provider as a way to get virtual currency.[50] Under this system, the virtual currency in "*Entropia Universe*" is directly convertible to cash and also the other way round.[51] Moreover, the provider of "*Entropia Universe*" will update their virtual world maps and create new places from time to time. It will also provide auctions to the general public.[52] In fact, the highlight of "*Entropia Universe*" is that strong players can earn real cash through completing various tasks. This is also the main source of income for "*Entropia Universe*."[53] In the end, it is submitted that the right to transfer virtual items is not granted to participants by the EULAs.

4.2 Power of the Provider to Terminate or Modify the Agreement

Since the relationship between the participants and the providers does not terminate after the rights have been allocated, their relationships are ongoing, it is hence necessarily to study beyond this initial allocation of rights. In fact, in all the EULAs that have been studied and analyzed, it is found out that all the providers add a term to alter the arrangement, including the right to forfeit virtual items, avatars, and user accounts as well as the right to unilaterally modify the EULA.

All the items, avatars, or accounts can be forfeited in various ways. Firstly, every EULAs has a term which let the provider to terminate the virtual world, in that way making the virtual world and all its respective virtual items and avatars not exist

50 MindArc, 'About Entropia Universe' <www.mindark.se/mindarks-offer/entropia-universe/> accessed December 3, 2013.

51 Entropia Universe, 'Account Pages' <http://account.entropiauniverse.com/account/> accessed December 3, 2013.

52 'Virtual Club to Rock Pop Culture' (BBC News.com, November 2, 2005) <http://news.bbc.co.uk/2/hi/technology/4385048.stm> accessed December 3, 2013.

53 Entropia Universe, 'More Than a Game: About' <www.entropiauniverse.com/entropia-universe/> accessed December 3, 2013.

anymore.[54] These termination clauses are more or less the same. All have the commonality that the providers may stop running a participant's account in the virtual world, if he or she chooses and that the participant in general can expect to receive compensation as a refund of the unused access fees. The only items that may vary between different agreements are the amount and type of notice that the providers give to participants.[55]

Secondly, forfeiture can happen when the provider chooses to terminate a player's individual account. Commonly, most EULAs will give the providers their power to terminate individual accounts if the player has either breached the rules of conduct or the terms of the EULA.[56] Apparently, this is an extremely broad discretionary power, where the provider can determine solely on its own on whether to terminate the account or not when such a breach is found. The rules applied by the providers are usually not spelt out to notify the players.[57]

---

54 A prototypical example of this clause, from *EverQuest II* EULA n.58 ("We may... terminate this Agreement if we decide, in our sole discretion, to discontinue offering the Game, in which case we may provide you with a prorated refund of any prepaid amounts."); *EverQuest II* User Agreement and Software License § 6 (Aug. 21, 2006) <http://help.soe.com/app/answers/detail/a_id/12248> [hereinafter EQ II EULA] accessed December 3, 2013.

55 cf *EverQuest II* EULA (providing no notice before termination) with *Second Life*®, 'Terms of Service', <http://secondlife.com/app/help/rules/tos.php> accessed December 3, 2013) ("Linden reserves the right to interrupt the Service with or without prior notice for any reason or no reason.") and *Dark Age of Camelot* 'End User Access and License Agreement' <http://camelotherald.wikia.com/wiki/EUALA> accessed December 3, 2013. ("In the event Mythic, in its sole discretion, ceases to provide any or all of the information services offered hereunder, then Mythic may terminate this Agreement... upon not less than thirty (30) days prior notice, which notice may be delivered via Mythic's patching system, or posted on Mythic's web site, or via electronic mail.").

56 See e.g., *EQ II* EULA, n.58 ("We may... terminate this Agreement if we decide, in our sole discretion, to discontinue offering the Game, in which case we may provide you with a prorated refund of any prepaid amounts.")

57 *Ibid.*

In truth, it would be a misperception to think that these provisions are only idle threats that are used as a means to make participants behave. Providers usually use this power to stop activity that is closely violating the rules of conduct. Taking Blizzard as an example, it is the company which created "*World of Warcraft.*" It is very famous for its super strict scrutiny in controlling users' behavior. In November 2006, Blizzard cancelled around 105,000 accounts for numerous activities that allegedly violated the terms of use including, but not limited to, exchanging virtual currency for real world cash and gold farming.[58] The extensiveness of Blizzard's interpretation of its terms of use recently was highly criticized. The incident originated from the fact that it threatened to terminate accounts that tried to recruit users for a league which would welcome gay, lesbian, bisexual, and transgendered people. Blizzard contended that this league would violate the terms of use and feared that it might provoke a negative response from other participants.[59] However, due to the controversies and criticisms Blizzard faced, it decided to retain the league in the end.[60] This is an example of the scope of activities that providers control under the rules of conduct.

The scope of this terminating power can be very wide. It can extend to associated player accounts which do not involve illegal conduct. Sometimes these EULAs would go so far in reserving the

---

58 Tobold's Blog, Blizzard Bans 105,000 in November (December 23, 2006) <http://tobolds.blogspot.hk/2006/12/blizzard-bans-105000-players-in.html> accessed December 3, 2013; Erik Cain, '"World of Warcraft" Sheds Another 600,000 Subscribers' (Forbes.com, July 26, 2013) <www.forbes.com/sites/erikkain/2013/07/26/world-of-warcraft-sheds-another-600000-subscribers/> accessed December 3, 2013.

59 Nate Anderson, 'Blizzard Bans Recruiting for Gay Guild' (arstechnica.com, February 8, 2006) <http://arstechnica.com/uncategorized/2006/02/6129-2/> accessed December 3, 2013.

60 See 'Blizzard CEO Responds to GLBT Issue' (March 13, 2006) <http://nonealcoholic.blogspot.hk/2006/03/blizzard-ceo-responds-to-glbt-issue.html> accessed December 3, 2013.

providers' right to terminate user accounts with no justification at all.[61] When termination happened, all the virtual items, avatars and accounts will be forfeited and the participant who owns these things would have no compensation for any possible resale value in the virtual goods or the access fees paid by the participant.[62]

Apart from the right to terminate accounts, all these EULAs retain the providers the right to amend the terms of the agreement unilaterally.[63] This right to alter the agreement is probably the widest power retained by the provider. This is because all of the other rights in the agreement are subjected to this right. Moreover, participants who are not satisfied with the amendments usually will only be provided with two options, either terminate the agreement and stop using accessing the virtual world or accept the changes and continue to participate.[64]

4.3 *Participant Remedies under the EULAs*

Furthermore, the EULAs may provide terms that will restrict players remedies available for them in the event of breach on the part of the provider. In most of the EULAs, the main remedies available for the players are "the rights to terminate the agreement" and "to recover a portion of any prepaid access

---

61 See e.g., *Entropia Universe* End User License Agreement § 16(n) <http://legal.entropiauniverse.com/legal/eula.xml> accessed December 3, 2013

62 See e.g., *Entropia Universe* EULA, § 6; Dark Ages of Camelot EULA § 6(D); But see *Second Life®* Terms of Service § 7.1

63 See e.g., *EverQuest II* User Agreement and Software License § 6 (August 21, 2006), <http://help.soe.com/app/answers/detail/a_id/12248>; See also § 3 ("We may amend this agreement at any time in our sole discretion.")

64 See eg, Ultima Online, 'Terms of Service' < https://help.ea.com/article/uo-terms-of-service> accessed June 20, 2013; cf *Dark Ages of Camelot* EULA § 5.

fees."[65] These remedies are usually insufficient for the participants in cases when they feel their rights to virtual goods have been infringed, because once the player has lost the access to his virtual items, he would not be able to retrieve or capitalize all the time, effort, and money he has invested in the virtual world. Moreover, since participants usually meet friends in the game, it would be very difficult for them to exit the game, because it will mean losing the social connections within the virtual space.[66] Also, a provider's behavior will not change when an individual player threatens to exit the game, unless that particular participant is very popular or influential in that virtual world.[67]

Except for the right to terminate the agreement, participants in general do not have other kinds of remedies, because the EULAs do expressly limit many other avenues of redress. Most of the EULAs provide provisions disclaiming participants any right to or value in virtual items, avatars, and accounts,[68] so that when there is any dispute between a participant and the provider, the EULA will serve as a safeguard for the provider by limiting the

---

65 See e.g., *EA.com*, 'Terms of Service' <www.ea.com/globallegal/tos.jsp> accessed December 3, 2013 ("You understand and agree that the cancellation of your Account or a particular subscription is your sole right and remedy with respect to any dispute with EA Online."); *DAoC* EULA § 10 ("In the event of a material breach of Mythic's obligations to provide access to and use of your account, ... your sole and exclusive remedy shall be a refund of any paid access fees attributable to the period of wrongful denial of service, or three-months' access fees, whichever is less.")

66 Jack M. Balkin, 'Law and Liberty in Virtual Worlds,' (2004) *49 N. Y. L. Sch. L. Rev. 63, 76–80* (2004).

67 James Grimmelmann, 'Virtual Worlds as Comparative Law,' *49 N. Y. L. Sch. L. Rev.* (2004) 147, 150–52, 173 (describing the situation in the world of *The Sims Online*, where influential participants constituting a "shadow government" are exerting increasing influence on the virtual-world provider).

68 e.g., *DAoC* 'EULA' n.58, § 10 ("You specifically acknowledge that the time you spend playing Dark Age of Camelot is for entertainment purposes only, and that you claim no interest in the value of such time as represented by the building up of the experience level of your character and/or the items your character accumulates during your time playing Dark Age of Camelot.") (emphasis omitted).

ways which he can pursue it. Similar to many other consumer contracts, the EULAs have clauses compelling arbitration,[69] specific venue, and choice of law, while a number of the EULAs contain provisions that waive particular forms of relief[70] or set liquidated damages at small amounts to avoid such clauses from being considered unconscionable.[71]

5. Conclusion

In sum, the nature of "goods" in the virtual world is very complex. Adopting the John Locke's theory on property, virtual goods can be regarded as a bundle of rights. This bundle of rights shares some similarities with personal property in terms of their exclusivity, persistence and transferability. To make the question more complicated, virtual world providers always make its participants to enter into license agreement with various provisions in an attempt to fight the potential liability and loss of control associated with the commodification of virtual goods. General property rights such as the right to exclude and the right to use are consistently retained by the providers.

While the providers are not consistent in how they treat the right to transfer, those who do give participants a right to transfer do so only in situations controlled by the providers. This in effect further limits the bundle of rights that participants own in the virtual goods and it does not seem that participants are entitle to own outright, in the legal sense, the virtual items and avatars they create and acquire while in virtual worlds. Furthermore, to make the situation worse, in addition to limiting participants' general

---

69 Frederick L. Miller, 'Arbitration Clauses in Consumer Contracts: Building Barriers to Consumer Protection' (1999) *78 Mich. B. J. 302, 302* (1999).

70 *EQ II* EULA, § 14.

71 *Ultima Online* Terms of Service, § 7 (limiting liability to the cost of the CD and fees paid for the service).

property rights, providers will also actively insert terms which will give limited remedies when participants try to seek protection for their interests under the contracts. This further deters them from claiming the property rights of the virtual goods, making their bundle of rights even smaller. Therefore, it is submitted that virtual property should be subject to certain regulations in order to protect the property rights that participants enjoyed within the virtual world.

5

Legal Protection for Virtual Property Rights: Rationale, Obstacles and Proposals

Lawrence Ka-yeung LAU

1. Introduction

Virtual worlds are computer-simulated environments consisting real world features.[1] They simulate three-dimensional graphical environments where players interact with each other through avatars.[2] The virtual worlds created by popular online games such as *Second Life*, *The Sims Online* and *Britannia*[3] incorporate virtual "goods" as an indispensable part of both the virtual world and the avatars occupying it.[4] These "goods" exist in various forms like clothing, cars, weapon and artwork.[5] Although virtual "goods" and real-life goods share some similarities, they are very

---

1 A. Chein, 'A Practical Look at Virtual Property' (2006) 80(3) *St. John's Law Review* 1059–1090.

2 S. K. Lowry, 'Property Rights in Virtual Reality: All's fair in Life and Warcraft?' (2008) 15 Tex. *Wesleyan L. Review* 109.

3 Dan F. Hunter & Gregory Lastowka, 'The Laws of the Virtual Worlds' (2004) 92 *California Law Review* 3–17.

4 Edward Castronova, *Synthetic Worlds: The Business and Culture of Online Games* (University of Chicago Press, US 2005) 1–2.

5 Samtani Anil, Angelia King, Wen Jie, Jeanne Soon Hui Min & Queenie Chew Wan Xiu, 'Virtual Property—A Theoretical and Empirical Analysis' (2012) *E.I.P.R.* 188, 189.

different in nature. For one, virtual goods are intangible. However, the sale of virtual goods generate tremendous amount of real-life income for virtual world users. It follows that users suffer real economic loss when their virtual goods or properties are lost by theft or the transfers of goods are not enforceable. Many scholars, thus, advocate for the legal protection for virtual property rights of the gamers.

The crucial question scholars and courts face is on what legal basis "virtual property rights" of users should be recognized and protected. Legal problems are posed by the contractual relationship between developers and gamers. While some scholars argue that real-life property rights should be extended to virtual property, this chapter argues that justifications for extending real-property rights to virtual goods are unsatisfactory. In fact, existing legislations and policies in some Asian civil law jurisdictions, such as China, Taiwan and Korea, should serve as good examples of legal recognition of users' virtual property rights. Additionally, the recognition of their rights by developers can also help protect the rights of users.

2. Nature of Virtual Goods

Before examining the question of whether the law should enforce "virtual property rights,, we should first examine the nature of virtual "goods." Virtual "goods" are items that can be purchased and transferred in virtual worlds.[6] They can be used, traded or thrown away like a real-life objects. The term of virtual "goods" is indeed misleading. The "goods" possessed or "owned" by gamers are all kinds of objects and assets ranging from weapons, clothing

---

6 Julian Dibbell, 'Dragon Slayers or Tax Evaders' (2006) *Legal Aff.* 47, 49.

and houses. While houses, as real properties,[7] are excluded from the meaning of "goods" under section 2 of Sales of Goods Ordinance.[8] Nelson even suggested the term of virtual "resources" in replacement.[9]

According to Fairfield, virtual "goods" and real-life goods are similar in three ways: exclusivity, persistence and transferability. Like real-life goods, virtual "goods" are exclusive to the use and control of a define number of persons. They also persistently exist which can be recalled by users every time they re-open the games. Lastly, they can be transferred from one user to another just like real-life goods.[10] In fact, the question of property rights in virtual "goods" would not exist if they could not be transferred.[11] There has to be an available market and the ability to trade to attach value to virtual "goods."[12]

Although closely mirroring real world goods in certain ways, virtual "goods" are of a very different nature. As Fairfield points out "virtual property is nothing more than a bundle of mathematic algorithms run through a computer to simulate the look and utility of a real world good."[13] The processing of computer codes mimics characteristics of real-world objects but

7 Julia Nissley, *How to Probate an Estate in California* (20th edn Nolo, USA 2009) 56.

8 "Goods" includes all chattels personal other than things in action and money. The term also includes emblements, industrial growing crops, and things attached to or forming part of the land which are agreed to be severed before sale or under the contract of sale. (emphasis added)

9 John William Nelson, 'The Virtual Property Problem: What Property Rights in Virtual Resources Might Look Like, How They Might Work, and Why They Are a Bad Idea' (2010) 41 *McGeorge L.Rev.* 281, 295.

10 Joshua A. T. Fairfield, 'Virtual Property' (2005) 85 *B.U.L. Rev.* 1054–55

11 Theodore J. Westbrook, 'Owned: Finding a Place for Virtual World Property Rights' (2006) Mich.St. L.Rev. 783.

12 N. DaCunha, 'Virtual Property, Real Concerns' (2010) *4 Akron Intellectual Property Journal* 35.

13 Fairfield (n 10) 1057, 1049, 1053–55.

they are nothing more than virtual representations of their real-world counterparts.[14]

For the purpose of this chapter, a more crucial difference is the lack of legal recognition of virtual "goods" as "goods". Courts and commentators refuse to extend the meaning of "goods" in law to virtual "goods." For example, in the U.S., Article 2 of the Uniform Commercial Code defines "goods" as "both existing and identified before any interest in them may pass." Accordingly, the section is not applicable to transactions of virtual "goods" without any physical manifestation.[15] As intangible items, virtual goods are "things in action"[16] which are also excluded in the meaning of "goods" under s2 of Hong Kong Sale of Goods Ordinance (Cap. 26).[17]

3. Virtual Property Rights Defined

Although not existing in a tangible form, scholars have argued that the law should protect users' property rights and interests in virtual goods. But how can virtual property rights be defined?

The traditional legal view of property is a "bundle of rights"

---

14 Gregory Lastowka & Dan F. Hunter, 'Virtual Crimes' (2004) 49 New York Law School Law Review 293-316

15 M.H. Passman, 'Transactions of Virtual Items in Virtual Worlds' (2008) 18 ALB.L.J. Sci. & Tech. 259, 271-72

16 According to Montana Code Annotated 2011 70-2-101, a thing in action is essentially a right to sue. It is an intangible personal property right recognized and protected by the law, that has no existence apart from the recognition given by the law, and that confers no present possession of a tangible object.

17 "goods" includes all chattels personal other than things in action and money. The term also includes emblements, industrial growing crops, and things attached to or forming part of the land which are agreed to be severed before sale or under the contract of sale. (emphasis added)

to a thing.[18] As stated by Stephen, "the concept of property simultaneously includes rights to a things and land, liability to another in tort, and obligations to others through contract."[19]

Extending property rights protection to virtual properties means imbuing them to the traditional property rights.[20] Suggested by Anil *et al.*, the virtual property rights of users should include the right to exclude, the right to transfer and the right to own and possess. The users should be able to exclude other users from trespassing. They should equally have the right to sell, trade, or transfer ownership of virtual property. This includes alienation in both in-game environment and in real-world auctions. Finally, they should enjoy ownership and possession of the virtual property in both the virtual environment and real world.[21]

4. Real World Economic Profits for Users

One may question the reason why virtual property rights should be protected and recognized in favor of the users. The rationale is simply that the virtual goods have an economic impact on the real lives of the users. As mentioned, virtual goods are transferred from user to user with a real-world monetary value. Thousands of auctions of virtual goods exist on the Internet. The avatars of the buyer and seller would meet in the virtual world and transfer the goods while real money payment is transferred through real-world bank accounts.[22] The profitability of sales of virtual goods has made some users become "pro gamers" who participate in the

18 G. E. Aylmer, *The Meaning and Definition of 'Property' in Seventeenth-Century England* (Feb. 1980) Past & Present 87.

19 Frank H. Stephen, *The Economics of the Law* (1988) 11.

20 Nelson (n 9) 295–296.

21 Anil *et al.* (n 5) 194.

22 Castronova (n 4) 149.

virtual world as an occupation.[23] Some companies are established with the sole business of buying and selling in-game items for real money.[24]

The income generated by sales of virtual goods is incredibly huge in figures. In 2009, the investment bank Piper Jaffray reported that sale of US virtual goods generated US$621 million, an increase of 134% from 2008 figures. The figure was estimated to rise to almost US$2.5 billion in 2013. According Linden Labs, the company that operates *Second Life*, 68,000 user accounts made profits from sales in August 2009. Almost 500 of those accounts made over $2,000 in the same month.[25]

5.   Effect of End-User-License-Agreements on Virtual Property

In view of the significant economic impact on users, scholars and users generally favor legal protection of virtual property rights of users. However, game developers argue that there are legal problems for recognizing such property rights in virtual goods.

Virtual properties do not confer upon their users exclusive usage rights like real world private property. Users are required to sign an End-User-Licensing-Agreement (EULA) contract drafted by the developer when they open an account in the virtual world.[26] The EULAs usually contain terms that give exclusive property rights to all aspects of the game to the corporation that

---

23 Leslie Brooks Suzukamo, 'Psst, Wanna Buy a Wizard' (Feb. 26 2001) St. Paul Pioneer Press, E1.

24 Castronova (n 4) 163–64.

25 Michael Capiro, 'Virtual Worlds with Real World Losses' (2009) *The Federal Lawyer* 12.

26 Hunter & Lastowka (n 3) 3–17.

created the virtual world.[27] As Westbrook suggested, the EULAs are designed to protect the software developer's interest in the foundation code of the game and to exclude potential liability for losses of virtual property suffered by users.[28] Virtual property rights, if the law in some way recognizes them, are mostly allocated to the game developers by EULA.[29]

Even worse for the users, developers disapprove the real world sales of virtual goods. The developer of *Everquest* attempted to remove online auctions for its virtual objects.[30] The developer of *World of Warcraft* even shut down accounts of users who engaged in real world transactions.[31] In the absence of any creation or invention of the users themselves, developers usually opt to disallow real-money trading for virtual goods.

These developers object to the real-money trading primarily out of fear of declining profits. As Stephens reasoned, players would improve his avatar by purchasing advanced virtual goods through real-money trading. Consequently, players would be spending less time on earning those advanced virtual goods through normal gameplay. The reduced game time also reduces the subscription revenue for developers.[32]

Due to the lack of judicial scrutiny,[33] it is doubtful whether these EULA conditions which deprive users of any ownership and property rights in virtual goods will be binding. According to contract law principles, courts are likely to find that the users

---

27 Lastrowka & Hunter (n 14) 293–316.

28 Westbrook (n 11) 787.

29 Anil *et al.* (n 5) 195.

30 Molly Stephens, 'Sales of In-Game Assets: An Illustration of the Continuing Failure of Intellectual Property Law to Protect Digital-Content Creators' (2002) 80 *Tex.L.Rev.* 1513, 1518–19.

31 Passman (n 15) 271–72.

32 Stephens (n 30) 1519.

33 Westbrook (n 11) 803.

are bound by the EULAs by clicking on "I Agree" appearing under the EULA terms and conditions.[34] However, Lastowkat and Hunter suggested that the courts are unlikely to uphold EULAs where they place excessive restrictions on the economic interests of users.

The all-encompassing scope of EULA restrictions are unfair when some developers run their in-game economies in ways contradicting their EULAs to exclude user's property rights. *Entropia Universe* boasts its own "Entropia universe Cash Card" which enable users to withdraw in-game currency from real-world ATMS. However, their EULAs stated that players "will not gain any ownership interest whatsoever in any Virtual item."[35] It appears to also be unfair to users who create in-game properties. The developers who enable the creation of intellectual property by users in the virtual world at the same time refuse the users the claim of ownership.[36]

6.   Theories Justifying Virtual Property Rights

To address the competing entitlement between users and developers, scholars have developed theories to justify the protection of virtual property rights in the favor of the users. The three main theories are the Lockean labor theory, the personality theory and the utilitarian theory.[37] Regrettably, these theories are flawed as illustrated below.

---

34 Raymond S. R. Ku *et al.*, *Cyberspace Law* (2nd edn Aspen Publishers, US 2006) 651–53.

35 Anil *et al.* (n 5) 192.

36 A. Jankowich, 'The Complex Web of Corporate Rule-Making in Virtual Worlds' (2006) 8 *Tul.J.Tech. & Intell.* Prop. 1

37 Hunter & Lastowka (n 3) 43–50.

6.1 Lockean "Labor" Theory

The theory of property proposed by John Locke revolves around the idea of labor. He stated that:

> "Every man has a Property in his own Person. This is no Body has any Right to but himself. The Labor of his Body, and the Work of his Hands, we may say, are properly his. Whatsoever then he removes out of the State that Nature hath provided, and left it in, he hath mixed his Labor with, and joined to it something that is his own, and thereby makes it his Property."[38]

Applying the theory, users deserve property rights in virtual goods since they have invested their time, skill and effort in earning virtual goods and upgrading their avatars.[39] The basis for their claim in virtual property rights are that "one's labor is the source of one's property" and that "one who has expended labor in the acquisition of a good is entitled to it over one who has expended little or no labor in its acquisition."[40]

The problem of the labor justification of virtual property rights of users arises out of the relationship between users and developers. In fact, the theory seems to support the claim of property rights by developers. Developers, too, have made contribution of labor on their part. As listed by Westbrook, they "created the virtual world, tis structure and rules, as well as the code that makes up the virtual object." It is their creation that allowed the users to obtain possession of the virtual object "through time, skill and money invested."[41] According to the

---

38 John Locke, *Second Treatise of Civil Government* (Cambridge University Press, UK 1690) 287–88.

39 Stephen J. Horowitz, 'Competing Lockean Claims to Virtual Property' (2007) 20(2) *Harvard Journal of Law and Technology* 443.

40 M. G. Veloso III, 'Virtual Property Rights, A Modified Usufruct of Intangibles' (2008) 82 *Philippine Law Journal* 37.

41 Westbrook (n 11) 802.

labor theory, the developers should have exclusive property rights in the virtual properties as their labor outweighs that of the users.[42]

6.2   *Utilitarian Theory*

Utilitarian theory focuses on the overall benefit of the society as a whole. The main goal for utilitarian theory is providing the maximum good for the greatest number of individuals.[43] Accordingly, it is appropriate to grant private property rights if it increases the overall social welfare (or utility).[44]

The Utilitarian theory avoids the clash between users and developers as it removes the focus from labor. The focus is, instead, the gains and losses brought about by the proposed system of recognizing the property rights of the users. Despite having little obvious value to the outside world, the creation of virtual properties is of high value to individual users. This is evident from the gigantic amount of real-world time and money invested by users on the creation of virtual properties.[45] With millions of users spending billions of hours per year within virtual worlds, the aggregated benefit of individual users obtaining property rights is huge.[46]

However, developers argue that giving property rights to users would reduce their welfare and would in turn reduce the overall utility of society.[47] Their main concern about virtual properties is the maximization of profits and the limitation of liability.[48] The

---

42   Horowitz (n 39) 443.

43   John Stuart Mill, *Utilitarianism* (Hackett Publishing Co., 2001) 7.

44   Hunter & Lastowka (n 3) 3–17.

45   Hunter & Lastowka (n 3) 59.

46   Westbrook (n 11) 795–796.

47   Hunter & Lastowka (n 3) 3–17.

48   Stephens (n 30) 1519–20.

recognition of virtual property rights of users would give them the right to transfer virtual goods.[49] As previously mentioned, the real money trading of virtual goods would lower the monthly subscription fees from users. The lost of monopoly over sales of in-game objects for cash will lower the profitability of developers.[50] Additionally, the developers may face claims over lost virtual properties against them.

The two-sided argument under the utilitarian theory illustrates the problem with the utilitarian justification. This method of justification brings about the consistent daunting task of identifying and weighing the benefits and losses of the proposed systems. Even after the enactment of the proposal, new benefits and losses may give rise to another evaluation.[51]

6.3 Personality Theory

The personality theory stems from the philosophy of G.W.F. Hegel.[52] Grey illustrates the theory by stating that "property was an extension of personality. Ownership expanded the natural sphere of freedom for the individual beyond his body to part of the material world."[53]

According to Hegel, private property rights are inseparably attached to personhood and identity. The property rights are an essential interest in protecting the basic nature of a person's humanity.[54] Hence, an object is actually part of the person

---

49 Anil *et al* (n 5) 194.

50 Westbrook (n 11) 797.

51 Jonathan Riley, *Utilitarian Ethics and Democratic Government* (1990) 100 Ethics 335, 338.

52 George Wilhelm Friedrich Hegel, *Hegel's Philosophy of Right* (Oxford Univ. Press 1821) 44.

53 Thomas Grey, *The Disaggregation of Property* (J. Roland Pennock & John W. Chapman, 1980) 74

54 Hunter & Lastowka (n 3) 3-17

possessing it in some way and the person enjoys the right to possess the object. Examples of such object include wedding rings[55] which can define a person's marital status, religious influence and socioeconomic status.[56]

Based on this theory, the avatar and its possession are extensions of a player's personality and personhood similar to real-life properties. Users are allowed to customize their own avatars and create their own inventions.[57] These virtual properties are, hence, deeply connected to the users' sense of self.[58]

As Latowska and Hunter noted, some may argue the personality justification has significant limitations on the alienability of the virtual properties.[59] This implies that the theory might not support a real-world transaction of virtual properties.[60] However, "just as our legal system supports the alienability of a wedding ring, it ought to support the alienability of a user's avatar."[61]

The real problem with the personality theory, like the above two, is that the user is unlikely to be considered the sole and complete owner of the virtual properties. At best, the user may be a co-owner of the avatar with the developers, entitled to certain rights to the use of those properties.[62] The flaws in these three theories imply that they might not serve as sound basis for the courts and the law to recognize virtual property rights.

---

55 Margaret Jane Radin, 'Property and Personhood' (1982) 34 *Stan L.Rev.* 957, 957–959, 965.

56 Hunter & Lastowka (n 3) 3–17.

57 Katie Hollstrom, 'Legal Conceptions of Virtual Property' (2008) 7 *Law & Soc'y J. UCSB* 59, 63

58 Anil *et al.* (n 5) 193.

59 Hunter & Lastowka (n 3) 68.

60 Ren Reynolds, IPR, Ownership and Freedom in Virtual Worlds <www.ren-reynolds.com/downloads/RReynolds-MMORPG-IPR.htm> accessed April 2, 2013.

61 Hunter & Lastowka (n 3) 48–499

62 Westbrook (n 11) 800.

7. Potential Economic Losses to Users

One of the implications of the EULAs is the potential economic losses to users. The EULAs seeks to deny users of their entitlement to virtual property rights. If they are held to be binding on users, users may be left without compensation in law in the event of fraudulent transactions and theft of virtual goods

Fraud in transaction of virtual goods may occur in a few forms. These include the non-payment for the transfer of properties, the non-performance of transfer after payment and the transfer of altered, duplicated, hacked or illegitimate virtual properties.[63]

Due to the restraints on transactions posed by EULAs, users must trade in black or grey markets with one another.[64] The trading in these relatively unsafe and illegitimate environments results in elevated levels of fraud and abuse.[65] Fraud in virtual good transactions is very frequent in some countries. According to the Korean Cyber Terror Response Center, an estimated 70% of teenage crime in Korea is somehow related to virtual property fraud, especially virtual property trade fraud. The number of Korean cyber fraud cases rose from 675 in 2000 to 10,187 in 2003.[66]

Theft of virtual goods means where a virtual world user's virtual goods are accessed and transferred by another without his/her consent.[67] Situations of this include where accounts are hacked and "where software exploits are used to get around a

---

63 Ian MacInnes, Y. J. Park, Sang-Min Whang, 'Virtual World Governance: Digital Item Trade and Its Consequences in Korea' (2004) *Virtual World Governance* 16.

64 Jason A. Archinaco, 'Virtual Worlds, Real Damages: The Odd Case of American Hero, The Greatest Horse That May Have Lived', (2007) 11 *Gaming L.Rev.* 21, 25.

65 Jeff W. LeBlanc, 'The Pursuit of Virtual Life, Liberty, and Happiness and its Economic and Legal Recognition in the Real World' (2008) 9 *Fla.Coastal L.Rev.* 256, 269.

66 MacInnes *et al.* (n 63) 17.

67 Nelson (n 9) 399.

virtual world's intended game mechanics to gain access to virtual resources."[68]

As argued by Nelson, "users need property rights in virtual goods in order to better protect against, punish and deter theft by people who illegally gain access to virtual world accounts."[69] Law enforcement bodies often refuse to investigate thefts of virtual goods with seriousness. In one such incident, a user of *Final Fantasy XI* lost his account and resources valued at US$3,800 to a hacker. The police declined to investigate for the reason that "points earned in games are devoid of monetary value."[70]

Regardless of how the users lose their virtual properties, by fraudulent transactions or theft alike, they are left without compensations. Since the victim gamers have no property rights under EULAs, they cannot seek remedies from the fraudsters nor the developers.[71]

8.   Existing Regulatory Models for Virtual Property Rights

The above theories might not satisfactorily justify the extension of property rights to virtual goods. Fortunately, there are existing regulatory models in various jurisdictions that protect or strive to protect the economic interests of the users. Some jurisdictions have begun to govern virtual property rights with a distinct set of legislations. These jurisdictions are discussed in further detail below.

---

68 Douglas Downing, *Dictionary of Computer and Internet Terms* (10th edn Barron's Educational Series, 2009) 223, 68.

69 Nelson (n 9) 293.

70 John Brewer, 'When a Virtual Crook Struck This Gamer, He Called Real Cops' (Jan 31, 2008) St. Paul Pioneer Press, A1.

71 Westbrook (n 11) 802.

8.1   United States

As covered above, virtual property rights in the U.S. are mainly governed by the law of contracts and privately enforceable EULAs.[72] The Computer Fraud and Abuse Act (CFAA) is the only existing legislation considered to be a potential fit for virtual property rights protection.[73] As reported by Anil *et al.*, "the CFAA safeguards against intrusions of computers with the intent to defraud where the perpetrator 'obtains anything of value'." However, some argued that the statute does not protect users with property on a computer that they do not own. Thus, only the developers can claim relief under the statute. Further, the low monetary value of the average each virtual property is unlikely to invoke the statute and investigation of the FBI.[74]

8.2   China

Chinese courts were one of the pioneers in offering virtual property rights to individuals and enforcing such rights against software companies.[75] China has over 26.33 million Internet users,[76] a population of over 1.3 billion people[77] and around 296 million players in 2012.[78] With a huge online gaming community, "Chinese action in regard to virtual property could act as a catalyst to spur growth in countries more averse to change" as pointed out by LeBlanc. China recognizes virtual property rights

72 Horowitz (n 39) 445.

73 DaCunha (n 12).

74 Anil *et al.* (n 5) 199.

75 'On-line Game Player Wins Virtual Properties Dispute', *China Daily*, Dec. 19, 2003, <www.chinadaily.com.cn/en/doc/2003-12/19/content_291957.htm> accessed April 2, 2013

76 Fairfield (n 10) 1061.

77 Central Intelligence Agency, 'The World Factbook: China', <www.cia.gov/library/publications/the-world-factbook/geos/ch.html> accessed April 2, 2013.

78 Anil *et al.* (n 5) 199

as part of its campaign to foster a domestic economy that focuses on the Internet and high technology. Chinese markets have created thousands of jobs for virtual property sales.[79]

In 2003, Beijing"s Chaoyang District People's Court ruled in favor of the virtual property rights of Li, a gamer, against the developer, Beijing Arctic Ice Technology Development Co. Ltd. The weapons and treasures of Li's avatar were stolen by another player due to programming loophole negligently created by the developer. Li filed a suit against the developer to recover the real world value of the stolen virtual property. Similar to other developers, Beijing Arctic Ice did not recognize any user property rights with the virtual world. Li stated to the press that he had "exchanged the equipment with my labor, time, wisdom and money, and of course they are my belongings." The Beijing court agreed that Li should be compensated for his stolen virtual property. This is an implicit legal recognition of the entitlement of virtual property rights for the reason of the user's labor.[80] In other words, it is a judicial recognition of the Lockean Labor Theory as a justification for users' virtual property rights.

In 2004, two Chinese teenagers were prosecuted for "theft of virtual property"[81] and police in Chengdu was actively investigating a virtual property theft case. The actions of Chinese law enforcement and judicial bodies have consistently recognized virtual property rights in China. Government officials also publicly called for legislation for the protection for virtual property rights.[82]

---

79 LeBlanc (n 65) 282–284.

80 LeBlanc (n 65) 282–283.

81 Fairfield (n 10) 1061.

82 LeBlanc (n 65) 283.

8.3 Taiwan

Taiwan is a leading jurisdiction in the recognition of virtual property rights.[83] Its courts have held that virtual property is property in the existing law.[84] According to figures in 2007, Taiwan less than 23 million residents but over 2 million were online gamers.[85]

The law enforcement and judicial bodies of Taiwan have routinely upheld virtual property theft and fraud. Its functioning and workable system has created enforceable virtual property rights through legislations.[86]

LeBlanc pointed out that "Taiwanese legislation recognizes the alienability and lawful existence of virtual property." In 2001, a Taiwanese Ministry of Justice Regulation expressly stated that virtual properties are alienable, transferable and protected by Taiwanese law.[87] The Taiwanese Ministry of Justice explained that:

> "The account and valuables of online games are stored as electromagnetic records in the game server. The owner of the account is entitled to control the account and valuables' electromagnetic record, to freely sell or transfer it. Although the above accounts and valuables are virtual, they are valuable property in the real world. The players can auction or transfer them online. The accounts and valuables are the same as the property in the real world. Therefore, there is no reason not to take the accounts and valuables of online games to be

---

83 Fairfield (n 10) 105.

84 LeBlanc (n 65) 282.

85 Ying-Chieh Chen *et al*, Nati'l Research Council Can, *Online Gaming Crime and Security Issue—Cases and Countermeasures from Taiwan* (2004) 1.

86 LeBlanc (n 65) 284–285.

87 *ibid.*

the subject to be protected by the larceny or fraud in criminal law."[88]

8.4 South Korea

Conversely, South Korean government has adopted strict measures to regulate economic activities of the virtual world. It has sought to discourage virtual property transactions with legislations.[89] Birch reported that "they have decided to pass a bill banning transactions between the real and virtual worlds. If the proposed 'Amendment for Game Industry Promoting Law' is passed by the National Assembly, then all kinds of businesses brokering between virtual money and real money could be fined. This clause is added to the bill prohibiting virtual world trading."[90]

It can be seen that the regulation of virtual property rights through legislation is a recent trend in Asian civil jurisdictions. The process of legislations in common law jurisdictions like Hong Kong and the U.S. might be lengthier. However, a proactive role of the legislative bodies and the positive support from law enforcement bodies are the keys to protection of the virtual property rights of the users.

9.   Alternative Proposal: Developer's Recognition

Alternative to legislation, the virtual property rights of users can be recognized by the developers. The difficulty in protecting the economic interests of the users is primarily due to the exclusion of their virtual property rights by EULAs. A logical solution for the problem is, hence, a change of the EULA terms or policy by the developers.

---

88 Taiwan Ministry of Justice Official Notation No. 039030 (90).

89 MacInnes *et al.* (n 63) 1.

90 D. Birch, 'Virtual Money: Money Laundering in Virtual Worlds: Risks and Reality' (2007) 9 *E-Commerce Law & Policy* 5.

Linden Lab, developer of *Second Life*, has an EULA with users that allow them to possess intellectual property rights in the virtual property they create. The CEO of Linden Labs stated that the adoption of such terms was intended to: "recognize the fact that persistent world users are making significant contributions to building these worlds and should be able to both own the content they create and share in the value that is created. The preservation of users' property rights is a necessary step toward the emergence of genuinely real online worlds."[91]

Another developer, Sony Online had suspended the accounts of players engaged in real money trading. However, they later realized the economic potential in virtual property trading. Since then, the company has provided an internal trading service. Sony acts a facilitator in the trades between players but does not sell virtual goods to users directly. Sony Online president John Smedley has commented that "the unsanctioned secondary market for online games is rapidly growing and more and more of our players are taking part in it. Not only are we answering the demands of a sizable portion of our subscriber base, but we are also set on establishing the standard for online game sales."[92]

10. Conclusion

As illustrated above, the intangible virtual "goods" are very different from real-life goods in their form of existence and recognition in law. In spite of their differences, the loss of virtual

---

91 Press Release, Linden Lab, Second Life Residents to Own Digital Creations (November 14, 2003) <http:///lindenlab.com/pressroom/releases/03 11 14> accessed April 2, 2013; Anil *et al.* (n 5) 195.

92 Fox News 2005, Sony Letting Everquest Players Buy, Sell Virtual Items, <www.-foxnews.com/story/0,2933,154206,00.html> accessed April 2, 2013; See also Michael Stikova, 'More than Just a Game: User Expectations v Operator Interests' (2010) 4 *Masaryk U.J.L. & Tech.* 47, 50

goods results in economic loss for the users in real life just as the loss of real-life goods do. The users face difficulties in claiming compensation in the event of losing them due to the contractual terms of EULAs. Theories have been developed by scholars to help advocate for the recognition of virtual property rights. These theories, however, are flawed and might not serve as good basis for the courts to recognize virtual property rights.

The Asian civil jurisdictions have developed regulatory models and enacted legislations in respect of virtual property rights. Their motives behind are the huge potential economic impacts on developers and users. Common law jurisdictions such as the U.S. and Hong Kong can follow their footsteps in enacting legislations and establishing regulatory systems. After all, the gamers and developers in those jurisdictions also face huge potential economic impacts. Alternatively, the developers can decide to recognize the users' virtual property rights through EULAs and in-game trading services. This could in turn enhance their profitability.

6

The Nature of "Goods" in the Virtual World:

Arguing for Recognition of Real Property Rights in Virtual Goods

Elke Ngai Ki LAU

1. Introduction

There has been a long debate on whether virtual goods[1] should attain real property rights like real world goods as virtual goods are also created by real life players. By understanding the legal nature of the goods in the virtual world, we may determine the conflict in order to reach a solution regarding appropriate regulation. We should not ignore the property rights on virtual goods just because they are intangible or considered not "real."[2] Indeed, virtual goods share many of the characteristics of real world goods and it is possible that they could carry some legal rights similar to that of tangible real world goods.

This chapter starts by discussing what a virtual world is, and then examines the nature of virtual goods, including their history, main characteristics, forms and legal status. Finally, it explains why virtual goods should attain real property rights.

---

1 In this chapter, I will refer 'goods' in the virtual world as 'virtual goods.'

2 Katie Hollstorm, 'Legal Conceptions of Virtual Property: Should Virtual Property Be Afforded The Same Rights As Its Real-World Counter-Part?' (2007–2008) 7 *Law & Soc'y J.* UCSB 59–60.

2.   What is a "Virtual" World

Before exploring the nature of virtual goods, it is important to first understand the place or environment where these goods are created, used and traded.

There is no single agreed upon definition of what a virtual world is.[3] This means that various legal scholars may use different definitions of "virtual world" when referring to certain aspects of these online spaces. Professor Lastowka defined "virtual world" as "Internet-based simulated environments that feature software-animated objects and events."[4] Similarly, Benjamin Duranske defined them as "avatar-based simulations where user alterations of the physical, social, or economic environment of the world are persistent."[5]

Some legal scholars define the term by its persistent and dynamic nature. For example, Juliet Moringiello identified a virtual world as "an online environment that is both persistent and dynamic. It is persistent because it does not cease to exist when the participant turns her computer off; it is dynamic because it is continually changing."[6] Richard Bartle, the co-creator of MUD1 (the first virtual world for computers), also described the virtual world as persistent as its environment "continues to exist and develop internally (at least to some degree) even when there are no people interacting with it."[7] Other definitions are close, and most of them include some descriptions of a simulated environment that is shared by multiple users, that is persistent,

---

3 M. Scott Boone, 'Ubiquitous Computing, Virtual Worlds and the Displacement of Property Rights' (2008) 4 I/S: J. L. & Pol'y Info. Soc'y 91, 109.

4 Greg Lastowka, *Virtual Justice* (Yale University Press 2010) 4.

5 Benjamin Duranske, *Virtual Law* (1st edn, Aba Publishing 2008) 4.

6 Juliet M. Moringiello, 'What Virtual Worlds Can Do for Property Law' (2010) 62 *Fla. L. Rev.* 159, 169.

7 Richard A. Bartle, *Designing Virtual Worlds* (New Riders 2004) 1.

and that can be affected by the users.[8]

To sum up, virtual world is a simulated depiction of our real world, which is a place online that enables users around the world to interact and communicate with each other in a persistence environment and can be accessed remotely by computers.

3.   What Are "Goods" in the Virtual World

3.1   Virtual Goods Are Not "Goods" under Section 2(1) of SOGO

"Goods" available for purchase and transfer in virtual worlds ("virtual goods") shall be distinguished from the definition of "goods" contained in the special laws governing the sales of goods, such as section 2(1) of the Hong Kong Sale of Goods Ordinance ("SOGO").[9] This is because "goods" in real world are specially defined in commercial law as existing objects that are identifiable and movable at the time of purchase,[10] whereas "goods" in virtual world are intangible objects which look and act like real things, but there is actually nothing truly real about them.[11]

3.2   A Brief History of Virtual Goods

The first virtual goods being sold are generally recognized to be the items use in MUD, a text-based multiplayer real-time virtual

---

8 M. Scott Boone, 'Virtual Property and Personhood' (2007–2008) 24 *Santa Clara Computer & High Tech. L.J.* 715, 718.

9 Sale of Goods Ordinance (Cap 26), s 2(1) ('goods' includes 'all chattels personal other than things in action and money. The term includes emblements, industrial growing crops, and things attached to or forming part of the land which are agreed to be severed before sale or under the contract of sale.')

10 Uniform Commercial Code, art. 2.

11 Greg Lastowka and Dan Hunter, 'The Laws of the Virtual World' (2004) 92 *Cal. L. Rev.* 1, 40–43.

world. Following the invention of massively multiplayer online role-playing game ("MMORPG"), more and more virtual goods are traded in the virtual worlds. Most of the role-playing games, such as *World of Warcraft*, use a mission-reward system, which players earn experience points and magical items when they defeat enemies.[12] The players' avatars, which are the players' manifestation in the virtual world, collect these items and can then use or trade them for other items. Since the virtual items enhance character attributes[13] but require time to obtain, they have become objects of value to players.[14] Eventually, an outside market—Real Money Trading—is generated which allows players to purchase virtual goods with real financial currency through websites like eBay and IGE.[15]

3.3   The Main Characteristics of Virtual Goods

Virtual goods are generally defined as "digital representation of objects (real or imaginary)…created for use with virtual worlds, video games or other social media applications."[16] They are intangible things created, simulated, or carried on by means of a computer or computer network.[17]

---

12 Justin A. Kwong, 'Getting The Goods On Virtual Items: A Fresh Look At Transactions In Multi-User Online Environments' (2010–2011) 37 Wm. *Mitchell L. Rev.* 1805, 1807.

13 Examples of attributes are strength, intelligence, wisdom, and stamina.

14 Andrea Vanina Arias, Comment, 'Life, Liberty, and the Pursuit of Swords and Armor: Regulating the Theft of Virtual Goods' (2008) 57 *Emory L. J.* 1301, 1302.

15 TNL.net Weblog 'Economic Activity in Virtual Worlds' <www.tnl.net/blog/2006/07/31/economic-activity-in-virtual-worlds/> accessed December 3, 2013.

16 James G. Gatto and Seth A. Metsch, 'Legal Issues with Virtual Worlds, Virtual Goods and Virtual Currencies' (2010) 1016 *Practising L. Inst.* 837, 849.

17 John M. Conley *et al.*, 'Database Protection in a Digital World' (1999) 6 *Rich. J. L. & Tech.* 2.

At their core, virtual goods are simply computer codes—lines of software code that exist within larger computer programs.[18] But contrary to computer codes that merely express ideas, virtual goods are "designed to act more like land or chattel."[19] The original virtual goods in the virtual world include domain names, uniform resource locators (URLs), websites and e-mail accounts. They can be owned and controlled exclusively; they do not go away when you turn off your computer; and they are interconnected.[20] Hence, Professor Fairfield states that virtual goods signify three key general characteristics: rivalrousness, persistence and interconnectivity.[21]

The "rivalrousness" of virtual goods simply refers to their exclusivity of use.[22] If a player has a unique virtual sword, other players cannot own the same exact sword at the same time. The sword is thus a rivalrous good.

The "persistence" of virtual goods refers to the fact that they remain available to users from one session to another.[23] This means that the virtual goods will not fade away after the users log off. They can access the goods again when they log back on, even by another computer.

Similarly, the "interconnectedness" of virtual goods merely refers to their presence in the virtual world.[24] A good is said to be interconnected if its existence is apparent to or impacts more than one user. This is essentially true for everything except for the interface features in most virtual worlds and games.

---

18   Lastowka (n 4) 50–53.
19   Joshua Fairfield, 'Virtual Property' (2005) 85 *B. U. L. Rev.* 1047, 1049.
20   *Ibid.*
21   *Ibid*, 1053.
22   Duranske (n 5) 87.
23   *Ibid.* 86.
24   *Ibid.* 86–87.

3.4   The Forms of Virtual Goods

Since the rapid development of virtual worlds, there is a great expansion in the varieties of virtual goods. Virtual goods take many forms and can include everything. They can be as simple as the free gift apps in the early days of Facebook;[25] weapons and potions which enhance the player's in-game abilities in multiplayer online role-playing games like *World of Warcraft*; accessories and cosmetic items for avatars in *Second Life*; and seeds and cows in online social farming games.[26]

Accordingly, virtual goods can be categorized into three types: collectible goods, consumable goods and customizable goods.

Collectible goods are things that can be purchased by users and are displayed to other users in the virtual worlds, such as virtual houses, cars, clothes and decorations. Users may even combine some of these goods to form a new object, which is unique and cannot be traded.[27]

Consumable goods are things that can only be used for a certain number of times and are then destroyed. They are usually items that grant the users more turns and lives, or access to some previously unavailable features.

Customizable goods are simply given virtual goods that can be customized by their owners. For example, owners can customize the way their avatars, farm animals or cards appear to the others.

Given the wide range of virtual goods available to trade, it

---

25 Jared Morgenstern, 'Last Call for Facebook Gifts' (Facebook.com, July 8, 2010) <www.facebook.com/notes/facebook/last-call-for-facebook-gifts/405727117130> accessed December 3, 2013.

26 Oliver Herzfeld, 'What Is The Legal Status Of Virtual Goods?' <www.forbes.com/sites/oliverherzfeld/2012/12/04/what-is-the-legal-status-of-virtual-goods/> accessed December 3, 2013.

27 F. Randall Farmer, KidTrade: A Design for an eBay-resistant Virtual Economy v 1.1 (2004) 5 <http://habitatchronicles.com/Habitat/KidTrade.pdf.> accessed December 3, 2013.

is observed that the economics of virtual goods, in terms of the number of transactions and the revenues, are growing at an astonishing rate.[28] For example, in China, it is estimated that the sales of game-based virtual goods have increased from $296 million in 2006 to $1.3 billion in 2009.[29] Hence, the trading of virtual goods has become one of the most important functions of virtual world economies, maybe as important as trading is for real world economies.[30]

3.5 The Legal Status of Virtual Goods

While people around the world have been spending large amount of real money and time on these intangible goods every day, the legal status of virtual goods remains uncertain. As a result, the rights of users with respect to these virtual goods are still not well defined and identified.

According to Oliver Herzfeld, there are four possibilities of the legal status of virtual goods, which include no legal significance, service, personal property, and intellectual property.[31]

A. No legal Significance

In most online games, like *Second Life*, players are required to sign the End User Licensing Agreement ("EULA") before they can open an account and start the game. The EULA is a form

---

28 KZero Worldswide, 'Virtual Worlds: 2011 and Beyond: Key Industry Trends and Market Developments' Slideshare (2009) <www.slideshare.net/nicmitham/virtual-worlds-2010-2098472> accessed December 3, 2013.

29 Morgan Stanley, 'The Mobile Internet Report 54' (2009) <www.morganstanley.com> accessed December 3, 2013.

30 Dominik Schrank, 'A Trustful Payment System for Virtual Worlds' (Masters Thesis, Graz University of Technology 2009).

31 Oliver Herzfeld, 'What Is The Legal Status Of Virtual Goods?' <www.forbes.com/sites/oliverherzfeld/2012/12/04/what-is-the-legal-status-of-virtual-goods/> accessed December 3, 2013.

of contract which usually states that the relevant virtual world makers have exclusive control and ownership of the games, thus the virtual goods possess no legal significance or status.[32]

This approach is favorable to the virtual world makers, who can avoid potential liability arising from conflicts over ownership of virtual goods. Nevertheless, this is completely divorced from the users' real world experiences and expectations. Users who invest significant amounts of money and time in the virtual goods will normally expect to have ownership over them. Further, if the virtual goods are of no legal significance, there will be no legal framework to deal with basic commercial disputes such as the purchases, sales and thefts of virtual goods.

B.   Service

Some people have suggested that virtual goods are a kind of service, because they are both intangible and insubstantial. Nevertheless, a service is usually time bound, inseparably delivered by the service provider to the service consumer, simultaneously provided and consumed, and unique in time, location and other circumstances. It can be seen that most virtual goods do not share many fundamental characteristics of service.

C.   Personal Property

Most users in the virtual worlds will probably support the view of treating virtual goods as personal property, because users will then enjoy property rights over the virtual goods. In effect, the purchases and sales of virtual goods become legitimate transactions, as users have the right to transfer the goods with each other and earn incomes from the goods. Moreover, users have the right to legal redress if the virtual goods are stolen, converted or misappropriated.

---

32 *Ibid.*

Virtual world makers will also be benefited by this legal treatment, because when users are granted with more rights in using the virtual goods, they will have more incentive to invest in the games, thus the market value of the games will increase. Nonetheless, personal property is usually tangible whereas virtual goods are intangible that can only exist on the screen and can only be called forth by computer commands.

D.   Intellectual Property

It is also suggested that virtual goods are more akin to intellectual property. This is because they are both intangible, can be reproduced and supplied for many times without extra costs as they are merely streams of code that can be injected at any time,[33] and may be combined with other virtual goods to create derivative work. However, virtual goods are fundamentally different from intellectual property because many contain minimal or no user creativity.[34]

Though virtual goods tend to have a legal status as personal property or intellectual property, they are only similar in some aspects but not all, thus they neither fit the profile of personal property nor intellectual property. But since virtual goods have clear value to users and match the society's usual definitions of "property" in most other respects, it is suggested that they should have some form of property law protection.[35]

---

33   Leah Shen, 'Who Owns The Virtual Items?' (2010) 11 *Duke L. & Tech. Rev.* 1.

34   Duranske (n 5) 81.

35   Lastowka and Hunter (n 11) 49.

4. Whether Virtual Goods Should Attain Real Property Rights as Real World Goods

It is argued that if a virtual world offered real property rights, it would have to reimburse them for any lost value if the world were to close or experience some technical problem,[36] and the costs, which would ultimately be borne by its consumers, would be substantially higher than they would be without such a right.[37] Nevertheless, we are of the view that the arguments made in favor of granting property rights to virtual goods are more compelling.

In the following section, I will first explain the effect of End User License Agreements on the ownership of virtual goods, and then examine the reasons to recognize real property rights in virtual worlds.

4.1 Understanding End User License Agreements ('EULAs')

Since the EULAs explicitly states that ownership of any rights remain with the virtual world makers, it generally removes the users' property rights to any virtual goods in the virtual world, including the goods that are built or created by the users themselves.[38] For example, the EULA for the MMORPG *World of Warcraft* reads as follows:

> "All title, ownership rights and intellectual property rights in and to the Game and all copies thereof (including without limitation any titles, computer code, themes, objects, characters, character names, stories, dialog, catch phrases, locations, concepts, artwork, character inventories, structural or landscape designs, animations, sounds, musical compositions and

---

36 Duranske (n 5) 99.

37 *Ibid.* 100.

38 Fairfield (n 19) 1082.

recordings, audio-visual effects, storylines, character likenesses, methods of operation, moral rights, and any related documentation) are owned or licensed by Blizzard."[39]

Under this kind of EULA, users do not have any property rights to the virtual goods, which are exclusively owned by the virtual world makers. The virtual world makers have considered any trades between users to exchange virtual goods for real money as illegal and potentially dangerous to the economy of virtual worlds.[40]

Nonetheless, some users who signed the EULAs still take the risk to engage in these kinds of trading in order to earn money. As a result, some virtual world makers like Blizzard Entertainment for *World of Warcraft* have attempted to enforce its claimed property rights by closing accounts of users who engage in impermissible transactions,[41] which lead to numerous disputes over the ownership of virtual goods. Such phenomenon reflects the fact that users are indeed seeking some kind of real property rights in the virtual worlds.

4.2 Reasons to Recognize Real Property Rights in Virtual Worlds

This section will discuss why virtual goods should be given the same property rights as goods in the real world.

---

39 Blizzard Entertainment, 'World of Warcraft End User License Agreement' <http:// eu.blizzard.com/en-gb/company/legal/wow_eula.html> accessed December 3, 2013.

40 Andrew E. Jankowich, 'Property and Democracy in Virtual Worlds' (2005) 11 *B. U. J. Sci. & Tech. L. 173,* 182.

41 Michael H. Passman, 'Transactions of Virtual Items in Virtual Worlds' (2008) 18 *Alb. L. J. Sci. & Tech.* 259, 264.

A.   Shared Characteristics of Virtual Goods and Real World Goods

As mentioned earlier, virtual goods represent three main characteristics: rivalrousness, persistence and interconnectivity. Professor Fairfield recognized that virtual goods actually share these three legally relevant characteristics with real world goods.[42]

Virtual goods and real world goods are rivalrous. In both virtual world and real world, users of the goods are able to exclude other people from using them.

Virtual goods and real world goods are also persistent. In virtual world, the goods remain the property of the users even they log out their computers. They do not go away after each use and do not run on only one computer. In real world, goods are simply persistent.

Virtual goods and real world goods are also interconnected. In virtual world, users of the goods are allowed to trade virtual goods with other users in either the virtual world or the real world. In real world, goods are naturally interconnected.

It can be seen that the characteristics of real world goods have been incorporated into the virtual goods. Hence, there is a tendency that virtual goods shall be treated as real world goods under the law.

B.   Three Theories of What Constitutes Property

Furthermore, there are three theories of what constitutes property that help to recognize real property rights in virtual worlds.

Under the Lockean Theory of property rights, whoever takes an item from nature in its original state and labors to improve

---

42 Fairfield (n 19) 1053.

it deserves to receive its benefits.[43] It is said that "Earning both real and virtual money share a common component — real-world time."[44] Therefore, where it is considered that users and gamers have spent significant amounts of time and efforts in obtaining the virtual goods in the virtual worlds, they should be granted with real property rights.

The Utilitarian Theory of property states that it is appropriate to grant private property interest if doing so would increase its overall utility or social welfare.[45] The granting of private property rights to users will obviously create the incentive of users to continue to play the games, thus create a better reality in the virtual worlds and benefit the overall utility of society.[46]

The Personality Theory of property provides that property is simply an extension of a player's personality and the expression of each player as an individual.[47] Hence, the real property rights are an essential interest in protecting the basic nature of a person's humanity.[48] Since players customize their avatars as well as create their own goods in the games, all these virtual goods can be treated as an extension of a player's personality, which should be granted with property interest like real world goods.

In essence, these three theories all together are in favor of the argument that virtual goods should attain real property rights.

C. *Laws against Criminal Activity Concerning Virtual Goods*

There are also persuasive public policy reasons to support the

---

43 Lastowka and Hunter (n 11) 3–17.

44 Andrew E. Jankowich, 'Property and Democracy in Virtual Worlds' (2005) 11 *B. U. J. Sci. & Tech. L.* 173, 183.

45 Lastowka and Hunter (n 11) 3–17.

46 *Ibid.*

47 *Ibid.*

48 *Ibid.*

granting of real property rights in virtual goods. Public policy generally does not tolerate consensual restraints on alienation and, hence, it should not tolerate EULAs, which are essentially consensual agreements that prevent the formation of property rights.[49]

Although the United States has not recognized any right to virtual goods yet, some courts in other countries such as China, Taiwan, South Korea and the Netherlands have already taken step to recognize and protect the ownership interests in virtual goods, hoping to attract the burgeoning industry of virtual worlds.[50]

In China, the court in *Li Hongchen v Beijing Arctic Ice Technology Development Co. Ltd.* found that the loss of items to a hacker was theft and ordered the game publisher to return the items and pay damages to a player because flaws in its servers allowed the theft.[51] This case is significant as it indicates that at least "some courts may be willing to view virtual property as property that is worthy of protection under the law".[52] The court protected the player's rights to own the virtual items exclusively from all others, including the game publisher.[53]

The Taiwanese government has enacted the Taiwanese Criminal Code to protect virtual goods. Under the Code, virtual goods are considered "property" if they possess characteristics similar to property, like if they are rivalrous, alienable and transferable.[54] The Code recognizes that "virtual property qualifies as

---

49 Fairfield (n 19) 1083–1084.

50 *Ibid.*

51 Will Knight, 'Gamer Wins Back Virtual Booty in Court Battle' New Scientist (2003) <www.newscientist.com/article/dn4510-gamer-wins-back-virtual-booty-in-court-battle.html> accessed December 3, 2013.

52 Theodore J. Westbrook, 'Owned: Finding A Place for Virtual World Property Rights' (2006) 3 *Mich. St. L. Rev.* 779, 805

53 Fairfield (n 19) 1085.

54 *Ibid.* 1086.

electromagnetic records and should be considered moveable property in cases of fraud and theft."[55] The right to control the electromagnetic record of the virtual goods is expressly granted to the owner the code, but "not the owner of the server on which the code happens to reside, or the intellectual property owner of the code."[56] The maximum penalty for offences regarding virtual goods is three years imprisonment.[57]

In South Korea, the Supreme Court has effectively struck down laws that banned real money trading, making it legal where online environment providers chose to offer it.[58]

Furthermore, two separate Dutch courts found that virtual items obtained through hacking or violent coercion were both theft.[59]

As pointed out by Professor Fairfield, the recognition of virtual goods has already existed and is not something new, as the law has moved to protect virtual goods like e-mail addresses and URLs long ago. With all the above reasons, it is foreseeable the more and more countries will follow the step to view virtual goods as property and to protect the users with relevant property rights.

---

55 *Ibid.*

56 *Ibid.* 1087.

57 *Ibid.*

58 Chris Pollette, 'Trading Virtual Money Is Legal in South Korea' How Stuff Works (2010) <http://blogs.howstuffworks.com/2010/01/20/virtual-money-is-legal> accessed December 3, 2013.

59 Benjamin Duranske, 'Netherlands Court Finds Criminal Liability and Sentences Two Youths for Theft of Virtual Goods' Virtually Blind (2008) <http://virtuallyblind.com/2008/10/22/netherlands-theft-virtual-good> accessed on December 3, 2013; 'Stealing in Virtual Worlds Is a Real Crime' Gossip Gamers (2009) <www.gossipgamers.com/stealing-in-virtual-worlds-is-a-real-crime> accessed December 3, 2013.

5. Conclusion

The argument that virtual goods should not enjoy real property rights because they are intangible and not "real" will no longer stand. It is noted that the ability of a person to assert true ownership rights over any goods to the exclusion of others is a fundamental right to efficient markets, and essential to the ongoing growth of the society. Therefore, where virtual goods share the major characteristics of real world goods, users shall possess ownership rights on their virtual goods as well as be protected by the law.

7

Massively-Multiplayer Online Role Playing Games and Ownership of Virtual Property: A Multi-Jurisdiction Perspective

Matthew Sin Lun MOK

1. Introduction

As information technology has developed rapidly, online games have become more popular. In online games, people can do almost everything they imagine: within the virtual world of online games, they can fight against evil masterminds from outer space in order to protect the earth. In non-game virtual worlds, they can have a second life similar to the real world where they can go fishing and shopping. Besides the sales of the games itself, computer games developers also make their money by selling virtual goods inside their games. As most online games allow exchange and transaction of virtual goods between players, computer game developers are no longer the only sellers of virtual goods. Today, there are massive transactions of virtual goods, not only with virtual currency but also with real money. There are even people who make a living by trading virtual goods. Consequently, the lines between real world and virtual world, real property and virtual property have been blurred.

Scholar Jack Balkin noted that if developers "encourage real world commodification of virtual worlds, encourage people in these worlds to treat virtual items like property, and allow sale and purchase of these assets as if they were property, they should not be surprised if courts, legislatures, and administrative agencies start treating virtual items as property."[1] However, how the law protects owners of virtual properties depends on the nature of virtual properties.

This chapter will comprise six sections. Here I refer online games players as "participants" and the online games developer as "proprietors."

2.   The Virtual World

In order to understand the nature of virtual goods, one must first understand the place in which they exist: the virtual world. Most of those virtual worlds are based on Massively-Multiplayer Online Role Playing Games ("MMORPGs"). Games such as *Second Life*, *World of Warcraft* and *SimCity* are all MMORPGs. Unlike traditional computer games where there is only one or two participant(s), MMORPGs provide a virtual world setting where thousands or even millions of participants interacted within the same virtual world at the same time through the Internet.[2] These virtual worlds are usually hosted and maintained by the proprietors and developers of the virtual world. Even if a participant is not playing, these virtual worlds still exist and continue to develop due to involvement by other participant.[3]

Usually a participant would see himself or herself as an avatar—"a three-dimensional persona with particular physical

1 Jack M. Balkin, 'Law and Liberty in Virtual Worlds' (2004) 49 *N. Y. Sch. L. Rev.* 63.

2 Mark J. P. Wolf and Bernand Perron, *The Video Game Theory Reader* (1st edn, Routledge 2003) 87.

3 Michael Meehan, 'Virtual Property: Protecting bits in Context (2006) 13 *Rich. J. L. & Tech.* 71.

traits chosen by the players."[4] The participant can control his avatar and direct it to do different things according to the nature of games. For instance, a participant's avatar in *World of Warcraft* has to fight against other races while a participant's avatar in *Second Life* lives in the virtual world as if it actually living in the real world.

In MMORPGs, like other computer games, players collect virtual items like weapons, jewelry, and customs in order to equip their character's ability or change the avatar's appearance.[5] These items are virtual goods and are one of the most important features of MMORPGs. In these games, the most powerful or special items are usually rare, or in limited quantity and availability. This requires players to spend a long time to acquire them. Furthermore, some of the items cannot be acquired simply by playing the game. These items can only be acquired by completing a mission within a specific time period. Thus, some of the items are valuable and of a considerable market value. As a result, participants started to exchange virtual goods as gifts or even sell their items both in the virtual world and the real world. This has generated an actual market for virtual goods transactions.

These markets are called Real Money Trading (RMT) where participants purchase virtual goods with real money.[6] Although goods sold only exist within the virtual world, there are a huge number of transactions in RMT. In 2005, the virtual goods market was worth around $200 million[7] while the industry estimated that trade in virtual goods exceeded $2 billion a year in

---

4 Andrea Vanina Arias, 'Life, Liberty, and the Pursuit of Swords and Armor: Regulating the Theft of Virtual Goods' (2007–2008) 57 *Emory L.J.* 1301, 1306.

5 *Ibid.* 1302.

6 Samtani Anil, *et al.*, 'Virtual Property: A Theoretical and Empirical Analysis' (2012) *European Intellectual Property Review* 34, 188–202.

7 Tom Leupold, 'Virtual Economies Break Out of Cyberspace' (Gamespot, May 6, 2005) <http://asia.gamespot.com/news/spot-on-virtual-economies-break-out-of-cyberspace-6123701> accessed December 2, 2013.

2008.[8] In addition to RMT, significant time is spent on acquiring these virtual items. For example, employees in Chinese companies are hired specifically to play these MMORPGs in order to acquire virtual items and later sell them within the virtual goods market in order to gain profit.[9] The above shows that transaction of virtual goods not only affect virtual world but also the real world.

3.   Why Do Participants Need Property Rights?

If virtual property could not be stolen, there is no such a need to acquire property rights in virtual goods. No one would claim property rights of virtual property in traditional computer games because those items could not be stolen by other participants. However, in MMORPGs, virtual goods can be stolen or obtained by the others in many ways so there is a need for property rights.

In MMORPGs, there is usually a limit in numbers of items that a participant can hold or carry. When a participant acquires a new item but his is full and can no longer hold any more items, he may ask another participant to hold it for him. He would then make rooms by discarding other items and asks the other participant to return him the new item.[10] However, a malicious or dishonest participant might not return such item and might retain it for his own use or sell it for profit.

Besides, participants can also deceive another participant in order to acquire their virtual goods. A dishonest participant may

8 Daneil Terdiman, 'Virtual Goods, Real Scams' (CNET, Sept 12, 2005) <http://news.cnet.com/Virtual-goods,-real-scams/2100-1043_3-5859069.html> accessed December 2, 2013.

9 David Barboza, 'Ogre to Slay? Outsource It to China' (*N.Y. Times*, Dec 9, 2005) <www.nytimes.com/2005/12/09/technology/09gaming.html?pagewanted=all&_r=0> accessed December 2, 2013.

10 F. Gregory Lastowka & Dan Hunter, 'The Laws of Virtual Worlds' (2004) 92 *Cal. L. Rev.* 1, 26–27.

suggest to trade with another participant, asking him to leave the item unattended or to transfer him the item and promise that his would afterward pay him back or exchange another item with him. Nevertheless, the participant may then walk away without keeping his promise.

In MMORPGs, there may also be robbery. A participant may threaten another participant that he would kill the other's avatar unless he transfers valuable items to him. Besides action within the virtual world, virtual goods can also be stolen by action in real world. Computer hackers may obtain another participant's login ID and password by hacking into that participant's computer.[11] He could then login to that participant's account and transfer all the items to him.

4. Who Owns Virtual Property?

It is necessary to know who the owner of virtual goods is in order to determine the nature of virtual property. If virtual goods are owned by proprietors, then property rights may not be necessary for the participants. To understand who is considered the real owner of such goods, one must begin by analyzing the agreement between the proprietors and the participants.

4.1 Proprietor Owns Virtual Property?

Rights and obligations between proprietors and the participants are usually determined and regulated by an agreement called the End-User License Agreement ("EULA").[12] Before playing MMORPGs, participants are required to agree to the EULA

---

11 Ruth Hill Bro, 'A Global View: U.S. and E.U. Approaches to Data Privacy' (2006) 878 *Practicing L. Inst.* 471, 483.

12 Jack M. Balkin, 'Virtual Liberty: Freedom to Design and Freedom to Play in Virtual Worlds' (2004) 90 *Va. L. Rev* 2043, 2049.

proposed by the proprietor.[13]

As proprietors invested much time and money in producing and maintaining MMORPGs and virtual worlds, it is reasonable that they wanted to retain any rights in the virtual world and the virtual goods within.[14] Therefore, EULAs usually "confirms the relationship between itself and the participants as a relationship of licensor-licensee.[15] Some EULAs even force participants to waive all the rights related to the virtual goods before they play.[16] In addition, some clauses in the EULAs state that participants agree to "transfer any rights in virtual property that could be recognized by law."[17]

By doing so, even if the court recognize that there are property rights in virtual properties, proprietors can still retain the rights over virtual properties for its interest.[18] Moreover, EULAs are created in a way that even if the virtual good is created by participants, proprietors would still hold rights over it.[19] Thus, EULA is used as a tool to help proprietor to obtain rights over virtual goods even if they are not the creator.[20] Besides, if participants hold rights in virtual goods, the proprietor can never shut down or stop running the virtual world as it may

13 Susan Abramovitch and David Cummings, 'Virtual property, real law: the regulation of property in video games: Part 2' (2010) *Ent. L. R.* 52.

14 Charles Blazer, 'The Five Indicia of Virtual Property' (2006) 5 *Pierce L. Rev* 137, 151.

15 *Ibid.*

16 Theodore J. Westbrook, 'Owned: Finding A Place for Virtual World Property Rights' (2006) 3 *Mich. St. L. Rev.* 779, 803.

17 Abramovitch and Cummings (n 13) 52 ; Sony Online Entertainment LLC, 'Terms of Service' (California, November 15, 2011) <www.station.sony.com/en/termsofservice.vm> accessed December 2, 2013.

18 *Ibid.*

19 Abramovitch and Cummings (n 13) 52 .

20 Blizzard Entertainment Inc., 'World of Warcraft End User Licence Agreement'(August 22, 2012) <http://us.blizzard.com/en-us/company/legal/wow_eula.html> accessed December 2, 2013.

lead to damage to participant's property which would lead to litigations.[21] In that sense, EULAs can help proprietors prevent potential litigation against participants.[22]

Some proprietors regard the transaction of virtual goods between participants with real money to be "potentially dangerous to the economy of their virtual worlds"[23] and they prohibit such transaction through EULA. For instance, Blizzard Entertainment, the proprietor of *World of Warcraft*, has shut down accounts of participants who involve in real money transactions of virtual goods.[24]

However, some proprietors started to grant participants more and more rights rather than restricting them.[25] For instance, Linden Labs, the proprietor of *Second Life*, provides intellectual rights of virtual goods created by participants to them.[26] The relevant clause of the Terms of Service of *Second Life* states that "You retain copyright and other intellectual property rights with respect to Content you create in *Second Life*, to the extent that you have such rights under applicable law. However, you must make certain representations and warranties, and provide certain license rights, forbearances and indemnification, to Linden Lab

21 Westbrook (n 16) 803; Blazer (n 14) 154.

22 *Ibid.*

23 Andrew E Jankowich, 'Property and Democracy in Virtual Worlds' (2005)11 *B.U. J. Sci. & Tech. L.* 173, 182.

24 Blizzard Entertainment Inc., 'Archived News, World of Warcraft Accounts Closed Worldwide' (December 10, 2006)< http://news.mmosite.com/content/2006-10-12/2 006101219505l254.shtml> accessed December 2, 2013.

25 Allen Chein, 'A Practical Look at Virtual Property' (2006) 80 *St. John's L. Rev.* 1059, 1088.

26 Ross Dannenberg, 'New Case: Eros v. Linden Research' (September 16, 2009), Patent Arcade, <www.patentarcade.com/2009/09/new-case-eros-v-linden-research. html> accessed December 2, 2013.

and to other users of *Second Life.*"[27]

Although rights are given to participants, one should be reminded that such rights are merely intellectual rights but not property rights. Participants who created the virtual good only have the right to "software patterns used in making virtual objects, but no rights to the objects themselves."[28] Thus, a participant who created a virtual object would only have the copyright of such object but not property right over such object.[29] As a result, Linden Labs is the one who possesses the actual virtual property. However, this still indicates that more and more rights are granted to participants rather than retained by proprietors.

Proprietors also changed their attitudes towards virtual property transactions. Rather than prohibiting virtual goods transactions, Sony Online Entertainment LLC created an official auction website where participants can trade and exchange virtual goods. By doing so, Sony provided a secure and safe platform for its users to conduct real money transaction.

4.2 Participants Own Virtual Property?

Although proprietors try to retain their rights over virtual goods, most participants believe that they have property rights over their virtual goods and have tried to protect such rights.[30]

Scholars argued that there are three reasons that participant should have retained property rights in their virtual goods:[31]

---

27 Linden Research, Inc. and Linden Research United Kingdom, Ltd, 'Second Life Terms of Service' (London, December 15, 2010) <http://secondlife.com/corporate/tos.php> accessed December 2, 2013.

28 Dannenberg (n 26)

29 *Ibid.*

30 Michael Passman, "Transaction of Virtual items in Virtual World" (2008) 18 *Alb. L. J. Sci. & Tech.* 259.

31 *Ibid.*

(A) EULAs are not always enforceable; (B) under labor-based property theory, participants should retain property rights in virtual goods due to the time and money spent and (C) policy considerations.

A.   EULAs Are Unenforceable

Proprietors only retain property right of virtual goods if EULAs are valid and enforceable. Generally, EULAs are enforceable as shown in the Canadian case of *Rudder v Microsoft Corp.*,[32] where the Canadian court held that terms and conditions of online agreement are enforceable as long as they are unambiguous and are presented fairly.[33]

However, scholars suggested that EULAs are not always enforceable. In considering whether EULAs are valid, one should first consider that who will be regarded as the owner of virtual goods if EULA does not exist. Then one has to consider that whether EULA has made any changes to the ownership of virtual goods. By then we can ask whether EULA is enforceable.[34]

It is suggested that if the EULA does not exist, property rights of virtual items are likely to rest in the participants as they spent time and money on it and had exclusory possession of them. It is only under the EULA which changed the ownership of such properties. Moreover, scholars pointed out that "some EULAs are clear contracts of adhesion."[35]

---

32 *Rudder v Microsoft Corp* [1999] 2 C.P.R. (4th) 474 (Ont).

33 Barry B. Sookman, *Computer, Internet and Electronic Commerce Law* (Scarborough, Carswell, 2007) 10–13.

34 Symposium, 'Rules & Borders — Regulating Digital Environments, Panel 3 – Ownership in Online Worlds' (2005) 21 *Santa Clara Computer & High Tech. L. J.* 807, 808.

35 Joshua Fairfield, 'Virtual Property' (2005) 85 *B.U.L. Rev.* 1047, 1083; Andrew Jankowich, 'EULAs: The Complex Web of Corporate Rule-Making in Virtual Worlds' (2006) 8 *Tul. J. Tech. & Intell. Prop.* 1, 7.

The Court in *Davidson & Associates Inc v Internet Gateway*[36] held that party's actual understanding of the agreement and the bargaining power of both sides are factors that the court would take into account.[37] There is no negotiation between proprietors and participants either at the time of the drafting of EULAs or before participants clicking the "agree button." In order to engage in virtual worlds, participants have no choice but are forced to agree with the EULA. Further, the terms and clause of the EULAs are always difficult to access. They usually contain difficult and complex terms which is hard to be fully understood. Some EULA even provides that proprietors can change the terms of EULA without notifying the participants.[38] Besides, scholars also suggest that there are limits on the terms that EULA can impose on users.[39] Thus, it is considered inequitable to hold the EULA as enforceable.

B.   Participant's Property Rights Are Supported by the Labor Theory

There is one element exists in earning money in real life and acquiring goods in virtual world: time and effort are spent.[40] According to labor theory, participants deserve property rights since they have invested time and effort in acquiring virtual goods.[41]

One may argue that it is the proprietor who created the whole

---

36 *Davidson & Associates Inc v Internet Gateway* 334 F. Supp. 2d 1164 (E. D. Mo. 2004).

37 Jon Festinger, *Video Game Law* (Markham: LexisNexis Canada, 2005) 101; Abramovitch (n13) 55–56.

38 Jankowich (n 23) 180–186.

39 Symposium (n 34) 808.

40 Jankowich (n 23) 183.

41 Steven Horowitz, 'Competing Lockean Claims to Virtual Property' (2007) 20(2) *Harvard Journal of Law and Technology* 443.

virtual world and wrote the codes of those virtual goods. The amount of time and effort spent by proprietor is much more than those of the participants and they should have hold rights in virtual goods.[42] However, it is argued that even the proprietor created and provided the virtual world, "it is largely through the labor of the users that dynamic identities and characters are created and that culture and community come to grow."[43] The most important feature of MMORPGs—interaction between participants, is the effort of participants instead of the proprietors.

It is the time and effort spent that participants believe that they should have property rights in those virtual items. Scholars commented that if there are a significant number of participants who think they hold rights in their virtual items, courts should satisfy such expectations and provide participants property rights over their virtual items.[44]

C.   Public Policy

Another factor supporting that participants being the owners of virtual goods is policy consideration.[45] As participants requires property right against theft or fraud, scholars suggested that EULAs are unenforceable as they are against policy consideration by failing to provide property right to participants. Moreover, participants spent much time and money in acquiring virtual items. If they are not granted rights over such items, it is likely that number of participants and number of virtual goods transaction would decrease. For countries trying to promote computer games industry like China and South Korea, this is not a result they would like to see.

---

42 *Ibid.*

43 Anil (n 6) 188–202; M. Grimes, 'Online Multiplayer games: a virtual space for intellectual property debates?' (2006) 8(6) *New Media & Society* 96.

44 Balkin (n 12) 2067.

45 Fairfield (n 35) 1083–1084.

5.   What Is Virtual Property?

5.1   *Characteristics of Virtual Property*

Scholars like Joshua Fairfield defined virtual property as "rivalrous, persistent and interconnected code that mimics real world characteristic."[46]

By looking at the virtual world's perspective rather than real world, they noted virtual goods are rivalrous rather than non-rivalrous. Although in real life such sequence of code can be used by one another, a particular virtual property in the virtual world can only be possessed by one participant to the exclusion of all others. If a participant transfers a virtual item to another participant, his possession to that particular item ceased. Virtual properties are also considered as persistent. Even when the participant is away from the game, the item would remain unchanged. Virtual property is considered as interconnected that other participants can experience a particular virtual property even if it is possessed by another.

The most important characteristic of virtual property is that they are transferable.[47] If virtual goods are not transferable, their value is insignificant since there would be no transaction with real money. As a result, the ability to be transferred is essential to provide virtual goods economic value.[48]

5.2   *Whether Virtual Goods are Recognized as Property*

The nature of virtual goods is of controversy. Scholars fell into

---

46 Fairfield (n 35) 1084; J. W. LeBlanc, 'The Pursuit of Virtual Life, Liberty, and Happiness and its Economic and Legal. Recognition in the Real World' (2008) 9 *Florida Coastal Law Review* 255.

47 Westbrook (n 16) 779.

48 N. DaCunha, 'Virtual Property, Real Concerns' (2010) 4 *Akron Intellectual Property Journal* 35.

two categories: some scholars believe that virtual goods cannot be regarded as property while the others considered that they can.

A minority of scholars suggested that virtual goods are not property in normal sense. They contend that virtual goods are simply piles of date that have no real world value. They also pointed out that virtual goods are non-rivalrous. While a participant is using such a sequence of code which represents a particular virtual item, another participant can also use the same sequence of code.[49] Thus, virtual goods do not fit the requirement of property.

On the other hand, Professor F. Gregory Lastowka and Professor Dan Hunter have made a "persuasive analysis that virtual items can be properly classified as property, but they concluded that virtual worlds should be left free from terrestrial law to develop their own norms and laws."[50]

Since virtual goods contain economic value, it should be regarded as property and protection is required. As mentioned above, since participants spent time and money in acquiring virtual items, these virtual goods possess certain economic values. Besides, there are people who make money in real world by selling virtual items. Apart from the virtual goods transaction market, secondary markets are generated. One of the examples is the Internet Gaming Entertainment Ltd (IGE), whose services include buying and selling of virtual games accounts, creating and design avatar for participants and providing technical support to participants.

Given the existing economic benefits that virtual property will possess, virtual property should be regard as property. However, the question is that what kind of property is it and what are its property rights.

---

49 Fairfield (n 35) 1048–49.

50 Lastowka & Hunter (n 10) 26–27.

5.3. Personal Property or Intellectual Property?

Some scholars argued that virtual goods are the subject of intellectual property rather than personal property.[51] However, some noticed that virtual goods fulfill the characteristic of chattels rather than of intellectual property's. Also, they pointed out that rights adhered to intellectual property is not sufficient to protect virtual goods against theft[52] but property rights in chattel can better protect virtual goods.

Virtual goods fit in the requirement of chattel rather than intellectual properties. Five characteristics of chattel are: "(1) the ability to be possessed; (2) the ability to be used; (3) the ability to be enjoyed; (4) the ability to be transferred and (5) rivalrousness."[53]

Participants possess virtual goods in the virtual world through their avatars. These virtual goods can be used and enjoyed by the participants. For instance, a virtual sword can be equipped to a participant's avatar to increase its ability. Moreover, as abovementioned, virtual goods can be transferred or exchanged with other participants. Further a participant have an exclusionary possession when he holds a particular item that other participants cannot possess it or use it at the same time. Therefore, virtual goods meet the five characteristics of a chattel.

Apart from having the five characteristic of chattel, scholars also noted that virtual goods are also similar to chattels regarding

---

51 Andrew D. Schwarz & Robert Bullis, 'Rivalrous Consumption and the Boundaries of Copyright Law: Intellectual Property Lessons from Online Games' (2005) 10 *Int. Prop. L. Bull.* 13, 18; Molly Stephens, 'Sales of In-Game Assets: An Illustration of the Continuing Failure of Intellectual Property Law to Protect Digital-Content Creators' (2002) 80 *Tex. L. Rev.* 1513, 1519–28; Lastowka & Hunter (n 10) 40–42.

52 Arias (n 4) 1306–1310.

53 Pamela Samuelson, 'Information as Property: Do Ruckelshaus and Carpenter Signal a Changing Direction in Intellectual Property Law?' (1989) 38 *Catt. U. L. Rev.* 365, 370; Fairfield (n 35) 1053.

persistence and interconnectivity. Virtual goods "do not fade after each use, and they do not run on one single computer."[54] As Fairfield stated, virtual property continues to exist even when participant is away from game. Further, although only one participant possesses a particular virtual item, other participants can still experience them as those items would also be shown in their computers.[55]

5.4 Property Rights of Chattel Can Better Protect Virtual Goods

Nature of property should be determined by the rights its owner seeks to protect.[56] Intellectual property rights usually "protect the authors' right of (1) adaptation; (2) distribution; (3) display; (4) reproduction and (5) performance."[57] In contrast, property rights in chattel includes: "(1) right to possess and own; (2) right to use; (3) right to manage how and by whom the property will be used; (4) right to income and profits generated by the property; (5) right to capital; (6) right to security which is immunity from involuntary transfer and expropriation; (7) right to transfer without limitation; (8) right to no durational limit to interest in property and (9) right to any residuary interest emerging from the property."[58]

From the above rights, one can observe that intellectual property rights aim to protect the author's rights in expression.[59] However, a right in expression is not what virtual goods owner

---

54 Fairfield (n 35) 1054.

55 Blazer (n 14) 141.

56 Arias (n 4) 1306–1310.

57 Arias (n 4) 1306–1310; Peter K. Yu, 'Intellectual Property and the Information Ecosystem' (2005) *Mich. St. L. Rev.* 1, 16–17.

58 Samuelson (n 53) 370; Timothy P. Terrell, '"Property", "Due Process", and the Distinction Between Definition and Theory in Legal Analysis' (1982) 70 *Geo. L. J.* 861, 869–70.

59 Susan A. Dunn, 'Defining the Scope of Copyright Protection for Computer Software' (1986) 38 *Stan. L. Rev.* 497, 518.

needs as this right would not prevent virtual items from being stolen from him. Rather, he needs rights similar to that of chattels. He needs rights to possess, to use and to transfer his virtual goods. Particularly, right of possession is of vital importance that this right can protect virtual goods against theft or fraud. Therefore, virtual goods should be classified as chattels or enjoy similar rights of chattel in order to protect virtual goods owners.[60]

6.   Multi-Jurisdictional Perspectives on Virtual Property

Property rights only exist if they are protected or enforced. Therefore, it is worth analyzing the statutes and case law of different jurisdictions.

6.1   Hong Kong

It seems that virtual property is recognized as property in Hong Kong. In 1993, the Computer Crimes Ordinance ("COC")[61] was implemented to protect against computer-related crime by amending the Crimes Ordinance and Theft Ordinance. The COC expended the meaning of "property" in Section 59 of the Crimes Ordinance[62] to include "any program or date held in a computer or in computer storage medium." It also extend the meaning of "criminal damage to property" to misuse of a computer program or date.[63] The COC also added a new offense of "access to computer with criminal or dishonest intent" in the Crimes Ordinance. Further, the COC also extend the meaning of "burglary" to include "unlawfully causing a computer to function

---

60   William S. Byassee, 'Jurisdiction of Cyberspace: Applying Real World Precedent to the Virtual Community' (1995) 30 *Wake Forest L. Rev.* 197, 214.

61   Computer Crimes Ordinance.

62   Crimes Ordinance, Section 59.

63   Crimes Ordinance, Section 60.

other than as it has been established and altering, erasing or adding any computer program or data."[64] As these ordinances protect owners' right of possession as if the goods are chattels, it indicates that virtual goods are recognized as property, not as intellectual property but chattel like property in Hong Kong.

Regarding commercial transaction of virtual goods, the position is still unclear. Under Section 2 of the Sales of Goods Ordinance ("SOGO"),[65] "goods" includes "all chattels personal other than things in action and money." As discussed above that virtual goods possess the characteristic of chattels rather than intellectual property, it is likely that virtual property would be considered as "goods" under SOGO. However, whether virtual property is protected by SOGO is still unclear in Hong Kong until relevant case arises.

6.2 United States

Courts in the United States have not yet recognize property rights in virtual property. There were two cases regarding this aspect but they were settled. In *BlackSnow Interactive v Mythic Entertainment, INC.*,[66] the plaintiff filed a lawsuit to confirm that participants have rights in selling their virtual goods. In that case, the plaintiff had hired others to play the game created by the defendant so that he can sell the virtual goods to other participants. However, this case was withdrawn because there was a clause in the EULA stating that any dispute arises have to be resolved be arbitration.

The next case regarding property rights in virtual property is

---

64 Theft Ordinance, Section 11.

65 Sales of Goods Ordinance, Section 2.

66 BlackSnow Interactive v Mythic Entertainment, Inc., No. 02-00112 (C.D. Cal. Filed 2002).

Bragg v Linden Research Inc.[67] The defendant, Linden Research Inc., was the proprietor of the MMORPG *Second Life*. In that case, the defendant shut down the account of the plaintiff since the plaintiff purchased a piece of virtual land, not through the defendant, but by way of an unauthorized auction. Although this case was also settled the District Court decided on two important issues: "*Second Life* Terms of Service's mandatory arbitration provision was unenforceable; and interaction with a person in a virtual world can satisfy a state's minimum contacts requirement for personal jurisdiction."[68]

6.3. China

At the moment, there is not law in China which explicitly recognizes virtual property rights.[69] However, the Chinese courts have acted to protect such rights. In *Li Hongchen v Beijing Arctic Ice Technology Development Co,*[70] the plaintiff's account was hacked by a third party and his virtual goods were stolen. The plaintiff then filed a lawsuit against the defendant, the proprietor of the game, claiming that the defendant failed to protect his virtual properties from theft. The trial court gave judgment in favor of the plaintiff and ordered to Defendant to "pay damages equal to the amount of money the Plaintiff had spent on game subscription fees."[71] Although in appeal the court only ordered the Defendant to restore the plaintiff's virtual items, this case indicated that "some courts may be willing to view virtual property as property that is worthy of protection under the law."[72] By recognizing the right of possession in virtual goods, the

---

67 *Bragg v Linden Research Inc 487* F, Supp. 2d 593 (E.D. Penn. 2007).
68 *Ibid.*
69 Anil (n 6) 188–202.
70 Fairfield (n 35) 1084.
71 Westbrook (n 16) at 805.
72 *Ibid.*

Chinese Court seems to accept virtual goods as property.[73]

Due to the rapid increase of online game theft[74], "China's Public Security Ministry published an advisory letter regarding virtual property theft in order to assist police with punishing such crimes."[75] Besides, a proposal was submitted in 2003 to the "Law Committee of National People's Congress seeking a law to protect virtual property."[76]

6.4. Taiwan

Unlike other jurisdiction, there is statute in Taiwan which recognizes virtual goods property.[77] The Taiwanese Criminal Code explicitly recognizes virtual goods as property. It provides that virtual goods are regarded as property since they have characteristics of chattels, such as "rivalrousness, are alienable and transferable."[78] The Taiwanese court held that theft of virtual goods is prohibited in Taiwan.[79] Under the Taiwanese Criminal Code, virtual properties are regarded as electromagnetic records thus they are considered as moveable property in case of theft.[80] As the participants can control the virtual properties' electromagnetic records, they are considered as the owner of

---

73 Fairfield (n 35) 1085.

74 Reuters, 'Verdict on Virtual Property Thief Upheld' (Sydney Morning Herald, 4 April 2006) <www.smh.com.au/news/breaking/verdict-on-virtual-property-thief-upheld/2006/04/04/1143916492279.html> accessed December 2, 2013.

75 *Ibid.*

76 P. Brown and R. Raysman, 'Property Rights in Cyberspace Games and Other Novel Legal Issues in Virtual Property' (2006) 2 *Indian Journal of Law and Technology* 87; Reuters, 'Verdict on Virtual Property Thief Upheld' (*Sydney Morning Herald*, April 4, 2006) <http://www.smh.com.au/news/breaking/verdict-on-virtual-property-thief-upheld/2006/04/04/1143916492279.html> accessed December 2, 2013.

77 Taiwan Ministry of Justice Official Notation No. 039030 (90) as cited in Fairfield (n 35) 1086.

78 Fairfield (n 35) 1086.

79 Taiwan Ministry of Justice (n 77).

80 Raysman and Brown (n 76) 17.

the virtual goods. Therefore, it is the participant but not the proprietor who owns the virtual property.[81]

6.5 South Korea

As one of the countries which have the highest population ratio of virtual world players,[82] South Korea also recognizes rights in virtual goods in order to protect its citizens and its computer game industry.[83]

South Korean court regarded that there is "no fundamental difference between virtual property and money deposited in the bank."[84] Similar to Taiwan, it was held that property rights are granted to the participants but not the proprietor.[85] The South Korean court also ruled that transaction of virtual properties is legal as participants spent money, time and effort in acquiring those items. However, such transactions have to be conducted through a legal channel as profits made from those transactions would be taxed.

6.6 Canada

Similar to the situation in China, Canadian law does not explicitly recognize property rights in virtual goods. However, scholars commented virtual property rights are recognized in Canadian Criminal Code as its provisions are wide enough to protect virtual property from theft.[86] It was suggested that virtual property code falls within the meaning of "data" which

---

81 Fairfield (n 35) 1087.

82 DaCunha (n 45) 35.

83 Fairfield (n 35) 1047.

84 P. Brown, 'Can Virtual Property Gain Legal Protection?', (IPLaw360, February 9, 2006), <www.law360.com/articles/5280> accessed December 2, 2013

85 P. Raysman and Brown (n 76) 87.

86 Canadian Criminal Code R.S.C. 1985, c. C-46.

is defined as "representations of information or of concepts that are being prepared or have been prepared in a form suitable for use in a computer system" under the Canadian Criminal Code.[87] In addition, the Canadian Code also provides that "any person who destroys, alters, interrupts, or denies access to the legal enjoyment of data is guilty of mischief and can carry a maximum penalty of two years imprisonment."[88] Further, the Canadian Code also prohibits fraudulent and unauthorized use of computer service and device.[89] Therefore, although Canadian Law does not explicitly recognize property rights in virtual property, it does appear to recognize property rights in virtual goods by providing protection against theft.

7. Conclusion

As MMORPGs are becoming more and more popular, the issue of recognizing rights in virtual goods becomes more and more important. One main controversy is identifying the real owner of virtual properties. Both participants and proprietors want to retain rights in virtual goods. Although proprietors tried to retain these rights through EULAs, majority of scholars suggested that participants should retain rights in virtual property since they need such rights to protect their virtual goods. Moreover, the time and effort spent by them also indicated that they deserve such rights.

Another controversy is the nature of virtual goods. Although a minority of scholars argued that virtual goods cannot even be regarded as "property," most scholars pointed out that virtual goods shard similar characteristics as chattels. In addition,

---

87 Canadian Criminal Code, s. 342.1(2).

88 Canadian Criminal Code, subss. 430(1.1), 430(4).

89 Canadian Criminal Code, s. 342.1(1).

rights of chattels such as right of possession are rights which participants required in order to protect their goods. Therefore, if the courts recognize rights in virtual goods, these rights should be similar to those of chattels.

However, a few problems would arise if there is property rights attached to virtual goods. Firstly, as participants possess rights in virtual goods, does shutting down the server of virtual world mean damaging property rights of participants? If so, does it mean that proprietors have to maintain virtual world forever even if there is only one participant still active in its virtual world?

Secondly, what if the nature of the game allows participants to rob or steal each other's item. For instance: participants can use "Robin Hood" as their avatars and steal properties from the rich. Does property right still exist in such kind of virtual worlds? If so, would a participant who steal items from another participant is this type of games commit theft?

The position regarding virtual goods remains unclear in Hong Kong. Nevertheless, the Taiwan model may be one that Hong Kong can use as a starting foundation. By regarding virtual goods as electromagnetic code, rights are granted to the participants but not proprietors. Besides helping participants to protect their items against theft, this act would also give confidence in participants thus promoting the growth of computer games industry.

8

Nature of Virtual Goods in a Virtual World: Ownership, Possession, or Nothing?

Michelle Wing Chi AU

1. Introduction

The virtual world is increasingly popular worldwide. Virtual worlds have helped real people become real-life millionaires, such as Anshe Chung, the avatar name for a real person. There are also individuals who can sustain their living through making real money in virtual worlds, varying from $10–$50 per month.[1] Its income-earning chances and high resemblance to the real world mean that more and more people devote time, money and effort to it. Professor Castronova calculated the Gross National Product (GNP) of virtual worlds and argued that it is greater than the GNP of Bulgaria.[2] To excel better in virtual games, players even make their own inventions and create their goods in the virtual world. These inventions are not only valuable because of the effort of the inventor. They are valuable also because they can be

---

1 Claude T. Aiken IV, 'Sources of Law and Modes of Governance: Ethnography and Theory in Second Life' (2008) *J of Tech L & Policy* 27.

2 Edward Castranova, 'Virtual Worlds: A First-Hand Account of Market And Society on the Cyberian Frontier' (2001) CESifo Working Papers <http://papers.ssrn.com/sol3/papers.cfm?abstract_id=294828> assessed December 2, 2013; Chesney, T., & Hannah N., 'Virtual World Commerce: An Exploratory Study' (2008) Nottingham University Business School Research Paper <http://ssrn.com/abstract=1286036> accessed December 1, 2013.

traded with high market prices. Due to such high resemblance of real goods, virtual thefts are also consequently on the rise. These incidents have caught some attention in different jurisdictions. Academic scholars also acknowledged the urgency for law intervention because, "[a]s a matter of policy, where a free market cultivates value, courts should protect that value, as long as other substantive rights are not infringed ... and should avoid excessive" restrictions on creativity.[3] However, should virtual world players own these goods to give them protection?

This chapter examines how goods are classified in the virtual world. It then analyses who should own the goods and what rights should be attached to these goods. This chapter concludes that full property rights should never be given to virtual world players. Only limited rights, including the rights to exclude and transfer, should be granted.

2. Overview of Virtual Worlds

Virtual worlds are environments that resemble in many aspects of real world but exist only within the computer world.[4] In general, the virtual worlds' games are often referred as "massively multiplayer online role-playing games" (MMORPGs) because millions of players create their own avatars to interact with each other. Like what Judge Posner had done, players can also choose the appearance of their avatars that resemble their face.[5] Some countries even established their virtual embassies in the virtual worlds in order to provide information about their countries to

---

3 Charles Blazer, 'The Five Indicia of Virtual Property' (2006) 5 *Pierce L Rev* 137, 146.

4 Allen Chein, 'A Practical Look at Virtual Property' (2006) 80 *St John's L. Rev.* 3 1059, 1090.

5 The Second Life of Judge Richard A. Posner, <http://nwn.blogs.com/nwn/2006/12/ the_second_life.html> accessed December 1, 2013.

interested travelers.

Virtual worlds also create money-making opportunities to different individuals. People are trying to view the virtual world as a real business to earn profits.[6] Nike and Reebok[7] commenced its virtual store in *Second Life*. Companies, mainly in Asia and Latin America, even employ workers to "farm" virtual resources and sell them for real currency.[8] Books are even published in teaching how people can become successful entrepreneurs to earn income from virtual worlds.[9] Thus, all these money opportunities, coming along with criminal offences of theft, increase the popularity of the virtual world.

3.   Goods Found in the Virtual World

The common law divides goods into personal property and real property.[10] Real property includes land and anything that is built on it. Real property is generally immovable and has a continuous lifespan. Personal property includes all other tangible and intangible properties but excludes real property. Therefore, intellectual property also belongs to the category of intangible

6 Erica Naone, 'Money Trouble In Second Life: A Series Of Upsets Could Spell Trouble For Second Life's Virtual Economy' *MIT Technology Review* (USA August 8, 2007), <www.technologyreview.com/Biztech/19193/page1> accessed December 1, 2013.

7 Chesney, T. (n 2)

8 The Leading MMORPG Services Company,<www.ige.com> accessed December 4, 2013.

9 Danie Terdiman 'Excerpts: The Entrepreneurs Guide to Second Life.' (CNET News, November 6, 2007)<www.news.com/Book-excerpt-The-Entrepreneurs-Guide-to-Second-Life/2100-1043_3- 6217117.html?part=rss&tag=2547-1_3-0-5&subj=news> accessed December 3, 2013.

10 Charles F. Floyd, Marcus T. Allen, *Real Estates Principles* (7th edn, Dearborn Real Estate Education 2002) 14.

personal property.[11] However, this classification is no longer applicable in virtual worlds.

3.1 Virtual Goods

Items in the virtual worlds that are for purchase and transfer are called "virtual goods.,"[12] Professor Hunter and Professor Lastowka noted that "[t]he real property systems within all these worlds mostly conform to the norms of modern private property systems, with free alienation of property, transfers based on the local currency, and so forth."

Virtual goods can be similar to stocks traded on real world stock markets.[13] They are intangible property and interests are represented by stock certificates. Accordingly all virtual items are intangible real property because all the goods exist only in a digital form. However, some think that the real world classifications cannot categorically address all property issues in virtual world. Virtual goods are not property because they are "simply 'piles of data' that have no real world value."[14] Virtual property is merely computer code and that "one person's use of code does not limit another person's use of the same code."[15] Thus, the real world classifications are inapplicable for the virtual world.

Thus, it has been proposed that virtual properties can be classified as collectables and consumables. Collectables are goods

---

11 Len Sealy and Richard Hooley, *Commercial Law: Text, Cases and Materials* (4th edn, OUP 2009) 55.

12 Caroline Bradley & A. Michael Froomkin, Virtual Worlds, Real Rules, (2005) 49 *N. Y. L. Sch. L. Rev.* 103, 132.

13 Reuters, "US Congress Launches Probe Into Virtual Economies" (October 15, 2006), Second Life News Center, <http://secondlife.reuters.com/stories/2006/10/15/us-congress-launchsprobe-into-virtual-economies> accessed December 4, 2013.

14 Jay Lyman, "Gamer Wins Lawsuit in Chinese Court over Stolen Virtual Winnings" Technewsworld.com (USA December 19, 2003) <http://technewsworld.com/story/32441.html> accessed December 4, 2013.

15 Joshua AT Fairfield, 'Virtual Property', (2005) 85 *B. U. L. Rev.* 1047, 1048–49.

of utilitarian in nature. They are mainly for the avatar's personal consumption or display purposes. Thus, collectable goods include vehicles and toys. Consumables are virtual items that are for limited and immediate use. These goods are consumed completely after using it for a fixed number of times including medicines and fuels.

3.2 Chose in Action in the Virtual World

Besides virtual goods, various chose in actions including money, bonds and agreements exist in virtual worlds because it cannot be enjoyed in specie and it is not capable of physical possession.[16]

Virtual worlds have their fictional currencies similar to the real world. Furthermore, these fictional currencies function equally of that in real world. In real world, money is a medium of exchange. It must be a measure of value to denominate and compare the value of goods and debts. Money must also be store of value for use in future trade. Yamaguchi similarly opined that money in the virtual world served all these purposes.[17] In one of the famous virtual games, Everquest, it also operates with Norrathian Currency. This Norrathian Currency at its peak was more valuable than Japanese yen against the US currency.[18] Furthermore, Linden Dollars in Second Life are even linked with the United States currency. Users can exchange what they have earned from Second Life back for US Dollars to earn a living. Accordingly, Professor Edward Castronova discovered that fictional currency is highly liquid not only in the virtual world; virtual players can also exchange such currency with

---

16 Jessica Young, 'Charge Over Book Debts—The Question of Control' (2004) 34 *HKLJ* 227.

17 Yamaguchi, H, 'An Analysis of Virtual Currencies in Online Games. The Japan Centre for International Finance' (2004) Soc Sci Research Inst. <http://papers.ssrn.com/sol3/papers.cfm?abstract_id=544422> accessed December 4, 2013.

18 Edward Castranova (n 2).

real currencies.[19] Thus, fictional currencies have their real-world values. Other chose in actions exist in the virtual world include also bonds and agreements. In 2007, the Ginko Financial bank created virtual bonds tradable on the World Stock Exchange in the world. Ginko stocks offer more than 100% interests rates annually in *Second Life*. However, unlike real banks, virtual banks in *Second Life* are not regulated at all. In 2007, approximately $750,000 of real currency was lost when the bank went insolvency, prompting cries for regulation.[20] Nevertheless, Linden re-iterated its position, that it did not regulate commercial deals between residents. Also there will be different agreements including lease agreement between the owner of the land and the leasee, employment agreement.[21] Land in virtual world is co-owned by Linden and private owners so private owners are required to purchase them in order to acquire ownership.

Goods found in virtual world resemble highly that of real life. They are like a "mini real world" except that everything happens in the Internet. As will be discussed below, despite the high resemblance of goods, it has come to a surprise that the current legal system is incapable of dealing with the rights and ownership attached to the goods.

4.   Who Should Own Property Rights Attached to Virtual Property

Virtual world transactions are largely conducted between virtual world players; between virtual world players and Non-

---

19 *Ibid.*

20 Bryan Gardiner, 'Bank Failure in Second Life leads to Calls for Regulation', WIRD, (USA 15 August 2007) <www.wired.com/gaming/virtualworlds/news/2007/08/virtual_bank> accessed December 2, 2013.

21 Yesha Sivan *et al.*, '3D 3C Real Virtual Worlds Defined', 1 *J. of Virtual World Research* 1.

Player Character (NPC); and between virtual world players and virtual world developers. Users can create almost any imaginable objects—varying from avatar accessories, houses to weapons to trade.[22] Despite all the objects are created by the players, nearly all virtual world developers prohibit virtual players having both property and intellectual property rights in virtual worlds. Upon signing up for accounts in virtual worlds, players agreed on "Terms of Use" (TOU) or the "End-user License Agreement" (EULA). They very often include the following clause:

> "You agree that you have no right or title in or to any such content, including the virtual goods or currency appearing or originating in the Game, or any other attributes associated with the Account or stored on the Service. Blizzard does not recognize any virtual property transfers executed outside of the Game or the purported sale, gift or trade in the "real world" of anything related to the Game. Accordingly, you may not sell items for "real" money or otherwise exchange items for value outside of the Game."[23]

All similar terms prohibit players from transacting goods in reality because they have no right property rights and intellectual property rights over their self-created virtual items. It is recognized that such clause constituted only a license.[24] As a result, all properties belong to the virtual world proprietor. Any violation will allow the virtual world proprietor "[to] suspend, modify, terminate, or delete the account at any time with any reason or no reason, with or without notice."[25]

---

22 Linden Lab, Scripting,<http://secondlife.com/whatis/scripting.php> accessed December 1, 2013.

23 World of Warcraft Terms of Use Paragraph 8.

24 Michael Passman, Transactions of Virtual Items in Virtual Worlds (2008) 18 *Alb. J. Sci. & Tech.*

25 Blazer (n 3).

However, *Second Life* is the only exception. *Second Life* distinguishes itself from its competitors[26] by granting players intellectual property rights for their creations:[27]

> "Users of the Service can create Content on Linden Lab's servers in various forms. Linden Lab acknowledges and agrees that, subject to the terms and conditions of this Agreement, you will retain any and all applicable copyright and other intellectual property rights with respect to any Content you create using the Service, to the extent you have such rights under applicable law."

As game creators have to rely on the participants to build virtual worlds and to modify the worlds they have created,[28] the encouragement of individual rights over the virtual items promotes more creation in the virtual world. *Second Life* succeeded in demonstrating how private intellectual property rights can promote the virtual world:

> "[R]ecognize the fact that persistent world users are making significant contributions to building these worlds and should be able to both own the content they create and share in the value that is created. The preservation of users' property rights is a necessary step toward the emergence of genuinely real online worlds."[29]

Every creator of objects in *Second Life* has ownership of their intellectual property rights over their virtual goods. The players can decide what rights to be attached with the virtual items—to

---

26 Symposium, Rules & Borders – Regulating Digital Environments, Panel 3— Ownership in Online Worlds, 21 *Santa Clara Computer & High Tech LJ* 809, 821. 807, 808 (2005).

27 Second Life Terms of Service Paragraph 3.2.

28 *Ibid.*

29 Press Release, Linden Lab, Second Life Residents to Own Digital Creations (November 14, 2003), <http://lindenlab.com/pressroom/releases/03 11 14> accessed December 1, 2013.

modify the product, to copy the virtual items by duplication, or to transfer the ownership of virtual item to another person[30] if there is any transfer or business transaction in the virtual world. This makes *Second Life* more attractive than its competitors' virtual world games as users now can "[m]ake real money in a virtual world."[31] *Second life* becomes a more attractive real-world business investment as intellectual property rights are retained by the players. Rights of users over their properties do not however extend to full property rights. Players only have rights to the "software patterns used in making virtual objects, but no rights to the objects themselves."[32] Coca-Cola had for instance participated in virtual worlds and sponsor events in virtual worlds and authorized *Second Life* users to use its trademark (freely) in the virtual environment.[33]

The labor theory stipulates that whoever have invested more time, skill and effort in developing their avatars and acquiring in-world possessions, they deserve property rights over the virtual items.[34] However, this theory can hardly be applicable in the conflict between the virtual world players and the virtual world proprietors. Both parties contributed to the virtual world differently.

Virtual world proprietor created the virtual world, structure, rules and codes to assist the creation of virtual items. Supporters that ownership rights still retained with the virtual world proprietors opined that since the labor effort of proprietors

---

30 Edward Castranova (n 2) 24.

31 Second Life. The Marketplace, <http://secondlife.com/whatis/marketplace.php> accessed December 3, 2013.

32 Dannenberg, "New Case: Eros v. Linden Research", Patent Arcade (USA September 16, 2009), <www.patentarcade.com/2009/09/new-case-eros-v-lindenresearch.html> accessed December 3, 2013.

33 Aiken (n 1).

34 Horowitz, 'Competing Lockean Claims to Virtual Property' (2007) 20 *Harvard J. of Law and Tech.* 2, 443.

clearly outweigh that of virtual game players, possession title should retain with the proprietors.[35]

Labor theory equally supports that virtual world players retain the ownerships with virtual players. Virtual world players build on the existing code and spend more time and effort to create virtual items.[36] They spent time and effort in creating their own properties.[37] Accordingly, these players deserve property rights over their items. Virtual world creators only laid down the foundation of creating virtual items. The creation of each virtual item should be traced back to the effort of each individual player and has nothing to deal with the proprietors. Consequently, the virtual items all come at a value—they are worthy in both fiction currencies and real currencies. Creators spent time and efforts in creating such inventions. It will be too inequitable if no personal remedies granted to them when their goods are being stolen.

In view of all these uncertainties, the best solution is to retain control and possession all with the virtual world developer and grant only licenses for the players in creating their virtual items.

5. Why Virtual World Creators Should Retain the Property Rights

5.1 Legal Uncertainty in Various Jurisdictions

Although countries try to retain the rights with the players, there are practical considerations for not granting the property rights and intellectual property rights with the virtual game players. First is the problem of forum-shopping. As virtual

---

35 *Ibid.*

36 *Ibid.*

37 Andrew E. Jankowich, 'Property & Democracy in Virtual Worlds' (2005) 11 *B.U. J. Sci. & Tech. L.* 173, 183.

world developer and disputing players can be from different jurisdictions, which jurisdiction will be appropriate in case of issue arise.[38] Furthermore, the legal paradigm for legal disputes arising out of the virtual worlds is still too pre-mature. Various jurisdictions, including Hong Kong, Canada and United States, merely extend the applicability of their present legislations to deal with the virtual world. These various jurisdictional perspectives are discussed below.

China was very keen to govern virtual world transactions judicially.[39] In *Li Hongchen v Beijing Artic Ice Technology Development Co*, a third party rogue hacked into Li's account in the game Red Moon and stole his virtual property. Li consequently sued Beijing Arctic, the developer of the Red Moon game, for not protecting his virtual goods from theft by a third party. Although there was a restrictive provision in EULAs like the Western EULAs, the courts still protected the virtual world players. The court held that the providers were responsible for the loss of virtual items and were required to compensate or restore the virtual players' loss of items.[40] There was also an appeal by Yan Yifan was dismissed by a Chinese court after the lower court had convicted and fined Yan for stealing and then selling his game identification names and online equipment belonging to players of the game Da Xihua Xiyou.[41] This judgment has a huge implication because it reflects the courts' attitudes "to view virtual property as property that is worthy of protection under the law."[42] The court protected the property owner's rights to exclusively own the piece

---

38 Coca Cola launches Second Life Contest for New Coke Machine <http://mashable.com/2007/04/17/coca-cola/> accessed December 3, 2013.

39 Joshua Fairfield, 'Virtual Property' (2005) 85 *B. U. L. Rev.* 1047, 1084.

40 Westbrook, 'Owned: Finding A Place for Virtual World Property Rights' (2006) 3 *Mich. St. L. Rev.* 779, 805.

41 Fairfield (n 14).

42 *Ibid.*

of virtual property contrary to all others, even to the third party that did not perpetrate the theft.[43]

However, despite the recent decisions in China, there is no explicit recognition of player's rights in virtual property. The court tried to rule virtual world proceedings pragmatically and tried to extend the applicability of Contract and Consumer laws as a legal basis for virtual property proceedings. The government only announced their desire to motivate investment in Chinese-based virtual worlds.[44] Legislatively, China's Public Security Ministry published an advisory letter regarding virtual property theft in order to assist police with punishing such crimes without legal effect.[45] Chinese lawyers called for refinement for virtual property laws and even submitted a proposal was submitted to the "Law Committee of National People's Congress in 2003. Further various articles laid down under Administrative Measures on Internationally Connecting of Computer Information and Internet Security, Protection and Management are targeted at computer crimes.

Like China, Taiwan is also very keen to protect virtual property ownership. The Taiwanese Criminal Code announced by the Ministry of Justice declared in 2001 that if virtual goods possess characteristics similar to property, such as rivalrousness, and are alienable and transferable, they should be protected. Thus, the theft of such property is fully punishable under criminal law.

> "The account and valuables of online games are stored as electromagnetic records in the game server. The owner of the account is entitled to control the account and valuables' electromagnetic record, to freely sell or

---

43 *Ibid.*

44 USITO China IT Weekly Briefing (October 15, 2004), <www.usito.org/uploads/269/weekly_oct15.htm> accessed December 1, 2013.

45 Fairfield (n 14) at 1085.

transfer it. Although the above accounts and valuables are virtual, they are valuable property in the real world. The players can auction or transfer them online. The accounts and valuables are the same as the property in the real world. Therefore, there is no reason not to take the accounts and valuables of online games to be the subject to be protected by the larceny or fraud in criminal law."

The right to control virtual property is acknowledged at the level of code and it is granted to the owner of the code [virtual world players] but "not the owner of the server on which the code happens to reside, or the intellectual property owner of the code." Thus, the Code recognizes theft of virtual property fully punishable under law because it "qualifies as electromagnetic records and should be considered moveable property." The maximum penalty for offences regarding virtual property in Taiwan is three years imprisonment.

South Korea is one of the leading countries with the most number of players in the virtual world. There were over 22,000 claims of virtual theft in 2003. As a result, the country took significant steps toward protecting ownership interests in virtual property. South Korea sees virtual property and money deposited with the bank identical. Thus, it is the rare country which contains law that instructs online virtual property with value independent of the game's developer. Since then, South Korea has enacted laws that make infringement of virtual property a crime. In September 2010, South Korea's top court ruled that acquiring game items takes time, effort and skill. Therefore selling them is legal.

In Hong Kong, the Crime Ordinance (Cap 200) extended the meaning of "property" to include any program or data held in a computer. Criminal damage has also extended the meaning of "criminal damage" to include any misuse of computer program or data. Thus, hacking into a player's computer for accessing online the virtual world for stealing any virtual items without consent now constitutes a criminal offence of theft.

In Canada, the Canadian Criminal Code again does not specifically deal with for virtual property issues. The provisions protecting computer use and data can potentially cover virtual property that is legally stored in a computer system. Consequently, it is wide enough to cover the situation when any person, who destroys, alters, interrupts, or denies access to the legal enjoyment of "data" is guilty of mischief and can be subjected to a maximum penalty of two years' imprisonment. However, such interpretation and applicability are not tested in courts.

Finally, litigants in the United States have to rely on the Computer Fraud and Abuse Act to protect virtual property. However, it was initially designed to prevent unauthorized breaches of government and financial institution computer systems and networks. Extending the statute to protect any intrusion of players' computers with intent to defraud when the perpetrator obtains anything in value may be too far reaching. Furthermore, all legal proceedings pursued under this act have been settled before the courts have made any decisions. For instance, Mr. Marc Bragg sued Linden Labs for confiscating his virtual property and disabling his account in 2007. However, this case resulted in out of court settlement already. Also in *Blacksnow Interactive v Mythic Entertainment, Inc*, Mythic was the developer of Camelot. Blacksnow was a virtual property farming company that "farmed" for virtual property in *Dark Age of Camelot*. Mythic told eBay to stop the auctioning *Dark Age of Camelot* items. Blacksnow sued Mythic for unfair business practices and interference with "prospective economic advantage." Blacksnow sought damages and a "court order declaring that the sale of items and accounts outside the game [did] not infringe onythic's copyrights." The case was again settled in Mythic's favor before judgment.

Except for Taiwan and South Korea, there is currently no definite legal system in different jurisdictions to govern particularly for virtual world transactions. Accordingly, the current judicial system is too immature to deal with virtual world conducts when property rights retain with players.

In view of the real world uncertainty and inconsistency governing the conducts of virtual world, it is more advisable to retain the property rights with the virtual games develop. This enables them to apply the rules and regulations developed by the virtual world developers in governing their self-created virtual worlds.

5.2 Practical Considerations

Granting virtual players property rights creates numerous concerns for the virtual game developers as well. If the virtual game developer decides to shut down the virtual world—for financial considerations, few players retained in world or bankruptcy of the developer for instance, should they indemnify the players? Avatars in the virtual world can choose to become thieves in this world. If the property rights belong to the virtual world players, how should the developer deal with the job selection? If thieves are to remain as a feasible option, then the virtual world developer will face numerous complaints for appropriating these assets.

Accordingly, scholars opined that the entire virtual world belongs to the virtual world proprietor. Thus, when user tries to gain access to the virtual world, they have to agree with the terms laid down by the proprietors. As a result of their mutual agreement, all these individuals should obey the rule of pacta sunt servanda that they all have to agree with the terms and conditions and should comply with them.

5.3 Other Rights that Should be Attached to Virtual Property

Although players should not enjoy the full property rights and intellectual property rights, they should be licensed by the virtual world developers in using the virtual goods with the right to exclusion and right to transfer.

The virtual world items should come along with the right to exclusion. Virtual items supplied by NPC are unlimited but have a very low utility level to virtual world players. The best items are owned and created by virtual players themselves. These self-created items in general can demand a high price. Joshua Fairfield described virtual property as "rivalrous" because when the property is possessed by one virtual player, it excludes all other players for gaining access to it.

Furthermore, the virtual items should be transferrable in the virtual world. To maintain the earning capacity for each player virtual world properties are transferrable so that players can transfer the limited and valuable title among themselves. This creates a market among players that create value as price to make it even more valuable. In view of the popularity of virtual world transactions, many countries started to extend the meanings of the present ordinance to cover the situations arose from the virtual world.

6.   Conclusion

Judge Posner viewed that "[w]ith real money being invested in virtual worlds, there need to be law-like rules to resolve disputes, protect property rights, enforce contracts, protect intellectual property and so forth." The virtual goods highly resemble that you find in real world. However, the impact of granting each player their right to legal possession and intellectual property rights can lead to legal uncertainty.

First, the EULAs and TOU are entered freely among the players so they should obey the terms stipulated in the agreements. Furthermore, the present legislations are insufficient to address other issues that arise when each individual player has property rights in the virtual worlds. There is still no uniform legal system to determine such issue. Most litigation dealing with virtual worlds issues were done by a mere extension of current legislations. Given the complexity of the virtual world, such extension is not able to cope with the issues arising out of the virtual world. In view of the labor theorists, the inconsistencies and legal immaturity among different jurisdictions, the ownership over the virtual property should remain with the virtual game developers.

I acknowledge the fact that the development of virtual world is becoming more rapid and prevalent. Thus, the right to transfer and the right to exclusion should be enjoyed by the players. However, unless there is a uniform legislative approach designated merely to address the virtual world issues, recognition of full property rights for each individual should still be avoided. The property rights and the intellectual property rights should remain with the virtual world developers to prevent all these uncertainties.

Part IV
Sale of Goods/Services Contract in the Virtual World

9

Improbable Real Sale of Virtual Goods

Felix Chin Kiu CHEUNG

1. Introduction

One of the most looming challenges to the existing system of commercial law is the advent of virtual worlds paralleled to the real world. Virtual worlds are online programs, supported by service providers, affording a 3D digital environment for their inhabitants. Individuals would set up avatars to represent themselves in the virtual worlds. Avatars are the virtual representations of the inhabitants within a virtual world.

Initially, virtual worlds were established merely for communications. Avatars were allowed to chat and render a series of postures and expressions. Recently, virtual worlds have increased rapidly in popularity, numbers and complexity. Newly developed virtual worlds support trading systems among avatars and manufacturing systems for creating new objects. Some develop into a comprehensive economic system resembling its equivalent in the real world. Business transactions and other kinds of commercial deals happened within virtual worlds are categorized by economics and legal scholars as v-commerce, as opposed to real-world commerce and e-commerce.

Given this emerging trend, there are heated debates as to the laws which should govern v-commerce. This article focuses on the sale of goods contract in the virtual worlds and argues that the Hong Kong Sale of Goods Ordinance (SOGO) or its equivalent in other commonwealth jurisdictions shall not be applied to govern the transactions of virtual items. To illustrate the arguments, two virtual worlds—*The Great Merchant* and *Second Life*[1]—will be examined for the purpose of a comprehensive and comparative analysis. At last, this chapter suggests the appropriate law for the purpose of governing transactions involving virtual items.

2.   Overview of the Two Virtual Worlds

2.1 *The Great Merchant*

The Great Merchant is an online game originated from Korea. It has a Hong Kong version, and therefore it fits into the local context of law and is subject to Hong Kong's jurisdiction.[2]

The Great Merchant is populated by avatars created by users. The avatars have a common goal of becoming the wealthiest merchant. It supports a trading system, whereby avatars can trade virtual items with other avatars for other virtual items or virtual money.[3] It also supports a manufacturing system, whereby avatars can invest in factories and decide the production lines.[4] The products could be sold in the market. The price fluctuates according to market supply and demand. Apart from that, users can use real money to purchase game points which could be used

---

1 For the sake of this paper, the author created an avatar in both virtual worlds, so as to closely interact with other virtual inhabitants and examine the structure of the two virtual worlds.

2 Rule 13(2) of the Terms of Service, <http://hk.beanfun.com/beanfun_web_ap/ signup/preregistration_join_law.aspx> accessed December 1, 2013; For the English reference of the Terms of Service, please refer to <www.thegreatmerchant.com/ terms-of-service.gs> accessed December 1, 2013. The English reference is not the same as the H.K. one, as it is provided by the US version, as opposed to the H.K. one, of *The Great Merchant*. The US version of *The Great Merchant* is governed by the US law (clause 8).

3 *The Great Merchant*, Economy System, <www.thegreatmerchant.com/> accessed December 1, 2013.

4 *Ibid.*

to purchase virtual items.[5] In this way, the market supply of a virtual item in the virtual world could be altered, and so its price.

2.2 Second Life

Second Life is an unrivaled virtual world in terms of size, popularity and economy.[6] It is based in the United States. US law is applicable to its governance.[7]

Second Life is too populated by avatars. However, it offers greater flexibility to the avatars than *The Great Merchant* does. Avatars in *Second Life* have no common goal. They enjoy their virtual life in a manner they wish. *Second Life* also supports a trading system. Added to this, avatars can own a shop to run its own business. They can also purchase a virtual plot of land to establish a home or a business as they wish.[8] What is more, *Second Life* allows DIY content. Users are allowed to create items of any shapes, colors and functions.[9] These user-generated items can be traded and distributed within the virtual world. Suffice it to say, the virtual world could be changed in light of the avatar's efforts to this end.

---

5 *The Great Merchant*, Item Shop, <www.thegreatmerchant.com/> accessed December 1, 2013

6 T. Linden, 'The Second Life Economy—First Quarter 2009 in Detail' (secondlife. com, April 16, 2009) <http://community.secondlife.com/t5/Features/The-Second-Life-Economy-First-Quarter-2009-in-Detail/ba-p/642113> accessed December 3, 2013.

7 Linden Labs 'Terms of Service' < http://lindenlab.com/tos> accessed December 1, 2013.

8 *Second Life*, Land Pricing & Use Fees, <http://secondlife.com/whatis/landpricing. php ; Second Life, Land, http://secondlife.com/community/land-islands.php> accessed December 1, 2013.

9 *Second Life*, Create: Coders, http://secondlife.com/whatis/create/coders.

3.   Nature of Virtual Items

The problem comes as to the appropriate law governing the trading of virtual items. Are such commercial transactions governed by SOGO or the equivalent legislation in other jurisdictions?[10] To answer this, the first and foremost question to determine is whether virtual items amount to "goods" for the purpose of the relevant statutes. According to section 2 of SOGO,[11] "goods" includes all chattels personal other than things in action and money. Academic views submit that non-physical items are things in action and excluded from the definition.[12] In section 2–105 of the Uniform Commercial Code (UCC), the US legislation governing sale of goods, "goods" is defined as both existing and identified before the property in it could be transferred. Both jurisdictions encountered difficulties deciding whether a computer program, where and only where virtual items exist, is a kind of "goods," as it unnecessarily involves a physical object, such as a disc, to be functional. A virtual world supported by an online browsing program is a case in point.

In *St Albans City and District Council v International Computers Ltd.*,[13] both Scott Baker J at first instance and Sir Iain Glidewell in the Court of Appeal held that a computer disk is within the definition of "goods," while the program in it is not "goods." In *Beta Computer (Europe) Ltd v Adobe System (Europe) Ltd*,[14] Lord Penrose held that the supply of computer software is a mere license as opposed to a sale of goods. However, this view sounded unattractive to some other judges, such as Stein J who uttered his powerful criticism in *Eurodynamics Systems plc v*

---

10 Sale of Goods Act (UK); Uniform Commercial Code (UCC) (US).
11 Sale of Goods Act (UK) s 61.
12 P. S. Atiyah, *The Sale of Goods*, (10th edn 2001) 66.
13 *St Albans City and District Council v International Computers Ltd* [1996] 4 All ER 481.
14 *Beta Computer (Europe) Ltd v Adobe System (Europe) Ltd* [1996] S.L.T. 604, [14].

General Automation Ltd,[15] holding that the disc and the program are inseparable, such as is in the case of a book and its content. Academic views are equally divided on this point.[16]

In U.S., the court encountered the same problem. In *Arbitron Inc v Tralyn Broad Inc,*[17] the court expressed the view that it was uncertain whether a computer program is "goods" *per se* for the purpose of UCC. In *Speeht v Netscape Commc'ns Corp,*[18] the court considered it to be not obvious that a computer program fits into the definition of "goods." Some court judgements tended to look at computer program as probably being "goods"[19] while some academics argued to the contrary that computer programs were not goods in the traditional sense.[20]

Provided that the position of computer programs is largely uncertain, the position of virtual items which exist only within a computer program is *prima facie* an uncertainty. If a computer program is not "goods," virtual items which could exist only within the program a fortiori cannot be "goods" *per se*. If otherwise, whether virtual items be "goods" remains an issue, which shall be dealt with again later.

---

15 *Eurodynamics Systems plc v General Automation Ltd* (unreported September 6, 1988)

16 e.g., P. S. Atiyah supporting the proposition that a computer programme is goods in P. S. Atiyah, *The Sale of Goods* (10th edn, 2001) 69–70 while Richard Morgan and Kit Burden are against this view in Richard Morgan and Kit Burden, Morgan & Burden on *Computer Contracts* (8th edn, 2009) Chapter 4.

17 *Arbitron, Inc. v. Tralyn Broadcasting, Inc.*, 400 F.3d 130, 138 n.2 (2d Cir. 2005).

18 *Speeht v Netscape Commc'ns Corp* 306 F.3d 17, 29, 31 n 13 (2d Cir. 2002).

19 e.g., *Berthold Types Ltd v Adobe Sys Inc*, 101 F Supp2d 697.

20 Claude T. Aiken IV, 'Sources of Law and modes of Governance: ethnography and Theory in Second Life' (2008) *J of Tech L & Policy* 27.

4. Nature of the Transactions

Whether a virtual item is goods or not, assuming it is, the transaction using the virtual item within the virtual worlds, whether it is part of a transaction in *The Great Merchant* or *Second Life*, cannot be a contract of sale for the purpose of SOGO or UCC.

According to Section 3(1) of SOGO,[21]

> "A contract of sale of goods is a contract whereby the seller transfers or agrees to transfer the property in goods to the buyer for a money consideration..."

According to Section 2–106 of UCC,

> "A "sale" consists in the passing of title from the seller to the buyer for a price."

The essence of both provisions lies in the passing of title or property in the goods. Pursuant to clause 8 of the Terms of Service of *The Great Merchant*, the users have no right or title to any content in the virtual world. It is further stipulated that the service provider solely owns all the property and the relevant intellectual property right of all the contents. The service provider has the absolute right to render any actions to the virtual items, including modification and even elimination. It is also stipulated that the users shall abandon any right to sue the service provider on ground of any property claim.

Pursuant to clause 7.7 of the Terms of Service of *Second Life*, the users are granted only a license to access and deal with the virtual items, not the property in them. Pursuant to clause 10.2 of the same document, the service provider is to provide the virtual world "as it is." It can make any changes at any time to the virtual world, or even cease to run it. All the content including

---

21   Sale of Goods Act (UK), s 2(1)

any virtual assets are thus subject to the service provider's action. Further, clause 7.1 only granted the users the right of intellectual property *vis-à-vis* the content they generated, not the property in or the title to it.

In summation, both service providers of the two virtual worlds retained the property in, if any at all, and the title to all the virtual items existing in the virtual worlds. As the users, and thereby their avatars, have no property in or title to the virtual items at all, there cannot be a contract of sale for the purpose of SOGO or UCC. As such, SOGO and UCC shall not be in operation to govern the transactions of virtual items.

5.   Reversed Offer and Acceptance

Aside from all the aforementioned, there are other observations that should preclude SOGO from being in operation, one of which is the reversed arrangement of offer and acceptance observed in *The Great Merchant*.

In *The Great Merchant*, there is a system of "trading in the Exchange."[22] In this system, avatars can set up a stand and display with price the items they seek to sell. Any other avatars can access the stand, and once they click the button of buying, the transaction is done, leaving the stand-seller no room to refuse to sell. The necessary conclusion of such a transaction is that the display of items is an offer, and any buyers could accept such an offer by clicking the buying button. This is contrary to the common law proposition that display of goods is merely an invitation to treat, and buying's purporting to buy is the offer, leaving the seller to decide whether to accept or not. It is submitted that the reverse is also contrary to the legislative intent of SOGO.

---

22 *The Great Merchant*, Economy System, <www.thegreatmerchant.com/> accessed December 1, 2013 .

The legislation of SOGO is necessarily based upon the long established arrangement of offer and acceptance in common law. SOGO implies into a contract of sale certain undertakings of the sellers that the goods sold must be of merchantable quality and fit for the particular purpose made known to the sellers.[23] It is submitted that such provisions are all based on the proposition that the seller is in a position to decide whether to sell or not after the buyer' purporting to buy. If this is not the case, such as in the case of *The Great Merchant*, the seller would easily be in breach of the implied condition of fitness when the buyer texts the seller about his particular purpose, then immediately clicking the button of buying, and the item turns out to be unfit for that purpose.

In other virtual worlds, many other ways of transaction could be implemented, and they all might be contrary to the arrangement of offer and acceptance in common law. SOGO, UCC and other relevant legislations' advent is not to deal with all those newly emerged vastly various means of v-transaction. Hence, the operation of those legislations should be avoided in the context of v-commerce.

6.　Users' Tolerance of Breach and Denial of Liability

Another observation that hinders the operation of SOGO and its kind is the users' tolerance of imperfect items. This is related to the reversed practice of offer and acceptance in the virtual worlds. The author has communicated with other avatars in *The Great Merchant*. A majority of the buyer-avatars do not communicate to the seller-avatars their purposes to buy the items.[24] They usually receive a mission from somewhere, or often plan to achieve a

---

23　Sale of Goods Act (UK), s16(2) and (3); Sale of Goods Act (UK) s14(2) and (3).

24　The author via his avatar interviewed 24 avatars in *The Great Merchant*. The 'majority' here refers to 21 out of the 24 avatars interviewed.

goal, and figure out the items that they seemingly need. Upon ascertainment of the required items, they seek them from the seller-avatars around, and would buy pending the price, rather than pending the intrinsic quality of the items. As the buyers searched for the items seemingly all by themselves, they usually expect to take the items at their own risk.[25]

On the other hand, the seller-avatars are unwilling to assume any responsibility as to the quality of the goods.[26] This is primarily because they usually have no knowledge of the particular purposes for which the buyer-avatars buy the items. Furthermore, in many cases, the seller-avatars are not only unwilling but also unable to guarantee that the items they sold are of merchantable quality, which is an implied undertaking of the seller under s16(2) of SOGO and s2–314(1) of UCC, because they themselves do not even have the knowledge as to what the items are for. The reason they want to sell it might simply be that the items are "useless," at least to them.[27] If the selling of a virtual item unfit for an unidentified purpose or not of merchantable quality would incur any legal liability at all, infinitely less avatars would dare to sell in any system alike to "trading in the Exchange."[28]

The necessary conclusion of the abovementioned observation is that the operation of SOGO and its alike, if at all, in the virtual worlds would cripple its economy because this would fundamentally defeat the design of transactional arrangement in those worlds.

---

25 23 out of the 24 avatars would tolerate virtual items not conforming to their own expectation.

26 All 24 avatars interviewed expressed that when they go into the shoes of a seller, they do not assume any responsibility.

27 This view was expressed by an avatar in *The Great Merchant* entitled 'jjethro.'

28 *The Great Merchant*, Economy System, <www.thegreatmerchant.com/> accessed December 1, 2013; 21 out of the 24 avatars claimed that they would refrain from 'trading in the Exchange' if they were to assume any liability under s16 of SOGO.

7.   Users' Expectation of Remedies

The last observation that tends to avoid the operation of SOGO and its alike is the fact that users of the virtual worlds do not expect the remedies set out in such statutes to be in force. Nor do they deem those remedies practical in the virtual worlds.

An example of the special remedies available to an unpaid seller is the right to exercise lien over the items. However, when a seller-avatar is not paid for the items, they expect the transaction to be immediately repudiated, rather than that the property in the items is transferred to the buyer-avatar and he holds the items in possession only as lien.[29] Certainly, if the case is based on the clause that no property in any virtual items capable of passing in a transaction is held by the avatars, no lien can ever be affected at all.

An example of the special remedies available to a buyer is the right to reject items not conforming to the contract of sale. This remedy is fundamentally unfeasible, on ground of the seller-avatars' denial of any liability as discussed above. Seller-avatars would basically not accept any rejection of items in the virtual worlds, where the buyer-avatars more often than not buy at their own risk.

Furthermore, as it is in *Second Life*, avatars are able to copy a virtual item fairly easily. It would be against justice if buyer-avatars are allowed to keep a copy and then reject the virtual item bought on ground of some beautifully made-up excuses.

8.   Supply of Service Contract

It is submitted that, in lieu of a contract of sale of goods, the transaction of virtual items in the virtual worlds should be one

---

29 This is the expectation of all the avatars interviewed.

of supply of service contract, which is in the form of license. It could be justified from the very outset since any avatars have made their first stride into the virtual worlds. Linden Lab's Terms of Service, applicable to users participating in *Second Life*, states that the terms must be agreed to by every would-be avatar before he can step into the virtual world, clearly stipulate that access and use of any virtual items in the virtual world is merely licensed by the service provider.[30] Property in any virtual assets is nowhere granted to the avatars. It thus follows that when an avatar purports to "sell" a virtual item to another avatar, he is intending in essence to sub-license the access and use of that item to the other avatar. This process of licensing can go repeatedly further without an end.

The rationale of license also makes more legal sense. License is a type of contract that "allocates rights to intangibles such as software, databases, and other forms of information."[31] When the actual form of a virtual asset within the virtual world is looked into, it is simply a piece of software code enabling the computer to produce relevant image. When the virtual asset is transferred, the position of the software code changes from one location to another within the entire program source code. It would be rather ridiculous to speak of owning the property in a piece of software code, so long as nobody is able to take the software code anywhere as they wish, not elsewhere away from the program.

A due analogy can be drawn between a virtual item and a Facebook emoticon. On Facebook, when you type in any chat box "<3", this "code" would be converted automatically to a pink heart shape "♡." It would be ridiculous to speak of it as "goods." Nor does it make sense for any Facebook user to own

---

30 Linden Lab, 'Terms of Service' <http://lindenlab.com/tos> accessed December 1, 2013.

31 Ray Nimmer, 'A Modern Template for Discussion' (2004) 2 *DePaul Bus & Com L J* 623.

the property in this heart, not to mention to enter into a contract of sale in relation to this heart.

In view of this, whether a computer program could be "goods" for the purpose of SOGO and UCC, virtual assets confined to it cannot possibly be one. No property in virtual items could be owned by any users. It follows that there cannot be a contract of sale of goods for this purpose.

9.   Conclusion

Although every virtual world provider aims to provide a world that is as realistic as possible, virtual can never become real. Virtual items are not goods in reality sense. It necessarily follows that there could be no actual sale of goods in terms of transferring title and ownership. Just as an apple in reality is capable of being sold, the virtual image of it in the mirror is incapable. However, the apple owner can license others to see the apple in the mirror! This is why, despite the uncertainty of the present legal position towards the transaction of virtual items in the virtual worlds, the contract law of license seems to fit into the context most.

10

Application of Real World Laws to Virtual World Sale of Goods and Services Contracts

Ken Wai Kin TANG

1. Introduction to Virtual Commercial Worlds

The term, "virtual worlds," is very familiar to online game fanatics. Indeed, a particular issue or event taking place in an online game portrays either part of, or sometimes, the whole of the real world in which human beings live. For instance, in a game in which an agent is obliged to complete several tasks assigned by his boss, the agent is driving his sports car on the road, different types of infrastructural facilities appear automatically and naturally on the screen. These items include parks, sports grounds and highways, as well as buildings, ranging from commercial, industrial to residential.[1] Since the above-mentioned facilities are commonly seen in the real world, "virtual worlds" are the very projection of the real world.

Undeniably and ordinarily, people from the real world interact with each other in different context in "virtual worlds." Commerce, which has been being regarded as one of the key

---

1 Second Life <http://secondlife.com> accessed December 1, 2013 ('virtual worlds' are important platforms where netizens, like those in Second Life, 'can socialize, connect and, in particular, create their own figures representing them (i.e., 'avatars') using various kinds of online tools, for example, 'free voice and text chat'.)

components of "virtual worlds,"[2] is one of the most salient forms of interaction that occurs every day and night. These virtual commerce transactions are shaping a fast-growing, vital virtual economy. For example, it is estimated that "gold-farming," which is real-world sale of virtual goods and services produced in online games, has a global value ranging from US$500 million to US$1billion and has created job opportunities for around 400,000 gamers.[3] These numbers are expected to skyrocket in the coming decades.

In virtual commercial worlds, people buy and sell goods, as well as provide various kinds of services for others. In the real world, sale of goods and provision of services are well governed by existing laws, including for example, the Hong Kong Sale of Goods Ordinance (Cap.26)("SOGO"), the Supply of Services (Implied Terms) Ordinance (Cap.457)("SSO") and common law. Superficially, it is not the case in virtual commercial worlds since they, in numerous persons' eyes, do not have any linkage with the real world. Nevertheless, in fact, it is possible for sale of goods and provision of services (for convenience, the term "commercial transactions" or "transactions" is used hereafter) in virtual commercial worlds to be protected by laws, rules and regulations from the real world, though it is a matter of degree.

The purpose of this chapter is to analyze the applicability of real world laws, rules and case law to virtual world commercial transactions. First, this article gives a brief introduction to virtual

---

2   Sivan Y, 'Real Virtual Worlds Defined: The Immense Potential of Merging 3D, Community, Creation, and Commerce' (2008) *Journal of Virtual Worlds Research* 7 (2008) <http://journals.tdl.org/jvwr/article/viewArticle/278> accessed December 1, 2013.

3   Richard Heeks, 'Current Analysis and Future Research Agenda on "Gold Farming": Real-World Production in Developing Countries for the Virtual Economies of Online Games' Development Informatics Working Paper Series #32 (2008) <www.sed.manchester.ac.uk/idpm/research/publications/wp/di/di_wp32.htm> accessed December 1, 2013.

commercial worlds by outlining the operation of commercial transactions among people from the real world (for convenience, the term "people" is used hereafter). Next, the article elaborates on the connection between transactions in virtual commercial worlds and the real world so as to show how laws, rules and regulations from the real world may apply to virtual world commercial transactions. The third section analyses potential problems invoked by the application of real world laws, rules and regulations to virtual world commercial transactions through means of contrasting the two worlds, with the provision of some feasible measures to deal with the identified problems. Finally, the article proposes practical steps to refine the existing system of local commercial law in a bid to facilitate the development of virtual world commerce.

2. Definition of Virtual Commercial Worlds

What are virtual commercial worlds? Simply speaking, they are "defined as an aggregation of individuals or business partners who interact around a shared interest,"[4] permitting users to sell their created content as well as alter the content before or after transactions occur. In other words, virtual commercial worlds are supercenters of commerce where people can trade their invented items, embracing both goods and services. Additionally, people can make any necessary and quick change(s) to their traded goods and/or services at an instant by, for example, giving orders/instructions using keyboards, mice or even voices, before or after transactions take place.

---

4 Dominik Schrank, 'A Trustful Payment System for Virtual Worlds Design and Implementation of a Payment System for Virtual Worlds' (Master's thesis, Graz University of Technology 2009) 11.

3.   Operation of Virtual Commercial Worlds

Based on the definition above and with the realization that virtual worlds represent a projection of the real world, in order to have good understanding of how commercial transactions may occur, let's take a real-world peasant as a typical example first. Suppose the peasant farms on a piece of land for water melons. After some time, he harvests the water melons and prepares to sell them in a mega market in the town center of the city in which he lives. Right before that, he realizes that part of the water melons have been rotten. In view of this, he picks off all the rotten water melons and abandons them, in essence altering the product before the transaction. After all of the remaining water melons are sold out, he spends part of the income purchasing fertilizers and farming machines of better quality in a bid to enhance the quantity, as well as quality of the water melons, thus altering the product after the transaction and retaining the opportunity to earn more money in the near future.

From the example above, it is not rare to see that people/ bodies create their own things and sell them to others for earning money in the real world. For instance, Nike, a clothing company, manufactures and sells sports shoes and sportswear. Bandai Asia, a toys manufacturer, makes and sells toys like Gundam, Powerranger, Digimon, Wonderswan and other items. The similar circumstance happens in virtual commercial worlds.

In virtual commercial worlds, people invent their own "representatives/agents," avatars, and create any thing they love and want, ranging from daily necessities, high-technological products to cleaning services. They can, if necessary, alter their creations anytime and anywhere.[5] Next, avatars sell the invented/ altered invented items to others directly or in a created open

---

5   Greg Lastowka, 'User-Generated Content and Virtual Worlds' (2008) 10(4) Vanderbilt. *J. of Entertainment and Tech. Law* 893–4.

market on behalf of and in accordance with the instructions given by their "masters/principals" for obtaining currencies, though in virtual form. After that, the 'masters / principals' use 'the money' they earn to buy some greater equipment for creating items with better quality and function(s), so that they can, like the real world peasant in the aforesaid case, generate more income in future.

4. Relationship between Commercial Transactions in the Virtual World versus the Real World

4.1 Overview

Referring to the said operation of virtual commercial worlds, it appears that transactions in virtual commercial worlds have nothing to do with the real world. The reason is crystal simple: People trade their created goods and services in abstract form using virtual currencies[6] in a platform which does not exist in the real world. To put it simply, nothing in virtual commercial worlds, including the worlds themselves has ever come into being in the real world where people live. Hence, as invented, traded goods and services in virtual commercial worlds are unreal, from countless persons' perspectives, there is no point in applying laws, rules and regulations from the real world to deal with those transactions. Furthermore, since it appears to the general public that people who control their own avatars indeed lose or suffer nothing in real monetary terms when breach of sale of goods/ provision of service contracts occurs, it will be ridiculous to order the "breaching parties" that they compensate the "victims."

For example, assume that A and B are virtual world users. A is a buyer and B is a seller. In their conversation conducted through a chat box, B agrees to sell a virtual television to A for

---

6 *Ibid.* 22.

12000 virtual dollars and the television is to be delivered on July 1, 2013. However, right after A pays B the money, B sells the television to a third party who is willing to pay more virtual dollars. A demands that B compensate A. In this situation, as a person from the real world, A actually loses nothing except for his time to indulge in virtual world games. Thus, from the general public's points of view, it is absurd to advise A that he applies to a real world court to either order B that he specifically perform the "contract" or pay damages to A.

Undeniably, what the general public perceive is justifiable, yet only to a certain extent. Indeed, such notion is rather superficial and impertinent, since it fails to present a comprehensive picture of the linkage between virtual world commercial transactions and the real world. As Matthew Ganis and David McNeill said, "...[r]esearch applied in this area of study would yield policy frameworks (for commercial entities) and help establish legal (legislative) baselines for how virtual worlds must behave when they are linked to the commerce of real-world goods and services...,"[7] it is implied that there is, to varying degrees, a relationship between virtual world commerce and the real world.

4.2   Human Beings: Masterminds of Commercial Transactions in the Virtual World

According to the above-mentioned discussion, in virtual worlds, avatars are people's representatives/agents. They trade on behalf of and according to people's instructions. Yet, it should never be ignored that those avatars are controlled by people. Without people, no avatars are able to engage in any commercial transactions in virtual worlds, not to mention how well virtual commercial worlds can function without human

---

7   Michael Gannis and David McNeill, 'Commercial and Business Opportunities and Problems of Virtual Worlds' in Mennecke *et al.*, *Second Life and Other Virtual Worlds: A Roadmap for Research* (2008) 22 (Article 20) 375.

beings. Therefore, metaphorically, the relationship between virtual commerce and the real world is the one between flesh and spirit. Since spirit is the "master" of flesh, without the former, the latter is no different from a corpse.

One point that is equally noteworthy is that, due to the fact that "human beings" are the "pivot" of the smooth operation of virtual commercial worlds, their misbehavior and exorbitance in the real world may cause tremendous detriment to the commercial transactions in virtual worlds. Such acts can be carried out in several ways. For instance, people maliciously hack into other virtual world users' accounts and steal their created items or intentionally deceive other virtual world users to deliver their virtual goods in exchange for nothing. Worse still, people may plant and spread computer viruses to virtual worlds in a bid to destroy their targeted transactions. Hence, it is mistaken to assert that virtual world commercial transactions are totally separated from the real world.

4.3 Bi-world Commercial Transactions: Conglomeration of Virtual Worlds and the Real World

There is a golden rule in the commercial world: the ultimate aim of every single commercial transaction is to gain profit. Otherwise, it will be pointless for people to trade.

In the old days, or even several decades ago, the platform for people's commercial transactions was confined to the real commercial world. They sold their goods, whether created themselves or not, to, as well as provided different types of services for others, either directly or indirectly. In today's globalized and digital economy, these transactions occur in different media. As Andrew Sparrow argues,

> "…It is possible to sell virtual world's assets purely in-world or into the real world…These contracts may be between the virtual world operator and its users, or

between users themselves—avatar to avatar. Finally contracts may be formed between users and the outside world…"[8]

Thanks to the fast and exciting development of science and technology, in the current information and electronic age, commercial transactions are no longer a privilege for the pure real world. Instead, virtual worlds are now playing a proactive role in facilitating commercial transactions which involve the "participation" of both virtual worlds and the real world.

Such participation can be presented in the following two forms:

(1) Virtual world operators and virtual world users.

(2) Virtual world users and virtual world users or the real world.

5. Forms of Virtual World Transactions

5.1 *Between Virtual World Operators and Virtual World Users*

As mentioned before, avatars are controlled by human beings. Virtual worlds are no exception. They do not operate automatically themselves all the times. They are rather functioned and monitored ultimately by their operators, which are, again, controlled by human beings.

Thus, in this case, contract law (e.g., common law) and laws relating to provision of service (e.g., the SSO) may apply because normally, a service contract is entered into between a virtual world operator and its users. For example, four key elements, embracing offer (i.e., becoming a user of a virtual world),

---

8 Andrew Sparrow, *The Law of Virtual Worlds and Internet Social Networks* (1st edn Gower, England 2010) 6.

acceptance of the offer (i.e., informing the operator that one agrees to join the virtual world as a user via e-mail or simply by clicking the button "I accept" online), consideration (i.e., users pay a certain amount of fee for creating a user account in real monetary terms) and intention to enter into legal relations, of the formation of contract must present. Besides, as far as sale of virtual goods is concerned, if a user buys a large number of virtual items, say, virtual weapons which are planned to be sold to another user for earning profit in real monetary terms, from a virtual shop monitored by the operator, the operator ought to deliver them to its user(s) according to the time for delivery stipulated in the service contract or within a reasonable period of time. Otherwise, breach of condition of contract may be committed by the operator, rendering the contract repudiated and consequently entitling the user(s) to obtain common law damages.

5.2 Between Virtual World Users

With respect to virtual commercial transactions between virtual world users, two scenarios must be considered: (1) when commercial transactions in virtual worlds involve the use of real world currencies being the medium of exchange; and (2) when commercial transactions in virtual worlds involves the sale of goods or provision of services in the real world.

In the first scenario, when commercial transactions in virtual worlds involve the use of real world currencies being the medium of exchange, it is well known that in plenty of virtual worlds like *Second Life*, *Entropia Universe* or *World of Warcraft*, virtual currencies are used to buy and sell virtual goods or provide services for avatars. As those goods/services do not exist in the real world, in case defects/problems arise during the course of dealing (e.g., there is late/, non-delivery of goods; there is late/non-performance of services), laws, rules and regulations from the real world cannot apply. Yet, it will be different provided that the real world currencies are used in virtual world commercial transactions.

Imagine an avatar controlled by J takes part in a virtual warfare. According to the rules of the virtual warfare, an avatar who aids his/her virtual nation in winning a war against another one created by another avatar will win several chances to use the virtual warfare as a platform to promote everything they need and want from the real world, for example, an event or a competition. Now, there is a great war being fought between two virtual nations, X and Y. J is the commander-in-chief of X. In order to enhance the chance of winning the battle against Y, X plans to purchase more high-tech, powerful and lethal military weapons from one of its allies. J, being the person-in-charge of the vital purchase, decides to buy several war crafts and super warships from one of X's allies, Z which is created and controlled by K, a real world person. To ensure that those war crafts and warships will not be purchased by X's enemy (i.e., Y), J has no choices but to buy them in real monetary terms. Before the purchase of the weapons, J and K enter into a sale of goods contract, in which J offers K $8,000 to buy the said weapons which must be delivered within two days. Based on such scenario, if K, upon receiving the payment, breaches the contract by selling the aforesaid weapons to X's enemy (i.e., Y), failing to deliver the weapons by the stipulated time,[9] delivering the wrong quantities,[10] or not delivering them to X at all,[11] the real world laws, rules and regulations, for example, the SOGO and relevant common law[12] may apply. Otherwise, the victim party, J, will suffer a great deal in real economic terms, since he, in addition to the loss of his money (i.e., $8,000), loses the precious chances to promote things that J needs and desires from the real world. Injustice will crop up.

---

9   Sale of Goods Ordinance 1896, s 12.

10   Sale of Goods Ordinance 1896, s 32.

11   Sale of Goods Ordinance 1896, s 53.

12   *Hadley v Baxendale* (1854) 9 Ex 341, *Wilensko Slaski Towarzystwo Drewno v Fenwick* [1938] 3 All ER 429.

Take the creation of virtual items as another typical example. Suppose L is a virtual world user. L is a great artist who has painted quite a number of pictures in the virtual world. Another virtual world user, M, who needs L's painting for promoting his personal webpage, agrees to offer L $5,000 to buy one. Suppose L encounters the same situations with K in the previous example. Again, it will be detrimental to L in real economic terms if M who breaches the contract does not compensate L.

In the second scenario, when commercial transactions in virtual worlds involve the sale of goods or provision of services in the real world, a salient example is illustrated as follows: assume that P is a virtual world user. He creates a virtual farm, which has fed various kinds of animals, such as goats, horses and oxen. When those animals grow up, P sells them to other users for earning virtual currencies which can then be converted to real money.[13] Owing to the fact that P will be busy working for the next couple of weeks, he will not be able to manage the farm. In addition, since part of the animals will be available for sale in the coming several weeks, P hires Q, who is a person from the real world, to manage the farm, as well as to argue for good prices for the potential sale of the animals. In return, Q gets $3,000 in real monetary terms.

In this case, there is indeed a real world service contract concluded between P and Q for the purpose of facilitating potential virtual world transactions (i.e., sale of goods—virtual animals).[14] If P breaches the contract by, upon Q's performance of the contact, say, refusing to pay Q the agreed service charge or failing to pay such charge by the stipulated time (if any) or within a reasonable time,[15] Q will be entitled to claim damages from P according to the laws of a jurisdiction, say, Hong Kong (e.g., the SSO and the common law).

---

13   Sparrow (n 7) 13.

14   Supply of Services Ordinance 1994, s 3.

15   Supply of Services Ordinance 1994, s 6.

Thus, in view of the examples of commercial transactions above, it has to be admitted that virtual world commercial transactions can hardly be separated from the real world thoroughly, since effective and smooth virtual transactions do, though not always, rely on the active "participation" of virtual world operators, users and the real world, which subsequently involves the application of the real world laws, rules and regulations once disputes and problems appear.

6. Potential Problems Arising from Application of Real World Laws, Rules and Regulations to Virtual World Commercial Transactions; and Possible Solutions

With reference to what has been illustrated above, it is concluded that, in principle, real world laws, rules and regulations may apply to commercial transactions in virtual worlds when those transactions involve the participants of the real world in terms of payment in real money and the sale of goods or provision of services in the real world. Yet, in practice, three potential problems, namely, (1) equivalence between virtual and the real world commercial transactions, (2) identity of parties to virtual commercial transactions, and (3) jurisdiction, may arise from such application, which is to dissect as follows:

Problem (1): Virtual Commercial Transactions: Do They Enjoy the Same Status with Real World Commercial Transactions?

As the names suggest, the terms "virtual" and "real" are two opposite nouns. "Virtual commercial transactions" are abstract and imaginary. They never exist in the real world. While goods are physically untouchable, services are merely provided for avatars, not real world persons. On the contrary, real world commercial transactions are genuine. They exist. While goods are physically touchable, services are provided for people in the real world. Thus, it seems unjustifiable to apply real world commercial law to virtual commercial transactions. Even if it is reasonable to do so, it appears that current real world laws, rules and regulations "express" clearly to us that they will not apply to virtual commercial transactions. I will take relevant laws of the U.S. and Hong Kong relating to sale of goods to illustrate the point.

In the US, according to Article 2 of the Uniform Commercial Code ("UCC"), goods means "both existing and identified before any interest in them may pass."[16] In Hong Kong, Section 2(1) of the SOGO provides, "goods include all chattels personal other than things in action and money... under the contract of sale." (Emphasis added). Upon reading these two pieces of legislation together, it is known that "goods" refer to all chattels personal which exist for sale. However, virtual goods, as said above, do not "exist," let alone sell them in the real world. Even they can be for sale, they (specifically referring to those created virtual items) can at best be classified as "intellectual property" (but whether they will be protected by real world intellectual property laws, rules and regulations still need ample discussion).[17] For these reasons, real world laws, rules and regulations may not apply to virtual commercial transactions.

Now, suppose real world laws, rules and regulations (e.g., the UCC and SOGO) apply to virtual commercial transactions. A head-aching question will crop up immediately: since virtual and real world commercial transactions are fundamentally different in nature, how can real world laws, rules, regulations and courts resolve disputes over problems concerning quality of virtual world goods and services? For instance, the quality of a real apple can be judged in terms of its color, size, taste etc. People may know the color and size of a virtual apple, but how can we know its taste? Regarding services, for example, in the real world,

---

16   Uniform Commercial Code Q 2–105(1) (2007).

17   Michael H. Passman, 'Transactions of Virtual Items in Virtual Worlds' (2008) 18 *Alb. L.J. Sci. & Tech.* 271–2.

people are able to know whether internet services provided by telecommunication companies are up to standard stipulated in service contracts by referring to the connection and browsing speed. Yet, it is impossible to do so in virtual worlds.

Since virtual goods, as said above, are physically untouchable, the term "quality" of virtual goods need some brand-new interpretation, which is different from that of real world goods. For instance, the quality of virtual goods may be determined in terms of price, whether such goods can help virtual word users achieve their purposes and/or whether such goods are exactly what have been described in, for instance, virtual advertisements, posters and brochures).

Problem (2): Identity of Parties to Virtual Commercial Transactions: Whom do People Actually Trade with?

It is assumed that problem (1) is solved, meaning that real world laws, rules and regulations apply to virtual commercial transactions. The second important question is as follows: who indeed possesses rights and/or bears legal liabilities in those transactions? In fact, this question stems from the difficulty to identify the actual parties engaging in the transactions to some extent.

In principle, in virtual worlds, avatars are the parties to commercial transactions. Nonetheless, in essence, virtual world users are the real traders in those transactions, since, as mentioned before, the former are controlled by the latter. Therefore, if real world laws, rules and regulations could apply to those transactions, the users would be the ones who possessed contractual rights and/or bore legal responsibilities derived from contracts they entered into. Yet, sometimes, it is hard to find out the "real traders" in a particular transaction. First, it is normal that virtual world users, before transactions, may not have seen each other. Since avatars representing the parties to transactions are "created" by the users, it is impossible for them to know who the real traders are. Worse still, if the users create multiple avatars to represent them, it will be even harder to spot out the real traders. Besides, as each user has an account in virtual worlds, what will be the consequence if the account is stolen?

To ensure that transactions are carried out with the real traders, first, a more sophisticated security system need be adopted to prevent virtual world users' accounts from being stolen. Besides, it is advised that each virtual world user is only allowed to create one avatar to represent him/her so as to avoid duplication or confusion.

Problem (3): Which Jurisdiction(s) Has/Have the Power to Govern Virtual Commercial Transactions?

Now, even both problems (1) and (2) have been successfully resolved; a vital issue is yet to be tackled: Which jurisdiction(s)' laws, rules and regulations shall apply to deal with virtual commercial transactions?

Such problem will be easy to resolve if those virtual transactions take place within one jurisdiction. For example, if transactions happen in Hong Kong, the SOGO, the SSO and relevant common law of Hong Kong will apply. If transactions occur in England and Wales, the Sale of Goods Act 1979, the Supply of Goods and Services Act 1982 and relevant common law of the area will apply. Yet, the said problem will become a lot more complicated when situations occur (not exhaustive) as follows:

(a) one of the parties to the transaction is situated in Jurisdiction A, but the other one is present in Jurisdiction B;

(b) one of the parties to the transaction, who is a national of Jurisdiction A, carries out the transaction in jurisdiction B;

(c) both parties to the transaction are the nationals of jurisdiction A, and they engage in the transaction in jurisdiction B.

(d) one of the parties to the transaction creates several virtual items in Jurisdiction A, sell them right away in Jurisdiction B to the other party who is a national of Jurisdiction C

To tackle this problem, it need be legally clarified that, when virtual transactions take place within one jurisdiction, say, Hong Kong, the laws, rules and regulations of Hong Kong will apply. Yet, for the other cases (For instance, when virtual transactions involve more than one jurisdiction (e.g., A virtual world user in Hong Kong trades with the one in the U.S.), internationally applicable laws, rules and regulations which need be enacted by nations/districts from all over the world beforehand will apply.

To be frank, the above-mentioned solutions are by no means a full-stop to the tackling of the said problems. In a bid to effectively govern commercial transactions in virtual worlds in the long run, a well-refined system of laws, rules and regulations based on real world legal model(s) ought to be established step by step.

First and foremost, the HKSAR government should appoint a relevant authority (i.e., The Commerce and Economic Development Bureau) or establish a specific statutory body to review the existing relevant laws, rules and regulations that apply to real world commercial transactions (e.g., the SOGO, the SSO etc.) in collaboration with the Department of Justice.

Then, after ample discussion and public consultation, the two bodies ought to decide on which part of laws, rules and regulations can be kept and which part should be abandoned or revised to fit in situations involving virtual commercial transactions.

Last but not least, after the newly-defined system of laws, rules and regulations regarding virtual transactions is established, comprehensive review over such system must be conducted on a regular basis by referring to the development of case law (e.g., how courts interpret "quality" in the facets of virtual transactions and under what circumstances will virtual transactions not be legally protected).

7.   Conclusion

Virtual commercial worlds are never separated from the real world as the operation of virtual transactions involves the "participation" of the real world in various terms. Thus, it is possible for laws, rules and regulations from the real world to apply to such transactions. Nevertheless, there are some problems that may arise from the application of real world laws, rules and regulations to virtual transactions since virtual and real world transactions are fundamentally different in nature. Hence, a decent tailor-made system of laws, rules and regulations based on the real world model(s) ought to be established to govern virtual transactions, followed by constant, comprehensive review, and revision when necessary.

11

Redefining the "Sale of Goods Contract" in the Virtual World: A US Legal Perspective

Darren Tak Long PO

1. Introduction

This chapter aims to redefine the definition of "sale of goods contract" in the virtual world by addressing relevant issues pertinent to the phenomenon of virtual items transaction against the backdrop of the US law. It will explain and expand on Michael H. Passman's theory with that there is no real "sale of goods contract" in the virtual world, but rather licenses of intellectual property.

The popularity of virtual worlds is ever growing. Millions of people around the world interact with each other in virtual worlds every single day; some even make a living from the trade of virtual items. It would be difficult to imagine 20 years ago today, trade of virtual swords and shields could support a person's life in reality. Regardless, there are more than one billion virtual world users around the globe at this moment,[1] heralding a "genesis of virtual societies with millions of dollars being spent for the production and preservation of these 'unreal' yet extremely

---

1 KZero, 'Virtual world registered accounts breakthrough 1bn' <www.kzero.co.uk/blog/virtual-world-registered-accounts-breakthrough-1bn/> accessed December 5, 2013.

lucrative worlds."[2] The amount of real money exchanged within virtual worlds is astounding. In 2001, a virtual world named *Norrath* was estimated to have a gross national product of $135 million, which means that each *Norrath* user had an average income of $3.42 per hour—a higher per capita income than that of Bulgaria.[3] Whereas in just the first quarter of 2010, there are over $160 million transferred among Second Life® users through the trade of virtual items.[4] The above figures highlight the tremendously lucrative new markets for transaction of virtual items.

1.1 What Is a Virtual World?

Before delving into the complex economic transactions among users within virtual worlds, it is paramount to define what exactly a "virtual world" is. Similar to other types of entertainment, virtual worlds are "communities that are premised on an escape to fantasy"[5] where one experiences "things not possible within the rules governing the real world."[6] Virtual worlds are driven by the users' appeal of the ability to "perform superhuman feats, develop completely anonymous relationships, or simply connect with friends who are thousands of miles away."[7]

---

2   J. Dibbell, 'The Life of the Chinese Gold Farmer' *New York Times* (June 17, 2007).

3   E. Castronova, 'Virtual Worlds: A First-Hand Account of Market and Society on the Cyberian Frontier'(2001) *CESifo Working Paper No. 618.*

4   'Virtual Economies' <www.kempedmonds.com/2010/05/digital-economies-gaming-and-gambling.html> accessed December 4, 2013.

5   G. Lastowka, *Virtual Justice* (Yale University Press 2010) 10.

6   *ibid.*

7   J. Ackerman, 'An Online Gamer's Manifesto: Recognizing Virtual Property Rights by Replacing End User Licensing Agreements in Virtual Worlds" (2012) *6 Phoen. L. R. 137, 140.*

While it is conceded that there is no single agreed upon definition of what a virtual world is,[8] a common definition of modern virtual worlds is the presence of "Internet-based simulated environments that feature software-animated objects and events."[9] Virtual worlds are "simulated social places" featuring software-animated objects and events whereby users interact with each other by employing "avatars."[10] A virtual world is also persistent in that users' actions and investments are expected to last some time, if not permanently.[11] Moreover, a virtual world offers an imitation of reality and allows users to affect the reality represented through interaction with each other.[12] In conclusion, virtual worlds can be observed as persistent places where a user creates a virtual self-representation known as an "avatar," interacts with other users' avatars, and make decisions that have permanent and lasting effects through those avatars.

1.2 Items in Virtual Worlds

Virtual items are designed to enhance and customize the user's experience in virtual worlds. The scope of the items' ability to modify that in-world experience depends on the nature of the world.[13] For example, in *World of Warcraft*, where missions are to be fulfilled by avatars, the bearer of certain items increase the avatar's abilities and powers hence its ability to complete missions.[14] The major differences among advanced players are mainly attributable to the items they have acquired during

---

8 J. Kwong, 'Getting The Goods On Virtual Items: A Fresh Look At Multi-User Online Environments' (2011) *37 WMLR 1805, 1813*.

9 Lastowka (n 5) 9.

10 Ackerman (n 7) 149 and Lastowka (n 5) 9.

11 Lastowka (n 5) 31

12 Lastowka (n 5) 31.

13 Kwong (n 8) 1816.

14 *ibid.*

missions and the battles.[15] Because of their rarity in the virtual worlds and the powers they convey, these items give the bearer a certain cache and status as a dedicated and highly skilled player since most items can only be acquired within the world. For example, *World of Warcraft* does not allow users to purchase virtual items with real money.[16]

On the other hand, items may have completely different uses or purposes depending on the theme of the world. For example in *FarmVille*, virtual items such as seeds and tractors can be earned or bought by users to improve their virtual farming.[17] Whereas in Sulake's Habbo.com, virtual items have no real "purposes" and are completely decorative.[18] Like most virtual items, those in Farmville and Habbo.com are created and sold to users by developers;[19] however in other virtual worlds, items can be created and marketed by users, such as those in Second Life®.[20] These items may include granting the user's avatar enhanced abilities through scripts of "genitalia" offered by Eros.[21] Contrary to mission-oriented worlds like World of Warcraft, the items in *Second Life*® are not required to advance through the world as there is an absence of "objective" in *Second Life*® other than "what

15 World of Warcraft, 'World of Warcraft Armory' <http://us.battle.net/wow Virtual Worlds: A Primer/en/game/armory> accessed December 3, 2013.

16 Blizzard Entertainment, 'World of Warcraft Terms of Use' <http://us.blizzard.com/en-us/company/legal/wow_tou.html> accessed December 3, 2013.

17 Insurance Journal, 'Farmers Insurance Offers Coverage in Virtual FarmVille' (Oct. 14, 2010) <www.insurancejournal.com/news/national/2010 Virtual Worlds: A Primer/10/14/114046.htm> accessed December 2, 2013. See also, (n 8) 1816.

18 Kwong (n 8) 1817.

19 Habbo.com, 'Terms of Sale' <https://help.habbo.com/entries/23071032-Terms-of-Sale-US> accessed June 26, 2013.

20 Second Life®, 'What is Second Life®?' <http://secondlife.com/whatis/?lang=en-US#Intro> accessed December 1, 2013.

21 Second Life® avatars are then allowed to engage in simulated sexual activity.

users decide for themselves."[22]

Soon, virtual world users realize that the virtual items they obtain represent the amount of time they have spent in the virtual world. Upon that realization, gamers started looking for ways to circumvent the countless hours required on their quest for the best items for their avatars. Rather than spending a tremendous amount of time, gamers started trading items for either virtual items/currency or real world money.[23] Today, the market for virtual items is huge and lucrative where there is a myriad of virtual items across a vast variety of virtual worlds.[24] Such expansion has tempted many developers to classify virtual items as a new form of property capable of being traded.[25] Despite the popularity of virtual items, no online environment has expressly acknowledged any such right to items within their world.[26] In the U.S., the right to virtual world assets has not, as yet, been recognized by the courts and the legislature. However such right is recognized in China, Netherlands and South Korea.[27] Arguably speaking, *Second Life*® is the closest of any other online environment in offering users something close to a legitimate right to property when it offered users the right to retain their own intellectual property rights.[28]

---

22 Kwong (n 8) 1818. See also, *Second Life*®, <http://secondlife.com> accessed December 3, 2013.

23 Kwong (n 8) 1808.

24 (n 20).

25 F. Lastowka & D. Hunter, *Virtual Worlds: A Primer, in The State of Play: Law, Games, and Virtual Worlds* (New York University Press 2006) 17.

26 Kwong (n 8) 1815.

27 Will Knight, 'Gamer Wins Back Virtual Booty in Court Battle' *New Scientist* (December 23, 2003) <www.newscientist.com/article/dn4510-gamer-wins-back-virtual -booty-in-court-battle.html> accessed December 1, 2013.

28 *Second Life*®, 'Terms of Service' s 7.1 <http://secondlife.com/corporate/tos.php> accessed December 1, 2013.

2.   Property Rights in Virtual Worlds

Before one enters a virtual world, he must have first entered into a contract with the developer. Typically, these contracts are titled "Terms of Use" or "Terms of Service" and very often an End User License Agreement ("EULA") are incorporated.

Generally speaking, EULAs are contracts that "remove the user's property rights to anything within the virtual world, including items the user builds or creates himself or herself using the tools the virtual world developer has provided."[29] Since under most EULAs a user has no property rights to in-game items, some virtual world developers regard transactions between users to sell virtual items in exchange of real money illegal and detrimental to the economy of their virtual worlds.[30]

The developer of *World of Warcraft*, Blizzard Entertainment, has arguably the most restrictive EULA. It states that "Blizzard repudiates any user property rights to virtual items and virtual currency."[31] In its Terms of Use it stipulates that "Blizzard does not recognize any virtual property transfer executed outside of the Game or the purported sale, gift or trade in the 'real world' of anything related to the Game."[32] To enforce its claimed property rights, Blizzard has shut down accounts of individuals who engage in allegedly illicit transactions.[33] In similar vein, Sony has enforced its claimed rights to *EverQuest II* by limiting sale of virtual items

---

29   J. Fairfield, 'Virtual Property' (2005) *85 B. U. L. Rev. 1047, 1082.*

30   A. Jankowich, 'Property and Democracy in Virtual Worlds' (2005) *11 B. U. J. Sci. & Tech. L. 173, 182.*

31   Fairfield (n 29) 1063.

32   *World of Warcraft* Legal: Terms of Use <www.worldofwarcraft.com/legal/termsofuse.html> accessed December 1, 2013.

33   *World of Warcraft*, Archived News, World of Warcraft Accounts Closed Worldwide <www.worldofwarcraft.com/news/rss-10-2006.xml> accessed December 1, 2013.

to its own website[34] and heavily prohibiting illegitimate sales.[35]

The developer of *Second Life*®, Linden lab claims itself to be a "virtual world entirely built and owned by its residents." *Second Life*® is one of the few virtual worlds which provide its users with property rights over virtual items within its virtual world.[36] It claims that users can "make real money in a virtual world."[37] Unlike most EULAs that are employed by other developers which essentially remove users' property rights, "Linden Lab's Terms of Service agreement recognizes residents' right to retain full intellectual property protection for the digital content they create in *Second Life*®."[38] Such has a resulted in a significant difference in the rights transferred during virtual item transactions.

2.1 Transactions of Virtual Items

Forbidding developers from the right of alienation of virtual items has led to an "artificial restraint on the transference of wealth between real and virtual worlds."[39] It is perfectly normal for users, who have devoted countless hours in virtual worlds to obtain scarce items, to wish to bring some of their virtual wealth into the real world.[40] However, as a result of the restraint imposed

---

34 Station Exchange, 'What is Station exchange?' <http://stationexchange.station.sony.com> accessed December 1, 2013.

35 B. Noveck, 'Trademark Law and the Scoial Construction of Trust: Creating the Legal Framework for Online Identity' (2005) *83 Wash. U. L. Q. 1733, 1735.*

36 *Second Life*®, 'What is Second Life®?' <http://secondlife.com/whatis/> accessed December 2, 2013.

37 *Second Life*®, 'The Market Place' <http://marketplace.secondlife.com> accessed December 4, 2013.

38 *Second Life*®, 'IP Rights' <http://secondlife.com/corporate/tos.php> accessed December 4, 2013.

39 J. LeBlanc, 'The Pursuit of Virtual Life, Liberty, And Happiness And Its Economic And Legal Recognition in The Real World' (2008) *9 FLCLR 255, 268.*

40 Y. Chen, 'Online Gaming Crime and Security Issue—Cases and Countermeasures from Taiwan' (2004) <www.iit-iti.nrc-cnrc.gc.ca/iit-publications-iti/docs/NRC-47401.pdf> accessed December 1, 2013.

by most EULAs, users' wishing to engage in trade of virtual items must do so in illegitimate or grey markets resulting in fraud and abuse.[41]

The issue of fraud and abuse in the transaction of virtual items will be revisited after the chapter makes clear the form of contract law governing transactions in virtual items.

3.   Transactions of Virtual Items are "Licenses," Not Sales

Michael H. Passman states that the "law of contracts generally enforces the reasonable expectations of the parties to the contract and that contract law should reflect the expectations of the parties. Therefore, when one looks at transactions in virtual world, the lens of the users must be worn in order to ascertain what their expectations really are so as to determine the appropriate form of contract law that should govern the sale of virtual items.[42] With reference to a survey that Passman conducted on *Second Life*®, he asked *Second Life*® users about their expectations regarding transferring rights upon sale, breaching of contract and revoking acceptance.[43] The survey concluded that user expectations align with the notion that transactions in virtual items are not sales of goods, but merely a license of intellectual property. Below we shall discuss this theory in detail.

3.1   Virtual Items Are Not "Goods"

A virtual item is generally defined as "a digital representation of

---

41 J. Archinaco, 'Virtual Worlds, Real Damages: The Odd Case of American Hero, The Greatest Horse That May Have Lived' (2007) *11 Gaming L. Rev. 21, 25.*

42 M. Passman, 'Transactions of Virtual Items in Virtual Worlds' (2008) *18 Alb. L.J. Sci. & Tech. 259–292, 267.*

43 Passman (n 42) 270.

objects (real or imaginary... created for use with virtual worlds, video games or other social media applications."[44] Virtual items may look and act like real things, but there is nothing truly real about them.[45] Both Passman and Justin A. Kwong have expressed concern over naming virtual items as "virtual goods" or "virtual properties."[46] Kwong expressly states: "the most common mistake made with respect to virtual items is the label "virtual goods."[47] He explains that "virtual items are not, and can never be, 'goods'." The use of the term "goods" invokes the special laws governing the sales of goods contained in Article 2 of the Uniform Commercial Code ("UCC") which "applies to transaction of goods."[48] "Goods" are specifically defined in Article 2 as existing objects that are identifiable and movable at the time of purchase."[49] As observed by Passman, even though some courts have applied Article 2 to software packaged in a physical form,[50] courts and commentators have struggled to apply Article 2 properly to transactions that are absent of physical manifestation.[51] To explain the distinction between a virtual item and a real world "good," Passman draws a compelling analogy:

> "Consider a sword in a virtual world. Very few people would confuse a real world sword with a virtual world sword. The two 'swords' might look similar and both be

44 J. Gatto & S. Metsch, 'Legal Issues with Virtual Worlds, Virtual Goods and Virtual Currencies' (2010) *1016 Practising L. Inst. 837, 849.*

45 Lastowka & Hunter (n 25) 40–43.

46 See Kwong (n 8) 1805; and M. Passman, 'Transactions of Virtual Items in Virtual Worlds' (2008) *18 Alb. L.J. Sci. & Tech. 259–292, 271.*

47 Lastowka & Hunter (n 25) 10–11.

48 Uniform Commercial Code (2010) s 2–105.

49 see Uniform Commercial Code (2010) s 2–105; and J. Kwong, ' Getting The Goods On Virtual Items: A Fresh Look At Multi-User Online Environments' (2011) *37 WMLR 1805 1811-1812.*

50 *ProCD, Inc v Zeidenberg* (1996) *86 F.3d 1447, 1450.*

51 See (n 42) 272; *Arbitron, Inc v Tralyn Broad. Inc.* (2005) *400 F.3d 130, 138*

> used for the same purpose in their respective worlds...
> However, the virtual swords is not a 'good' as that term
> is used in Article 2 because it is not moveable at the time
> of identification[52] in a physical sense."[53]

As such, virtual items are not "goods" under the U.C.C..

3.2   Virtual Item Transactions Are Licenses, Not Sales

Passman proposes that even if virtual items were goods under
Article 2, their purchase may not qualify as a "sale."[54] A "sale
consists in the passing of title from the seller to the buyer for a
price..."[55] The seller of a virtual item does not always grant full
title to the buyer. In fact, the majority of virtual world users do
not expect the buyer to acquire full rights in the item at purchase:
72% of the users interviewed expected the seller to retain some
rights over an item when "selling" it.[56] It is explained that
contrary to a sale, a license "allocates rights in intangibles such
as software, databases, and other forms of information."[57] While
a sale "centers on qualitative warranties or remedy limitations...
a license focuses instead on delineating the scope of permitted
use of the licensed subject matter."[58] As such, the license contains
"no assurance that the licensee can actually use the subject matter
without infringing another's rights."[59]

Licenses also differ significantly from sales of goods in that
the licensed product "can be transferred and simultaneously

---

52   Uniform Commercial Code (2010) s. 2–05.

53   Passman (n 42) 272.

54   *ibid.*

55   Uniform Commercial Code (2010) s. 2–106(1).

56   Passman (n 42) 273.

57   R. Nimmer, 'A Modern Template for Discussion' (2004) 2 *DePaul Bus. & Com. L. J.*
     623.

58   *ibid.*

59   Nimmer (n 57) 627.

retained by the transferor." [60] Since a license limits the rights of its buyer, the buyer of a license should not expect the same level of complete ownership that a buyer of goods should expect. [61] Hence transactions of virtual items in virtual worlds are not sales but licenses. Kwong agrees with Passman's theory and concedes that such labeling can be confusing because many scholars or developers themselves refer to them as "virtual goods." Most consumers do not understand that there is a distinction, but legally, goods are specific kinds of commercial items that are addressed by the U.C.C.. The distinction is sometimes expressed by developers in the EULAs, [62] but since users tend to overlook license agreements, their assumptions about virtual items being "goods" can be explained by common practice within the industry where terms such as "sell and buy" of "goods" are used because those words are "convenient and familiar," but developers are actually aware that "all software… is distributed under license." [63] Kwong asserts that most purchases of virtual items are licenses to access certain features of an ongoing service (the game), rather than acquisition of goods where there is a formal transfer of title. [64] It could be argued that nearly every aspect of a virtual world is a software service provided on condition of compliance with the terms of a license agreement. [65] This could be confusing sometimes because virtual items appear to be discrete objects that are "separate, identifiable, and moveable" at the time of purchase which are similar to the features of goods under U.C.C. Article

60   Nimmer (n 57) 629–630.

61   *ibid.*

62   R. Hillman & J. Rachlinski, 'Standard-Form Contracting in the Electronic Age' (2002) *77 N. Y. U. L. Rev. 429, 445-50.*

63   Kwong (n 8) 1824.

64   Terms of Service, Second Life®, s 4-7 <http://secondlife.com/corporate/tos.php> accessed December 3, 2013.

65   Kwong (n 8) 1825.

2.[66] Nonetheless, it is worth noting that unless title is transferred, there is no true sale.[67]

A. Kwong explains that pub loyalty schemes are analogical to the license nature of virtual items:

> "Many pubs offer loyal patrons the opportunity to join a mug club. Each year, patrons get the chance to buy into the club by paying a nominal fee, in exchange for which they get a numbered mug. The patron is the only person who can use the mug, but he or she does not own it—the mug must stay in the pub. However, the patron does receive larger, lower priced drinks throughout the subscription period. The subscription fee guarantees the bar a minimum amount of revenue up front and imputes a certain amount of loyalty from the patron in order to recoup his or her 'investment'."[68]

A Kwong's "numbered mug" perhaps best illustrates the situation where someone pays money for a separate and identifiable item and has almost exclusive possession of it.[69] The almost part is confusing because of the fact that the pub is still the owner of the mug. Therefore when the pub shuts down, the patron cannot take the mug to another pub and receive the same treatment—he must start the process all over again in the new pub.[70] The membership therefore is effectively a license to access a service and not a sale. Virtual items are analogous to the mugs because they only exist within the virtual world created and are incapable of being moved outside the realm for which they were created.[71]

---

66 Uniform Commercial Code (2010) s. 2–105.

67 Uniform Commercial Code (2010) s. 2–106(1).

68 Kwong (n 8) 1825–1826.

69 *ibid.*

70 Kwong (n 8) 1826.

71 *ibid.*

Similarly, a shirt or a car created/ bought in *Second Life*® cannot be brought to use by an avatar in the *World of Warcraft*. Each virtual world is a "separate and discrete software program that uses proprietary computer programming code to generate images and transfer information."[72] Not only would allowing users to move items and avatars from one environment to the next create technical issues, it would also defeat the provider's goal of keeping users invested in its platform.[73]

A distinction between a software purchase and a typical sale of goods could be made based on the fact that the nature of digital content is such that it can be transferred to someone without affecting the ability of the owner to possess it at the same time.[74] Such is the essence of licensing. Licenses allow people to see movies or buy music albums without owning them. They cannot walk out of the theater with a copy of the movie or music and sell it to a stranger. This is also true with music album and DVDs. But according to Kwong, this has led to confusion among consumers about their ability to actually "own" virtual items due to their similar characteristics as a U.C.C. Article 2 good without realizing their right to the item is only a limited license.[75]

The situation is a bit different in *Second Life*® however. As mentioned earlier, *Second Life*® is different from most other virtual worlds as it expressly guarantees users' intellectual property rights to the items they have created. Since users retain intellectual property rights of the virtual items they have created, under US law, those rights can be sold or licensed.[76] While such

---

72 Kwong (n 8) 1826.

73 *ibid.*

74 R. Nimmer, *Law of Computer Technology: Rights, Licenses, Liabilities* (4th edn, 2010).

75 Kwong (n 8) 1827.

76 Kim Shiffman, '*Second Life*®: Real Sales in Fake World' (2008) Rogers Business Resources.

transaction may qualify as a "sale," it is still unlikely to fall within the tradition definition of "sale of goods." The fact that Linden Lab retains complete ownership and absolute control through exclusive control of user's access to the world mirrors the aforementioned pub mug analogy—even though users have intellectual property rights to their items, their access to those rights can be eliminated by Linden Lab at any time.[77]

4.   Enforceability of Contracts between Users

After establishing that transaction of virtual items in virtual worlds are contracts of license rather than contracts of sale, this paragraph discusses the scenario where there is a breach of contract. Surprisingly, as observed by Passman, many virtual world users do not expect to receive the exact item they paid in a transaction with another user highlighting a lack of enforceability of contract in the virtual world.[78]

On one hand, virtual worlds may be better suited to the resolution of contract disputes than the real world: First, record keeping in virtual worlds is generally automated and accurate. Second, in many worlds, the code itself handles transactions in a way that everyone assents to before making a transaction.[79] On the other hand, in terms of users' ability to create long-term contracts, virtual worlds and games are currently limited for several reasons, most notably, the current expectation of pseudonymity in most virtual worlds. An example would be a user of a virtual world who wants to build a villa. The construction will require virtual building tools to build the frame of the villa, the garden, etc. It may also involve programming light sources,

---

77   *Bragg v Linden Research, Inc* 487 F. Supp. 2d 593 (E.D. Pa. 2007).

78   Passman (n 42) 276.

79   B. Duranske, *Virtual Law* (American Bar Association 2008) 135.

fans and other interactive objects. In the context of *Second Life*®, the user may not have the necessary knowledge to use scripting tools to build everything himself, and may probably hire or buy from other experts in the virtual world. In such cases, there is no reason that the employer and the contractor/buyer and seller cannot form a binding contract using communication tools within the virtual world, which are similar to real life telephones and e-mails, to negotiate the terms. Parties can even draft a written document memorializing all the terms if necessary.

The most significant problem with the enforceability of between-users contract is the pseudonymity inherent in virtual worlds.[80] Even though it is not legally necessary for one party to know the real name of the other party to the contract, it would still be practical if you know who the other party is in order to enforce the contract. EULAs typically only govern the contractual relationships between users and developers; however upon breaches of contract between users, parties to the contract will most probably resort to real world remedies.

The problem is minimized in cases where both parties to the contract have associated their avatars with real identities. However, most virtual items transactions between users involve more than one anonymous party hence they are mostly "point-of-sale transactions, with payment and purchase changing hands at essentially the same time."[81] Fraud and abuse are rampant under such circumstances.

4.1 Fraud

A typical virtual item transaction fraud takes place where A, a virtual user who wants to buy an item, contacts B, a user who wants to sell an item. Fraud may occur when B has transferred

---

80 *ibid* 136.

81 Duranske (n 79) 137.

the item to A and A fails to pay for the transfer; or B may transfer an item other than the one requested by A to him after he has paid; or B may transfer an illegitimately obtained item to A.[82]

4.2 Black Markets

As illustrated in the chapter concerning EULAs, black markets for transaction of virtual items are a result from the constraint of economic liberty.[83] In order to circumvent the restraint imposed by EULAs, users have to trade in black markets, which are often more costly than a legal free market.[84] While black market for virtual item transaction is actually thriving, users subject themselves to fraud and abuse since there is a lack of control by the government and virtual world developers.[85]

4.3 Breach of Contract

As mentioned earlier, transaction of virtual items are not, strictly speaking, sale of goods. Breach of contract of sale between users cannot fall neatly into the normal standards of breaching for either goods or non-goods contracts.[86] While Article 2 cannot be properly applied to transactions of virtual items within the United States, we now look at international transactions which are common among virtual world users.

In terms of international transactions, it is governed by the Convention on Contracts for the International Sale of Goods

---

82 I. MacInnes, 'Virtual World Governance: Digital Item Trade and its Consequences in KOREA' (2004) <http://web.si.umich.edu/tprc/papers/2004/382/ppr%20 Korea%C2008%C20TPRC%C20final%20revised.pdf> accessed December 2, 2013.

83 *Black's Law Dictionary* (8th ed. 2004) 988.

84 E. Castronova, *Synthetic Worlds: The Business and Culture of Online Games* (2005) 149–51.

85 LeBlanc (n 39) 273.

86 Passman (n 42) 276.

("CISG"). However transactions of virtual items do not fall into the definition of "sale" under the CISG because they are in the form of licenses. Furthermore, CISG does not apply to sales of "goods bought for personal…use" and presumes that the contracting parties have some knowledge of international law. It is quite markedly different from the reality where international transactions of virtual items are often among unsophisticated parties who purchase the items for person use.[87] Hence CISG do not govern international transactions in virtual items.

The only possible way to redress the issue of unenforceability of contract within virtual worlds appears to be a liquidated-damages contract with the amount in question held by a neutral third party (e.g., one who has associated his avatar with his real-life identity) until both of the parties have fulfilled the contractual terms or, in case of a breach, an arbitration proceeding has been decided.[88]

5.   Future of Virtual Goods Transactions

While EULAs strip most virtual world users of their virtual property rights, the recognition of those rights may actually benefit both users and developers.

Virtual items transactions are a growing business with real world value of over 1 billion US dollars.[89] If developers can remove the black market by legitimizing in-world items transactions, additional revenue could be generated from the already existing auction-house technologies within virtual worlds when the supply chain is moved from black markets back to

---

87   Passman (n 42) 284.

88   Duranske (n 79) 137.

89   E. Castronova, *Synthetic Worlds: The Business and Culture of Online Games* (2005) 13.

legitimate arenas within virtual worlds.[90] Rather than driving the huge amount of profits generated from virtual items transactions to "black market alleyways of the Internet," effective control of an open, predictable and safe marketplace should be utilized by developers to effectively remove externalities like fraud and abuse and maximize profits from such booming business.[91] Therefore, this essay advocates the legal alienability of virtual items by recognizing virtual property rights, which would ultimately benefit both virtual world users and developers.

5.1 Recognition of Virtual Property Rights

In the United States, contract law and privately enforceable EULAs govern virtual property rights which usually result in the lack of the rights themselves. However, other jurisdictions have begun to recognize virtual property rights to virtual world users regardless of the restrictions imposed by EULAs.[92] Indeed, courts in China have offered and enforced virtual property rights to users against developers in various cases[93] and Taiwan has explicitly covered virtual property in its law.[94] In 2003, Beijing's District People's Court held that victim to virtual item theft should be compensated by the developer, Beijing Arctic Ice, which had expressly stated any property rights would not be recognized within its game.[95] The holding implicitly recognized that through the application of the victim's "labor, time, wisdom and money,"[96]

---

90 LeBlanc (n 39) 273.

91 LeBlanc (n 39) 274.

92 LeBlanc (n 39) 282.

93 Y. Chen, 'Online Gaming Crime and Security Issue--Cases and Countermeasures from Taiwan' (2004) <www.iit-iti.nrc-cnrc.gc.ca/iit-publications-iti/docs/NRC-47401.pdf> accessed December 1, 2013, IV.

94 *ibid.*

95 China Daily, 'On-line Game Player Wins Virtual Properties Dispute' (19 December 2003) <www.chinadaily.com.cn/en/doc/2003-12/19/content_ 291957.htm> accessed December 1, 2013.

96 *ibid.*

he had acquired certain property rights in his virtual item in the virtual world.

In the United States, *Bragg v Linden Lab*[97] has illustrated the conflict between users and developers inherent in EULAs on the status of virtual items. The case concerns a suspended *Second Life* user, Bragg who claimed compensation for approximately US$8,000 worth of virtual land that was in his account at the time when the account was closed by Linden Lab. Bragg claimed that Linden Lab has breached the terms in the EULA of *Second Life* which promises users they can retain intellectual property rights in virtual land, property and goods.[98] However, the case did not progress to trial which rendered the unfortunate lack of progress as regards the clarification of the status of virtual property in the U.S.. In this regard, China is many steps ahead of the United States in terms of recognition of virtual property rights.

Taiwan is considered a leading jurisdiction in the recognition of virtual property rights[99] where the alienability and lawful existence of virtual property are recognized.[100] As early as 2001, a Taiwanese Ministry of Justice Regulation expressly stated that virtual property is alienable and transferable and is protected by Taiwanese law.[101] Indeed, some commentators have suggested if the United States were to create a system recognizing virtual property rights,[102] it could learn from Taiwan's experience where prosecutions for virtual property theft and fraud have been upheld.[103]

---

97 *Bragg v. Linden Research, Inc.* (2007) 487 F. Supp. 2d 593.
98 *ibid.*
99 Fairfield (n 29) 1050.
100 Fairfield (n 29) 1086.
101 *ibid.*
102 LeBlanc (n 39) 285.
103 Fairfield (n 29) 1087.

6. Conclusion

The current virtual item transaction governed by a multitude of EULAs is far from being economically efficient and effective. In addition, it does not answer to the realistic needs of people to trade virtual items for real world money.[104] Some recognition of property rights, which have been inherent in virtual items, must be recognized by legislations in order to provide a more effective platform for virtual items transactions. Pushing virtual item transactions into black markets is an unhealthy practice within the industry, which is not only detrimental to both virtual world users and developers, but also tampers with the overall maturation of the virtual world business. Virtual world users' right to alienate virtual property obtained through the application of skill and labor and engage in legitimate trades with other users should be recognized and protected.[105]

Ultimately, a delicate balance must be struck between the recognition of the user's virtual property rights and the developer's legitimate need to exercise protection against breaches of intellectual property rights. The time has come for a more vibrant market for virtual item transaction and reform in the American law must not delay any further.

---

104 LeBlanc (n 39) 286.
105 LeBlanc (n 39) 290–291.

Part V
Transfer of Property and Risk in the Virtual World

12

Transfer of Risk
in Real World Commercial Transactions
and Its Application to Virtual Transactions

Cybele Cin Cam LO

1. Introduction

In *Head v Tattersall*,[1] a horse which did not fit its sale description
was sold to the Plaintiff. The horse later sustained an injury in
an accident, and the buyer sought to return the horse within the
warranty period set out at the time of sale. The court held that the
buyer should be allowed to return the horse under a contractual
right. Had the horse been a virtual horse, would the buyer still be
allowed to return the horse?

With the growing popularity of virtual worlds,[2] it is inevitable
that issues stemming from transactions in the virtual world should
be of concern to academics[3] and the courts.[4] In this chapter, I will

---

1 *Head v Tattersall* (1871) LR 7 Exch 7.

2 Dan Hunter and Greg Lastwoka, 'The Laws of the Virtual Worlds' (2004)
California Law Review 92.

3 Brian Mennecke, Ben Konsynski, Anthony Townsend, David Bray, John Lester,
Edward Roche, and Michael Rowe, 'Second Life and other Virtual Worlds: A
Roadmap for Research' (2007) *ICIS 2007 Proceedings*.

4 Brian E. Mennecke, William D. Terando, Diane J. Janvrin, and William N. Dilla,
'It's just a game, or is it? Real money, real income, and real taxes in virtual worlds'
(2007) 20 *Communications of the Association for Information Systems*, Article 15;
See also *Bragg v. Linden Research, Inc.*, 487 F. Supp.2d 593 (E.D. Pa. 2007).

look into the transfer of property and risk in virtual transactions. I will first consider the transfer of risk in the real world and discuss its application to virtual transactions. I will argue that the current rules that deal with transfer of risk are not suitable for virtual transactions and suggest a model for addressing transfer of risk in virtual transactions.

2.   Transfer of Risk

Risk, in terms of the sale and transfer of goods, is a negative concept defined by a party's existing rights, duties and remedies.[5] At any given transaction, when does a buyer lose his right to demand a refund? When does a seller lose his right to keep a payment? In Hong Kong, the general rule for the passing of risk is provided in section 22 of the Sale of Goods Ordinance ("SOGO"), which states:

> "Unless otherwise agreed, the goods remain at the seller's risk until the property therein is transferred to the buyer, but when the property therein is transferred to the buyer the goods are at the buyer's risk, whether delivery has been made or not."[6]

Thus, the general rule provides for the passing of risk along with the property, and is a reflection of the civil maxim "*res perit domino*," or, in other words, a property is lost to the owner at the time it is lost or destroyed. As J. Blackburn put it, "when you can show that the property passed, the risk of the loss prima facie is in the person in whom the property is."[7] However, while in many instances risk is tied to property, risk can be transferred

---

5 Len Sealy and Richard Hooley, *Commercial Law* (Oxford University Press 2008) 299.

6 Sale of Goods Ordinance (Cap 26) (SOGO) s 22.

7 *Martineau v. Kitching* (1872) LR 7 Q B 453.

separately from property. This is evident in cases such as *Head v Tattersall* (above) and *Castle v. Playford*[8] where, when a ship sank along with a shipment of ice, the buyer was liable for the "fair estimation of its value" even though the ice had, obviously, not been transferred. The second part of SOGO section 22 provides for this:

> "Provided that where delivery has been delayed through the fault of either seller or buyer, the goods are at the risk of the party in fault as regards any loss which might not have occurred but for such fault:
>
> Provided, also, that nothing in this section shall affect the duties or liabilities of either seller or buyer as a bailee of the goods of the other party."[9]

3. Virtual Property and Legal Property

Virtual worlds allow individuals to log in and interact with one another. This may involve games where players role play and fight battles,[10] or simply be a place where people virtually co-inhabit and socialize with each other.[11] The property in these worlds is regularly traded between players using online currency,[12] which

---

8 *Castle v. Playford* (1872) LR 7 Ex. 98.

9 Sale of Goods Ordinance (Cap 26) (SOGO) s 22.

10 'World of Warcraft' (World of Warcraft) <http://us.battle.net/wow/en/> accessed December 1, 2013.
   'Diablo III' (Diablo III) <http://us.blizzard.com/en-us/games/d3/> accessed December 1, 2013.

11 'Second Life' (Second Life) <http://secondlife.com/> accessed December 1, 2013.

12 'Currency in World of Warcraft' (World of Warcraft Universe Guide) <www.wowwiki.com/Currency> accessed December 1, 2013.

may be converted to US dollars,[13] or via other online mediums such as eBay.[14] Despite the prevalence of trade, however, it has yet to be decided whether players should have legal interest in the virtual property. This is especially problematic in discussing risk as there is still no consensus as to whether virtual property should be treated as legal property, and if so, to what extent. While risk can be transferred separately from the transfer of property, it is doubtful whether the topic exists when neither the seller nor the buyer own the property — or worse, the property does not even exist under law. To complicate things further, SOGO itself only applies to "goods,"[15] that is to say, tangibles or tangible property.[16] As the opinions on whether and why virtual property should/should not be considered property under the law differs widely amongst academics, I will provide a few examples below to illustrate the debate. Current opinions on whether virtual property should be considered legal property can be categorized into three groups, discussed in detail below.

3.1   If Jellyfish Are Not Really Fish...

Benkler[17] argues that virtual property does not really exist, that "there are only social relations mediated by a richly rendered communications platforms."[18] A virtual spoon, in the physical, tangible sense, does not really exist. Whether or not property

---

13   'Buying and Selling Linden Dollars' (Second Life) <http://community.secondlife. com/t5/English-Knowledge-Base/Buying-and-selling-Linden-dollars/ta-p/700107> accessed December 1, 2013.

14   'eBay Banned World of Warcraft Virtual Goods Auctions' (Softpedia, January 30, 2007) <http://news.softpedia.com/news/eBay-Banned-World-of-Warcraft-Virtual-Goods-Auctions-45809.shtml> accessed December 1, 2013.

15   Sale of Goods Ordinance (SOGO) s 2 ("Goods' includes all chattels personal other than things in action and money.")

16   Sealy and Hooley (n 5) 268.

17   Jack M. Balkin and Beth Simone Noveck (eds) *The State of Play: Law, Games, And Virtual Worlds* (NYU Press 2006) Chapter 11.

18   *ibid.*

rights should be part of the framework in any given virtual platform should depend whether property rights would benefit the platform. It is, in Benkler's view, a matter to be dealt with by the End User License Agreement rather than law since the user has the option of choosing which, if any, virtual worlds he joins.

Lawrence takes a different approach and argues that providing independent property rights in virtual property would be incomparable with the nature of retail software.[19] Virtual property is dependent on the medium in which it is created. For example, the existence of a spoon in *Second Life* is dependent on the existence on *Second Life*. Lawrence argues that the changing nature of software ensures that currently existing virtual property will be incompatible with future versions of the software. As a new software version is rolled out, resources will be directed toward the new version and the old software will eventually be phased out and shut down. A user will eventually be unable to enjoy any virtual property created in the old version. Therefore, in Lawrence's opinion, property rights in virtual property merely provide short term solutions, and create problems in the long run.

3.2 If It Looks Like a Duck...

With the increasing number of transactions related to virtual property, some academics have advocated for the protection of rights related to virtual property under common law.

Lim[20] argues that the virtual property provided in some virtual platforms, such as *Second Life*, fit the known characteristics of property: A player may, for example, control the land he owns by excluding trespassers, controlling what sound enters the land,

---

19 Dan E. Lawrence, 'It Really Is Just a Game: The Impracticability of Common Law Property Rights in Virtual Property' (2008) 47 *Washburn L. J.* 505, 541

20 Lim Yee Fen 'Virtual World, Virtual Land but Real Property' (2010) *Singapore Journal of Legal Studies* 304.

controlling whether his land should be publicly listed etc. As virtual property fits the description of property, and there is an expectation amongst players that the virtual property should be treated as property, legal rights should be invested in virtual property to protect players.

3.3 It Is Neither a Jellyfish Nor a Duck

Some academics have on one hand acknowledged that virtual property exists within the confines of virtual platforms, but on the other hand try to strike a balance by suggesting restricted property rights for virtual property.

Hunt[21] argues that intangibility and impermanence are not reasons to exclude virtual property from being considered property. The law recognizes intangibles such as copyright and mortgages, so it is feasible that virtual property be treated as property under common law. Further, not only will ownership facilitate creative innovation, but the sheer scale of virtual transactions demands that there be legal protection.[22] Hunt suggests a "rule of permeability" where virtual property within a game should not be protected while virtual property sufficiently intertwined with the real world should be regulated by common law. Hunt provides a three pronged test in measuring whether property is intertwined with the real world, and believes that property rights should only be applied to worlds (1) that are open, (2) where there is commodification of the property, and (3) where there is collaboration by the players in developing the virtual world.

---

21 Kurt Hunt, 'This Land Is Not Your Land: Second Life, CopyBot, and the Looming Question of Virtual Property Rights' (2007) 9 *Tex. Rev. Ent. & Sports L.* 141.

22 'The value of this market was estimated in 2005 at approximately US$880 million' Lim Yee Fen (n 20) 304.

4. Applying Real World Rules to Virtual Worlds

Looking at risk in current transactions involving virtual property, the risk lies mostly on the buyer. As SOGO only pertains to tangible assets, and there has yet to be a separate acknowledgement of virtual property as a form of property, at present there is no recognition of virtual property as property under the law. Without recognition of virtual property as legal property, it is impossible for buyers to seek legal recourse when transactions go wrong. In cases such as *Head v Tattersall*,[23] where the seller holds the risk, the property is deemed to have passed defeasibly to the buyer, but the seller continues to bear the risk. Should there be damage to the property, the seller is retrospectively burdened with the loss. This is not the case in transactions involving virtual property. More often than not, buyers first pay the seller either through a third party such as eBay, or a private transaction, then virtually meet with the seller in order to obtain the virtual property concerned.[24] There is not much a buyer can do should something go wrong with the property after payment has been made. In fact, buyers do not expect risk to remain with the seller and no not expect to be able to make refunds.[25]

Perhaps due to the fact that the courts around the world have yet to catch up with the relatively new concept of virtual property, the options with regard to risk are similar whether the parties are from China or a common law jurisdiction. In China, it was held that a player's sword in the game "*Legend of Mir II*" was not considered property, and so there was no remedy for the player's

---

23 *Head v Tattersall* (1871) LR 7 Exch 7.

24 Garlick 'Player, Pirate or Conducer? A Consideration of the Rights of Online Gamers' (2005) 7 *Yale J. L. & Tech.* 422, 428 <http://yjolt.research.yale.edu/files/garlick-7-YJOLT-422.pdf > accessed December 1, 2013.

25 Michael H. Passman 'Transactions of Virtual Items In Virtual Worlds' (2008) 18 *Alb. L.J. Sci. & Tech.* 259

stolen sword.[26] Chein, in *A Practical Look at Virtual Property*,[27] puts forward that had the events occurred in the U.S., a US court would also fail to find property rights in the virtual sword. Hints toward the lack of a concept for virtual property as real property may also be found in the fact that in *Bragg v. Linden Research, Inc.*,[28] a case concerning virtual land, much of the discussion was based on contract law rather than the nature of virtual property.

In real life transactions where the buyer assumes the risk, the buyer "waives all claims and rights which arise from the non-performance by the seller of his obligations in so far as this is attributable to such loss or damage."[29] In virtual transactions, this waiver of claims and rights is not voluntary, but constrained by the process of virtual transactions and limitations for recourse. Without acknowledgement of property rights in virtual property, the buyer has no choice but to accept the loss which comes with non-performance on part of the seller.

5. Beyond Contract Law

Whether a buyer is protected under contract law depends, of course, much on the contract he signed. In many cases this may be the End User License Agreement between a company and a user. While contract law may provide some protection to a buyer, without a concept of risk in virtual property, a buyer continues to hold the burden of risk and in many cases may not be able to attain the same amount of protection given to buyers of transactions involving real property. Turning back to the question

---

26 Allen Chein 'A Practical Look at Virtual Property' (2006) 80(3) *St. John's Law Review*, 1059.

27 *ibid.*

28 *Bragg v. Linden Research, Inc.*, 487 F. Supp. 2d 593 (E. D. Penn. 2007).

29 Sealy and Hooley (n 5) 237.

posed in the beginning of this essay: Had the horse in *Head v Tattersall*[30] been a virtual horse, would the seller still assume the risk? Arguably no. Without a concept of risk in virtual property, the risk would have shifted to the buyer as soon as he had made payment. It would be difficult for the buyer to find remedy under contract law as the contract did not provide for damaged horses.

A concept of property and risk needs to be developed for virtual property in order to protect the rights of buyers in transactions involving virtual property. The courts have already started to take steps in this direction. In *Bragg v. Linden Research, Inc.*,[31] for example, while the court did not recognize independent property rights in Bragg's virtual assets, they did recognize that virtual property has value within in a virtual environment. For transactions that involve real world currency and spill into the real world, perhaps a more realistic concept of property and risk will have to be provided to protect the buyers in these transactions.

6. Reducing Risk

Given the limited legal recourse in terms of risk under SOGO and the common law, a buyer in a transaction involving virtual property may attempt to find some protection under contract law.

6.1 Unconscionable Contracts

The End User License Agreement which a user signs will dictate much of the rights a user has in any given virtual world. However, a court will not uphold an unconscionable agreement. That is to say, the courts will not allow agreements where the terms are

---

30 *Head v Tattersall* (1871) LR 7 Exch 7.
31 *Bragg v. Linden Research, Inc.*, 487 F. Supp. 2d 593 (E.D. Penn. 2007).

unreasonably favorable to one party to the detriment of the other party who has no meaningful choice in the matter or a real chance to negotiate. The principles governing unconscionable contracts are independent of decisions pertaining to the nature of virtual property and this has provided protection to users in situations like *Bragg v. Linden Research, Inc.*[32] where the seller is the party providing the End User License Agreement and the buyer is the party signing the agreement. For a buyer to rely on the argument of unconscionable agreement, the agreement must be one-sided and excessively unfair.[33]

6.2 Misrepresentation

A buyer may rely on misrepresentation if the seller makes a statement which is inconsistent with the facts which induces the buyer to act in reliance of the statement. Hunt[34] gives the example of a company, which states in its End User License Agreement that players may not "own" virtual property. If a subsequent agreement between the company and the user refers to virtual property in the language of property, and the language leads the user to believe and rely upon the idea that the virtual property is property, the language in the contract may consist of a misrepresentation.

7. Conclusion

As the prevalence of trading virtual property grows, it is important that a consensus be made on how virtual property should be considered under the law in order to protect the rights of buyers and sellers. In the meantime, buyers and sellers will have to rely on contract law in their attempt to protect their rights.

---

32 *ibid.*
33 Hunt (n 21) 154.
34 *ibid*

13

Transfer of Property and Risk in the Virtual World: Challenges to the Current Legal Framework

Winnie Wing Yee CHUNG

1. Introduction

Since the invention of computers and the rise of the Internet era, the virtual world has become increasingly multi-functional and popular among the new generation. With the promotion of economic globalization and trading, it is not surprising to find myriads of commercial activities taking place in the virtual world. Nevertheless, seldom do people question the process of these virtual transactions from a legal perspective, in particular the passing of property and risk therein.

This chapter provides a critical analysis of how traditional commercial law regarding the transfer of property and risk can be applied to the emerging commercial transactions in the virtual world. In order to establish a concrete foundation for further development of the chapter, part 2 will provide a definition of the virtual world and explain the commercial transactions therein. Parts 3 and 4 will discuss the transfer of property and risk while distinguishing the virtual world from the real world, thereby questioning the applicability of, for example, the Hong Kong Sale of Goods Ordinance (Cap 26) ("SOGO"). Part 5 will compare the legal positions in Hong Kong to those in other jurisdictions. Finally, part 6 will evaluate the need of new rules to govern this specific commercial aspect and part 7 will conclude the essay by offering a brief summary.

2.   Commercial Transactions in the Virtual World

A virtual world is a synchronous and persistent online digital 3D environment, accessed by a website or a computer program, where people can communicate and interact with each other.[1] In general, virtual worlds are categorized into (1) structured or closed massively multiplayer online games ("MMOGs"), and (2) unstructured or open multi-user virtual environments ("MUVEs").[2] Examples of the latter include *Second Life*, *Kaneva* and *Active Worlds*. They serve as business platforms and are the key study of this essay.

MUVEs enable users to exchange virtual objects or services. Users are usually represented as avatars and can create, buy or sell items, through which they earn virtual monies that may have exchange rates with and can be converted to real-world currencies. For instance, users of *Second Life* can enter stores, try on and purchase products by Linden Dollar, and talk to salespeople or other shoppers via voice-chat.[3] This deviate commercial transactions in the virtual world from basic online shopping through e-commerce and seems to bring it closer to the

---

1   Michael H. Passman, 'Transactions of Virtual Items in Virtual Worlds' (2008) 18 *Alb LJ Sci & Tech* 259, 261; Mark W. Bell, 'Toward a Definition of "Virtual Worlds"' (2008) 1 *Journal of Virtual Worlds Research* 1, 2.

2   Brian E. Mennecke *et al.*, 'Second Life and other Virtual Worlds: A Roadmap for Research' (2008) 22 (Article 20) *Communications of the Association for Information Systems* 371, 373.

3   Dominik Schrank, 'A Trustful Payment System for Virtual Worlds: Design and Implementation of a Payment System for Virtual Worlds' (September 2009) <https://eportal.cityu.edu.hk/bbcswebdav/pid-1546984-dt-content-rid-10473896_2/courses/201302LW4658/2009_Schrank%20Thesis%20Commerce%20in%20Virtual%20Worlds.pdf> accessed December 3, 2013, 2, 30.

real world. Virtual economies may or may not connect to in-game needs like food or equipment. Successful stories include the one of Anshe Chung who symbolizes an avatar attached to *Second Life* real estate mogul and has become a real-world millionaire in virtual land assets.[4] It is believed that the total volume of sales in virtual goods would top $1 billion in the United States alone.[5]

3.   Transfer of Property

Virtual objects designed by corporate owners or users of the virtual world dominate virtual transactions. Since each object carries with it property which is defined by section 2(1) of the SOGO as "the general property in goods" and differs from "title," one shall ask how and when the property of virtual objects passes between the sellers and the buyers.

3.1 Property in the Virtual World

There are three main types of virtual objects: (1) collectible objects, such as virtual cars and clothes, can be purchased by users and are displayed to others; (2) consumable objects permit a limited number of users and are destroyed afterwards; (3) customizable objects can be controlled by its owners through varied permissions.[6] Their trading is divided into business to consumer and consumer to consumer.[7]

---

4   Claude T. Aiken IV, 'Sources of Law and Modes of Governance: Ethnography and Theory in Second Life' (2009) *Journal of Technology Law and Policy* 1, 27.

5   Mikhail Reider-Gordon, 'Real World Risk in Virtual World Gaming: Virtual Currencies, Money Laundering, and the Hidden Risks to Game Companies' <www.navigant.com/~/media/WWW/Site/Insights/Disputes%20Investigations/Real%20World%20Risk%20in%20Virtual%20World%20Gaming.ashx> accessed December 3, 2013, 12.

6   Dominik Schrank (n 3) 23.

7   *ibid.*

Due to the widespread usage by virtual-world-makers of End User License Agreements ("EULAs") which basically remove users' property rights to all virtual items,[8] scholars have doubted whether users do ever possess any property right to virtual objects. The rationale of EULAs is that all raw materials and tools for users to build their own items are provided by virtual-world-makers. In case the property of these items never belongs to the users, it would be theoretically impossible and illegal for them to engage in any trade of the virtual items.[9] Hence, the fundamental question is: who has the property in virtual objects.

Michael Passman has offered three reasons to support users' property rights in virtual objects,[10] and I am prepared to agree with him. First, EULAs may sometimes be unenforceable because they are pre-drafted by virtual-world-makers and users have no bargaining power or real negotiation with the makers. Second, users may have legitimate expectations under traditional property theory[11] to benefit from their efforts and labors.[12] Third, public policy may be reluctant to recognize EULAs or deny the formation of property rights in favor of the users.[13] While it is true that nothing would exist without the creation of the virtual games or environments by its operators, it is fair and in the interests of the society to grant some property rights to the users so as to encourage the production and sale of virtual items.

---

8 Joshua A. T. Fairfield, 'Virtual Property' (2005) 85 *BU L Rev* 1047, 1082.

9 See Andrew E. Jankowich, 'Property and Democracy in Virtual Worlds' (2005) 11 *BU J Sci & Tech L* 173, 182.

10 Michael H. Passman (n 1) 265-267.

11 C. B. Macpherson (ed), John Locke: Second Treatise of Government (Hackett Publ'g Co Inc 1980) proposes that property can be created by the mixing of work with an object.

12 Jack M. Balkin, 'Virtual Liberty: Freedom to Design and Freedom to Play in Virtual Worlds' (2004) 90 *Va L Rev* 2043, 2067.

13 Joshua A. T. Fairfield (n 8) 1083–1084.

3.2 *Applicability of the Sale of Goods Ordinance (HK)*

Recognizing property rights in virtual objects has remained unsettled law.[14] Courts have simply equated virtual properties to real-life personal properties owned by users regardless of their substantial differences in nature.[15] Although this line of ruling may not be entirely satisfactory, it seems to be the only workable way under the present legal regime which has no guidance for property in virtual items. It follows that the most relevant ordinance governing the transfer of property in the virtual world in Hong Kong might be the SOGO, but academics have expressed worries about its applicability.

Sections 18–21 of the SOGO contain rules which regulate the passing of property in goods sold from the seller to the buyer. It is important to understand that the SOGO solely applies to any sale of goods under its own interpretation. According to section 2(1) of the SOGO, "goods" comprises "all chattels personal other than things in action and money" and "sale" means "a bargain and sale as well as a sale and delivery." Arguably, "goods" connotes certain physical manifestation[16] and is lacking in virtual items which resemble intangible intellectual property to some extent. As far as "sale" is concerned, it often impliedly carries a passing of title from the seller to the buyer in return for the payment of a contractual price.[17] Yet, this may be false in the "sale" of the three major types of virtual objects where sellers intend to retain part of the rights in the items. As such, the SOGO, which is the embodiment of Hong Kong's existing commercial law on sale of

---

14 Leah Shen, 'Who Owns the Virtual Items?' 2010 *Duke L & Tech Rev* 11.

15 Mari Yamaguchi, 'Angry Online Divorcee "Kills" Virtual Ex-Hubby' (October 23, 2008, MSNBC News) <www.msnbc.msn.com/id/27337812> accessed December 3, 2013.

16 See *Arbitron Inc v Tralyn Broad Inc* 400 F 3d 130, 138 n 2 (2d Cir 2005) cited in Michael H Passman (n 1) 272.

17 Cf Uniform Commercial Code 2007, §2–106(1).

goods and services, may not be wholly applicable to commercial transactions in the virtual world. Enactment of new law has been proposed, the possibility of which will be explored below.

3.3   Effects of the Classification of Virtual Items

Assuming the SOGO applies to the virtual world, the next question to ask in order to determine the transfer of property is the legal characteristics of the virtual objects. In other words, are the virtual items unascertained or specific goods?

A.   Unascertained Goods

Unascertained goods are not defined in the SOGO, yet they may be interpreted as bearing an opposite meaning to specific goods. Hence, unascertained goods are "not identified at the time of the contract but depend on some subsequent agreed act of appropriation."[18] They comprise wholly unascertained goods and quasi-specific goods which are partially identified due to a designated source of supply.[19]

Section 18 of the SOGO stipulates "[w]here there is a contract for the sale of unascertained goods, no property in the goods is transferred to the buyer unless and until the goods are ascertained." Goods can be ascertained through physical separation from the bulk as in *Gillett v Hill*.[20] Methods of ascertainment include exhaustion,[21] segregation[22] and consolidation. Pearson J in *Carlos Federspiel & Co SA* held that there must be an irrevocable act binding the seller to deliver a

---

18   Ewan McKendrick ed., *Goode on Commercial Law* (4th edn, Penguin Books 2010) 230.

19   *ibid.* 231.

20   *Gillett v Hill* (1834) 2 C & M 530, 535.

21   *Wait v Midland Bank* (1926) 31 Com Cas 172.

22   *Re Stapylton Fletcher Ltd* (in administrative receivership) [1995] 1 All ER 192.

certain portion of the bulk to which the buyer must assent.[23] Mere setting aside or selection of goods by the seller is insufficient.

Despite the apparent simplicity of the above principle, it is remarked that its application and the classification of virtual goods may bring about much confusion. In light of the unique nature of the virtual world, it may be hard to tell whether a particular virtual object is an unascertained goods or not in the first place. There may be inadequate information for users to know exactly the total number of certain virtual products or the details of their source or storage. Even in a case where the seller originally has only one item for sale, she can always copy the item and change them to generic or unascertained goods. The multitudinous functions provided by the computer and the Internet together with the speed of information transmission and virtual transactions rule out the possibility for one to figure out the nature of virtual objects which may alter instantly.

Failing to identify the characteristics of the virtual goods — the starting point of the test, the entire section 18 of the SOGO becomes meaningless and inoperative. Even if the goods, say two swords from manufacturer X, are successfully classified as unascertained goods and thus fall within section 18 of the SOGO, the lack of transparent information and the changing nature of virtual environments would equally render it impossible to decide if the goods are ascertained.

An additional problem associated to the determination of ascertainment is the minimal time taken for users to complete a transaction in the virtual world, i.e., to sell, buy, ascertain and deliver a virtual item. The normal process may take seconds unless there are delays or technical problems. The question then is: at which point is the virtual goods ascertained? In practice,

---

23 *Carlos Federspiel & Co SA v Charles Twigg & Co Ltd* [1957] 1 Lloyd's Rep 240, 255.

the time of the formation of a contract for the sale of the goods may overlap that of the ascertainment of the goods (which may not really exist). All that a user is required to do is to press one single button to confirm the transaction; the rest are done by the computer program. When the virtual item displays in the buyer's virtual environment, it is of course ascertained and its property is transferred from the seller to the buyer. Therefore, the application of section 18 of the SOGO would become purely academic.

In any event, once an unascertained goods is ascertained, its property will pass to the buyer "at such time as the parties to the contract intend it to be transferred" under section 19 of the SOGO. An in-depth discussion of the section is to be found below.

Section 20 rule 5 of the SOGO, applying to both unascertained and future goods, further offers assistance for one to ascertain the parties' intention "as to the time at which the property in the goods is to pass to the buyer."[24] Rule 5(1) points out: where the goods of that description in a deliverable state are unconditionally appropriated[25] by either party with another's assent, the property passes to the buyer. The seller is deemed to have unconditionally appropriated the goods under rule 5(2) by delivery to the buyer or carriers.

One may argue that appropriation in the virtual world may not be irrevocable since buyers may purchase items same as those that they have chosen but are actually duplicated by the computer program. Yet, what rule 5(1) requires is merely an intention for irrevocable appropriation and an unchanged mind on the part of the seller. Nonetheless, sellers usually do not intend to pass the

---

24 Sale of Goods Ordinance (Cap 26), s 20.

25 *Carlos Federspiel & Co SA v Charles Twigg & Co Ltd* (n 23) 255 where Pearson J expressed 'the parties must have had … an intention to attach the contract irrevocably to those goods, so that those goods and no others are the subject of the sale and become the property of the buyer.'

property until payment of the price as in *Stein Forbes*,[26] which avoids the appropriation from being unconditional. By contrast, rule 5(2) is relatively easy to be fulfilled for goods are often free from any right of disposal[27] when they are delivered. In that regard, property in unascertained goods generally passes upon delivery.

B.   Specific Goods

According to section 2(1) of the SOGO, specific goods are "identified and agreed upon at the time a contract of sale is made." They may include future goods where the seller does not own but has to acquire the goods.[28] No later selection from the stock by either the seller or the buyer is needed.[29] For example, if a buyer enters a shop, purchases and takes away a pair of shoes at that moment or at a later time, the shoes are specific goods. It is highlighted that the fact of specificity is concerned rather than the contract formulation.[30]

Section 19 of the SOGO relates to the sale of specific or ascertained goods, subsection 1 of which reads "the property in them is transferred to the buyer at such time as the parties to the contract intend it to be transferred." Section 19(2) of the SOGO further lists out factors to be considered for the purpose of ascertaining the parties' intention. This general rule is applied in cases such as *Seath v Moore*[31] and *Re Goldcorp Exchange Ltd.*[32]

---

26 *Stein Forbes & Co Ltd v County Tailoring Co Ltd* (1916) 86 LJKB 448, 449.

27 Sale of Goods Ordinance (Cap 26), s 21; Cf *Gilman & Co Ltd v Yokohama Musen Industrial Co (HK) Ltd* [1976] HKLR 821.

28 The Honourable Mr Justice Ribeiro PJ *et al.*, *Chitty on Contracts: Hong Kong Specific Contracts* (3rd edn, Sweet & Maxwell 2013) [11–018].

29 Ewan McKendrick (n 18) 228.

30 *ibid.* 229.

31 *Seath v Moore* (1886) 11 App Cas 350.

32 *Re Goldcorp Exchange Ltd* [1995] 1 AC 74.

Due to similar reasons as mentioned above, the nature of the virtual world causes quite a few problems in defining virtual objects as specific goods. Other than that, sellers of virtual items usually possess more than one of each item but may simply display a sample in the window. When a buyer click on a certain item to enter into a contract for the sale of that item, there is no clue if she is in fact buying and obtaining that specific item, especially because the whole process of selection and delivery of the goods (if any) are carried out by the computer program or the internet. This is completely contrary to buying and selling in the real world.

Upon overcoming the obstacles to the classification of virtual goods, another problem may arise in ascertaining the intention of the parties. Sellers and buyers in the virtual world are usually anonymous as no personal detail is swapped during transactions.[33] Sometimes, there may not be any communication between the parties, let alone any negotiation of contract terms. Moreover, as pointed out by Lord Wright in *Smyth & Co Ltd*, parties often do not have or express any clear intention in relation to the passing of property in virtual items.[34] With so little or vague evidence of the parties' conduct and silent or ambiguous terms of the contract, it would be difficult to construe the parties' intention in accordance with section 19(2) of the SOGO.

In view of the above problems, section 20 of the SOGO may kick in to help ascertain the parties' intention as to the transfer of property. Any expression of intention by the parties will have no effect if the property has already passed under section 20 of the SOGO.[35] This is illustrated in *Dennant*[36] where the property in the

---

33 Dominik Schrank (n 3) 31.

34 *Smyth & Co Ltd v Bailey Son & Co Ltd* [1940] 3 All ER 60, 67.

35 P.S. Atiyah, John N. Adams and Hector MacQueen, Atiyah's Sale of Goods (12th edn, Pearson 2010) 311.

36 *Dennant v Skinner and Collom* [1948] 2 KB 164.

cars had been transferred on the fall of the hammer in an auction. The expression of an intention in a subsequent document that the ownership would not pass until the proceeds of the cheque were credited to the auctioneer was too late to avoid the passing of the property to the bidder.

Section 20 of the SOGO contains five rules, the first three of which concentrate on specific goods. It is emphasized that all these rules are merely presumptions capable of being rebutted by any opposite intention.[37]

Rule 1 stipulates that the property in the goods passes to the buyer when an unconditional contract for the sale of specific goods in a deliverable state is made. The time of payment or delivery is immaterial as evidenced in *Dennant*.[38] The word "unconditional" inclines to mean the transfer of property is not subject to any fulfillment of conditions.[39] Concerning "goods in a deliverable state," section 2(4) of the SOGO states that "they are in such a state that the buyer would, under the contract, be bound to take delivery of them." In *Underwood Ltd*,[40] the engine was attached to the premises and must be dismantled before delivery. It was held not to be in a deliverable state which depended on the actual state of the goods at the time of the contract.[41]

Rules 2 and 3 require the seller to do something before the property passes and the buyer must have notice thereof. More specifically, the seller is bound to put the goods into a deliverable state under rule 2 and to ascertain the price under rule 3. Where the weighing is only a way to prove the buyer has what he

---

37 Section 20 of the Sale of Goods Ordinance (Cap 26) begins with '[u]nless a different intention appears;' see, for example, *The Tang He* [2000] 4 HKC 701.

38 *Dennant v Skinner and Collom* (n 36).

39 The Honourable Mr Justice Ribeiro PJ (n 28) [11–169].

40 *Underwood Ltd v Burgh Castle Brick and Cement Syndicate* [1922] 1 KB 343.

41 *ibid.* 345.

bargained for as in *Nanka-Bruce*,[42] the condition would not suspend the passing of property.

Though these rules may be quite useful in the real life, they do not fall short of criticisms in terms of the virtual world. First, no contract would be unconditional in the face of EULAs. Second, the lack of information may not allow one to know if certain goods are in a deliverable state. Third, the stage of putting goods into a deliverable state may last for such a short period of time that it can be overlooked. Buyers would clearly not be notified of it; even if sellers intend to do so, they do not have sufficient time and any notice would look redundant when the buyers have already "received" the goods. Fourth, the price is in most cases, if not all, fixed or agreed by the parties without any need to weigh, measure or test the goods. The virtual world is after all not markets in the real world. As a result, rules 2 and 3 may not have any practicality in ascertaining the parties' intention in virtual transactions.

Moreover, the presumptive force of the rules enables them to be displaced easily, which further casts doubts on the necessity of rules 1–3. The high technology enables goods to be delivered almost instantly. Where goods have been delivered to the buyer and their property has already passed as in *Kershaw v Odgen*,[43] it does not matter if they still need to be put into a deliverable state or measured by the seller. On some occasions, once the buyer has purchased an item in a virtual environment, she may receive an automatic electronic acknowledgement of the transaction or that the goods are held to the buyer's order, similar to the situation in *Howes v Watson*.[44] As such, the property may be held to have passed.

---

42 *Nanka-Bruce v Commonwealth Trust Ltd* [1926] AC 77.

43 *Kershaw v Odgen* (1865) 3 H & C 717.

44 *Howes v Watson* (1824) 2 B & C 243.

For the sake of completeness, rule 4 concerns goods delivered on approval or on sale or return. The property in the goods passes to the buyer if she approves or adopts the transaction, or retains the goods without giving notice of rejection. However, this rule may have little applicability in the virtual world for the subject matters rarely or never exist. Delivery often takes place at the same time as the conclusion of a transaction. No expression of acceptance is generally expected from buyers other than their original agreements to purchase the goods. Buyers may also find no way to return the goods to sellers and thus are forced to "retain" the goods, making rule 4 infeasible.

4. Transfer of Risk

The *res perit domino* rule stipulated in section 22 of the SOGO is that the risk of damage, deterioration or loss of the goods *prima facie* passes to the buyer along with the property in the goods. In other words, risk is linked to property and independent of delivery. There are three exceptions to this principle: (1) any contrary agreement between the parties, say the property and risk is separated by agreement;[45] (2) the fault of either party in causing the delay of the delivery; and (3) the duties or liabilities of either party as a bailee of the goods. In *Sterns Ltd*,[46] risk was transferred upon the buyers' acceptance of the delivery warrant, i.e., before the property passed.

Professor Sealy explains the meaning of "risk" as a derivative concept that "either or both of the primary obligations of one party shall be enforceable, and that those of the other party shall be deemed to have been discharged, even though the normally

---

45 *Castle v Playford* (1872) LR 7 Ex 98.
46 *Sterns Ltd v Vickers Ltd* [1923] 1 KB 78.

prerequisite conditions have not been satisfied."[47] In effect, where the goods are at the seller's risk, she cannot recover the price from the buyer or compel the latter to take delivery of any remaining goods.[48] On the other hand, buyers who bear the risk should pay the price and sellers are released from their duty of delivery.[49]

In view of the many problems in determining the transfer of property in the virtual world, it may be equally, if not more, difficult to decide the passing of risk under section 22 of the SOGO. Besides, the exceptions provided in the section may rarely apply in the virtual world. Sellers and buyers seldom form extra agreements other than standard contracts, let alone specific agreements as to the passing of risk. Moreover, goods are usually delivered immediately by the computer program or the Internet after they are sold to the buyers. Any delay of delivery may be caused without any fault of the parties and no bailment may involve during the process.

One may argue that section 22 of the SOGO produces an unfair result to buyers. A buyer may acquire the property and risk in goods which remain in the seller's possession but are accidentally destroyed without fault.[50] Hence, it has been suggested that a more reasonable rule would be to connect risk with control.[51] However, the second rule may make no difference to the original situation in the virtual world. The transfer of property is safely assumed in a majority of cases to take place

---

47 L. S. Sealy, 'Risk in the Law of Sale' [1972] 31 *CLJ* 225, 226.

48 L. S. Sealy and R. J. A. Hooley, *Commercial Law: Text, Cases, and Materials* (4th edn, OUP 2009) 303.

49 *ibid.*

50 Ewan McKendrick (n 18) 265.

51 United Nations Commission on International Trade Law, United Nations Convention on Contracts for the International Sale of Goods (Vienna, November 2010) <www.uncitral.org/pdf/english/texts/sales/cisg/V1056997-CISG-e-book.pdf> accessed December 3, 2013.

upon delivery when buyers would have physical possession and thus control over the goods. Risk may pass to buyers at roughly the same moment no matter which route or rule is adopted.

In addition, one of the purposes of section 22 of the SOGO is to settle which of the parties should take proper steps for their protection and cover losses by insurance. Although insurance may act as a remedy for the suffered party, virtual items are seldom insured. Ewan McKendrick is also correct to comment that "the existence of insurance has not eliminated issues of risk and liability between seller and buyer but has merely shifted the interest in them from the insured to the insurers."[52]

Section 9 of the SOGO codifies the doctrine of frustration which has a wider scope than the rules of risk. Where certain specific goods perish without any fault of the parties before the risk passes to the buyer, the agreement for the sale of such goods is avoided in the sense that both parties are discharged from their obligations. It appears that section 9 of the SOGO is sort of limited.[53] Not only does it solely cover "specific goods" which "perish,"[54] but it is also restricted to cases where risk has not yet passed, and is therefore not applicable to fully executed contracts as the Court of Appeal in *Re Shipton Anderson & Co Ltd*[55] thought. This poses problems for the application of the section to virtual transactions in which property and risk often pass together. It may be impossible for virtual goods to perish, too. Where section 9 of the SOGO is not applicable and the risk has not passed to the buyer, the common law rules of frustration

---

52 Ewan McKendrick (n 18) 283.

53 P. S. Atiyah, John N Adams and Hector MacQueen (n 34) 349.

54 For the meaning of 'perish,' see *Asfar & Co v Blundell* [1896] 1 QB 123; *Oldfield Asphalts v Grovedale Coolstores* (1994) Ltd [1998] 3 NZLR 479; *Barrow, Lane & Ballard Ltd v Phillip Phillips & Co Ltd* [1929] 1 KB 574.

55 *Re Shipton Anderson & Co Ltd and Harrison Bros & Co Ltd* [1915] 3 KB 676.

concerning other unforeseeable events may come in force.[56] Any computer or Internet problem may then fall within these rules.

5. Positions in the United Kingdom and the United States

From the outset, the position of the Sale of Goods Act 1979 ("SOGA") in the United Kingdom seems rather similar to the SOGO in Hong Kong as to the transfer of property and risk, but the former differs from the latter in the following five ways. First, section 18 rule 5(2) of the SOGA adds custodians to the group of persons who can hold goods for transmission to buyers. Second, section 18(3) and (4) puts the doctrine of "ascertainment by exhaustion" into statutory form.[57] Third, the insertion of section 20A into the SOGA enables property in undivided shares in goods forming part of an identified bulk to pass before ascertainment. Fourth, section 20B lists the types of dealings in bulk goods which are deemed to be valid based on the consent of co-owners. Fifth, section 20(4) of the SOGA distinguishes the transfer of risk in consumer cases from non-consumer cases. Where the buyer deals as a consumer, the risk remains with the seller until the goods are delivered to the consumer.

Though the first two differences may not have much influence on the transfer of property and risk in the virtual world, section 20A and 20(4) of the SOGA may carry some significance. Virtual items are often mass-produced, stored in a defined virtual environment and interchangeable with each other, thereby constituting a "bulk."[58] Section 20A of the SOGA greatly

---

56 Ewan McKendrick (n 18) 284–285.

57 For instance, Sale of Goods Act 1979 s 18(3)(a) reads 'the remaining goods are to be taken as appropriated to that contract at the time when the bulk is so reduced.'

58 Sale of Goods Act 1979, s 61(1).

simplifies the process of passing of property under the SOGO. Only three conditions are required in the SOGA, including a sale of a specified quantity, an identified bulk and the payment of goods. Regarding section 20(4) of the SOGA, millions of the buyers of virtual goods may be considered "consumers" and the section may be broadly applied to virtual transactions.

On the contrary, article 2 of the American Uniform Commercial Code 1952 ("UCC") does not adopt the concept of property[59] but tends to equate "property" to "title."[60] This is not a pure matter of label and has two consequences: (1) detailed terms are needed to replace and explain "property;" and (2) new rules are required to handle any new situation.[61] The UCC also deals with the transfer of risk in merchant cases individually as opposed to other transactions.[62]

6.   Possibility of the Formation of New Rules

The court in Hays quoted "[t]he concept that a contract is to be interpreted in light of the parties' reasonable expectations lies deep in contract law."[63] Contract law aims to reflect and enforce the reasonable expectations of the parties to a contract.[64] Given the distinct nature of commercial transactions in the virtual world, the rules governing such transactions should change

---

59 L.S. Sealy and R.J.A. Hooley (n 48) 298.

60 Uniform Commercial Code 2007, §2–401.

61 L.S. Sealy and R.J.A. Hooley (n 48) 298; see *The Odessa* [1916] 1 AC 145.

62 Uniform Commercial Code 2007, § 2–509(3) reads: 'In any case not within subsection (1) or (2), the risk of loss passes to the buyer on his receipt of the goods if the seller is a merchant; otherwise the risk passes to the buyer on tender of delivery.'

63 *Hays v Pacific Indem Group* (Cal Ct App 1970) 8 Cal App 3d 158, 162–163.

64 See Michael H. Passman (n 1) 269; Melvin Aron Eisenberg, 'The Bargain Principle and Its Limits' (1982) 95 *Harv L Rev* 741, 788–789, 794–797.

accordingly to meet the unique expectations of the buyers and sellers.

To begin with, scholars such as Passman argue that transactions involving the sale of virtual goods are merely licenses of intellectual property instead of ordinary sale of goods transactions as understood by current commercial law.[65] Sealy lists out the differences in the transfer of property between an agreement to sell and a sale.[66] In agreements to sell, the seller retains property in the goods until such time as the goods become ascertained and appropriated to the buyer. In a contract of sale, the seller generally parts with the property in goods in favor of the buyer.[67] Transactions in the virtual world fall between the two as sellers expect to pass some property in the goods to the buyers while retaining part of the property. Indeed, a better approach may be to treat virtual items as licensed products which "can be transferred and simultaneously retained by the transferor."[68]

A license, as a kind of contract, allocates rights in intangibles and delineates the scope of permitted use of the subject matter.[69] In virtual worlds like *Second Life*, buyers may acquire the rights to copy, give away or modify the items depending on sellers' permissions. Further, most users expect a market pervaded by *caveat emptor*, i.e., purchasers buy at their own risk,[70] and never think of returns on demand.[71] One of the reasons is because, with the help of technology, buyers can easily make a copy of a virtual item, return one of the items to the sellers and sell the rest.

---

65 Michael H. Passman (n 1) 271.

66 L. S. Sealy and R. J. A. Hooley (n 48) 295–296.

67 *ibid*. 296.

68 Ray Nimmer, 'A Modern Template for Discussion' (2004) 2 *DePaul Bus & Com LJ* 623, 629–630.

69 *ibid*. 623, 627.

70 Bryan A Garner *et al.*, *Black's Law Dictionary* (8th edn, Thomson 2004) 236.

71 Michael H. Passman (n 1) 278, 290.

Strictly speaking, commercial transactions in the virtual world are not covered within the scope of the present legislation or law on the sale of goods as discussed above. This is especially true where the virtual world users' expectations have not been fully recognized. Therefore, one may consider the possibility of forming a new set of rules for the transfer of property and risk in the virtual world. The author is not against separating the rules of virtual transactions from traditional commercial principles, similar to the emergence of cyber law which was not anticipated decades ago. There is in fact such a need to legislate these booming virtual dealings.

What the author wishes to draw the legislators' attention to is the features of the proposed new rules. It is put forward by Passman that the statute should be "fair, flexible and narrow."[72] Differences between users' expectations in diverse virtual worlds should be taken into account, and in the meantime interests of operators and users as well as sellers and buyers should be balanced. It is also noted that the existing commercial law on the transfer of property and risk differs in varied jurisdictions. Should new rules be formulated in the context of the virtual world, it is desirable to be a uniform law that applies internationally, eliminating any possible problem of jurisdiction. In the real world, nations are separated by boundaries; in the virtual world, nations are united where people can trade with each other regardless of their skins, languages or physical barriers.

7.   Conclusion

Following the above arguments, one may conclude that the intended application of commercial law in the aspect of the transfer of property and risk to commercial transactions in

---

72   *ibid.* 285–288.

the virtual world is highly unsatisfactory. Aside from the use of EULAs and the fact that virtual dealings do not fall within the definition of "sale of goods" under the SOGO, the artificial application of the SOGO to virtual transactions brings about countless difficulties with the problems in first classifying the items and then determining the ascertainment of unascertained goods and/or the parties' intention as to the passing of property in specified or ascertained goods. The conclusion on the transfer of property would greatly affect the question of risk which passes with property in general. This reveals the danger of the link between property and risk and the forced use of the SOGO. The different commercial laws in various jurisdictions further confuse and complicate their applications.

Against such a backdrop and to recognize the fundamental purpose of contract law, it seems ideal to establish a new set of rules for the reflection of the expectations of virtual world users and the true nature of virtual transactions. Drafters should devote to creating a uniform regime for the passing of property and risk in the virtual world, possibly through incorporation and modification of present commercial laws in various regions.

PART VI
PAYMENT METHODS AND ISSUES IN VIRTUAL WORLD TRANSACTIONS

14

Payment Methods and Issues in Virtual World Commercial Transactions

Sherwin Chiu Wing YAM

1. Introduction: The Existence of Virtual World

With the advancement of technology, online communications nowadays are not only restricted to email, instant messengers and chartrooms. 3D Internet platform games such as other massive multiplayer online role playing games ("MMORPGS")[1] also come into play. Linden Labs created the virtual world called *Second Life*,[2] which enables users to have their virtual characters interact with one another on a face-to face basis in the 3D world. Because the creators of *Second Life* strongly emphasize that the *Second Life* virtual world resembles the real world, it is reasonable to think that real commercial transactions do happen in the virtual world.

A virtual world is a place online, accessed by either a computer program or website, which offer users a platform to interact with one another, meet new people and deal with business via enter

---

1 David Assalone, 'Law in the virtual world: Should the surreal world of online communities be brought back to earth by real world laws?' (2009) Vol. 16 Issue 1 *Vill. Sports & Ent. L.J.* 163.

2 Daniel Terdiman, *The entrepreneur's guide to second life making money in the metaverse* (Wiley Publishing 2008) 4.

into transaction with new e-commerce and applications.[3] One common way users made interaction is through the buying or selling of items they make or find in the virtual world setting. For example, online characters in *Second Life*, just like real human beings, need all sorts of daily necessities ranging from clothes to food and furniture. These virtual goods, in fact, cost real money. Entrepreneurs sell these products for genuine US dollars which adds a sense of reality in the fantasy world.[4] In another words, it is a common phenomenon that commercial transactions take place in these virtual environments.

This may trigger a number of questions: if commercial transactions take place in the virtual world just as in real life, how is payment made in these virtual settings? How is it different or similar to real life payment method that we made every day? These issues will be dealt with in this chapter. We will also examine the possible risks in making payments in virtual world transactions.

This chapter aims at exploring the virtual world economy and its commercial implications with respect to payment methods and systems. Firstly, it explores *Second Life*'s economy and its hidden risks related to payment in the virtual avatar setting. Secondly, it examines how transactions in virtual world take place. It will then draw a comparison with real life to examine to what extent virtual payment methods mirror payment methods in real life. Thirdly, this chapter will explore the possible obstacles in enforcing payments in virtual world. Last but not least, it aims to shed lights on how to impose a higher enforceability of commercial transactions via payment in virtual world.

---

3 Edward Castronova, 'Virtual Worlds: A First-Hand Account of Market and Society on the Cyberian Frontier' (2001) CESifo Working Paper No 618 <www.international.ucla.edu/media/files/SSRN_ID294828_code020114590.pdf> accessed December 3, 2013.

4 Michael S. Rosenwald, 'Second's Life Virtual Money Can Become Real Life Cash' (*Washington Post*, March 8, 2010) <www.washingtonpost.com/wpdyn/content/article/2010/03/07/AR2010030703524.html> accessed December 3, 2013.

2. Second Life's Economy in the Virtual World Setting

A virtual economy is an emergent economy existing in a persistent and perpetual virtual world. It usually involves an exchange of virtual goods in the online Internet game setting. On the other hand, a real economy is the part of the economy that is concerned with actually producing goods and services.[5] *Second Life* is an example of a virtual economy. It appears in a virtual three-dimensional world run by Linden Lab, in which virtual currency is used in order to facilitate business among users of the virtual world and to attract new users to this online platform.

With the advancement of technology, *Second Life*'s economy blossomed, with user-to-user transactions worth over $567 million in actual US currency. It was found that about 770,000 unique users made repeated visits to *Second Life* by the end of 2009. The users cashed out $55 million of their *Second Life* earnings and transferred that sum of money to their PayPal accounts.[6]

As is evident from the transactional values and the monetary value of *Second Life*'s virtual economy, there is a significant number of virtual currency and payments being made.

---

5 Dr. Veronica Adriana Popescu and Dr. Christina Raluca Popescu, 'Manager: Real economy versus virtual economy—New challenges for nowadays society' No.13 2011 <http://manager.faa.ro/archive/manager_13/articles/1303.pdf> accessed October 1, 2013.

6 Michael S. Rosenwald, 'Second's Life Virtual Money Can Become Real Life Cash' (*Washington Post*, March 8, 2010) <www.washingtonpost.com/wpdyn/content/article/2010/03/07/AR2010030703524.html> accessed December 3, 2013.

3.   Hidden Risks Related to Payments in Virtual World Commercial Transactions

3.1   *The Use and Legal Status of Virtual Goods and Currencies*

"Virtual goods" are defined as items available for purchase and transfer in the virtual worlds.[7] Virtual goods are non-physical objects purchased for use in online games as well as real world environments, such as *Second Life*. Virtual goods have no intrinsic value and are intangible. Virtual currency, on the other hand, is an online, intangible currency typically used to purchase virtual goods. Virtual currency is partly a subset of virtual goods.[8]

3.2   *Transactions of Virtual Items are not considered as "Sale" and "Goods" but merely "License"*

Under the Sale of Goods Ordinance (Cap.26), a sale is defined, in part, whereby "the seller transfers or agrees to transfer the property in goods to the buyer for a money consideration, called the price."[9] The seller of a virtual item does not always grant full title to the buyer; therefore a sale does not take place. Instead, a license limits the rights of the buyer. It "allocates rights in intangibles such as software, databases, and other forms of information." Items purchased and transferred in virtual world are purely virtual properties because they have no physical manifestation. They also do not fall under the definition of goods in section 2 of the Uniform Commercial Code, which defines "goods" as "both existing and identified before any interest in

---

7 Michael H. Passman,'Transactions of virtual items in Virtual World' (2008) 18 Vol.18 *Alb. L.J. Sci & Tech.* 259.

8 Jas Purewal, 'The use and legal status of virtual goods and currency' (Social Gaming 2012, October 30, 2012) <www.slideshare.net/fullscreen/jaspurewal/the-use-and-legal-status-of-virtual-goods-and-currencies/1> accessed December 3, 2013.

9 Section 3(1) Sale Of Goods Ordinance (Cap.26).

them may pass." In addition, virtual goods do not seem to fit within section 2 of the Sales of Goods Ordinance, which defined goods as "all chattels personal...and things attached to or forming part of the land which are agreed to be severed before sale or under the contract of sale."

3.3   Second Life's Virtual Money is a Reflection of Real Life Cash

The Linden currency is a reflection of *Second Life*'s economy. Users may opt to trade their US Dollars for Linden Dollars (L$) on the Linden Dollar Exchange (LindeX).[10] LindeX charges are generated on a per-transaction basis and once an exchange occurs, charges will be made. Users can purchase Linden Dollars on the Internet just by clicking a button that allows them to buy Linden dollars.[11] Some argue that the *Second Life* economy is more stable as its currency, Linden dollar (L$), is fairly stable over its lifetime.[12] Despite the fact that Linden dollar is a virtual currency, one can use it for shopping in the eBay or trade it back to US dollars in the official LindeX currency exchange. As proclaimed by virtual economies expert Edward Castronova, so long as the virtual dollar is associated with value, it operates just as real money. On the other hand, some have criticized that the Linden dollar's development in the virtual world impedes the development of a sophisticated private law (such as contract, intellectual property law) in real life.[13]

---

10   'Billing'<http://community.secondlife.com/t5/English-Knowledge-Base/Billing/ta-p/700037#Section_.1.2.6> accessed December 3, 2013.

11   Michael S. Rosenwald (n 4).

12   Daniel Terdiman (n 2) 4.

13   Claude T. Aiken IV, 'Sources of law and Modes of Governance: Ethnography and theory in Second Life' (2008) 10 *University of Pittsburgh Journal of Technology Law and Policy* 1.

3.4 Legal Precedent Reveals Virtual Currency Linked to Real Money

Participation in a virtual economy is not without danger. It may lead to criminal acts. In *R v Ashley Mitchell*, a former council accounts clerk hacked into Zynga, which is an American Poker company. He disguised himself as two employees of his company and stole 400bn virtual gaming chips. He then transferred chips worth more than $7 million to himself through the social media site, Facebook. He was imprisoned for two years after admitting that he committed an offence pertaining to computer misuse and four counts of money laundering.[14]

This case shows that virtual poker chips have a significant value which can be converted to real cash. There is just a thin blurred line between virtual and real money which can lead to possible financial crimes. This triggers the issue of how commercial transaction in the virtual world took place and what are the hidden risks in payment in virtual world commercial transactions.

3.5 Risks of Financial Crimes Involving Virtual Money

With the increasing popularity of settling payments through electronic cash and e-banking, there has been increased interest in the concept of virtual banks. Virtual banks are banks that do not have a branch in Hong Kong and its entire distribution system is based on the Internet.[15] A virtual bank is defined by the Hong Kong Monetary Authority (HKMA), Guideline 9.1, as "a company that delivers banking services primarily through the Internet or other electronic delivery." In another words, it operates in an individual capacity by conducting business entirely

---

14 Steven Morris, 'British hacker jailed over £7m virtual gaming chips scam' *The Guardian* (United Kingdom, March 18, 2011) (also known as *R v Ashley Mitchell* heard by the Exeter Crown Court on 03/02/2011).

15 David Ellis, 'Regulation of Virtual Banks' (August 2000) *Hong Kong Lawyer*.

in the cyberspace. The advantage is that it allows 24-hour access and facilitates international transactions. To ensure the soundness of the virtual banks, the HKMA issued guidelines to specify that applicant should attach equal importance to the management of conventional banking risks, such as credit, liquidity, and interest rate risks. In addition, it also issued guidelines to maintain a level of security that is appropriate to the type of business that is intended to be conducted.[16]

Unlike real world banks, virtual exchanges and operations are not subject to the same regulatory oversight.[17] There is a minimum regulation of these payment systems due to the arbitrary nature of their creation. As a result, cyber-criminals could take advantages of these online sites to perpetrate crimes. The most common crimes relating to payment in virtual world are money laundering and phishing.

In order to commit money laundering in the virtual world, all one needs is just a computer, an Internet connection and a stolen credit card number. Credit card numbers can be easily stolen through a phishing scheme. Phishing schemes are situations where computer users are easily tricked into entering passwords and credit card information that appears to be legitimate.

For example, a cyber-criminal may use a stolen credit card to purchase virtual items. It can then sell the virtual goods to other users in return for "clean money." After obtaining Linden currency, they can then transfer value into real cash and launder funds. On the other hand, PayPal payment method seems to provide a wider sense of protection to its virtual online users. For example, if a fraudster created a PayPal account with a stolen

---

16 Andrew Abraham, 'The Regulation Of Virtual Banks: A Study of the Hong Kong Perspective' (June, 2007) 10 No.12 *J.Internet* L.3.

17 'Our digital playground: Real crimes in virtual world' (BJA, March 2012) <http://drakontas.com/articles/Real%20Crimes%20in%20Virtual%20Worlds.pdf> accessed December 3, 2013 .

credit card, PayPal would be held liable for removing the payment from the original owner. PayPal advertises itself as a company with a safe and advanced technology to protect against fraud. Furthermore, there is a verification method to ensure the person who opens the account is the real owner. For example, there is an email notification for every payment made via PayPal and if two avatars exchange goods, the bank account number or bank information will not be revealed to the transaction parties. This reveals that PayPal's general security system seems to prevent fraud and can bring a positive impact on virtual world users and virtual world commercial transactions.

4. How Virtual World Transactions are Made via Various Payment Methods

Second Life has introduced Linden Dollars. Cyworld trades in Acorns and virtual gold is the currency in *World of Warcraft*. An efficient payment mechanism has to be established within the virtual world to make transactions possible.[18]

There are several features of *Second Life*'s virtual currency. Firstly, it can be bought from real life currencies. By the same token, virtual currency can also be converted back to real life currencies, thereby allowing consumers to extract money from the virtual world and convert it to real world dollars. One US Dollar is worth 270 Linden dollars;[19] however, the exchange rate fluctuates depending on the demand and supply of the virtual currency. The payment instruments that enforce these transactions are often restricted to credit cards, which are usually used to

---

18 Andrea Kaminski, 'Exchanging Real money in Virtual World' (E-Commerce Times, March 3, 2008) <www.ecommercetimes.com/story/61893.html> accessed December 3, 2013.

19 'Transactions of virtual items in Virtual World' (2008) Vol.18 *Alb. L.J. Sci. & Tech.* 259.

convert real money into virtual currency in order to fund the account. Besides, Internet wallet type of payment instruments (such as PayPal) is used to fund virtual accounts.

5. Payment Methods Used in E-Commerce Dominates Virtual World Transactions

The use of e-commerce is applicable as a means of payment to enforce transactions in the virtual world. Specifically, credit cards and the PayPal system are usual payment instruments that virtual world users use in their transactions. Research shows about 62% of North American virtual good sales are facilitated by PayPal or credit cards.[20] In virtual transactions, the payment prompts within each app make the payment options available. For instance, in an Australian study of financial transactions in virtual environments, the researchers found that several MMORPGS had a virtual reality space created by its account holders to trade virtual property with others through the use of a currency system based on credits, promotional credits and developer tokens purchased with real-world currency.[21] Some of the most common payment options which facilitate transactions in *Second Life* will be discussed in detail below.

5.1 Credit Card

Visa, MasterCard, American Express, to name but a few can be

---

20 Dean Takahashi, 'Paypal 12M Monthly users are paying for virtual goods' (VB News, Aug 1, 2011) <http://venturebeat.com/2011/08/01/paypal-says-there-are-12m-monthly-users-paying-for-facebook-games-exclusive/> accessed December 3, 2013.

21 Irwin S. M. Angela, 'Are the financial transactions conducted inside virtual environments truly anonymous? An experimental research from an Australian perspective' (2013) Vol 16 (1) *J.M.L.C* 6.

used directly for transactions and in-game purchases.[22] A credit card enables the holder to whom such a card is issued to obtain goods and services without payment in cash or by cheque and it allows users to also obtain cash. A credit card gives the holder a revolving credit facility with a monthly credit limit.[23]

An example of virtual goods monetization platform is PlaySpan, which is acquired by Visa, the credit card company.[24] PlaySpan is, in fact, part of Visa. Merchants nowadays use PlaySpan's technology to enable their consumers to make safe and convenient purchases online for items such as game credits, premium memberships and digital goods in different countries worldwide.[25] The advantage of PlaySpan is that it has security features. For instance, users can save their credit card information for future purchases through a pop-up PlaySpan window.

Payment by credit card involves four parties, namely the card issuer (i.e., the financial institution or another company), the cardholder (i.e., virtual online games users), merchant (i.e., the online virtual website) and the acquirer (i.e., the financial institution that provides card-processing services to the merchant).[26]

Transactions start when the virtual user decides to place an order online from a virtual world webpage at the merchant's website. The merchant's commerce application prompts the buyer

---

22 'Pay via PlaySpan', <http://worldoftanks.com/game/guide/en/payments_instruction/playspan> accessed December 3, 2013 .

23 Sealy and Hooley, *Commercial law Text, Cases and Materials* (3rd edn, Oxford University Press 2009) 808.

24 Martin Schuppelius, 'Virtual Goods Spending in the US to Exceed 2$B Says PlaySpan Study' (Payment Observer, March 5, 2012) <www.paymentobserver.com/tag/virtual-goods> accessed December 3, 2013.

25 'Visa to acquire PlaySpan' (Visa Inc, 09 Feb 2011) <http://corporate.visa.com/newsroom/press-releases/press1099.jsp> accessed December 3, 2013.

26 D.K. Srivastava, *Business Law in Hong Kong* (3rd Edition, Sweet & Maxwell 2012) 302.

to insert payment information concerning the credit card (such as credit card number, cardholder ID, and expiry date). The buyer will then enter payment information into a form secured by secure sockets layer (SSL).[27] With the secure form, the payment information is protected when it is sent to the merchant.

After filling out payment information, virtual goods are sent to the online user immediately: similar to the purchase of physical goods with a credit card in real world. Upon receiving the order, the merchant server sends the payment information to the acquirer processor for authorization, using dedicated and secured lines.[28] The acquirer will then ensure that there are sufficient funds to cover the transaction.[29] The acquirer's role is to authorize a certain amount of money or declines the transaction. After the transaction has been authorized, the merchant charges the authorized amount to the buyer's credit card.

5.2 Mobile Commerce

Mobile Payment is also made available to transactions of virtual goods. The idea behind is virtual goods can be bought online, which billed to one's wireless account. The plus point is that many virtual users are kids or adolescents, they might not have a credit card,[30] and therefore payment through their smart phone might be more user-friendly.

The phone number will either bill directly to a user's mobile phone bill or in some cases serve as a proxy for additional payment methods such as credit cards and Automated Clearing

---

27 Weidong Kou, *Payment Technologies for E-Commerce* (Springer 2003) 229.

28 Weidong Kou (n 27) 230.

29 *ibid.*

30 Peter Kafka, 'Virtual Goods and Mobile Payments = Small Market Worth Fighting For?' (*WSJ*, June 16, 2009) <http://allthingsd.com/20090616/virtual-goods-mobile-payments-small-market-worth-fighting-for/> accessed December 3, 2013.

House (ACH).[31] An example of such mobile payment is *Boku*[32] which provides direct billing through wireless account. *Boku* is in fact expanding its business from virtual goods to real world goods.

The advantage of mobile payment is that users simply have to provide their phone. No additional information is required. Transactions are carried via text message and it will appear on the consumer's phone bill.[33] For this reason, it is not common for hackers to break into the database to obtain the mobile phone number as there is no connection to other personal data such as address and bank account information. Besides, mobile payment requires authorization meaning one must access the mobile phone in order to make a valid purchase, whereas, credit card purchase can be done by hackers since one does not necessarily need to possess the credit card in order to place a purchase.

5.3 PayPal

PayPal is a subsidiary of eBay. It is not only restricted to settling transactions on auction sites. It is also an instrument used to settle payment for digital goods, such as virtual goods sold in Facebook's games.[34]

---

31 Dan Butcher ,'Mobile payment for Virtual Goods to grow exponentially in 2010: Boku' (*Mobile Commerce Daily*, January 5, 2010) <www.mobilecommercedaily. com/1b-virtual-goods-space-will-continue-explosive-growth-boku> accessed December 3, 2013

32 Lauren Goode, 'Boku Takes "pay any way You want" Approach with mobile Payment' (*WSJ*, February 23, 2012) <http://allthingsd.com/20120223/boku-takes-pay-any-way-you-want-approach-with-mobile-payments/> accessed December 3, 2013.

33 Kolja Reiss, 'Why mobile Payment are the Safest Solution for Online Transactions' (Mashable, June 11, 2011) <http://mashable.com/2011/06/10/mobile-payments-security/> accessed December 3, 2013.

34 Weidong Kou (n 27) 230.

An online user who would like to purchase virtual goods via PayPal can simply open a PayPal account by giving their credit card or bank information in a simple transaction.[35] In daily life situations, as the account is created, the online user can send money to the merchant with their email address and place the money in an online form. After payment is made, the merchant will receive email notification. Anyone who has to receive money via PayPal must open a PayPal account. The money is taken from the sender's bank account and deposited in the PayPal account of the intended recipient. PayPal consumer can keep the money in their PayPal account or choose to credit into their bank account. PayPal does not disclose the account information to both parties in order to ensure security of the transaction.

Regarding the special circumstances of virtual transactions which take place in an online platform, it is undoubted that PayPal dominates this market. The rationale is that PayPal permits online purchasers to engage in transactions "without mailing a check or sending a credit card number to an unknown person or a website,"[36] PayPal acts as if an intermediary in transactions between two avatars, thus safeguarding security as they do not have to disclose account information to one another.

There are several attractive features of using PayPal to settle transactions in virtual world. Firstly, payments can be made directly. Payments for virtual goods do not necessarily have to be made in the PayPal Homepage.[37] This facilitates the process of

---

35 Andrés Guadamuz González, 'PayPal and eBay: The legal implications of the C2C electronic commerce model' (18th BILETA Conference: Controlling Information in the Online Environment) <www.era.lib.ed.ac.uk/bitstream/1842/2259/1/eBaylaw.pdf> accessed December 3, 2013.

36 *Ibid.* (n 34)

37 'Paypal's New Virtual Goods Payment System: User Experience and Implementation' <www.insidesocialgames.com/2010/10/27/paypals-new-virtual-goods-payment-system-user-experience-and-implementation/> accessed December 3, 2013.

payment whilst playing online games. Upon choosing the virtual goods through PayPal, users can see a pop-up mini-browser in which transaction can be carried out, thereby online players can make payment directly on their online video games where they need to buy goods. This feature can accustom to the needs of virtual users as they will not lose the page which they are playing after making the payment. Besides, PayPal is a way that users could purchase directly for virtual currencies in games. PayPal API (Application Programming Interface) is the application which allows direct payment.[38] In order to use this function, merchants must first registered and embed the JavaScript behind the"Pay with PayPal" buttons on their game or site. The transaction flow is as follows. Firstly, a buyer has to initiate a PayPal purchase on a merchant's site. Then the merchant makes an API request from the PayPal. The merchant then receives a pay key. After that, the merchant launches the mini-browser, which does not redirect the user to the homepage of PayPal. As the buyer authorizes the purchase, PayPal will send an email notification to both the buyer and the merchant. The advantage of the application API is that as the buyer closes the mini-browser, he will still be on the same site.[39]

Secondly, payments made are guaranteed to be cost-efficient and without additional fees. For example, virtual goods payment system includes automatic selection of the appropriate merchant account, therefore it minimizes users' fees, subscription and recurring payment support, which is a donation made to the charity.[40]

Finally, *Second Life* transaction history feature allows user to track their Linden dollar economic activity in their account within

---

38 *ibid.* (n 36).
39 *ibid.*
40 *ibid.*

the last 45 days.[41] In addition, PayPal also provide transaction history for all accounts, which allows user to track their payment history with virtual transactions easily.[42]

6. Differences and Similarities of Payment Methods between Real and Virtual World

The special circumstances of a virtual world are that transactions happen without direct physical contact of buyer and seller. Therefore, payment has to be made through an intermediary such as credit cards, PayPal and mobile phone for direct billing.

The aforementioned payment method in virtual transactions is also available to the purchase of physical goods in real life. Contrasting to the virtual world, most commonly held payment method includes currency and negotiable instrument as parties have direct physical contact.

Currency is the most widely and commonly used method of payment. The note issuing is discharged by three leading banks in Hong Kong namely, the Hong Kong and Shanghai Bank, Standard Chartered Bank and the Bank of China, whereas, coins are issued by the Hong Kong Monetary Authority.[43]

Negotiable instruments are documents which are evidence of contractual rights, it guarantees payment of a specific amount of money, either on demand or a set time, without condition imposed on the payer. It is a document that can be owned like any other tangible thing, it can also transfer its rights by delivery or endorsement.[44]

---

41 Daniel Terdiman (n 2) 31.

42 Daniel Terdiman (n 2) 2.

43 D. K. Srivastava, (n 26) 301.

44 *ibid.* (n 42).

A cheque is an example of negotiable instrument. Section 3 of the Bills of Exchange Ordinance[45] (BEO) defines a bill of exchange as "an unconditional order in writing,[46] addressed by one person to another, signed by the person giving it,[47] requiring the person to whom it is addressed to pay on demand or at a fixed or determinable future time."[48] There must be a certain sum of money and there must be a bearer or specified person. If the cheque is payable to a specified person, according to section 7 of the BEO, the payee must be named with certainty of the BOEO.[49]

In a nutshell, the most common form of payment methods available for physical goods commercial transactions can be made by cash and cheque. Whereas, for virtual goods commercial transactions, payment methods are restricted to credit card payment, paypal or even mobile phone payment due to their constraints in time and space in the virtual world, yet these transaction methods are also available when one purchases real goods via online through auction websites.

7. Possible Obstacles in Enforcing Payments in Virtual Transactions

7.1 *Problems of Legal Enforcement of Payments as Revealed in the Terms of Service (ToS)*

As with all available payment methods, their ultimate goal is to settle transactions. However, according to the Terms of Services

---

45　Bills of Exchange Ordinance (Cap 19)

46　*Atlas Overseas v Tratmann & Co* [1952] HKLR 60.

47　Bill of Exchange Ordinance (Cap 19), s 97 Signature.

48　*Korea Exchange Bank v Debenhams* [1979] 1 Lloyd's Rep 548.

49　Bills of Exchange Ordinance, s 7(1) (Certainty required as to payee: where a bill is not payable to bearer, the payee must be named or otherwise indicated therein with reasonable certainty).

(TOS) of the *Second Life*, one can see there are loopholes on the legal enforcement of payments. For instance, even if Linden Dollar is purchased, it only constitutes a limited license with permission for one to trade goods with other users and use the service of the Linden Lab.[50] In other words, payment in the virtual world does not guarantee virtual users' rights on virtual goods or currency.

Despite the fact that virtual currency can be traded back into real money, it is neither issued by the government nor through central banking authorities. This means that the virtual money that one possesses may vanish at any point if the *Second Life* website shuts down. According to the terms of service, Linden Labs may revoke the Linden Dollar License at any time without notice, refund or compensation when the Linden dollar program is suspended or discontinued, or when there is alleged fraud on the account holder. Users are forced to acknowledge the unconscionable terms that Linden dollars are not real currency or any type of financial instrument, and as a result, they are not redeemable from the Linden Lab.[51]

These are the possible sub-issues arise as to the flaws of payment, as "virtual currency" is a sub-set of "virtual goods." After all, there is still no recognition of the property rights of the virtual online users in most virtual environments. This is readily seen in the End Users License Agreement (EULA) of most virtual environments. Virtual goods at most only have a "limited license right, not an ownership right."[52] Therefore, no matter how sound the payment methods in the virtual world transactions are, the crux of the problem related to payment lies on the issue of

---

50 'Terms of Service of Second Life 5.1' <http://secondlife.com/corporate/tos.php> accessed December 3, 2013.

51 *ibid.* (n50).

52 David Sheldon, 'Claiming Ownership, But Getting owned: Contractual Limitations on asserting Property Interests in virtual goods' (2006–2007) 54 *UCLA L. Rev.* 751.

property rights of virtual goods. In a word, the unconscionable terms of payments raises a sub-issue of legal enforcement of property rights.

7.2 The Cost of "Commodification" in the Virtual World Implies Stricter Legal Regulatory Regime of Property Right in Virtual World is Necessary

One can see that lawsuits pertaining to virtual property are on the rise due to "commodification" in virtual world. Commodification is defined as the process in which virtual goods are transformed into marketable item for genuine money to satisfy virtual users' wants or needs. For example, in China, when an online gamer's account was hacked, the virtual merchants were held liable for the loss of virtual property because it failed to provide a safe server system, making it easy for hackers to break in.[53] This shows there is a pressing social need for law to regulate property rights in order to give business efficacy in payment.

As there are different medium of virtual world available these days, some are "non-commodified" where users are not allowed to make money from it and they are merely a fantasy. On the other hand, some are "commodified" such as Linden's Lab Second Life which enables users to make money through selling virtual goods and in turn transfers into real American Dollars. If so, "commodified" virtual online games, should be regulated by law due to their commercial nature which resemblances real life transactions.

The traditional position that property rights does not exist in virtual world as reflected in "*World of Warcraft*"[54] should be changed due to the rising popularity of virtual world nowadays.

---

53 'Online Gamer in China wins virtual theft suit' (CNN.com, December 20, 2003) <http://edition.cnn.com/2003/TECH/fun.games/12/19/china.gamer.reut/> accessed December 3, 2013.

54 Andrew Jenkowich, 'Property and democracies in virtual world' (2005) Vol.11:2 *BUJ SCI & TECH L.*

There should be legal regulation in order to give effect to payment and commercial transactions in the long run.

In *Bragg v Linden Research Inc*,[55] the court held that the EULA concerning arbitration provisions was both procedurally and substantively unconscionable. Despite the EULA claimed that virtual users do not have property rights, this remains controversial as the court in Bragg reconsidered the issue of property rights based on the development of *Second Life* which repeatedly emphasized Linden Lab have the possibility of ownership rendering it different from other virtual worlds.[56] Therefore, it will be unreasonable to deny virtual users to their property rights as the idea expressed by creator of *Second Life* contradicts with the terms in EULA. Scholars like Lastowka and Hunter[57] also claimed that people should have property rights in items existing in virtual worlds; they opined that if regulation is not developed by courts, there should be legislation to regulate this area. For example, administrative agencies, such as the Federal Trade Commission can change the law in "commodified" virtual online games in order to recognize and protect property rights in virtual worlds.[58] Besides, the court may strike down the terms of EULA whenever necessary or there should be legislature to override them in order to protect consumers. Only by having stricter legal regulatory regime in the commercialized aspects of virtual world relating to property rights can payment systems used in virtual world commercial transactions be truly enforced without any restraints.

---

55 487 F. Supp. 2d 593.

56 Ryan Kriegshauser, 'The Shot Heard Around Virtual Worlds: The Emergence and future of unconscionability in agreement relating to property in virtual worlds' (2008) 76(4) *UMKC Law Review* 1077.

57 Jack M. Balkin, 'Virtual Liberty: Freedom To Design And Freedom To Play In Virtual Worlds' (December 2004) 90 *Virginia Law Review* 2043.

58 Andrew Jenkowich, 'Property and democracies in virtual world' (2005) 11(2) *B.U. J. Sci. & Tech. L.*

8. Conclusion

To conclude, the most prominent payment method to settle transaction in virtual world includes credit cards, PayPal and mobile commerce due to the Internet setting of the virtual world. These payment methods are also available in real life transactions which provide more variety for payers to choose their means of payment to accommodate their needs. Despite the fact that money laundering is possible in these payment methods as criminals may hack users' information through phishing, the advanced technology of PayPal's security features has kept these issues at bay for the moment. Lastly, possible obstacles relating to payment are due to the nature of virtual goods where currently there are no property rights. Therefore, stricter law enforcement either by rectification of legislation or judicial activism to strike down relevant terms of EULA is necessary in order to make sure that payment systems in virtual commercial transactions are binding upon users and give business efficacy in the long run.

15

Supervising Economic Transactions and Payments in the Virtual World: An Asia-Pacific Perspective

Raymond SIN

1. Introduction

In virtual worlds, people participate in fantasy adventures or socialize in visually immersive online environments. Whereas the settings of virtual worlds may be whimsical or in some cases fantastic, the economic activity is quite real. Many virtual worlds have their own internal trade-based economies in which participants trade virtual weapons, armor, t-shirts or shoes with computer-controlled non-player characters or other human participants.[1] Virtual worlds have established their own currencies that function like real money to facilitate these trades. While most online economies do not facilitate real money transactions, a few have implemented real cash economies by allowing two-way conversions of virtual currencies for real money.[2]

Globally, the virtual world market has exploded in the last decade and was estimated, as of June 2009, to exceed 186 million

---

1 Steven Chung, 'Real Taxation of Virtual Commerce' (2009) 28 *Virginia Tax Review* 733, 735.

2 *ibid.*

unique registrations worldwide.[3] Experts anticipate virtual worlds will continue to develop, with future generations approaching virtual reality. The primary market of virtual worlds — meaning the subscription cost for one to participate in game-play — is in itself overwhelming. However, it is the amount of real money that revolves within the games themselves that makes the industry genuinely intriguing. In 2001, a fantasy world called *Norrath* in the U.S. was estimated to have a gross national product of US$135 million wherein each of the 430,000 subscribers theoretically had an average income of US$3.42 per hour.[4] In 2009, the *Second Life* economy grew to US$567 million, which amounts to 25% of the entire US virtual goods market.[5] Today, the aggregate gross domestic product of virtual economies may range between US$7 to US$12 billion dollars.[6]

As more people are reportedly earning real money through their virtual-world activities, governments are looking into whether virtual world transactions should be subject to regulations, even if the participants do not convert their virtual income into cash. The policy reasons behind, if any, might be to provide more consumer protection measures, to curb gambling and illicit trade, or even to stop financially-motivated cybercrime, money laundering and terrorism financing.[7]

---

3 Peter J Quinn, 'A Click Too Far: The Difficulty in Using Adhesive American Law License Agreements to Govern Global Virtual Worlds' (2010) 27 *Wisconsin International Law Journal* 757, 758.

4 Edward Castronova, 'Virtual Worlds: A First-Hand Account of Market and Society on the Cyberian Frontier' (2001) *CESifo Working Paper No 618* <www.international.ucla.edu/media/files/SSRN_ID294828_code020114590.pdf> accessed December 3, 2013.

5 Samtani Anil, Angelia King Wen Jie, Jeanne Soon Hui Min and Queenie Chew Wan Xiu, 'Virtual Property — A Theoretical and Empirical Analysis' (2012) 34 *European Intellectual Property Review* 188.

6 *ibid.*

7 Mark Methenitis, 'Virtual World Money Laundering' (June 3, 2009) <http://lawofthegame.blogspot.hk/2009/06/virtual-world-money-laundering.html> accessed December 3, 2013.

This chapter is organized into five parts. After this introduction, Part 2 provides a general account of virtual worlds by distinguishing them from traditional video games. It is followed by subcategorizing virtual worlds into structured and unstructured ones with a view to understand how virtual wealth with real-world value is indeed accumulated by virtual world users. Subsequent to the appreciation of virtual economies, Part 3 takes virtual world providers and online financial service providers in turn, reserving an in-depth discussion of various payment methods in virtual world transactions. A total of eight real-life examples are given here as an illustration of how real and virtual currency can be transferred between user's accounts. Part 4 adopts an interpretative approach to look at the regulations implemented by three Asian countries—Japan, South Korea and China—on supervising economics transactions and payments in the virtual world. Part 5 provides a summary of the chapter.

2. General Description of Virtual Worlds

Virtual worlds provide a forum for people to engage in a wide variety of activities through the Internet, ranging from role-playing in medieval fantasy worlds to social networks within a virtual environment.[8] Among other things, these worlds offer their users a new way to make friends, be creative and even trade products. Since every virtual world is unique,[9] the description here is necessarily general.

---

8 Adam S Chodorow, 'Ability to Pay and the Taxation of Virtual Income' (2008) 75 *Tennessee Law Review* 695, 696.

9 Leandra Lederman, 'Stranger than Fiction: Taxing Virtual Worlds' (2007) 82 *New York University Law Review* 1620, 1625–30.

Fulfilling the function of online spaces that allow people to interact with one another through characters they create,[10] virtual worlds are different from traditional video games in several prominent aspects. First, since virtual worlds continue to run even if a user stops playing online,[11] a returning user may be surprised to see things change significantly since he or she last visited it.[12] Second, the experience enjoyed by participants in a given world is as much an outcome of theirs initiative as the developer's, for most worlds are programmed to allow users to create their own and unique life within the world. Third, most worlds even process a virtual economy, where users can manufacture, locate, purchase, sell and exchange virtual goods.[13] Fourth, to gain access to virtual worlds, users have to sign End User License Agreements or Terms of Service agreements in order to establish their rights with respect to the virtual goods created and obtained within those worlds.[14]

Virtual worlds can be divided into two categories: structured and unstructured.[15] In both categories, participants can acquire their virtual wealth in a number of different ways, many of which are analogous to real-world wealth acquisition. People often create their own virtual goods for exchange, earn salaries for

---

10 Woodrow Barfield, 'Intellectual Property Rights In Virtual Environments: Considering the Rights of Owners, Programmers, and Virtual Avatars' (2006) *39 Akron Law Review* 649, 653–54.

11 F. Gregory Lastowka and Dan Hunter, 'The Laws of Virtual Worlds' (2004) *92 California Law Review* 1, 5–6.

12 *ibid.* 6.

13 Edward Castronova, 'Virtual Worlds: A First-Hand Account of Market and Society on the Cyberian Frontier' (n 4) 6.

14 Andrew Jankowich, 'EULAw: The Complex Web of Corporate Rule-Making in Virtual Worlds' (2006) *8 Tulane Journal of Technology & Intellectual Property* 1, 7–11.

15 Bryan T. Camp, 'The Play's the Thing: A Theory of Taxing Virtual Worlds' (2007) *59 Hastings Law Journal* 1, 4.

working, and receive gifts.[16] Over the past years, players have begun to amass significant virtual wealth, which has significant real-world value.

2.1 Structured Virtual Worlds

Structured worlds are highly scripted environments where the virtual-world-maker provides a content-rich setting with scenery, pre-existing characters, plot lines, and rules for interaction.[17] Players, often joining together with others, are given a wide variety of tasks to complete, with the hope of searching for treasure. As they acquire more virtual currencies, virtual goods and experiences in the world, they are able to do more within the context of the game, often rising to a new "level" and undertaking more difficult quests.[18] *World of Warcraft*, *Lineage* and *Dark Age of Camelot* are some of the most popular structured worlds in this day and age.

The purpose of most current structured worlds is for players to experience the unique world constructed by the developers, who would normally supervise the in-world activities just to ensure users do not sabotage the setting for others or otherwise compromise the world's integrity. Because of that, developers generally reserve the right to force out troublemaking players, intending to retain all property rights in the virtual goods created. What is more, to stop users from deploying their real-world wealth to alter their in-world status, developers often limit users' capabilities to exchange virtual items outside the context

---

16 See Buzzard Entertainment Inc, 'World of Warcraft Beginner's Guide' <http://us.battle.net/wow/en/game/guide/> accessed February 16, 2013; Linden Research Inc, 'What is Second Life?' <http://secondlife.com/whatis/> accessed December 3, 2013.

17 *ibid.* 4–6.

18 *ibid.* 6.

of virtual world, resulting in a "closed" system.[19] For instance, Blizzard Entertainment, which operates *World of Warcraft*, strictly prohibits the sale of virtual goods or currencies for real money and reserves the right to take legal action against those who violate its rules.[20]

Despite these restrictions, people can still in reality buy and sell items associated with these worlds on eBay, Itembay.com, Internet Gaming Entertainment (IGE.com), and similar sites.[21] In a practice known as "gold farming," players even play solely to acquire virtual goods and currencies that they then sell for real-world currency to other players who are too impatient to work through the game to gather virtual wealth and experience necessary to play at an advanced level.[22]

2.2 Unstructured Virtual Worlds

By comparison, unstructured worlds provide a platform for users to interact without presetting any plot line and roles.[23] As a result, these worlds transform in accordance with the preferences and fondness of those who participate.[24] *Second Life* and *The Sims Online* can be cited as two well-known examples of unstructured worlds.

---

19 Michael Zenke, 'SOE's Station Exchange — The Results of a Year of Trading' (February 7, 2007) <www.gamasutra.com/view/feature/1716/soes_station_exchange__the_.php> accessed December 3, 2013.

20 Edward Castronova, 'Blizzard Goes to War' (December 12, 2004) <http://terranova.blogs.com/terra_nova/2004/12/blizzard_goes_t.html> accessed December 3, 2013.

21 Dustin Stamper, 'Taxing Ones and Zeros: Can the IRS Ignore Virtual Economies?' (2007) *114 Tax Notes* 149, 150.

22 Julian Dibbell, 'The Life of the Chinese Gold Farmer' *New York Times Magazine* (New York, June 17, 2007) <www.nytimes.com/2007/06/17/magazine/17lootfarmers-t.html?pagewanted=all&_r=0> accessed December 3, 2013.

23 Bryan T Camp (n 15) 7.

24 *ibid.* 7–8.

The purpose of most unstructured worlds is for the users to create their own experiences. Almost all goods in unstructured worlds are manufactured by those who take part using constituent building blocks made available in the given world.[25] Because unstructured worlds are designed to allow users to act freely, virtual world makers take a far less active role in managing what goes on in-world.[26] In addition, they tend to grant users significantly greater rights in their creations than is typical in structured worlds and are generally more "open" to exchanges between virtual and real worlds. For example, *Second Life* operates the LindeX, an official exchange that facilitates people buying and selling virtual currency.[27]

Although many people spend time in unstructured worlds as an escape from reality, at least some of these worlds begin to look more like an alternate forum to conduct real-world activities. For instance, Nissan, IBM and Nike have already established a presence in *Second Life* to market their real-world goods.[28] And various universities have set up virtual sites to promote themselves, to allow students to interact, and even to hold classes and other meetings.[29]

---

25 Cory Ondrejka, 'Escaping the Gilded Cage: User-Created Content and Building the Metaverse' (2004) *49 New York Law School Law Review* 81, 87–88.

26 See Linden Research Inc, 'Second Life Community Standards' <http://secondlife.com/corporate/cs.php> accessed February 16, 2013.

27 Timothy J. Miano, 'Virtual World Taxation: Theories of Income Taxation Applied to the Second Life Virtual Economy' (August 2007) <http://works.bepress.com/cgi/viewcontent.cgi?article=1000&context=timothy_miano> accessed December 3, 2013.

28 Allison Enright, 'How the Second Half Lives' Marketing News (February 15, 2007) <http://us.i1.yimg.com/us.yimg.com/i/adv2/pdf/brainfood/second_life.pdf> accessed December 3, 2013.

29 Andrew Johnson, 'Business and Education Test Online Virtual World's Real-World Potential' *Wisconsin Rapids Tribune* (November 16, 2007) A11.

3.   Payment Methods in Virtual World Transactions

Virtual world providers and online financial service providers (OFSPs) are the two main sectors to economic transactions in virtual worlds. On the one hand, virtual world providers offer the possibility to use money to purchase goods within the simulated setting.[30] The main difference between virtual world currencies and real world currencies is that there is no monetary control in virtual worlds.[31] Within virtual worlds, users earn money by selling objects and there is no measure which controls the supply of money, such as central bank issues currencies. Accordingly, the amount of money and objects in a virtual world depends solely on the users of such world.[32] And it is the task of game makers to integrate currency in the economy of their virtual world.[33] On the other hand, OFSPs allow the rapid transfer of real and virtual currencies between player's accounts across international borders.

In this part, only virtual world providers that possess their own internal economy with in-world currencies which can be purchased and sold inside the virtual environment or traded using the OFSPs, and only OFSPs that can be used to place funds into these virtual environments, are selected for discussion.

3.1 *Virtual World Providers*

Three specific virtual world providers are selected here as

---

30 Jun-Sok Huhh, 'Effects of Real-money Trading on MMOG Demand: A Network Externality Based Explanation' (November 4, 2006) <http://papers.ssrn.com/sol3/papers.cfm?abstract_id=943368> accessed December 3, 2013.

31 Hiroshi Yamaguchi, 'An Analysis of Virtual Currencies in Online Games' (September 1, 2004) <http://papers.ssrn.com/sol3/papers.cfm?abstract_id=544422> accessed December 3, 2013.

32 *ibid.*

33 Dominik Schrank, '*A Trustful Payment System for Virtual Worlds: Design and Implementation of a Payment System for Virtual Worlds*' (Mater's thesis, Graz University of Technology 2009).

examples to illustrate various virtual world transactions.[34]

By allowing account holders to create virtual items for sale, *Second Life* has its own internal currency (called Linden Dollar) which can be used to carry out in-world transactions with others. Such internal currency can be traded for real-world cash or exchanged for other virtual world currencies under different exchange rates.[35] Although *Second Life* is free to use, account holders can purchase a premium membership package which gives them access to increased levels of customer support and other membership benefits.[36] If an account holder wishes to perform financial transactions through his or her account, he or she must add contact and billing details to his or her account profile, within which four different account types are provided—resident, business owner, enterprise and currency trader.

Similar to *Second Life*, *InWorldz* is a simulated reality space created by its account holders, who can meet to chat, create virtual goods or places, and socialize with each other. *InWorldz* has an active and diverse economy where account holders can create and sell goods and services to other account holders. The currency inside can also be traded for real-world cash or exchanged for other virtual world currencies. Although this world is also free to use, it is tailored for the users who are about the age of 18.[37]

Lastly, *IMVU* is an online social entertainment website in which

34 Angela S. M. Irwin, Jill Slay, Kim-Kwang Raymond Choo and Lin Liu, 'Are the Financial Transactions Conducted inside Virtual Environments Truly Anonymous? An Experimental Research from an Australian Perspective' (2013) *Journal of Money Laundering Control* 6, 14–15.

35 Linden Research Inc, 'Second Life Terms of Service' <http://secondlife.com/corporate/tos.php?lang=en-US> accessed February 17, 2013.

36 Linden Research Inc, 'Second Life Premium Membership' <http://secondlife.com/premium/?lang=en-US> accessed December 3, 2013.

37 InWorldz, 'InWorldz Terms of Service' <http://inworldz.com/tos.php> accessed February 16, 2013.

account holders can make new friends, create virtual items and play virtual games. Like the previous two virtual worlds, *IMVU* has an active economy where account holders can create and sell goods and services to other players. It contains its own economy with a currency system based on standard credits, promotional credits and developer tokens.[38] For in-world standard credits which are usually used by account holders to buy virtual items such as clothing, pets, property and land, they can be purchased using real-world currency either directly from the game makers on gift cards available from retail outlets such as department stores or from third party resellers. Unused standard credits can only be re-sold to other registered users who will purchase them for real-world currencies, but cannot be refunded by *IMVU*. As for promotional credits which can also be used to buy virtual products, they can be earned by participating in partner promotions. Promotional credits are similar to standard credits in that a given number of promotional credits equate to the same number of standard credits, and that they cannot be traded back to *IMVU* for real-world currencies. Promotional credits can then be exchanged into developer tokens when transactions take place. Developer tokens are not equal in value to promotional credits, because developers receive only a single developer token per purchase regardless of the price of the product bought.

3.2   Online Financial Services Providers (OFSPs)

Five identifiable OFSPs are chosen here as illustrating examples for different payment methods in virtual world transactions.[39]

First, PayPal is a global e-commerce business allowing online payments and money transfers to be made through the Internet. Originally, a PayPal account only supported payments with an

---

38   IMVU Inc, 'IMVU Information' <www.imvu.com/catalog/web_info. php?section=Info&topic=terms_of_service> accessed December 3, 2013.

39   Angela S. M. Irwin, Jill Slay, Kim-Kwang Raymond Choo and Lin Liu (n 34) 15.

electronic debit from a bank account or by a credit card at clients' choice. But some time in 2010 or early 2011, PayPal began to require a verified bank account after the account holder exceeded a predetermined spending limit.[40]

Second, Moneybookers is an Internet payment and eWallet service with over 17 million account holders worldwide and provides more than 100 payment options, with 41 currencies covering 200 countries and territories.[41] The Moneybookers payment system offers account holders an online deposit account and a low-cost, Internet-based alternative to traditional money transfer methods such as cheques and money orders. It enables customers to make online payments conveniently, securely and economically.

Third, the Pecunix system allows account holders to make and receive payments instantly via the Internet. Pecunix account holders can convert national currencies (i.e., cash) to Pecunix, convert Pecunix to most national currencies, and convert Pecunix to gold and gold to Pecunix.[42] The Pecunix system does not sell its currency directly to account holders. Instead, it uses numerous virtual currency exchangers to assist account holders to put value into their Pecunix account or convert Pecunix's value back into their national currency. All virtual currency exchangers used by the Pecunix system are independent businesses which are not affiliated with such system.

Fourth, IGE.com is a diversified service provider operating the world's largest secure network of buying and selling sites for

---

40 PayPal, 'About PayPal' <www.paypal-media.com/about> accessed December 3, 2013.

41 Marie Lizette, 'Moneybookers' <www.confessionsofapokerprowannabe.com/p/moneybookers.html> accessed December 3, 2013.

42 Pecunix Inc, 'Buy and Sell Pecunix' <http://pecunix.com/money.cfm...buysell> accessed December 3, 2013.

virtual currencies.[43] IGE.com provides debit cards where virtual currency can be transferred from a player's electronic account straight to cash to be withdrawn in real-world currencies at most automated teller machines worldwide.

Fifth, VirWoX is a top European exchange which allows account holders to directly trade the Euro (EUR), British Pound (GBP), and Swiss Francs (CHF) against many virtual currencies, thus eliminating the cost by having to convert local currency first to US$ before exchanging to virtual currencies. Say, a *Second Life* player has 100 Euros in his VirWoX account and wants to get Linden dollars for it. After checking the current market and seeing that the rate is near 400 (Linden dollars per Euro), he decides he wants to sell his Euros for not less than 400 Linden dollars per Euro. Commissions aside, this would give him 40,000 Linden dollars if executed.[44]

In sum, there are a myriad of online financial services provides who cater to virtual world transactions. The next section provides a comparative analysis of how several Asia-Pacific jurisdictions are using real world regulations to handle virtual world economic transactions and whether such attempts are feasible in light of the unique characteristics of virtual world economies.

4.   Comparative Analysis of Real World Regulation of Virtual World Economic Transactions

Due to the existence of virtual economy and currency exchange policy in a number of virtual worlds (as discussed in Part 2) together with the convenience of money transfer in virtual world

---

43 IGE.com, 'IGE—About Us' <www.ige.com/about.html> accessed December 3, 2013.

44 Virtual World Services GmbH, 'How to Exchange' <www.virwox.com/help. php?drgn=1> accessed December 3, 2013.

transactions because of the OFSPs (as discussed in Part 3), virtual world providers in Asia have been successful in making substantial profits by selling virtual currency for real cash.[45] Asian gamers have found Real Money Trade (RMT), a secondary market for virtual items which are exchanged for real cash, profitable, and some players even commit to RMT excessively. According to a study from the research firm In-Stat, virtual goods revenue from online social games and social networking exceeded US $7 billion in 2010, of which Asia accounted for about 70%.[46]

As more users spend real cash to purchase virtual currencies in virtual worlds, more governmental supervisions and controls may be warranted. Indeed, some Asian countries have begun regulating economics transactions in the virtual world. This part seeks to examine the different regulations adopted by Japan, South Korea and China.

4.1 Japan

There are two types of pre-payment services in Japan: certificate and server. Whereas monetary values are recorded on certificates in Certificate Type services, such are recorded only on a server on the Internet in Server Type services.[47] To purchase these services, users of Certificate Type services were provided with paper, cards or cell phone chips (Certificate Type Instruments), and users of Server Type services are provided with numbers or codes (Server Type Instruments).[48]

---

45 Akky Akimoto, 'Japan's No.1 Social Network — Gree And Mobage Town Competes' (February 4, 2011) <http://asiajin.com/blog/2011/02/04/japans-no-1-social-network-gree-and-mobage-town-competes/> accessed December 3, 2013.

46 Brian Hong, 'Regulation of Virtual Currencies in China and Korea, Asian Gaming Giants Eye the US Market' (November 28, 2012) <http://legalbrainz.blogspot.hk/2012/11/regulation-of-virtual-currencies-in.html> accessed December 3, 2013.

47 Takashi Nakazaki, 'Real World Excessive Regulations Might Kill Economic Transactions in Virtual Worlds' (2011) *14 Journal of Internet Law 3.*

48 *ibid.*

In March 2009, Japan promulgated regulations on pre-payment services and fund transfer services under the Payment Service Act 2009 (PSA), which came into effect on April 1, 2010. For pre-payment services, the PSA replaces the Prepaid Certificate Act 1989 that used to apply only to Certificate Type services but not to Server Type services.

In the past, the Prepaid Certificate Act imposed an obligation on the prepaid certificate issuers by requiring them to deposit with the Legal Affairs Bureau half of the outstanding balance of the issued amount. However, this practice was not required for the Server Type services. This preferential treatment might be problematic in terms of consumer protection and might lead to the imposition of unfair burdens on prepaid money service providers.

Currently, the PSA treats Certificate Type Instruments and Server Type Instruments the same. First, it prohibits cash-out and refunds of prepaid money, unless in situations where a service provider closes down its business or the amount to be refunded is insignificant. Second, it forbids foreign prepaid money service providers which are not registered under the PSA from seeking clients to use their services in Japan. Since a virtual world currency system, where a user can pay real-world cash in exchange for virtual currencies to purchase virtual items and services, could fall within the definition of "Server Type Instruments," an issue emerges as to whether in-world currency systems will be regulated by the new legislation.

While both the Prepaid Certificate Act and the PSA include explicit provisions exempting their application to admission tickets, these exemption provisions cannot be found when it comes to virtual currencies. On top of that, both the Order for Enforcement of the PSA and the Guidelines for the PSA clearly excludes application of such exemption to virtual world services. As a result, Japanese virtual world service providers, including those involved in the online gaming industry, should consider the impact of the PSA regulations on their business operations.

That said, article 4 of the PSA stipulates the types of Prepaid Payment Instruments that are not subject to PSA regulation. They include Prepaid Payment Instruments which are used only within a period of six months starting from the issuance date.[49] Because of this, some virtual world providers in Japan began shortening the effective duration of their virtual currencies to only six months.

It should also be noted that the situation is different should the Prepaid Payment Instrument be offered for the issuer's own business as opposed to for a third party's business. Where a virtual currency is provided as a favor for playing and working in the virtual world and cannot be purchased using real-world currencies, such a virtual currency system would be deemed a form of reward program not caught by the PSA. In a reward program, points which can be used for in-world transactions are given at no cost. Such is different from points issued for a price paid by users, which would fall under the definition of 'Prepaid Payment Instruments' under the PSA.

In conclusion, foreign companies offering virtual world services to Japanese players might have to stop using virtual currencies issued in exchange for real money. For foreign operators issuing virtual currencies to players in Japan, the issuer would be required to comply with the PSA requirements, such as obtaining registration under the PSA and prohibiting any cash-out policy. Following this, if the Linden Dollar falls within the definition of "Prepaid Payment Instruments" under the PSA and *Second Life* still wants to continue to issue Linden Dollars to users in Japan, *Second Life* would have to register under the PSA by establishing a subsidiary office in Japan, and would have to abstain from providing any exchange services for converting Linden Dollars into real money.

---

49 *Cabinet Office Ordinance on Prepaid Payment Instruments*, art 4 para 2.

4.2 South Korea

In South Korea, real money trading of virtual currencies, simulated items in virtual betting games and computer-generated items produced illegally by way of copying, adapting, hacking, or abnormal game-play in virtual worlds is prohibited by the Game Industry Promotion Act. The Game Industry Promotion Act, adopted in April 2006 by Korean Congress, was originally intended to cover mundane matters such as content ratings. The Act was, however, amended in January 2007 to directly address RMT of virtual goods. With the amendments coming into effect in May 2007, the Act was the first attempt by the Korean Government to regulate RMT.[50]

The amended Act makes it illegal to trade virtual items for real money if the items are either used as an instrument in a game of chance, such as a virtual betting game, or obtained through the exploitation of security loopholes by using computer-controlled characters or other abnormal play.[51] Online gambling and virtual worlds have thus been classified into different categories. Those who violate the Act can be sentenced to a maximum of five years in prison or a fine not exceeding 50 million KRW (approximately US$45,000). In this way, the legislator has attempted to curb some of the negative consequences of secondary market trading while leaving trading activities pertaining to normal players and virtual worlds untouched.[52]

Although the Act was criticized for containing some ambiguous expressions such as "abnormal" and "game of chance," these

---

50 Vili Lehdonvirta and Perttu Virtanen, 'A New Frontier in Digital Content Policy: Case Studies in the Regulation of Virtual Goods and Artificial Scarcity' (September 16, 2010) <http://microsites.oii.ox.ac.uk/ipp2010/system/files/IPP2010_Lehdonvirta_Virtanen_Paper.pdf> accessed December 3, 2013.

51 Unggi Yoon, 'Selective Bombing of RMT in Korea' (May 13, 2007) <http://terranova.blogs.com/terra_nova/2007/05/s_koreas_bancan.html> accessed December 3, 2013.

52 Vili Lehdonvirta and Perttu Virtanen (n 50).

terms were clarified in 2009 when the South Korea Supreme Court sought to give relevant interpretation.[53] In this case, the two suspects surnamed Kim and Lee allegedly purchased an amount of "Aden," the virtual currency of an online multiplayer role-playing game "Lineage," worth 234 million KRW (approximately US$208,000) from various sources and resold it to individual players for a profit of at least 20 million KRW (approximately US$18,000).[54] Since no evidence was put forward at any point during the proceedings purporting that the currency was originally generated by any other means than normal game play, the case turned on whether Lineage was a "game of chance." The prosecutor asserted that luck is an element in the game in the same way as it is in poker, even though its role is less clear.

The first instance court found the suspects guilty in March 2008. An appellate court later overturned the decision in July 2009, explaining that Lineage is a time consuming game: Aden can only be earned through expending time and effort by hunting monsters, fighting against other players, or profiting through trade on virtual marketplaces.[55] In December 2009, the South Korea Supreme Court confirmed the appellate court's ruling, finding the traders not guilty.[56] The Supreme Court conditioned its ruling upon the situation where cyber money was earned through skill, not luck.

Following such decisions, the contours of South Korea's statutory regulation of second-hand virtual item marketplaces

---

53 Park Si-soo, 'Ruling to Boost Sale of Cyber Money' The Korea Times (South Korea, January 10, 2010) <www.koreatimes.co.kr/www/news/nation/2010/01/116_58775.html> accessed December 3, 2013.

54 Choe Sun-uk and Lee Min-yong, 'Supreme Court Acquits Two in Cyber Money Game Case' Korea Joongang Daily (South Korea, January 11, 2010) <http://koreajoongangdaily.joinsmsn.com/news/article/article.aspx?aid=2915126> accessed December 3, 2013.

55 Klint Finley, 'South Korea Considering Virtual Currency Real' (January 20, 2010) <http://technoccult.net/archives/2010/01/20/south-korea-considering-virtual-currency-real/> accessed December 3, 2013.

56 *ibid.*

were clearer. While selling virtual goods obtained through cybercrime activities or computer-controlled characters were prohibited by law and subject to fines or imprisonment, selling virtual goods obtained through normal game play was not illegal. Trading game money for cash was punished only in cases where it was obtained by online gambling games such as poker or other card games.

That said, in June 2012, the Korean Government ultimately decided to ban all virtual item trades with a new law effective from the second half of 2012 as a measure aimed at encouraging students not to waste time.[57] The Government official stressed that collecting items for commercial use is a serious hindrance in creating a healthy game culture. Those who violate this law will face up to a KRW 50 million fine and a maximum of five years in jail.

4.3 China

According to the China Internet Network Information Center, the market for virtual currency trading in China increased from 10 billion to 13 billion yuan in 2008, and China has over one million virtual world users who earn online money by playing.[58] In the past, Chinese online game players could use virtual currencies to purchase virtual items such as clothes, cars, and houses for their virtual avatars, as well as real items and exchange virtual currencies for cash in a second market. However, since November 2006, virtual money trading has drawn official attention, with the Chinese Government demanding tighter controls as such trading became an avenue for gambling and illicit trade.[59]

---

57 Cho Mu-hyun 'Korea Prohibits Trade of Online Game Items' The Korea Times (South Korea, June 13, 2012) <www.koreatimes.co.kr/www/news/tech/2012/06/129_112964.html> accessed December 3, 2013.

58 China Internet Network Information Centre, 'Statistic Report' <www.cnnic.net.cn/gjymaqzx/aqzxtjbg/> accessed December 3, 2013.

59 People's Republic of China Ministry of Commerce, 'China Bars Use of Virtual Money for Trading in Real Goods' (June 2009) <http://english.mofcom.gov.cn/aarticle/newsrelease/commonnews/200906/20090606364208.html> accessed December 3, 2013.

In September 2008, the Chinese Government imposed a 20% tax on income generated from the trading of virtual currencies.[60] Tax authorities generally took the view that all income from online business should be taxable, even if profits were derived from virtual worlds.[61] While taxation may be an effective means of bringing down such economic activities initiated by the virtual world operators, there are enforcement issues arising from the transactions between players because of the difficulties of identifying each individual real-world users.

Subsequently, in June 2009, the Chinese Government issued new regulations aimed at restricting the trading and use of virtual money. Virtual currencies "which is issued by an online game operator, purchased by a game user with real cash, electrically kept in a server provided by the operator, and indicated in the form of prepaid amount or points" would be banned from being exchanged for goods.[62] This definition does not encompass virtual items earned within the gaming world.

The circular addresses and clarifies several key issues. First, it prohibits one entity from providing both a virtual currency issuing service and an exchange market platform service for virtual currency transactions among users. Second, it limits the use of virtual currency to trades of virtual goods and services only for the original issuer. The purpose of this restriction was to limit the possible impact of the rapidly growing online gaming market on China's real financial system. Third, game operators must provide virtual currencies to users only in exchange for real money and it must be purchased at a reported price. This means that a game operator cannot give virtual currencies as a prize for

---

60   Mure Dickie, 'China in Web Money-making U-turn' *The Financial Times* (Beijing, November 3, 2008) <www.ft.com/intl/cms/s/0/ba1cfc30-a946-11dd-a19a-000077b07658.html#axzz2O5yOZ100> accessed December 3, 2013.

61   Mure Dickie, 'China U-turn on Online Money-making' *The Financial Times* (Beijing, November 2, 2008) <www.ft.com/cms/s/0/2b2a3030-a90d-11dd-a19a-000077b07658.html#axzz2O5yOZ100> accessed December 3, 2013.

62   David Barboza, 'In China, New Limits on Virtual Currency' *The New York Times* (New York, June 30, 2009) B4.

in-game contests or as a benefit. When a game operator wants to change an exchange rate, including promotional discounts, it must file an application with the authority. Fourth, it requires virtual currency exchanging platform service providers to require a user, who sells virtual currencies, to register with a real ID and use a real domestic bank account associated with the real ID. Fifth, it prohibits virtual currency exchanging platform service providers from providing their services to minors.

In June 2010, the Chinese Government announced that starting from August 1, 2011, it would prohibit companies that operate on platforms for online virtual currency transactions from providing services to minors in an effort to prevent abuses.[63] In addition, all online game players must register using a real name including a valid identification. The People's Bank of China, as the Chinese central bank, also stated that non-financial institutions should obtain a payment business license in order to provide payment services including issuing prepaid money and online payment.[64]

5.   Conclusion

At first glance, economic transactions and virtual worlds do not seem to fit well together. Yet, since the main activities of current virtual world users are creating objects for trading and real-world currencies are capable of being incorporated into a virtual world, there exists a huge potential for e-commerce applications in virtual worlds nowadays. To manage money transactions, a number of payment processors such as PayPal started to allow the transfer of real and virtual currencies between players' accounts across international borders.

---

63 Mark Lee, 'China Government Bans Online Virtual-Currency Dealing Platforms for Minors' Bloomberg (Hong Kong, June 22, 2010) <www.bloomberg.com/news/2010-06-22/tencent-shares-fall-after-china-announces-virtual-currency-ban-for-minors.html> accessed December 3, 2013.

64 *ibid.*

Subsequently, in many virtual worlds, both businesses and individual users can profit from economic transactions. This means that a large number of consumers who are unfamiliar with the rules on economic transactions in virtual worlds may become virtual world entrepreneurs. What is more, uncontrolled online gambling may prevail in society which lacks regulation, adversely influencing future generations. Such consumers need laws to enable them to navigate the online business environment and to appreciate the legal ramifications of their online transactions.

In Japan, virtual world operators that receive consideration from their users for virtual currency are regulated for compliance with consumer protection laws. On the other hand, the South Korea Government has prohibited certain types of in-game currency transactions through amendments to the Game Industry Promotion Act. In contrast, the Chinese Government announced rules that prohibit virtual currencies, including the Linden Dollars of *Second Life* and "QQ Coins" of *Qzone*, from being exchanged for any real items, thereby limiting their use to purchasing virtual items.

As economies around the Asia-Pacific region start to recognize the impact of virtual world commercial transactions, it will become more important for legislators and lawyers to better understand the need for clear legal frameworks for supervising economic transactions and payments in the virtual world.

PART VII
REMEDIES FOR BUYER/SELLER IN THE VIRTUAL WORLD

16

Remedies Available for Buyers and Sellers in Virtual Commercial Transactions

Austin YIU

1. Introduction

This chapter shall explore remedies available for buyers and sellers in the emerging commercial environments of virtual worlds. First, we will examine the nature of virtual worlds and goods, with reference to applicable commercial law principles in real-life. Disputes often arise in commercial dealings, and in the real world, buyers and sellers are provided with the avenue to resolve such through established procedures and safeguards provided in practice and law. In virtual transactions however, these safeguards are yet to exist. For example, parties to a transaction for real goods have the ability to examine and test them, but in contrast, virtual goods in virtual worlds, by their very nature, cannot allow one to do so. It is therefore paramount that remedies are available for proper settlement of disputes when any arise in virtual worlds.

As this topic remains an emergent field of law, this chapter then undertakes a comparative approach by analyzing the different remedies to which one can avail themselves in different jurisdictions. In particular, we will focus on the experiences of the United States, European, and Chinese/Hong Kong courts in facing virtual worlds. The international nature of virtual worlds, their relevance towards commercial law, and the importance as to why remedies are needed to arbitrate disputes shall conclude this chapter.

1.1 Definitions

The emergence of the Internet as a commercial arena has led to difficulty where commercial disputes arise; most jurisdictions' laws were originally designed to deal with problems grounded in reality, not virtual reality. The amount of "precedence, pronounced judgments, and case laws" for electronic transactions for real goods continues to be relatively low in number and remains in its "infancy."[1]

This problem has been no less exacerbated with the emergence of virtual worlds, wherein virtual goods are traded. A virtual world is not necessarily a game, but is instead a "complete virtual world in which participants can do just about anything—play and be entertained, have relationships," and also to conduct "mundane businesses and meetings and even attend university courses."[2] This latter part of this statement is what concerns here—because the conduct of businesses, even virtual ones, necessarily involves commercial relationships. Where these virtual commercial transactions go wrong, the question arises: how does commercial law grounded in the real world apply?

2. The Nature of Virtual Worlds and Goods

As more "people flock to virtual worlds and invest their time and resources there," the legal regulation for transactions in such worlds is increasingly seen as necessary.[3] To determine the proper remedies available to participants in these transactions, one must first ascertain the nature of virtual goods.

---

1 B. H. Agalgatti and S. Krishna, *Business Ethics: Concepts and Practices* (4th edn, Nirali Prakashan, Mumbai 2007) 261.

2 Harry Henderson, *Encyclopedia of Computer Science and Technology* (Rev edn, Infobase Publishing New York 2009) 347.

3 Angela Adrian, 'Intellectual Property or Intangible Chattel' (2006) 2 *Journal of International Commercial Law and Technology 52, 53.*

Several legislations in Hong Kong provide protection for electronic commerce. Prominently, the Electronic Transactions (Amendment) Ordinance 2004 (ETO) regulates transactions made electronically. This corresponds with the United States' Electronic Signatures in Global and National Commerce Act. According to section 5 of the Ordinance and §7001 of the Act, electronic records are valid as evidence in the courts, and the Ordinance itself provides that Internet transactions have the same validity as contracts made in writing on paper in real life. In essence, this Ordinance provides the same legal rights for parties to an Internet transaction as those commercial transactions made in real life.

In addition to this are the laws in force prior to the 2004 enactment of the Ordinance, which also act to guarantee the rights of parties. The keystone to any commercial transaction is the contract of sale. Such a contract involves several elements to be valid. In Hong Kong, these requirements are listed in section 3(1) of the Sales of Goods Ordinance (SOGO), "whereby the seller transfers or agrees to transfer the property in goods to the buyer for a money consideration, called the price." It is also relevant to examine the United Nations Convention on Contracts for the International Sale of Goods (CISG), due to the multi-border nature of virtual worlds. The CISG's article 1 states that the Convention "applies to contracts of sale of goods between parties, whose places of business are in different States," but however does not define what exactly a contract of sale of goods is.

Considering that both the SOGO and CISG were drafted in times prior to virtual worlds or even the Internet, one must decide whether the notion of "virtual goods" can be included under the idea of "goods" that the legislation imposes as a crucial element to the formation of a contract of sale. Necessarily this involves one to determine the definitional ambit of what exactly is a "good," and whether virtual world goods can be classified into that.

Section 2(1) of SOGO defines "goods" as including "all chattels personal other than things in action and money." What is problematic is the issue of whether virtual goods made by players in virtual worlds can be seen as personal chattels. This has been a difficult question for many jurisdictions. In the European Courts, it was said in *Football Dataco Ltd and others v Sportradar GmbH*[4] that these old legal categories of property, "based on concepts, such as time and space" are not helpful as "the meaning of which becomes highly ambiguous in the world of virtual reality" and this new medium of trade is "highly resistant to the discipline of a legislative framework that can be effective and efficient only if it is set up with the support of the international community of States as a whole."[5]

In the United Kingdom, it seems that virtual goods can be seen as personal property for tax reasons under *Westone Wholesale Limited v The Commissioners for Her Majesty's Revenue and Customs VAT*.[6] There, the judges held in obiter and in comparing real goods that "virtual goods can just be jettisoned, and more virtual goods can be brought in"[7] for the purpose of taxation. Whether this means that the Sales of Goods Act extends to virtual goods for commercial purposes however remains to be seen. The fact that this was a decision from a Tax Tribunal in addition to being obiter rather than a ratio from the higher courts also means it is not a decision to put much weight upon as conclusive to the nature of virtual goods.

In contrast, in the United States, the corresponding section 2 of SOGO requiring "goods" to form a contract of sale is set out in article 2 of the Uniform Commercial Code (UCC). The courts there have however found it difficult to find the UCC applicable to virtual goods too. This is seen in *Arbitron Inc v Tralyn Broad*

---

4 [2013] 1 CMLR 29.

5 *ibid.* [AG55].

6 [2009] UKFTT 218 (TC).

7 *ibid.*

Inc,[8] where it was held that "it is not clear whether 'license' agreements (which virtual worlds use)... are contracts for the sale of 'goods' and therefore within the UCC's purview."[9] The issue still has not been brought up before the Hong Kong courts.

But let one consider, say hypothetically that the contract for a sale of good for virtual goods in the determination of remedies is a relevant investigation. Virtual goods are birth of software and computer code, and so are any transactions amongst players or between the developers and players. They are regulated by computer code rather than by words. To argue that one can spawn appropriate remedies from conduct derived from code is difficult plainly from just the interface of a virtual world, which may or may not allow extensive social interactions culminating in transactions inherent in real life sale; i.e., negotiation, discussions of supply and delivery. A real life commercial transaction is not only commercial, but also a social transaction, and whilst a "judge might at least hope to sort through conflicting versions of a story... software is necessarily blind to the social meaning of events."[10] To regulate such transactions within the virtual world is ill suited for software and attempting to craft remedies from that may perhaps be fanciful.

To affect a contract of sale of goods, the general rule requires a transfer in the good.[11] The relevant maxim is expressed as *nemo dat quod non habet*, or as succinctly explained by Lord Denning in *Bishopgate Motor Finance v Transport Brakes:*[12] "no

---

8 400 F3d 130 (2nd Cir 2005).

9 *ibid.* 138.

10 James Grimmelmann, 'Virtual Worlds as Comparative Law (2004) *49 New York Law School Law Review 147, 157–159* in Paul Schiff Berman (ed), *Law and Society Approaches to Cyberspace* (Ashgate, Aldershot 2007).

11 Sale of Goods Ordinance (Cap 26), s 3(1).

12 [1949] 1 KB 322.

one can give a better title than he himself possesses."[13] This is statutorily affirmed and reflected in sections 23 of SOGO and 27 of the corresponding English Act. The *nemo dat* rule is especially relevant for transactions made amongst players in the virtual world, for in many a virtual world; restrictions mean that players do not own the goods that they purport to sell. Therefore, as a result buyers acquire no better title than sellers. This results in confusion and faulty transactions, and a host of legal problems that shall be discussed in length below.

Thus generally, to most, virtual goods are still seen as "things" that cannot be governed under contract of sale of goods because they "do not fall under this definition" of goods under a sales contract. A proper contract "frees the buyer from restrictions as to the use of the product bought."[14] In contrast, most worlds wherein virtual goods are traded "are in the form of licenses, not sales," which means that the "producer or developer" of the virtual world can still "exercise control over the product down through the licensing chain."[15]

3.   Contractual Remedies

Although it appears the contract of sale of goods is not an applicable way to deal with virtual goods, this does not mean that contractual remedies are irrelevant in resolving disputes in virtual worlds. Contract remedies are still relevant, but in the form of the End User License Agreement (EULA) or Terms of Service (TOS) instead. This agreement, commonly required to be accepted by the user before entering a virtual world, is one that "generally

---

13   *ibid.* 336–337.

14   United Nations, *United Nations Commission on International Trade Law Yearbook* Volume XXXII: 2001 (United Nations Publications, New York 2001) 298. A/CN.9/SER.A/2001.

15   *ibid.* 298–299.

removes the user's property rights to anything within the virtual world, including items the user builds or creates"[16] themselves. These are "standardized contracts" offered to players on a "take it or leave it basis" without any bargaining opportunity between the parties.[17]

For players in virtual worlds, these agreements often withhold rights to virtual goods from players for the purpose to "protect corporate investment."[18] This means that remedies afforded to buyers of virtual goods subjected to EULAs are often extremely biased to the developer, or even non-existent at all. For players, this may appear to be an extremely unfair starting position. After all, it is a general principle that "the law of contracts generally enforces the reasonable expectations of the parties to the contract."[19] Unfortunately for players in most virtual worlds, they are not afforded property rights under the EULA of the virtual world in which they agreed to participate in. Presently, this means that if a player creates something inside the virtual world, according to the usual EULAs that restricts property rights, this may mean that the player does not own any proprietary right inherent in his creation (i.e., intellectual property rights or copyright). If he sells his creation to another, the buyer does not acquire or retain property or ownership over the item bought either. This may not be of particular concern where "players do not care about" their rights where the virtual world is "used for entertainment not income," but this is increasingly untrue as "business is booming in virtual worlds."[20]

---

16 Michael Passman, 'Transactions of Virtual Items in Virtual Worlds' (2008) *18 Albany Law Journal of Science and Technology 259, 263.*

17 *Cubic Corp v Marty* (1986) 185 CA 3d 428.

18 Angela Adrian, 'Contract Law and Virtual Worlds' in Angela Adrian, *Law and Order in Virtual Worlds, Exploring Avatars, Their Ownership and Rights* (IGI Global, New York 2010) 154.

19 Passman (n 16) 269.

20 Adrian (n 18).

It seems the likeliest way for buyers and against developers to obtain a proper remedy and to safeguard their rights over virtual goods transactions upon a contractual basis with the EULA is to argue that the EULA is "unconscionable" and imposes overly "onerous conditions."[21] The case law has indicated that this is an allowable remedy under real life contracts. It was held in *Progress Bulk Carriers Ltd v Tube City IMS LLC*[22] by Cooke J that where the stipulations in a contract "provoked such a sense of moral outrage and appeared so unconscionable" or were "so manifestly beyond the norms of ordinary commercial practice"[23] then a contract could be held illegitimate.

To do so, according to Roth J in *Slocom Trading Limited, Derbent Management Limited v Tatik Inc, Sibir Energy plc, Maritime Villa Holdings SCI*,[24] "it is necessary to demonstrate that it would be unjust or unconscionable for one of the parties"[25] of the contract. He concedes however that before one can decide whether these conditions have been met, one must "bear in mind that the individuals involved conducted their affairs in a manner and in a commercial and social environment that is very different from that which prevails in the United Kingdom."[26] Hence, whether it is unjust must take into account the circumstances at the time when a contract was made and agreed to. Hong Kong law generally follows these English principles.

The difficulty in allowing this remedy to cross the barrier into virtual worlds is multi-faceted however. First is the fact that almost all virtual worlds follow the practice of employing restrictive EULAs. It is an industry standard. Furthermore, the

---

21 *ibid.*
22 [2012] EWHC 273 (Comm).
23 *ibid.* 373.
24 [2012] EWHC 3464 (Ch).
25 *ibid.* [282].
26 *ibid.* [5].

international scope of the Internet means that it would be an arduous fact finding exercise for the courts to determine how and where the contract was draft and why people all over the world would agree to such unfair conditions in the EULA for the mere purpose of joining a virtual world. Moreover, despite the fact that most parties to virtual good transactions have similar expectations to contracts made in the real world, this does not translate to the fact that their expectations can be enforceable in a court of law. It has been observed that "it is not at all clear what form of contract law should govern transactions in virtual items,"[27] and this is certainly true due to the lack of cases brought to court.

The only case brought forward successfully was *Bragg v Linden Research*[28] from the United States. The plaintiff had agreed to the EULA of the virtual world *Second Life*, in which one term of the EULA required arbitration whenever any dispute arose. Bragg contended that this term was unenforceable, and that the developer of *Second Life*, Linden had "unlawfully confiscated his virtual property."[29] Judge Robreno in his judgment ruled that the EULA provision was both procedurally and substantively unconscionable. Procedural unconscionability in American law concerns "surprise" or as explained in, *Guiterrez v Autowest*,[30] "the extent to which the supposedly agreed-upon terms of the bargain are hidden"[31] in the contract, whilst substantive unconscionability dealt with the reasonableness of the term.

In *Bragg*, it was found that "Linden buried the arbitration provision in a lengthy paragraph under the benign heading

---

27 Passman (n 16) 271.

28 487 F Supp 2d 593 (2007).

29 Jane Kaufman Winn and Benjamin Wright, *The Law of Electronic Commerce* (4th edn, Wolters Kluwer Law & Business, New York 2008) 6–52.

30 7 Cal Rptr 3d 267 (2003).

31 *ibid.* 275.

'GENERAL PROVISIONS'," with "nothing in the Agreement," bringing "the reader's attention to the arbitration provision."[32] This satisfied procedural unconscionability. Even so, the EULA "may nonetheless be enforceable if the substantive terms are reasonable."[33]

Judge Robreno further found that the EULA provided "Linden with a variety of one-sided remedies to resolve disputes, while forcing its customers to arbitrate any disputes with Linden,"[34] which is exactly the case in *Bragg*. Linden's terms included instances of reservation of unilateral rights such as the ability to confiscate players' virtual property on the mere suspicion of fraud or similar situations.[35] This lack of mutuality led the Judge to conclude that the EULA arbitration provision was substantively unconscionable, and hence unenforceable against Bragg.

To conclude, the EULA was criticized as providing "one-sided means, which tilts unfairly in almost all situations to Linden's favor" and that its use was Linden's attempt to "insulate itself contractually from any meaningful challenge to its alleged practices."[36] In this instance, Bragg was successful. There was not much of a remedy other than to hold that the provision as unenforceable against Bragg. Bragg did however get a confidential settlement of an undisclosed amount with Linden, which perhaps could be seen as a "remedy" technically. [37] There does not however, appear to be similar successful instances to his since. It is hard for one to advise a client on how the courts would treat similar facts as no comparable cases have arisen in the

---

32 Bragg (n 28) 606.

33 *ibid.* 607.

34 *ibid.* 608.

35 *ibid.* 611.

36 *ibid.*

37 Andrew Murray, *Information Technology Law: The Law and Society* (Oxford University Press, Oxford 2010) 564.

United Kingdom or Hong Kong either since *Bragg*. The American experience also seems to indicate the sums from settlement rather than litigation is the general remedy sought by disgruntled parties and is often awarded as so.

Predominantly this is due to the reason that most virtual good transactions are of such a low value that bringing a lawsuit to resolve any dispute would be wholly disproportional as to cost. The remedies that one can obtain under a contractual basis do not seem to be entirely satisfying and grounded in a multitude of authority either. Instead, perhaps it is prudent to look into the rights and remedies available to licensors and licensees afforded under the EULA rather than the validity of the agreement's provisions or the agreement as a whole.

4.   Intangible Remedies

As mentioned, the inherent characteristics of virtual goods make them difficult to be classified as personal chattel. It is noted, "in many respects, virtual goods are more similar to intellectual property than personal property."[38] After all, "virtual goods are intangible, may be copied an infinite number of times without any additional cost or material expenditure of time, effort or resources, and may be combined with other virtual items to create derivative works."[39] It is not that personal property cannot be intangible, but to address virtual goods as proper personal "goods" and follow a contractual approach leads to difficulty in obtaining remedies as addressed above. If one were to view it through the intellectual property lens however, remedies through such an avenue are relatively easier to obtain under the law.

---

38   Oliver Herzfeld, 'What is the Legal Status of Virtual Goods?' (Forbes, April 12, 2012 New York) <www.forbes.com/sites/oliverherzfeld/2012/12/04/what-is-the-legal-status-of-virtual-goods/> accessed December 3, 2013.

39   *ibid.*

It is a well-known fact that, buyers and independent sellers (which are both "buyers" in the face of the developer) in the virtual world face a strenuous struggle against the creator of the virtual world in obtaining remedies. This relationship between individuals and the creators of the virtual world is generally in the form of the license. The participant to the virtual world, (the licensee) "is motivated to ensure that the license" he is given "adequately describes the operating environment" of the virtual world, while conversely, the developer (the licensor) of the virtual world would seek to protect his proprietary rights such as the right to derivative works.[40] The license delineates the "scope of permitted use of the licensed subject matter,"[41] which in the present discussion is the virtual world.

Creators of virtual worlds that sell their products for use to participants are likely to codify their obligations into the EULA, which as seen, are generally quite restricted. For most, this means that buyers' rights are "dependent on what the seller is willing to give."[42] The agreement to this EULA can be challenged contractually on the basis that it is unconscionable, but also on the fact of the developer's failure to follow the obligations set out in the license.

As virtual worlds' quality largely depends "on periodic services and enhancements that the licensor provides over the term during which the licensee uses the software,"[43] it is possible to argue that a developer's failure to satisfy this ongoing obligation a breach. As the buying of the license is regulated by law, in particular the ETO and SOGO, if the virtual world software is not fit for purpose, maintained or developed, the buyer is entitled to at the

---

40 Ronald Mann, *Electronic Commerce* (3rd edn, Aspen Publishers, Austin 2008) 534.
41 Passman (n 16) 273.
42 *ibid.* 275.
43 *ibid.* 539.

very least "repair or replace"[44] remedy. If this is not possible, and if the courts find that the developer had failed "its essential purpose" to do so, the courts can "void the licensee's" contractual agreement and award damages[45] to them.

In contrast, the developer of the virtual world, as the seller, is in the advantage with remedies. As the licensor of the virtual world, the developer often would have a "well-capitalized company" with "relatively limited ongoing obligations."[46] The most obvious source for seeking a remedy is where the participant to the virtual world "fails to make a payment due to the licensor."[47] This may either be for the subscription for continued involvement in the virtual world, or the buying of a virtual good from the developer. In such a case, developers, as sellers can of course, seek a lawsuit to recover the money rightfully owed to them. However, as this concerns an intangible world with intangible goods, the "more effective remedy often would be to" simply "terminate the licensee's ability to use the software."[48]

In short, this is to banish the licensee defaulter from the virtual world. This in effect allows the licensor to take the goods away from the licensee without any legal action[49] and is most effective for those that have thoroughly invested in their character in the virtual world. The legality of this remedy although undoubtedly effective, does not seem to have a strong basis again, on authority. The only case found where such action was held legal was *American Computer Trust Leasing v Jack Farrell Implement*,[50]

---

44 Ward Classen, 'Fundamentals of Software Licensing' (1996) 37 *Journal of Law and Technology* 1, 13.

45 *ibid.* 13–14.

46 Mann (n 40) 554.

47 *ibid.*

48 *ibid.* 545.

49 *ibid.*

50 763 FSupp 1473, 1492–493 (D Minn 1991).

(which concerned software and not specifically virtual worlds) which has been regarded as a case that is not highly authoritative considering the situation was only mentioned in the hypothetical and in obiter.[51] Considering the "unduly harsh"[52] nature of this remedy, it remains to be seen whether the British or Hong Kong courts would allow this either.

As to participants in the virtual world who create and sell virtual goods amongst themselves, the remedies available to disputes between them are again, as mentioned briefly, dependent upon the generosity of the EULA in which the developer or seller bestowed upon them. For example, Sony's virtual world, *EverQuest*, allows the "real money transfers of virtual objects, with Sony taking a ten percent commission."[53] However, the EULA specifically "wants it both ways" by expressly and strictly disclaiming "any right of a player to establish a virtual property interest."[54] But by making money of the "existence of saleable virtual property and directly profiting from it," Sony for all intents and purposes is actually admitting and condoning property right interests and their transactions whilst simultaneously denying such rights exist within the framework of its EULA. This rather inequitable arrangement opens up the argument of "equity"[55] and equitable remedies. It must be said that it is only a matter of time before this practice is challenged, and it is noted that the "courts are fully capable of finding the equitable situation"[56] in such instances, although again, cases need to be litigated in full and not settled for this to be found.

---

51 *ibid.*

52 Mann (n 40) 546.

53 Adrian (n 18) 159.

54 *ibid.* 160. See also, Terms of Service, VI Our Sales Policies, On Virtual Goods Generally, available here: <www.soe.com/termsofservice.vm> accessed December 3, 2013

55 Adrian (n 18) 159–160.

56 Leah Sheen, 'Who Owns the Virtual Items' (2010) *11 Duke Law and Technology Review [20].*

In contrast, the virtual world *Second Life*'s EULA specifically allows players to retain the intellectual property rights and copyright to any virtual goods made. The "application of these rules to transactions in virtual items could be easy" then since the rules are similar to "outside of [the] virtual world."[57] Therefore, such interests can be sold or transferred to others, creating property rights, relationships and bringing in the applicability of commercial law in such transactions. Instead, what is difficult is to determine what relevant jurisdictions' commercial law and its allowed remedy is to be applied. This is due to the fact that SOGO, the ETO, and other Hong Kong laws only apply to transactions in the jurisdiction of Hong Kong. This is the same for other countries' legislation. They remain largely jurisdictionally limited legislation backed by old notions of territorial boundaries, something that the Internet does not recognize. Virtual good transactions are likely international transactions and a conflict of law is likely to arise which affects the remedies to which parties may have access.

Unfortunately, the CISG is unable to assist for article 2(a) states that the Convention cannot apply to sales "for personal, family, or household use" which is exactly what the copyright, and intellectual property rights of virtual goods generally fall into. On the whole it must be said that the remedies generally available to parties remain limited and largely dependent upon the text of the EULA in each specific virtual world.

5.   Self-Help and Public Law

Obviously other than resorting to legal action, the most reasonable form of achieving remedies for both buyers and sellers is to engage in dispute resolution. This is especially true for virtual

---

57 Passman (n 16) 281.

worlds and goods. Considering the medium of the Internet, disputes are much more quickly tended to and resolved where the parties engage in negotiating out of disputes. This should obviously the first recourse that parties should seek as the "dispute remain private and the individual parties to the transaction remain in control of the process."[58] It is also incidentally, free.

Nonetheless, self-help is never exactly the best nor the safest way of seeking remedies. A case in China tragically highlights the increasing need for the law to provide adequate remedies to parties in virtual worlds. Qui Chengwei was a player in the virtual world *Legend of Mir II*, where he, after dedicated playing, won a rare virtual sword.[59] He lent it to his friend Zhu Caoyuan, who, without informing him, then sold it on for "£480 in real-world money and ran."[60] He reported this to the authorities but to no avail, being "given no remedy since Chinese laws did not recognize his virtual goods as a type of property."[61] Without a proper remedy, he therefore found and confronted Zhu, and enacted what he felt to be a just remedy—he stabbed Zhu to death. Qui was subsequently sentenced to a "suspended death sentence"[62] for his actions.

The tragic case of Qui clearly shows the increasingly prevalent aspects of virtual worlds and goods in people's lives. People do view goods, even as virtual, as property of theirs. The danger of the virtual world spilling into the real world is very real where the position of buyer and sellers are extremely unbalanced and

---

58 Robert Bradgate and Fidelma White, *Commercial Law* (Oxford University Press, Oxford 2007) 483.

59 Adrian (n 18) 137.

60 Aleks Krotoski, 'Chinese gamer gets suspended death sentence for stabbing a player who stole his virtual sword' (*The Guardian*, London June 9, 2005) <www.guardian.co.uk/technology/gamesblog/2005/jun/09/chinesegamers> accessed December 3, 2013.

61 Adrian (n 3).

62 Krotoski (n 60).

skewed in favor of either one side. Proper remedies are needed for all parties to virtual worlds so as to ensure that disputes are resolved peacefully and in a manner that is fair and impartial. Courts can do that, but only to the extent of their interpretation in legislation and commercial law principles allows them to do.

The United States has strikingly little actual legislation dealing with and regulating virtual property goods and transactions, considering it is one of the biggest markets for virtual worlds. In contrast, Mainland China has started to recognize the existence of virtual property rights and have provided remedies in the criminal law where virtual property has been obtained fraudulently or stolen from their legitimate owner. For example, in *Li Hongchen v. Beijing Artic Ice Technology Development Co*, the plaintiff had spent years spending real money and amassing virtual goods, which was subsequently stolen.[63] The plaintiff then sought help from the developer, who refused, saying that 'the virtual property was merely data and had no real world value' whilst having pocketed some $1200 from the plaintiff in sales.[64] The Supreme Court of China disagreed, and ordered "all game winnings and weapons that had been stolen" to be reinstated to Mr. Li.[65]

The Republic of China (Taiwan) has likewise done so in recognizing property rights in the context of criminal laws,[66] so that those with their virtual goods stolen can seek redress in the sphere of public law. It is uncertain whether this translates to property rights of virtual goods in the context of private and especially commercial law however, although the implementation of such would not require be extremely hard

---

63 Andrea Vanina Arias, 'Life, Liberty and the Pursuit of Swords and Armor: Regulating the Theft of Virtual Goods' (2008) *57 Emory Law Journal 1320, 1321.*

64 *ibid.*

65 *ibid.*

66 *ibid* 1322; See also *Procurator v. Lin Qunzhi,* 82, 777 (Taiwan Nantou District Court)

absent the restrictions given in the EULA. The approaches taken by the courts there that have provided remedies can be said to be creative, and one cannot say it is applicable to Hong Kong, although the courts can take reference to them. Most legislation here in Hong Kong, in the United Kingdom, and the United States however are still inept in dealing with virtual goods and needs reform so as to encompass this ever-increasing aspect of people's online lives.

6. Conclusion

The remedies available for parties in virtual worlds are regrettably quite limited. The very nature of virtual goods makes it difficult to classify as to what exactly they are on a legal basis, which therefore inevitably leads one to provide an analysis that is largely based upon rhetoric and logic rather than sound legal authorities that are directly applicable. Nonetheless, parties do have recourse to some remedies, particularly with reference to contract law due to the prevalence of EULAs in the governance of most virtual worlds. The contractual relationship of licensor and licensee is also a helpful tool for parties to seek remedies in the course of their disputes, though it must be said that the highly unequal power position between buyers versus sellers makes enforcing such remedies quite difficult. This is especially pronounced in virtual world due to the many privileges withheld from licensees by licensors, and is an exciting area for development, especially in Hong Kong law. One of the main reasons for the lack of litigation is because most virtual goods that are part of a commercial transaction in the virtual world have a low monetary value. As such, parties are not likely to engage in expensive litigation when disputes arise. The few cases provide scant guidance as to what remedies are available. This lack of authority and precedence is the most prominent difficulty facing parties in seeking remedies in virtual worlds. Therefore, this is an area that is ripe for reform in commercial law, considering the crucial aspects that virtual worlds are evolving to play in the lives of many individuals and businesses.

17

Second Life, Second Remedies

Anita JAY

1. Introduction

Virtual cash could replace money.[1] Virtual video games are used by governments to train soldiers and promote patriotism.[2] Virtual world is blended with physical and networked environments, where avatars and people interact through "mixed-reality portals."[3] The world of tomorrow is virtual.[4]

A virtual world is defined as "a synchronous, persistent network of people, represented as avatars, facilitated by networked computers."[5] There are 'hundreds of publicly accessible virtual worlds [for] a variety of functions as well as a diverse set of target markets" and it is evident that its popularity is on the

---

1 Joe Lynam, 'Bitcoins: Could Virtual Cash Replace Money?' (BBC, March 31, 2013) <www.bbc.co.uk/news/technology-21990136> accessed December 3, 2013.

2 John Sudworth, 'Chinese Government Promotes Patriotism with Video Game' (BBC, April 2, 2013) <www.bbc.co.uk/news/world-asia-22001123> accessed December 3, 2013; also used to train in the U.S.

3 'Michael Takeo Magruder—Visions of Our Communal Dreams' (FACT) <www. fact.co.uk/projects/robots-and-avatars/michael-takeo-magruder-visions-of-our-communal-dreams/> accessed December 3, 2013.

4 Angela Adrian, 'Law and Order in Virtual Worlds: Exploring Avatars, Their Ownership and Rights' (IGI Global 2010).

5 Mark Bell, 'Toward a Definition of "Virtual Worlds"' (2008) 1(1) *Journal of Virtual Worlds Review* 1, 2.

rise.[6] The wide-ranging functions are reflective of the real world and include economic, military and vocational training, social, entertainment, commercial, education, professional, tourism, medical consultation and psychotherapy.[7]

Virtual commercial transactions are a significant aspect of various virtual worlds, where approximately $1.5 billion worth of user-to-user transactions take place annually.[8] In 2009, a total of $567 million (increased by 65% from 2008) in user-to-user transactions occurred just within *Second Life*.[9] Such trend has continued, where $45 million per month has been recorded in 2010.[10] It is likely that transactions will increase due to the popularity rise of virtual worlds and its users.

Second Life, developed and launched by Linden Lab (LL) in 2003, is the world's leading 3D virtual world environment[11] and the "Next Big Thing."[12] It allows its avatar-represented users (residents) to, *inter alia*, create content and trade virtual property

6 Brian Mennecke *et al.*, 'Second Life and Other Virtual Worlds: A Roadmap for Research' (2008) 22 (Article 20) *Communications of the Association for Information Systems* 371, 372.

7 Michael Passman, 'Transactions of Virtual Items in Virtual Worlds' (2008) 18 *Alb LJ Sci & Tech* 259, 262.

8 Albert Lin, 'Virtual Consumption: A Second Life for Earth?' [2008] *BYU LR* 47, 85.

9 T. Linden, '2009 End of Year Second Life Economy Wrap up' (Second Life, January 19, 2010) <http://community.secondlife.com/t5/Features/2009-End-of-Year-Second-Life-Economy-Wrap-up-including-Q4/ba-p/653078/page/3> accessed December 3, 2013.

10 'Virtual Worlds—Changing the Way Brand Owners Do Business and Protect Their IP' (White & Case, November 2010) <www.whitecase.com/articles-12232010-3/#.UVbED7vnY3k> accessed December 3, 2013.

11 Linden Lab, 'A Vibrant Community and Mixed-Reality Events for Virtual World Business and Policy: Metanomics in Second Life' (2009) <http://secondlifegrid.net.s3.amazonaws.com/docs/Second_Life_Case_Metanomics_EN.pdf > accessed December 3, 2013, 7.

12 Teddy Sherrill, 'A Crisis of Identity: Anonymity and Decision-Making in a Pseudonymous Economy' <www.eecs.harvard.edu/cs199r/fp/Teddy.pdf> accessed December 3, 2013.

and services. These virtual property and services are traded using its own virtual currency (Linden dollars or L$).[13] As Linden dollars are exchangeable for real money (about 250–300 L$ per US dollar) and subject to currency exchange fluctuations,[14] this further encourages commercial ventures.

Residents can buy "just about anything you can imagine" from "thousands of items to choose from," in order to "expand and enrich" their adventures and express themselves.[15] Besides land, residents may purchase clothing, accessories, vehicles, Easter décor and many more. These may be purchased from shops in *Second Life* as well as the official web-based *Second Life Marketplace*.[16] An ideal transaction would involve a deduction of L$ from the buyer and the appearance of the item in the buyer's inventory. However, a virtual world user (who wishes to remain anonymous) has experienced problems of others "taking money and not giving items and taking items and not giving money [yet] cannot do anything about it." This user has clearly highlighted the issues of non-delivery and non-payment between a seller and a buyer as well as the lack of regulation on this.

Despite the many and increasing numbers of commercial transactions, there is, unfortunately, no regulation for any such transactions in the virtual worlds. Where numerous virtual worlds mimic the real world and even use an exchangeable currency, is the lack of regulation justified? If not, what is the way forward? Accordingly, this chapter will examine the current absence of regulation on commercial transactions, notably

---

13   'Shop: Learn' (Second Life) <http://secondlife.com/shop/learn/> accessed December 3, 2013.

14   *ibid.*

15   'Shop: Frequently Asked Questions' (Second Life) <http://secondlife.com/shop/faq/> accessed December 3, 013.

16   'Second Life Marketplace' (Second Life) <https://marketplace.secondlife.com/> accessed December 3, 2013.

sellers' and buyers' remedies, and the need for such remedies. The applicability and practicality of the Hong Kong Sales of Goods Ordinance (Cap 26) (SOGO) will be examined before proposing the way forward. *Second Life*, a virtual world with millions worth of transactions, will be used to exemplify the abovementioned issues. Having said that, an analysis of these issues is applicable to other virtual worlds involving commercial transactions.

2. Absence of and Need for Regulation and Remedies

2.1 *Absence of Regulation and Remedies*

In the virtual world, the concept of law is "rather turbulent."[17] *Second Life* is governed by Linden codes including the Terms of Service (TOS) and Community Standards (CS). While the TOS mainly addresses resident-Linden relationship, the CS deals limitedly with resident-resident relationship. Each potential resident must agree to the terms of these documents in order to gain access to the virtual world.[18]

Disappointingly, the concept of law and regulation is totally absent with regards to virtual transactions. LL adopts a "very laissez-faire approach to how commerce is transacted in the world."[19] *Second Life* Shopping Safety Tips warns that LL "cannot verify, enforce, certify, examine, uphold, or adjudicate any oath, contract, deal, bargain, or agreement made between *Second Life* Residents."[20] The TOS expressly states that "interactions with

---

17 Claude Aiken IV, 'Sources of Law and Modes of Governance: Ethnography and Theory in Second Life' [2009] *Journal of Tech Law & Policy* 1, 10.

18 Aiken (n 17).

19 *ibid.* 13.

20 Jeremy Linden, 'Second Life Shopping Safety Tips' (GuideScroll, September 5, 2011) <http://guidescroll.com/2011/09/second-life-shopping-safety-tips/> accessed December 3, 2013.

other users and your use and purchaser of User Content or user services are entirely at your own risk" (4.3) and LL is "NOT liable for its users' actions."[21]

Simply put, Linden Lab disclaims responsibility for virtual transactions between residents and will not intervene. Moreover, the CS deals with resident-resident misconduct "that is not commercial in nature," including prohibition of intolerance, harassment, assault, unreasonable disclosure of communication, indecency and disturbing the peace (Big Six).[22] To sum up, virtual sellers and remedies are therefore left with no remedies. LL recommends the residents to contact each other to resolve their issues[23] and to submit a support case requesting redelivery;[24] however, these may not always cure faulty transactions. It is useful to note that the recent launch of Direct Delivery, which is simpler, faster and more reliable than the previous Magic Box, is likely to prevent future faulty transactions arising from technical issues.[25] However, such improvement does not exclude the need for regulation.

The opening of Field Fisher Waterhouse, the first major law firm in *Second Life*, is recognition that "[b]usinesses are moving increasingly rapidly into *Second Life* and other 3D Internet environments and their advisers should be there with

---

21 'Terms of Service' (Second Life, December 15, 2010) <http://secondlife.com/corporate/tos.php?lang=en-US> accessed December 3, 2013.

22 Aiken (n 17) 12–13.

23 Linden (n 20).

24 *ibid.*

25 Linden Lab, 'A Look Back at Improvements to Second Life in 2012 and Forward to 2013' (Second Life, December 20, 2012) <http://community.secondlife.com/t5/Featured-News/A-Look-Back-at-Improvements-to-Second-Life-in-2012-and-Forward/ba-p/1775925> accessed December 3, 2013.

them."[26] Despite that, it does not seem to resolve the root of the problem—what will virtual lawyers advise them on if there is no "law" on virtual transactions?

2.2 Need for Regulation and Remedies

As our presence in virtual worlds increase and the numbers and amounts of virtual transactions grow, with real money being invested, so will the likelihood of disputes. As Attorney Claude Aiken IV emphasized, "[a]s commerce in the world increases in quantity and sophistication, users will expect an equally sophisticated method for dealing with disputes."[27] Such expectation is much more than the current absence of remedies, thus urgently calls for reform. Currently, there is a great need for "law-like rules to resolve disputes,"[28] regulate transactions and provide remedies for virtual sellers and buyers.

Virtual transactions are different, yet arguably similar, from real world transactions and e-commerce. Although goods are traded through a different platform and method, virtual worlds such as *Second Life* were designed to mimic the real world. In addition to other facially similar characteristics, virtual goods "just like real-life stuff"[29] are transacted with the use of exchangeable virtual currency. As a parallel to the real world, virtual worlds should have similar remedies for its sellers and buyers. The idea that virtual property is indistinguishable from traditional forms of

---

26 'Field Fisher Waterhouse is First Major Law Firm to Launch Second Life Presence' (Field Fisher Waterhouse, April 23, 2007) <www.ffw.com/latest-news/2007/apr/field-fisher-waterhouse-is-fir.aspx> accessed December 3, 2013.

27 Aiken (n 17) 5.

28 Passman (n 7) 268.

29 Mark Wallace, 'The Game is Virtual. The Profit is Real' (*NY Times*, May 29, 2005) <www.nytimes.com/2005/05/29/business/yourmoney/29game.html?pagewanted=print&_r=0> accessed December 3, 2013.

property is also widely accepted.[30] Residents also acknowledge the notions of fairness in commercial transactions, notably one should get what one bargained for[31] and will want "more nuance and certainty in the enforcement of their expectations."[32] Otherwise, virtual world service providers risk users turning elsewhere, such as real world legal systems or "leaving the world altogether."[33] The provision of guidance on commercial transactions and remedies are, in my opinion, not inconsistent with the overriding philosophy of "hands off" policy; the enforcement of a basic set of guidelines does not restrict residents from transacting freely. Instead, it will ensure smooth transactions and a harmonious community.

3. Applicability and Practicality of Hong Kong Sale of Goods Ordinance

Where *Second Life* mimics the real world and involves transactions of "just like real-stuff" using exchangeable currency, a good starting point would be to consider and compare the Hong Kong Sale of Goods Ordinance (SOGO) with the UK Sale of Goods Act (SOGA)) since the Hong Kong SOGO effectively derived from SOGA. It seems that the "real world law is necessary to some extent to regulate virtual worlds."[34] Residents have also expressed, "I don't see any reason [why] normal laws wouldn't

---

30 Jacob Rogers, 'Note: A Passive Approach to Regulation of Virtual Worlds' (2008) 76(2) *The George Washington LR* 405, 419.

31 Aiken (n 17) 28.

32 *ibid*. 30.

33 *ibid*. 31.

34 Bettina Chin, 'Regulating Your Second Life: Defamation in Virtual Worlds' (2007) 72 *Brook LR* 1303, 1308.

apply."[35] The analysis of the applicability and practicality of SOGO remedies (and duties) of sellers and buyers to virtual worlds will be based on the assumption that "goods" is wide enough to cover virtual goods. Although further discussion is beneficial, virtual goods arguably fall under "chattels personal other than things in action and money [including] emblements, industrial growing crops, and things attached to or forming part of the land which are agreed to be severed before sale or under the contract of sale" (s 2 SOGO, s 61(1) SOGA). There are many parallels between real and virtual property; the intangible nature of the latter should not exclude the possibility of "treating virtual property akin to physical property for legal purposes."[36] Likewise, virtual goods may be existing goods (s 7 SOGO, s 5(1) SOGA) or future goods, to be "created" or acquired by the virtual seller after the making of the contract (s 2 SOGO, s 61(1) SOGA). Having said that, inclusion of virtual goods does not amount to total application of SOGO to the virtual worlds.

As in the real world, virtual sellers also transfer or agree to transfer the property in goods to virtual buyers for a money consideration (s 3(1) SOGO, s 2(1) SOGA). In many cases, virtual buyers are "dealing as a customer" (s 2A SOGO, s 61(5A) SOGA). It is important to note that although residents are represented by avatars, the "substance of their interaction satisfies the legal tests for formulation of viable contracts, with certain other necessities … can form binding relations."[37] In virtual worlds, an offer may be made by in-world email, spoken words or conduct and positive

---

35 Henri, 'Virtual World Transactions' (Google, 19 May 2008) <https://groups.google.com/forum/?fromgroups=#!topic/misc.legal.moderated/zjRop5Ttz8Q> accessed December 3, 2013.

36 Susan Abramovitch and David Cummings, 'Virtual Property, Real Law: The Regulation of Property in Video Games' (2007) 6(2) *Canadian Journal of Law & Tech* 1, 21.

37 Andrew Sparrow, 'The Law of Virtual Worlds And Internet Social Networks' (Gower 2010) 9.

response to that would culminate an agreement to transfer the goods.[38] However, it is unlikely that such virtual contracts will contain elaborate contractual terms. As such, residents should fall back on the basic duties—to deliver (s 29 SOGO, s 27 SOGA), to deliver exact quantity (s 32 SOGO, s 30 SOGA), to pay and accept delivery (s 30 SOGO, s 28 SOGA)—and implied conditions—undertaking as to title (s 14 SOGO, s 12 SOGA) and sale by description and sample (s 15 SOGO, s 13 SOGA). A discussion on the virtual contracts highlights the increasingly important need for virtual contracts "law" and regulation, which is also absent.[39]

Where there is a contract of sale of goods, "[i]t is the duty of the [virtual] seller to deliver the goods, and of the [virtual] buyer to accept and pay for them, in accordance with the terms of the contract of sale" (s 29 SOGO, s 27 SOGA). In addition to that, "[virtual] seller[s] must [also] be ready and willing to give possession of the goods to the [virtual] buyer in exchange for the price" (s 30 SOGO, s 28 SOGA).

Whilst the stipulation of sellers' and buyers' duties and implied conditions deal with the question of what is required of them, the stipulation of their remedies enable them to take action in event of a breach of duty.

4. Applicability of Seller's Remedies under Hong Kong Sale of Goods Ordinance

SOGO provides unpaid sellers with real remedies, which are exercisable against the goods (lien, stoppage in transit, resale) as well as personal remedies, which are enforceable against the buyers (action for price and damages for non-acceptance).

---

38 *ibid.* 10.

39 Passman (n 7).

4.1 Lien

Section 43 SOGO (s 41 SOGA) states that "unpaid seller of goods who is in possession of them is entitled to retain possession of them until payment or tender of the price" where (a) goods have been sold without any stipulation as to credit, (b) goods have been sold on credit, but the term of credit has expired or (c) buyer becomes insolvent. Although not a prominent problem in virtual worlds, unpaid virtual sellers may also exercise lien over the goods in possession and retain for price in the abovementioned situations. Similarly, such a lien should be lost when the seller delivers goods to buyer without reserving the right of disposal, the buyer lawfully obtains possession of goods or by waiver (s 45 SOGO, s 43 SOGA). Although a contract of sale is not rescinded by the mere exercise of an unpaid seller' right of lien (s 50(1) SOGO, s 48(1) SOGA), *RV Ward v Bignall*[40] held that upon notice to the buyer, subsequent failure to pay within by the stipulated date amounts to repudiation.

4.2 Stoppage in Transit

Under s46 SOGO (s44 SOGA), "when the buyer of goods becomes insolvent, the unpaid seller…may resume possession of the goods as long as they are in course of transit, and may retain them until payment or tender of the price." Section 47(1) SOGO (s 45(1) SOGA) clarifies that "[g]oods are deemed to be in course of transit from the time when they are delivered to a carrier by land or water, or other bailee for the purpose of transmission to the buyer, until the buyer…takes delivery of them." The concept of "course of transit" is inapplicable to virtual worlds where virtual sellers send the virtual goods directly to virtual buyers, which

---

40 [1967] 1 QB 534.

will appear in the buyers' inventory.[41] Until virtual worlds have adopted methods of delivery to carriers and bailees, provisions on stoppage in transit will not be an available remedy to virtual sellers.

4.3 Resale

Besides a right of withholding delivery (s 42 SOGO, s 39(2) SOGA), sellers have a right to resell the unpaid goods in possession and recover damages from the breach of contract if such goods are "perishable … or where the unpaid seller gives notice to the buyer of his intention to re-sell, and the buyer does not within a reasonable time pay or tender the price" (s 50(3) SOGO, s 48(3) SOGA). As of now, none of the virtual "perishable goods" including fruits indicate that they are perishable in nature, hence the first ground would not be available. However, virtual sellers may, after giving notice to virtual buyers and the latter fail to pay within a reasonable time, resell the virtual goods to other residents and claim damages from the original virtual buyer. Sellers may also resell and claim damages where there is an express right of re-sale in event of default and the buyer defaults (s 50(4) SOGO, s 48(4) SOGA). This provision is less applicable since, as mentioned earlier, residents are unlikely to stipulate elaborate contractual terms, including the right of re-sale.

4.4 Action for Price

Sellers have an action for price where "property in the goods has passed to the buyer [who] wrongfully neglects or refuses to pay for the goods according to the terms of the contract" (s 51(1) SOGO, s 49(1) SOGA). As stated above, some residents take items without giving money. This failure to pay breaches the

---

41 Dominik Schrank, 'A Trustful Payment System for Virtual Worlds' (Master's Thesis, Graz University of Tech 2009) 30.

buyer's duty to "accept and pay for the goods." In virtual worlds, it is highly likely that the price was part of the contract, where prices are shown with the item (in virtual shops and Marketplace) or was orally agreed. Similarly, sellers may maintain an action for price if buyer fails to pay the price "payable on a day certain irrespective of delivery" (s 51(2) SOGO, s 49(2) SOGA).

4.5 Non-Acceptance Damages

In event of buyers' wrongful neglect or refusal to accept and pay for the goods, sellers may, under section 52(1) SOGO (s 50(1) SOGA), maintain an action for the damages for non-acceptance. Section 52(2) SOGO (s 50(2) SOGA) provides that "the measure of damages is the estimated loss directly and naturally resulting…from the buyer's breach." Such damages are often less than the price and sellers have the burden of reselling to another buyer.[42] In virtual worlds, virtual sellers may also arguably maintain an action for damages for non-acceptance of goods, however, any damages must arise directly and naturally from the buyer's breach. Like the real world, virtual worlds have their own virtual markets.[43] Where there is an available market for the goods, damages are to be assessed according to the least onerous performance—the difference between the contract price and the market price at the time of supposed acceptance or refusal of acceptance (s 52(3) SOGO, s 50(3) SOGA).

Moreover, buyers may be "liable to the seller for any loss occasioned by his neglect or refusal to take delivery, and also for a reasonable charge for the care and custody of the goods" (s 39 SOGO, s 37(1) SOGA) as well as "interest or special damages" (s 56 SOGO, s 54 SOGA). In *Second Life*, there is no restriction

---

42 Paul Dobson and Rob Stokes, *Commercial Law* (Textbook Series, 8th edn, Sweet & Maxwell 2012) 229.

43 Mark Lemley, 'The Dubious Autonomy of Virtual Worlds' (2012) 2 *UC Irvine LR* 575, 578.

as to how much content you have and all items are placed your private storage area (inventory) and goods will not perish.[44] As such, it is unlikely that any charges will be incurred for the care and custody of the non-accepted goods.

5.   Applicability of Buyer's Remedies under Hong Kong Sale of Goods Ordinance

SOGO provides buyers with remedies including rejection of goods, action for non-delivery or late delivery, action for breach of warranty and specific performance. In the U.K., there are additional remedies for consumers which requires seller to repair or replace or claim reduction in price.

5.1 Reject Goods

Where the seller has breached a condition, the breach of which is fundamental and "may give rise to a right to treat the contract as repudiated" (s 13(2) SOGO, s 11(3) SOGA), such as delivering goods not of contractual description, the buyer is entitled to reject such goods. Such right only exists when the buyer has had a reasonable opportunity of examining the goods (s 37(2) SOGO, s 35(2) SOGA) and not accepted them. The buyer has the right to reject when he has not intimated to the seller that he has accepted them, or, upon delivery, does not do any act which is inconsistent with the ownership of the seller (s 37(1) SOGO, s 35(1) SOGA). Moreover, buyers are not bound to return rejected goods (s 38 SOGO, s 36 SOGA), but must do so upon request, even if purchase money has not been returned, as held by the court in *JL Lyons & Co Ltd v May & Baker Ltd* [1923] 1 KB 685. As in the real world, virtual sellers may deliver goods which do not match the contractual description, thus virtual buyers should equally

---

44 'Shop: Learn' (n 13).

have the right to reject such goods. Without such rights, there is a risk of an increase in (intentional) misdeliveries.

5.2   Non-Delivery Damages

An example that entitles the buyer to reject goods is the delivery of wrong quantity (s 32 SOGO, s 30 SOGA). This includes the delivery of "less than" and "more than" the amount he contracted to sell as well as delivery with "mixed goods of a different description not included in the contract." The court in *Shipton Anderson & Co Ltd v Weil Bros & Co Ltd* [1912] 1 KB 574 held that amount in excess is subject to the *de minimis* rule, where buyers are not entitled to reject if the quantity in excess was so trifling and sellers have not claimed for the price. Equally, in virtual worlds, virtual sellers may deliver less than, more than or mixed goods than the ones contracted, thus virtual buyers should be entitled to reject such wrong deliveries, recover paid amounts or not required to pay.

5.3   Breach of Warranty Damages

In the event of sellers' wrongful neglect or refusal to deliver the goods, buyers may, under s 53(1) SOGO (s 51(1) SOGA) maintain an action for damages for non-delivery. This is akin to the sellers' right to maintain an action for the damages for non-acceptance, with the same measure of damages (s 53(2)–(3) SOGO, s 51(2)–(3)). As stated above, some residents take money without giving items. The failure to deliver breaches the seller's duty to "deliver the goods." As such, residents should be able to maintain an action for the damages of non-delivery, "interest or special damages" (s 56 SOGO, s 54 SOGA) as well as specific performance, discussed further in the next section.

5.4   Specific Performance

Under s 54 SOGO (s 52 SOGA), "[i]n any action for breach of

contract to deliver specific or ascertained goods, the court may, if it thinks fit, on the application the plaintiff, by its judgment direct that the contract shall be performed specifically, without giving the defendant the option of retaining the goods on payment of damages." Such judgment may be conditional on "terms and conditions as to damages, payment of the price, and otherwise." It is not disputed that virtual goods are capable of being specific or ascertained. With regards to the different roles, the virtual buyer should "apply" to LL or a future virtual court for it to determine and direct the contract to be performed specifically, without giving the virtual seller the option of retaining the goods on payment of damages. However, it should be noted that, as held in the case, *Behnke v Bede Shipping Co* [1927] 1 KB 649, specific performance would only be granted where damages are an inadequate remedy, due to the uniqueness of the goods. Whilst a certain virtual good may be rare and unobtainable, it can arguably be (re) created.

6. Additional Remedies for Consumers

The UK Sale of Goods Act (SOGA), unlike the Hong Kong Sale of Goods Ordinance (SOGO), gives additional rights to buyers in consumer cases (Part 5A SOGA). These rights include the right to repair or replace the goods (s 48B SOGA), and right to reduce the purchase price by an appropriate amount or rescind the contract (s 48C SOGA). Whilst the concept of "repair" has limited applicability, it seems reasonable to allow virtual buyers to request and have a replacement of goods that do not conform to the contract of sale. This is to be done "within a reasonable time but without causing significant inconvenience to the buyer" (s 48B(2)(a) SOGA). The failure to do so will give rise to the right to require the seller to reduce the purchase price appropriately or rescind the contract. Such right is not unlimited because sellers are not required to replace goods where it is impossible, disproportionate to other remedies, to an appropriate reduction in purchase price or rescission (s 48B(3) SOGA). Although not provided in SOGO, the right to replace is likely to be useful in virtual worlds. However, the right to rescind the contract may seem to be an over-regulation of commercial transactions (contrary to the hands off policy) and does not seem necessary at this stage.

7. Conclusion: A Proposed Way Forward

There is an emerging trend of virtual worlds as well as increasing numbers and amounts of transactions. This evolution should not be hindered by the lack of regulation in virtual transactions and the absence of remedies, thus the *laissez-faire* attitude adopted by Linden Labs has got to change.

The analysis of SOGO (and SOGA) has provided invaluable insight into the possible remedies to virtual sellers and buyers. Due to the unique nature and hands off policy of virtual worlds, SOGO should be adapted to the virtual needs.

A "virtual SOGO" should include the basic duties and remedies of virtual sellers and virtual buyers:

1. It is the duty of the virtual seller to deliver the goods and of the virtual buyer to accept and pay for them, in accordance with the agreed terms of sale.
2. A virtual seller may maintain an action for price where the virtual buyer wrongfully neglects or refuses to pay for the goods according to the agreed terms of sale.
3. A virtual seller may maintain an action for the direct and naturally arising damages for non-acceptance where the virtual buyer wrongfully neglects or refuses to pay for the goods according to the agreed terms of sale.
4. A virtual seller may, after giving notice to the virtual buyer and the latter fail to pay within a reasonable

time, resell the goods to another and claim damages from the original virtual buyer.

5.   A virtual seller may maintain an action for damages for non-delivery where the virtual seller wrongfully neglects or refuses to deliver the goods according to the agreed terms of sale.

6.   A virtual seller may apply for the specific delivery of the goods.

7.   A virtual buyer may replace (where a consumer) or reject goods that are inconsistent with the agreed terms. In a breach of warranty, a virtual buyer may claim diminution of price or maintain an action for damages.

It should be noted that the virtual SOGO is a proposed way forward, subject to further research, modification and precise formulation. Linden Labs should regulate these general principles, where it considers the actions and applications. This may be easily done through the inclusion in the TOS, CS and/or separate policies, where LL reserves the right to change its codes at any time. Ideally, the duties and remedies of virtual sellers and buyers should be regulated and abided in all virtual worlds involving virtual transactions, across different jurisdictions.

In extreme cases where sellers and/or buyers have continuously breached their duties, a transactional blacklist can be introduced to track fraudulent business, and LL should also be able to reprimand, suspend and kick them out of the game entirely.[45] These are additional to the core duties and remedies of virtual sellers and buyers, which, if properly regulated, will undoubtedly, improve the smoothness and success of virtual transactions. Where there is a Second Life, there should be Second Remedies.

---

45   Aiken (n 17) 13.

Part VIII
Use of Real and Quasi Securities in Virtual World Transactions

18

Real and Quasi Security in Virtual World Transactions: Charting New Reforms in Law for a New Reality

Brian Man Ho CHOK

1. Introduction

The emergence of virtual worlds has been remarkable in recent years. It no longer offers simply a platform of entertainment, but also provides a business opportunity for game developers and users to make a fortune. In 2001, the gross domestic product (GDP) of one of the virtual worlds, Noarrath, was equivalent to that of a nation, Bulgaria.[1] In 2005, the size of the trade in virtual items amounted to approximately $200 million US Dollars.[2] In 2008, 40 virtual goods-related businesses shared a total of over $408 million in sales of virtual goods and currencies.[3] These

---

1 Edward Castronova, 'Virtual Worlds: A First-Hand Account of Market and Society on the Cyberian Frontier' (2001) *CESifo Working Paper Series No. 618, 33* <http://papers.ssrn.com/sol3/papers.cfm?abstract_id=294828> accessed December 3, 2013.

2 Tom Leupold, 'Virtual Economies Break Out of Cyberspace, Gamespot' (2005) <www.gamespot.com/news/2005/05/06/news_ 6123701.html> accessed December 3, 2013.

3 Tim Williams, '$408 Million Invested in 40 Virtual Goods-Related Businesses in 2008' (2008) <www.virtualworldsmanagement.com/2008/vgoods2008.html> accessed December 3, 2013.

figures illustrate the trend of growth of virtual world transactions. Since the commercial significance of virtual items has been emerging rapidly, it may enhance the use of security to facilitate transactions in virtual worlds as far as valuable and scarce virtual items are concerned.

In this chapter, the main discussion revolves around the applicability of real-world laws of security on items purchased or sold in the virtual worlds. The first part defines different types of security which may be applied in virtual world transactions and the characteristics of virtual worlds. In the second part, we explore the applicability and suitability of real-world security in nascent virtual worlds and predicts its future application. Lastly, this chapter concludes with recommendations as to how to improve the facilitation of real-world security and corresponding legal reform.

2.   Definitions and Types of Real Security

In *Bristol Airport plc v Powdrill*, the Court adopted the following definition of real security:

> Security is created where a person to whom an obligation is owed by another by statute or contract, in addition to the personal promise of the debtor to discharge the obligation, obtains rights exercisable against some property in which the debtor has an interest in order to enforce the discharge of the debtor's obligation to the creditor.[4]

It is held that real security refers to security in an asset, granting an interest in the assets of the debtor to the creditor with

---

4   [1990] Ch 744 (CA) 760 (Browne-Wilkinson VC).

the aim to secure the debtor's obligations.[5] There are four types of consensual security that are created by agreement between the parties i.e., pledge, contractual lien, mortgage and charge.[6] Other consensual forms of security are considered as quasi-security. On some occasions, real security arises by operation of law (e.g., lien). Among all real security, two further categories generally exist: possessory security (e.g., pledges and common law liens) and non-possessory security (e.g., mortgages and charges).[7] These are discussed in detail below.

2.1 Mortgage

A mortgage involves the transfer of the title to an asset as security for a liability.[8] In *Santley v Wilde,* Lindley MR defined a mortgage as "a conveyance of land or an assignment of chattels as a security for the payment of a debt or the discharge of some other obligation for which it is given…the security is redeemable on the payment or discharge of such debt or obligation…."[9] An equitable mortgage means "a contract which creates a charge on property but does not pass a legal estate to the creditor."[10] Both real and personal property can be subject to a mortgage.[11] No delivery of possession of the mortgaged property is necessary, which means the property concerned may be tangible or intangible.[12] It is noteworthy that the goods to be mortgaged, be it tangible or intangible, must satisfy the definition of "property" at

---

5 Len Sealy and Richard Hooley, *Commercial Law: Text, Cases and Materials* (4th edn, Oxford University Press 2009) 1081.

6 *Re Cosslett (Contractors) Ltd* [1998] Ch 496 (CA) 508 (Millett LJ).

7 Sealey and Hooley (n 5) 1082.

8 Richard Calnan, *Taking Security: Law and Practice* (2nd edn, Jordan Publishing Limited 2011) 39.

9 [1899] 2 Ch 474 (CA) 474 (Lindley MR).

10 1993] AC 295 (PC) (Lord Templeman).

11 Sealy and Hooley (n 5) 1124.

12 *ibid.* 1124.

common law.[13] For tangible assets, they must be capable of being possessed. The mortgagor must transfer his title to an asset to the creditor,[14] by way of security.[15] The purpose of such mortgage is not, *per se*, to grant the mortgagee the absolute entitlement to the asset. Once the debt concerned has been discharged, the debtor is entitled to have the asset re-transferred to him, which is considered as the "equity of redemption."[16]

If the mortgagor defaulted in payment, there are several remedies available to the mortgagee such as power of foreclosure, power of sale, power of appointment of a receiver and power of possession.

2.2 Charge

In *Re Bank of Credit and Commerce International SA (No 8)*, the House of Lords characterized a charge as "a security interest created without any transfer of title or possession to the beneficiary... but is subject to the doctrine of purchaser for value without applicable to all equitable interests."[17] Moreover, in *Carreras Rothmans v Freeman Mathews Treasure*, Gibson J stated that a charge is formed "by an appropriation of specific property to the discharge of some debt or other obligation without there being any change in ownership either at law or in equity."[18] The crux of the statement of Gibson J gives rise to the main difference between a mortgage and a charge. The latter does not involve a right of redemption, but only grants "certain rights to the charge over the property as security for the loan," since there is no

---

13 Calnan (n 8) 44.
14 *ibid.* 39.
15 *ibid.* 40.
16 *ibid.* 40.
17 [1998] AC 214 (HL) (Lord Hoffmann).
18 [1985]1 Ch 207 (Ch) 227 (Gibson J).

transfer of proprietary interest in the assets.[19] A chargee does not possess the right of foreclosure or the right to take possession, but can only apply for an order for sale or appointment of a receiver.

There are two types of charges: fixed and floating. A fixed charge is attached to "ascertained and definite property," while a floating charge is "ambulatory and shifting in its nature… floating with the property which it is intended to affect until some event occurs…"[20] The events referred to is the crystallization of a floating charge, resulting in the transformation of a floating charge into a fixed one. Events such as the appointment of a receiver, liquidation of a company, when the company ceases to run its business[21] or put its business on sale,[22] and automatic crystallization clause[23] gives effect to crystallization.

2.3 Lien

A common law lien is defined in *Hammonds v Barclay*, as "a right in one man to retain that which is in his possession belonging to another, till certain demands of him the person in possession are satisfied."[24] Further in *Tappenden v Artus*, the Court of Appeal held that lien is "the exercise of a right to continue an existing actual possession of the goods, it necessarily involves a right of possession adverse to the right of the person who, but for the lien, would be entitled to immediate possession of the goods."[25] Different from a pledge, a lien requires the retention

19 *Re Bond Worth Ltd* [1980] Ch 228 (Ch) 250 (Slade J).

20 *Illingworth v Holdsworth* [1904] AC 335 (HL) 358 (Lord Macnaghton).

21 *Re Woodroffes (Musical Instruments) Ltd* [1986] Ch 366 (Ch).

22 *Re Real Meat Co Ltd* [1996] BCC 254 (Ch).

23 *Re Brightlife Ltd* [1987] Ch 200 (Ch) 214–15 (Lord Hoffmann J); See also *Fire Nymph Products Ltd v Heating Centre Pty Ltd* (1992) 7 ACSE 365 (Court of Appeal of New South Wales).

24 (1802) 2 East 227 (KB) (Grose J).

25 [1964] 2 QB 185 (CA) (Diplock LJ).

of possession of goods, but not delivery. A common law lien gives rise to "a personal right of the retention to the person in possession of goods belonging to another."[26] In this regard, the lienee is not entitled to dispose if his interest and he does not any implied right to sell the goods which is subject to the lien.[27] There are several categories of liens: common law, statutory, equitable and maritime. The most common statutory lien is the unpaid seller's lien, pursuant to sections 41 and 43 of the Hong Kong Sale of Goods Ordinance (Cap 26). Equitable lien is similar to an equitable charge e.g. the lien of the unpaid vendor of land.[28]

2.4 Pledge

In *Halliday v Holgate*, the court defined pledge as "where by contract a deposit of goods is made a security for a debt, and the right to the property vests in the pledgee so far as is necessary to secure the debt…until the debt is paid off the pledgee has the whole present interest."[29] According to the long-standing ruling in *Coggs v Bernard*,[30] only goods which are transferable by delivery of possession can be pledged. Neither land nor intangibles, such as information,[31] are capable of being pledged.[32] Furthermore, the pledgee is granted a "special interest" in the goods pledged such the power of sale or power of assignment at common law, while the pledgee has no right of foreclosure and can never become the

---

26 *Legg v Evans* (1840) 6 M & W 36, 42 (Parke B).

27 *Donald v Suckling* (1866) LR 1 QB 585 (QB) 604, 610, 612; See also *Halsbury's Laws of England: Vol 28* (4th edn, LexisNexis Butterworth 2009) [719].

28 Louise Gullifer and others, *The Law of Personal Property Security* (Oxford University Press 2007) [4.105].

29 (1868) LR 3 Exch 299 (Exchequer Chamber) (Willes J).

30 (1703) 2 Ld Raym 909.

31 Norman Palmer and Alistair Hudson, 'Pledge' in Norman Palmer and Ewan McKendrick (eds), *Interests in Goods* (2nd edn, Informa Law 1998) 635.

32 Calnan (n 8) 17.

owner of the goods as a pledgee. However, the pledgee is allowed to "exercise the proprietary and possessory remedies against a third party wrongdoe...to recover damages...as if he were the owners."[33]

3.   Definitions and Types of Quasi-Security

Quasi-security has a function as a security. However, it does not confer any security interest in the assets to the creditor since no rights in an asset which bind third parties is involved. Types of quasi-security include, for example, contractual set-off,[34]subordination agreements, flawed assets, and retention of title clauses.[35]

Although the creditors possess a right in the asset, such right is retained by them but not granted by the debtors. Only those rights which are granted by the debtors are categorized as rights by way of security. In *Armour v Thyssen Edelstahlwerke AG,* the House of Lords held that an all monies reservation of title clause did not create a right of security. Lord Jauncey opined that "it is of the essence of a right of security that the debtor possesses in relation to the property right which he can transfer to the creditor, which right must be retransferred to him on payment of the debt."[36] It further commented that without an interest in the asset or the power to dispose of the asset, a debtor cannot use

---

33   Norman Palmer, *Palmer on Bailment* (2nd edn, Sweet and Maxwell 1991) 1382–83.

34   Roy Goode, 'Security: A Pragmatic Conceptualist's Response' (1989) *15 Monash University Law Review 361, 362.*

35   Roy Goode, *Legal Problems of Credit and Security* (3rd edn, Sweet & Maxwell 2003) 12.

36   [1991] 2 AC 339 (HL).

such assets as security.[37]

4.   Virtual Worlds

Virtual worlds are "computer-based interactive environments that simulate real life,"[38] including "community and commerce-focused worlds like *Second Life*."[39] Most virtual worlds share the following characteristics: (1) "a share space, allowing multi-user access; (2) a 3-D graphical user interface that depicts the world visually; (3) immediate and simultaneous interactions; (4) interactivity, allowing users to change or create customized content; (5) social interaction, allowing in-world social groups such as clubs or neighborhoods,"[40] and (6) "the use of an avatar."[41]

Take one of the virtual worlds, *Second Life*, as an example. Users may engage in transactions of virtual products and services with *Second Life's* virtual currency, Linden Dollar.[42] Virtual money earned in the *Second Life* can be converted into US Dollars.[43] In 2008, the exchange rate between Linden Dollar and US Dollar is around $L265 to $1.[44] ($L260 in 2010). Users have

---

37 Fidelis Oditah, *Legal Aspects of Receivables Financing* (Sweet & Maxwell 1991) 5–8.

38 Shannon Thompson, 'Securities Regulation in a Virtual World' (2009) *UCLA Entertainment Law Review 89, 90.*

39 *ibid.*

40 *ibid.* 91.

41 Virtual Worlds Review, 'What is a Virtual World?' (2008) <www.virtualworldsreview.com/info/whatis.shtml> accessed December 3, 2013.

42 Second Life, 'Economy' (2008) <http://secondlife.com/whatis/economy.php> accessed December 3, 2013.

43 Second Life, 'What is Second Life?' (2008) <http://secondlife.com/whatis/> accessed December 3, 2013.

44 Second Life, 'LindeX™ Market Data' (2008) <http://secondlife.com/currency/market.php> accessed December 3, 2013.

an in-world job such as wedding planner, clothing designer, and detective.[45] They can design their own products and own them. To own a piece of land, one must pay a monthly membership fee (e.g., a premium account), or to pay a rent for the land, or buy the land from another users in the *Second Life*.[46]

5. The Nature and Characteristics of Virtual Property and the Suitability of Real and Quasi Security

In determining which type of security can be applied to the assets in virtual worlds, we must first establish the nature of those assets, notably whether the assets can be owned and the status of the users. It is also useful to explore whether the users can own their virtual property in legal sense. These issues are to be discussed in the following sections.

5.1 Intellectual Property?

Prior to the emergence of "virtual-item commodification," game developers generally depended on existing intellectual regimes to safeguard the value and to protect the context of their world.[47] Nonetheless, it has been debated that such regime no longer offered comprehensive protection to game developers, as well as users. For example, although the developers attempted to make it harder to prevent users from including copyrighted art in their

---

45   Second Life, 'Business Opportunities' (2008) <http://secondlife.com/whatis/businesses.php> accessed December 3, 2013.

46   Second Life, 'Frequently Asked Questions from Beginning Landowners' (2008) <https://support.secondlife.com/ics/support/default.asp?deptID=4417&task=knowledge&questionID=5198> accessed December 3, 2013.

47   David Sheldon, 'Claiming Ownership, But Getting Owned: Contractual Limitations on Asserting Property Interests in Virtual Goods' (2007) *54 UCLA Law Review 751, 762.*

advertisement, the result was not entirely desirable.[48] It is further challenged that on the other hand, the "time and creativity used by participants while interacting with the virtual world" might allow them to "seek intellectual protection for the personality of their avatars."[49]

This struggle is highlighted in the *Second Life* situation. The website of *Second Life* specified that "[r]esidents retain intellectual property rights in the original content they create... If you create it, you can sell it, trade it, and even give it away for free...."[50] Meanwhile, section 2.6 of the Terms of Service says that "Linden Lab has the right at any time for any reason or no reason to suspend or terminate you Account...."[51] Section 3.3 furthers states that "[y]ou agree that even though you may retain certain copyright or other intellectual property rights with respect to Content you create..., you do not own the account you use to access the Service... Your intellectual property rights do not confer any rights of access to the Service or any rights to data stored by or on behalf of Linden Lab."[52]

The implication of these conflicting provisions indicates that while recognizing the intellectual property rights within the virtual world, Linden Lab "strived" to protect itself in the way that "such property rights would lessen its control over the game's

---

48 Molly Stephens, 'Sales of In-Game Assets: An Illustration of the Continuing Failure of Intellectual Property Law to Protect Digital-Conttent Creators' (2002) *80 Texas Law Review* 1513, 1521–23.

49 Kelly Slavitt, 'Gabby in Wonderland – Through the Internet Looking Glass' (1998) *80 Journal of the Patent and Trademark Office Society* 611, 619.

50 Second Life, 'IP Rights' (2008) <http://secondlife.com/whatis/ip_rights.php> accessed December 3, 2013.

51 Second Life, 'Terms of Service' (2008) <http://secondlife.com/corporate/tos.php> accessed December 3, 2013.

52 *ibid.*

platform."[53] That leaves the users with a "rusted pistol." That means he holds the intellectual property rights in the products he created, which are assumed to be valued only in *Second Life*, and such rights remain enforceable against any infringers, but he could be denied access at any time without any reason. These rights are of "no value to the users since he could neither sell nor derive value from their rights anymore."[54]

What makes the situation even more ambiguous is that there is a tendency that the courts would equate intangible property to intellectual property "because intangibility has been considered as a "bad proxy" for intellectual property."[55] It is argued that "commercial law must discard distinctions based on physical manifestations of assets and focus instead on the legal qualities of those assets."[56] Such proxy system fails to recognize a certain number of intangible assets which do not fall within the category of intellectual property interests, for instance, domain names, bank deposit accounts, stocks, non-IP virtual property, etc.[57] Thus, it is unclear whether the intellectual property in virtual assets, if any, can still be owned by the users.

5.2 Contract Rights?

Approximately all game developers such as Sony Online Entertainment for "*the EverQuest*", Mindark for "*the Entropia Universe*," and Blizzard Entertainment for "*the World of*

---

53 Steven Horowitz, 'Competing Lockean Claims to Virtual Property' (2007) *20 Harvard Journal of Law and Technology* 443, 448.

54 Megan Caramore, 'Help! My Intellectual Property Is Trapped: Second Life, Conflicting Ownership Claims and the Problem of Access' (2008) *15 Richmond Journal of Law and Technology* 3, 7.

55 Juliet Moringiello, 'False Categories in Commercial Law: The (Ir)relevance of (In) tangibility' (2007) *35 Florida State University Law Review* 119, 137.

56 *ibid.* 120.

57 Joshua Fairfield, 'Virtual Property' (2005) *85 Boston University Law Review* 1047, 1057.

Warcraft" etc., attempt to dismiss the notion that users may have any property rights in the property they own in the virtual worlds by means of End-User License Agreements (EULAs). EULAs are the terms of service between the game developers and the users explicitly stating that no one can own the property in the virtual worlds other than the game developers.[58] Users are refrained from engaging in real-world sale of in-game property.[59] The game developers also reserve the right to remove any account of the users if impropriety arises, or cancel the account without reason.[60]

On the other hand, the game developer of "*Second Life,*" LindenLab, distinct from other game developers, announced on its website that "Second Life's Terms of Service now recognize the ownership of in-world content by the subscribers who make it," and it further stated that "once you've built something, you can easily begin selling it to other residents, because you control rights of your creations."[61] Particularly, in the context of purchasing land, Linden also assured users that "owning land lets you control what happens on that land"[62] including "the rights to exclude, i.e., to prevent others from visiting or building, and the right to alienate, i.e., to sell it."[63]

---

58 Sharon Lowry, 'Property Rights in Virtual Reality: All's Fair in Life and Warcraft?' (2008) *15 Texas Wesleyan Law Review* 109, 119.

59 Bobby Glushko, 'Tales of the (Virtual) City: Governing Property Disputes in Virtual Worlds' (2007) *22 Berkeley Technology Law Journal* 507, 514–17.

60 Entropia Universe, 'End User License Agreement' (2007) <www.entropiauniverse. com/pe/en/rich/107004.html> accessed June 23, 2013, [3]; Second Life, 'Terms of Service' (2008) <http://secondlife.com/corporate/tos.php> accessed June 23, 2013, [2.6]; EverQuest, 'User Agreement and Software License' (2006) http:// help.station.sony.com/cgi-bin/soe.cf.g/php/enduser/std_adp.php?p_faqid=16210> accessed December 3, 2013, 9; World of Warcraft, 'Terms of Use Agreement' (2007) <http://www.worldofwarcraft.com/legal/termsofuse.html> accessed December 3, 2013, 7.

61 Linden Lab, 'Press Release: Second Life Residents to Own Digital Creations' (2003) <http://lindenlab.com/pressroom/releases/03_11_14> accessed December3, 2013.

62 Second Life, 'Knowledge Base' (2009) <http://support.secondlife.com/ics/support/ kbAnswer.asp?questionID=4058> accessed December 3, 2013.

63 Juliet Moringiello, 'What Virtual Worlds Can Do for Property Law' (2010) *62 Florida Law Review* 159, 172.

However, confusion arises since while the website makes reference to the land ownership, the actual Terms of Service does not.[64] The Terms of Service, on its face, only confer a license right to "use the Linden Software and the rest of the Terms of Service."[65] Regrettably, there is no mention of "land" under the definition of "service."[66] It only refers to "servers, software, application program interfaces, and websites."[67]

Looking at the Terms of Service provided for by different game developers, there are reservations as to whether virtual property, including land can be owned by the users. What has been illustrated is that the Terms of Service in *Second Life* "creates and conveys novel and confusing property rights"[68] and also for Microsoft software, the transfer of several crucial rights of "an owner of the material embodiment of the software" to the transferee is recorded in an agreement entitled "license."[69] Although most game developers have chosen to transfer rights in the virtual worlds by way of a license,[70] it failed to define the scope of property rights granted to users.

In the context of software transactions denominated as a "license," courts are generally of opinion that "there is no transfer of ownership of the material object on which the software is

---

64 Second Life, 'Terms of Service' (n 51) [3.1].

65 *ibid.*

66 *ibid.* [1.1].

67 *ibid.*

68 Moringiello, 'What Virtual Worlds Can Do' (n 63) 191.

69 Microsoft, 'Microsoft Office 2008 for Mac Home & Student Edition: Microsoft Software License Terms' (2008) <http://download.microsoft.com/documents/useterms/Office%20for%C20Mac%C20Home%C20and% 20Student_2008_English_8e9a97ac-8ca6-47bc-8039-fc6048a94cdc.pdf> accessed December 3, 2013.

70 Michael Madison, 'Reconstructing the Software License' (2003) *35 Loyola University Chicago Law Journal* 275, 291.

embodied.[71] In *Mai Sys Corporation v Peak Computer, Inc,*[72] the defendants were held not to be the owner of the software on the basis that he had entered into license agreements with the producers. In *Network Solutions, Inc v Umbro International Inc.,* where a judgment creditor applied to garnish Internet domain names to set off debt owed to him by the defendants. The court categorized the name as "the product of a contract for services," which was of great economic value.[73] Thus, the names were not eligible to be subject to garnishee order. The reason why the distinction between contract and property has become cardinal is because creditors only have the rights against property that can be seized or garnished.

Another landmark case is *Bragg v Linden Research Inc.*[74] This case is concerned about virtual real estate in *Second Life*. The Plaintiff, Mr. Bragg, purchased some parcels of land for US$300. Later, LindenLab, discovered that Mr. Bragg has engaged in some inappropriate activities and subsequently decided to eject Mr. Bragg from his $300-worth land based on a claimed violation of its policies. It is reasonable for Mr. Bragg to assume that if a person has ownership over a property, such property cannot be confiscated or taken away by others in the absence of legal process.[75] It is further commented that "even if one's property is subject to a lien or mortgage and one is not living up to ones obligations under the agreement, the other party cannot simply show up and physically remove the occupant from the

71 John Rothchild, 'The Incredible Shrinking First-Sale Rule: Are Software Resale Limits Lawful?' (2004) *57 Rutgers Law Review* 1, 33.

72 991 F 2d 511, 519 (9th Cir 1993).

73 529 S E 2d 80 (Supreme Court of Virginia) 81.

74 487 F Supp 2d 593 (E D Pa 2007).

75 Steven Hetcher, 'User-Generated Content and the Future of Copyright: Part Two— Agreements between Users and Mega-Sites' (2008) *24 Santa Clara Computer and High Technology Law Journal* 829, 835.

property."[76] Mr. Bragg, as a result, contended that his piece of virtual land shall not be removed from him without the inference by the legal system.

Conversely, Linden might rebut on the point that it was crystal clear on the Terms of Service that Linden reserved the rights to deactivate any users at any time. However, such argument attracts criticism. First, if Linden did not expect the users to own the property in a way similar to how it can be owned by a person in real life, it should have laid it down in an unambiguous manner. Secondly, Linden should have notified users that there is a possibility that the property purchased by the users with real US Dollars would be taken away subject to the discretion of Linden and the leave the users no avenue of redress.[77]

Normally the distinction between property and contract is negligible in the context of conveyancing. The law will only enforce a certain types of contract promises because "contracts create in personam rights which bind only the parties to the contract."[78] Apart from the issues of public policy and unconscionability, contract rights are infinitely customizable.[79] This distinction becomes significant only when parties have not agreed to the scope of the right.[80] For instance, when a third party wishes to or is compelled to deal with the right in the property, including "by purchasing it, lending against it, or enforcing rights in it," they must appreciate the scope of the right

---

76 *ibid.*

77 *ibid.* 835.

78 Thomas Merrill and Henry Smith, 'The Property/Contract Interface' (2001) *101 Columbia Law Review* 773, 776–77.

79 Henry Hansmann and Reinier Kraakman, 'Property, Contract and Verification: The Numerus Clausus Problem and the Divisibility of Rights' (2002) 31 *Journal of Legal Studies* 373, 373; See also Thomas Merrill and Henry Smith, 'Optimal Standardization in the Law of Property: The Numerus Clausus Principle' (2000) *110 Yale Law Journal* 1, 3.

80 Moringiello (n 63) 180.

in question and identity the holders of that right.[81] The Brag case was settled before the final judgment. Although there was no case law guidance pertaining to virtual worlds, the District Court for Eastern District of Pennsylvania shared the following insights:

> We believe our new policy recognizes the fact that persistent world users are making significant contributions to building these worlds and should be able to both own the content they create and share in the value that is created. The preservation of users' property rights is a necessary step toward the emergence of genuinely real online worlds.[82]

Concluding from the foregoing analysis, there is a likelihood that future courts will not accept the argument that simply a Terms of Service, which is similar to that of the *Second Life*, would be sufficient to demarcate the rights of the users over the property in the virtual world since "they place excessive restrictions on the economic interests of users."[83] Further, customization of property rights through Terms of Service or other random forms of contract is not permitted at law. Scholars questioned the allowance to virtual world developers to "prevent formation of property rights in the first instance any more than we tolerate other consensual restraints on alienation."[84] There should be a recognized form[85] publicizing such rights.[86]

---

81 Hansmann and Kraakman (n 79) 382–83.

82 *Bragg* (n 74) 596.

83 Gregory Lastowka and Dan Hunter, 'The Laws of the Virtual Worlds' (2004) *92 California Law Review 1*, 50–51.

84 Joshua Fairfield, 'Virtual Property' (2005) *85 Boston University Law Review* 1047, 1083–84.

85 *ibid.* 1084.

86 Richard Epstein, 'Notice and Freedom of Contract in the Law of Servitudes' (1982) *55 Southern California Law Review* 1353, 1357.

5.3   Personal Property?

Commentators have also suggested that virtual property should be justifiably categorized in accordance with property theory and law.[87] As far as the scope of application of property law is concerned, the property in question may not necessarily be real, as noted by the High Court of Australia in *Yanner v Eaton*, that "the concept of property may be elusive … and it may be … that 'the ultimate fact about property is that it does not really exist: it is mere illusion'."[88] It is further commented that property is concerned about "socially approved and power relationship in respect of socially valued assets" in essence, but not simply just a thing.[89] In *Western Australia v Ward*, the High Court of Australia noted the essence of property theory and law, which is to "identify property relationships between people and places or things as rights of control over access to, and exploitation of, the place or thing."[90] These remarks may provide some guidance as to the core features of property i.e., a presumptive right to exclude others (or control over access) and discretion in the manner of exploitation.[91]

In determining whether virtual property e.g., land, would satisfy the definition of property under property law in the real world, it is of great assistance to explore the characteristics of property in the virtual worlds, for example *Second Life*, and compare them with those in the real world.

---

87   Gregory Lastowka and Dan Hunter, 'The Laws of the Virtual Worlds' (n 83); See also Daniel Miller, 'Determining Ownership in Virtual Worlds: Copyright and License Agreements' (2003) 22 *The Review of Litigation* 435.

88   [1999] 201 CLR 351 (High Court of Australia) [17], citing Kevin Gray, 'Property in Thin Air' (1991) 50 *Cambridge Law Journal* 252.

89   Kevin Gray, 'Equitable Property' (1994) 47(2) *Current Legal Problems* 157, 160.

90   *Western Australia v Ward* [2002] 213 CLR 1 (High Court of Australia) [88] (Gleeson CJ, Gaudron J, Gummow J and Hayne J).

91   Hannah Lim, 'Virtual World, Virtual Land but Real Property' (2010) *Singapore Journal of Legal Studies* 304, 316.

First, owners can permit or refuse others from, editing, building, erecting objects upon the land. This is the exclusive right for the owners to carry on construction works or place any objects on it.[92] This is analogous to the fact that anyone, other than the owner or persons with the owner's permission, cannot infringe the use of land belonging to the owner e.g., to erect a statute in one's garden without the permission of the owner.

Secondly, the owner is entitled to bar other users from entering onto the land. The owner may choose to deny access to the public or confined the number of visitors to 50 users. He is also allowed to sell passes to access the land and determine the price of the passes, as well as duration of stay.[93] The ability to restrict access to the land is conspicuously comparable to the ownership of land in the real world where the owners can decide who to get access to his place and who to eject.

Thirdly, owners of land can change the land by "terraforming."[94] "Terraforming" refers to "flattening, raising, lowering, smoothing or roughening the land."[95] They have the choice to change the land in parts or in whole. Further, owners at any time can subdivide his land or resell the land. The liberty to alter the outlook of land and the subdivision of land is similar to the real-life situation, given the permission of relevant authorities.

Last but not least, landowners are liable for a monthly charge called "Land Use Fee" to the producer, Linden, if the land owned by a user in total exceeds 512 square meters.[96] The charge will increase proportionally to the size of the land. This may also be a reflection of land tax in real-life practice.

---

92 *ibid.* 317.

93 *ibid.* 318.

94 *ibid.*

95 *ibid.*

96 Second Life, 'Mainland Pricing and Fees' (2008) <http://secondlife.com/whatis/landpricing.php> accessed December 3, 2013.

These are forceful indicators proposing that the owners of virtual land in *Second Life* possess a presumptive right to exclude and eject other users. It can also be shown that the landowners have the discretion in the manner of exploitation since landowners are permitted to convert the land into any form as they wish. All these similarities in nature between the property in virtual and real world would suffice to give rise to some "some kind of property rights" in many Commonwealth jurisdictions, such as mortgages and leases, in relation to virtual property.[97]

6.   Implications

Having established the difficulties in defining virtual property, the questions remain: "Who has the right to subject the property to security?" and "Can virtual property be a subject matter of security?"

The key concern is that most forms of security require a person who wants to have their virtual property mortgaged or charged to have the title in the property. This is where the fallacy emerges. It is far from settled as to who owns the property in virtual worlds, the game developer or the user? The situation will be the same if the property concerned is intellectual property. If the goods are non-intellectual property, confusion remains, especially when it comes to land. If it is contract right which is similar to what the foregoing section has established, it is very likely that the owners will not have title.

Another striking concern is the nature of virtual property. For some types of security such as pledge and lien, it is required to have physical possession or retention of the tangible assets. There is no room for virtual property to be pledged or subject to a lien since they are intangibles. It may be contended that

---

97 Lim (n 91) 319.

virtual assets can be mortgaged because not only tangible assets, some intangibles can be subjected to mortgages. Nonetheless, the fundamental problem remains that "the common law only recognizes limited categories of intangible asset as constituting property, e.g., shares and debentures of companies, intellectual property. But it is not possible to transfer contract rights or receivables at common law. They are regarded as being purely personal rights, which not capable of being transferred."[98] However, the notion of intellectual property is unclear, as previously illustrated. Even some virtual property, e.g., land in *Second life*, share similarities with land in the real world to a great extent, there exist several difficulties in subjecting virtual land to a mortgage.[99] For instance, there is no registration mechanism of virtual land to illustrate the encumbrances attached to the land in order to determine priority. It is unsettled whether an owner would be able to initiate a claim against other virtual world users when the land is destroyed or ownership is fettered.[100]

The chance of using quasi-security is slimmer since it does not confer any interest in the assets to the creditors. As the situation in virtual world is yet to be clear, creditors will not wish to bear an extra risk to give away its money without having his interest in the assets secured.

There is also uncertainty as to the practicality of the use of security in virtual world transactions. Are there any financial justifications to use security in virtual world transactions and how often does it take place? While acknowledging the potential of generating a greater sum of revenue in the area in the future, there are reservations concerning the need to use security in purchasing

---

98 Richard Calnan, *Proprietary Rights and Insolvency* (Oxford University Press, 2010) 59.

99 Lyria Moses, 'The Applicability of Property Law in New Contexts: From Cells to Cyberspace' (2008) *30 Sydney Law Review* 639, 646.

100 *ibid*, 646.

virtual property. If a user wishes to mortgage his virtual land to a virtual or real bank, a series of implications will follow. There are ambiguities as to how and where the banks could apply for foreclosure of the property when the mortgagor has defaulted on payments. Literally, there are no courts in *Second Life* which would avail mortgagee to exercise that right.[101] In addition, as far as the price of the property is concerned, it is incomparable to that of property in parallel in real life. How economically viable for a real bank to provide a loan in return for a mortgaged virtual land for security when the piece of virtual land is only worth several hundreds or thousands US Dollars, after taking into account the handling charge and administrative cost? If the same application is made to a virtual bank, it may be questioned how administratively workable and practicable it is for the virtual bank to conduct background investigation regarding the ability of the mortgager to repay the loan before approving the application for mortgage. Even though a background check is possible, is it the earning capability in virtual or real world of the applicant that the virtual bank has to take into consideration? The ambivalence suggests that the use of security in virtual world transactions may not be as productive as predicted.

7. Conclusion

Judging from the economic benefit and revenues inherent in the virtual world, "commerce has arisen in virtual worlds and proven hard to destroy."[102] The definition of property and some features of security, for example transferability by delivery, hinder the broader application of real and quasi-security in virtual world transactions. One should bear in mind that "property concerns

---

101 Hetcher (n 75) 835.
102 Andrew Jankowich, 'Property and Democracy in Virtual Worlds' (2005) 11 *Boston University Journal of Science and Technology Law* 173, 179.

relations among people...and property rights do not concern 'things' at all, but intangible resources, e.g., copyright or interests in an ongoing business."[103]

The law must change in order to regulate the relations among people that exist in new forums, such as virtual worlds. These reforms are inevitable because activities and items in the virtual world share many common features to those in real life. For example, banking services in the real world, including the form of deposit services, credit cards, corporate banking and currency exchange, are similar to those offered by banks in virtual world, namely ABN Amro and ING.[104] In response to this, some areas of law have already been altered to adapt to the new environment. One notable example is "prohibition of gaming within the U.S. through gambling regulations, and the regulation of virtual banks and the auctions of land and property in the *Second Life*."[105] Thus, refinement of existing legal doctrines or, adventurously, development of new legal doctrines, are both highly anticipated areas in charting a course for law reforms in a new commercial reality.

---

103 Joseph Singer, *Introduction to Property* (2nd edn, Aspen Law & Business 2005) 231.

104 Essvale Corporation Limited, B*usiness Knowledge for IT in Retail Banking: A Complete Handbook for IT Professionals* (Essvale Corporation Limited 2007) 4.

105 Norman Palmer, *Palmer on Bailment* (3rd edn, Sweet & Maxwell) 1547.

19

Taking Security over Virtual Assets: Is It Really Practical?

Leo Lut Pong YAU

1. Introduction

A virtual world is an online space where people interact with each other and their environment.[1] People usually join the virtual world by making a contract, which contains the terms of services agreement, with the operator of the virtual world. The terms of services agreement outlines the rights and obligations between the service provider and an individual, but there remain some legal vacuums regarding the rights and obligations between one avatar and another avatar in a virtual world.

Linden, of Linden Labs, Inc., has been successful in creating *Second Life*, a highly sophisticated virtual world with a virtual economy, including a virtual bank, virtual land and other virtual properties. In addition, *Second Life* has user created avatars. In the wake of this virtual world, the question of what law governs the commercial transactions in the virtual world is an interesting issue. Some have suggested that the form of contract law should govern the transactions in virtual world. However, there is some uncertainty because the value of virtual items is likely to be below

---

1 Richard A Bartle, 'Virtual Worldliness: What the imaginary Asks for the Real' (2004–2005) *49 NYL Sch L. Rev 19.*

the cost of bring a lawsuit. In addition, most users are generally ignorant about whether law in real world is applicable to virtual worlds.[2] Despite these challenges, the steady increase of virtual commercial transactions means that law must begin to look at whether existing commercial law is sufficient to address these issues.

When the virtual economy becomes more developed and virtual property becomes increasingly more valuable, a set of detailed rules should be put in place to govern virtual transactions, in particular the money lending activities and the lender's rights to secure the payment of a monetary liability. This chapter aims to address the practicability of taking security of virtual assets. The first part will discuss what security means, the nature of quasi-security and the formalities of creating security interest. The second part will focus on applying the concept of real security and quasi-security in virtual world transactions as well as the challenges in application.

2.   What is Security and Quasi-security?

2.1   Security

Security is an advanced and complicated area of law. Professor Goode commented that "[t]he primary purpose of security is to reduce credit risk and obtain priority over other creditors in the event of the debtor's bankruptcy or liquidation."[3]

Real security gives the holder of security a proprietary claim over asset of the debtor and over third parties to secure a debt or

---

2 Michael H. Passman, 'Transaction of Virtual Items in Virtual Worlds' (2008) *18 Alb.L.J. Sci & Tech* 252–292, 271.

3 Louise Gullifer, *Goode on Legal Problems of Credit and Security* (4 edn, Sweet & Maxwell 2008) 1.

obligations, whereas quasi-security does not give the holder of security a security interest because it does not create any rights over asset which binds third party.[4]

In *Bristol Airport plc v Powdrill*, Browne-Wilkinson VC said "security is created where a person to whom an obligation is owed by another by statute or contract, in additional to the personal promise of the debtor to discharge the obligation, obtains rights exercisable some property in which the debtor has an interest in order to enforce the discharge of the debtor's obligation to the creditor."[5]

The definition of quasi-security is not precisely defined; however, Lord Simon said in *National Westminster Bank v Halesowen Pressword and Assemblies*, "quasi-anything gives uncertain guidance in the law."[6] It generally refers to the transaction having the same economic effect as the creation of real security.[7] Quasi-security is intended to fulfil a security function but the creditor has no right in any asset.[8] It is a way of enhancing a creditor's protection against a debtor without creating a security interest.

Personal security is a form of quasi-security, that is a personal undertaking that reinforce the debtor's undertaking to repayment and it is usually given by a third party. A guarantee, indemnity, contractual set-off, subordination agreements, hire purchase agreement, conditional sale agreement and retention of title clause are examples of quasi-securities. In *Armour v Thyssen Edelstahlwerke AG*, the House of Lords held that only rights

---

4 Len Sealy and Richard Hooley, *Commercial Law: Text, Cases and Materials* (4 edn, Oxford 2008) 1082.

5 [1990] Ch 744 (CA), 760.

6 [1972] AC 785 (HL), 808.

7 Richard Calnan, *Taking Security Law and Practice* (2 edn Blackwell, London 2011) 170.

8 Sealy and Hooley (n 4) 1082.

created by debtor can be regarded as rights by way of security. Lord Jauncey of Tullichettle ruled that "it is the essence of a right of security that the debtor possess in relation to the property a right that which he can transfer to the creditor, which right must be retransferred to him on payment of the debt."[9]

2.2 Creation of Real Security

Len Sealy suggested that the process of creation of security interest includes attachment, perfection and priority.[10] Attachment is a process that fastens the security interest on the asset offered as security, thus give the creditor interest in rem against the debtor personally. Perfection is an additional step prescribed by law, so that the security interest can bound third parties. Priority rules are developed through the common law and the law of equity, it determines the ranking of the security interest among rival claims over the debtor's asset.[11]

2.3 Creating Security over Tangible and Intangible Assets

In English law, there are four types of consensual security in English law, namely pledge, lien, mortgage and charge. Pledge and lien are created and taken over tangibles whereas security interests over intangible property can only be created by charge or mortgage.[12]

9 [1991] 2 AC 339 (HL).

10 Sealy and Hooley (n 4) 1084.

11 Sealy and Hooley (n 4) 1086.

12 Gullifer (n 3).

3. The Virtual World

3.1 The Sources of Law in the Virtual World

When users join in a virtual world, individual user makes a contract with the service provider. An End User License Agreement (EULA), the agreement made between a service provider and a user, generally removes the user's property right in virtual world and declares that user has no property rights over virtual items but some service providers recognize the property rights over virtual items in the virtual world.[13] The only source of law in the virtual world would probably be the terms of services agreement or the EULA. Taking *Second Life* as an example, the terms of services agreement outlines the relationship between the user and the developer, Linden.[14]

The agreement recognized that users may have a limited property right on the virtual items, yet Linden reserved the rights to reproduce the contents for marketing and the rights to terminate and delete the contents for whatsoever reason.[15] However, the EULA governs the relationship between an individual user and the service provider, it seems that there are no rules governing the commercial transactions between one avatar to another avatar, and some argued that the regulation in this area is incomplete.

3.2 Virtual Property

Some EULA suggested that a user has no property right to virtual items, and those virtual items are defined as the intellectual property of the service provider. However, there are service

---

13 Passman (n 2) 267.

14 Claude T Aiken IV, 'Sources of Law and Mode of Governance: Ethnography and Theory In Second Life' (2009) *10 PGH. J. Tech. L. & Pol'y*

15 Aiken (n 14) 11.

providers, such as Linden Lab, recognized that users may own a limited property right in the virtual items. It is suggested that the existence of property right is the necessary condition of the system of real and quasi-security. In order to create a security over an asset, the debtor must have property right over the asset being taken as security. If the debtor does not have property right, it would be impossible to create security interest over certain property or the class of property.

However, the nature of transactions in virtual items is an issue of license and not sale. It is argued that "seller's preservation of rights in virtual worlds is based on the fact that the items are parts of computer programs that can be easily copied when permission granted."[16] Because a license is an intangible property, and property rights can be subsisted in the license, the necessary condition of creating security interest is satisfied. The outstanding issue is how do these license rights be transferred inside and outside the virtual world.

3.3 Virtual Currency

Linden Dollars, a virtual currency, is the medium of transaction in *Second Life*, avatars may do simple transactions in the virtual world with Linden Dollars. Virtual currency is generally regarded as virtual token instead of real money or financial instruments, and they are not redeemable for money. According to the terms of services of the Linden Dollar program:

> "Linden Lab hereby grants you a limited license to use the Linden dollars as a virtual token to be held, bartered, traded, and or transferred in second life with other users in exchange for permission to access and use content, applications, services and various user created features, in accordance with these terms of services...

16 Passman (n 2) 275.

> You acknowledge that Linden Dollars are not real currency or any type of financial instrument and are not redeemable for any sum of money from Linden Lab at any time. You agree that Linden Lab has the right to manage, regulate, control, and or modify the license rights underlying such Linden dollars as it sees fit and that Linden Lab will have no liability to you based on its exercise of this right."[17]

Alek Felstiner suggested that, in some situations, users may exchange virtual asset for real money through authorized transaction or grey market transaction yet the game developers do not treat virtual currency as real currency in order to retain full control of those license.[18]

Regardless whether developer named it token or Linden Dollars, the terms of services suggested that it is a limited license granted to the users and such license right could be exercised in the virtual world. In real world, Linden Dollars may be regarded as a property because license right is a form of property.

3.4 Cashing Out

Converting virtual currency to real currency is either limited or prohibited in some jurisdictions. In Japan, the Payment Services Act (Act No.59 of 2009, PSA) prohibits service providers to provide exchange services for converting virtual currency to real currency.[19] It is estimated that the virtual market in China was worth 13 billion yuan in 2008. However, the trade of virtual goods and services among users is prohibited by the Chinese

---

17 Jason D. Arnold, 'Licensing Concerns for Virtual Worlds' (2011) *14(11) J. Intl. Law* 3, 7.

18 Alek Feistiner, 'Regulating In-game Work' (2012) 16(2) *J. Intl. Law* 3, 15.

19 Takashi Nakazaki, 'Real World Excessive Regulations Might Kill Economic Transactions in Virtual Worlds' (2011) 14(12) *J. Int. Law.* 3.

government and the use of virtual currency is restricted to transactions between the issuer and the end users.[20]

The nature of the virtual currency and restrictions of cashing out may not prevent the rules of real and quasi-security to be applicable. The law of security does not require the existence of money. It requires the existence of an obligation to the creditor and that the debtor has property rights over certain asset or class of assets which can satisfy the obligation. Arguably the transaction of virtual assets can be done perfectly within the virtual world notwithstanding the prohibition of cashing out. For example, avatar A wants to buy a sword (a license to use the sword), and avatar B borrows A 5 Linden Dollars (a license to use the Linden Dollars), B may create a charge over A's sword to secure that A will repay the 5 Linden Dollars. The idea of creating a charge looks possible, so long as the user controlling avatar A has some property interest in the sword. Even if virtual currency is merely a license, it does not prevent the concept of security to be applicable in the virtual world.

4.   Whether the Concept of Security Is Applicable in the Virtual World

Like real world, when it comes to commercial transactions, certain rules shall be made and enforced in order to provide a legal framework for virtual transactions. This part will discuss whether the concept of security itself is applicable to virtual world. Look at the concept itself, the purpose of security is to reinforce an obligation. In a well-developed virtual world, where avatars can communicate and trade with other avatars, it is possible that one avatar may borrow from another avatar. If this situation happens, the concept of security may be applicable in order to secure an obligation.

---

20 Nakazaki (n 19).

4.1 Real Security

Professor Goode commented that "All forms of real security... confer on the secured creditor at least two basic real rights, right of pursuit, and the right of preference. The secured party can follow his asset, and its product and proceeds, into the hands of any third party other than one acquiring an overriding title by virtue of some exception to the nemo dat rule; and the secured party is entitled to look to the proceeds of the asset to satisfy the debt due to him in priority to the claims of other creditors."[21]

4.2 Possessory Security

Turning to possessory form of real security, English authorities suggested that pledge and lien is not applicable in the virtual world because pledge and lien required uninterrupted physical possession of the item. In virtual world, assuming the users have a limited property, no users could have physical possession of a virtual item.

Creation of pledge require delivery, it is suggested that "only chattels which are capable of actual, constructive or symbolic delivery can be pledged. Intangible property, such as information cannot be pledged."[22] In *Official Assignee of Madras v Mercantile Bank of India*,[23] Lord Wright ruled that "if the pledgor had the actual goods in his physical possession, he could affect the pledge by actual delivery..." Similar to intangible information, virtual assets or licensed rights of the virtual assets do not have physical existence and, thus, cannot be pledged.

Like a pledge, a lien also relies on the physical possession of the item. In *Hammonds v Barclay*,[24] Grose J ruled that "A lien

---

21 Roy Goode, *Goode on Commercial Law* (3 edn, Butterworth 2004) 623.

22 Sealy and Hooley (n 4) 1094–1095.

23 [1935] AC 53 (PC).

24 (1802) East 227 (KB).

is a right in one man to retain that which is in his possession belonging to another, till certain demands of him the person in possession are satisfied."

Physical possession is the pre-requisite of creating a pledge or lien over certain assets, but virtual items are itself source code or data in the computer system. Virtual items and virtual currency do not have physical existence, they are generally regarded as a right or license or intellectual property of the users, since no one could have a physical possession over those virtual items, possessory security is not applicable in virtual world.

4.3 Non-Possessory Security

Mortgage and charge are categorized as non-possessory security, that is physical possession is not the essence of the creation of such security. In *Santley v Wilde*, Lindley MR ruled that "mortgage is a conveyance of land or an assignment of chattels as a security for the payment of a debt or the discharge of some other obligation for which it is given."[25] Lord Templeman in *Downsview Nominees Ltd v First City Corp Ltd*, ruled that mortgage is "security for repayment of a debt. The security may be constituted by a conveyance, assignment or demise or by a charge on any interest in real or personal property..."[26]

As for equitable charge, *Buckley LJ in Swiss Bank Corp v Lloyds Bank Ltd*, ruled that an equitable charge is said to be created "when property is expressly or constructively made liable, or specially appropriated, to the discharge of a debt or some other obligation, and confers on the charge a right of realization by judicial process, that is to say by the appointment of a receiver or an order for sale..."[27]

---

25 [1889] 2 Ch 474 (CA).

26 [1993] AC 295 (PC).

27 [1982] AC 584 (CA).

If the virtual property, or the license to use that property, is an asset of an avatar or an user, it seems there is theoretically possible to create a charge on a virtual property, virtual land or virtual building. For example, user A who controls avatar A may want to purchase a virtual land and avatar B financed the purchase. Therefore avatar A has an obligation to repay the purchase price of the virtual land in terms of virtual money, and the virtual land purchased, in real world terms, is the right or license to enjoy that virtual land subject to a mortgage or charge. It seems to me that all elements of creating a mortgage or charge are presence. Though real world court may regard the virtual land and virtual currency as a license, there is no common law rule to prevent the creation of a charge over a license to secure the performance of an obligation of repayment of the virtual currency (license).

4.4 Quasi-Security

Quasi-security generally refers to personal promises that may reinforce the debtor's obligation. It does not create the creditor any real interests in the asset. Guarantee is "a contract whereby the guarantor promises the actual or potential creditor of a third person to be responsible to him, in addition to the principal debtor…"[28] It seems to me that no rules could prevent the concept of quasi-security to apply in virtual world.

4.5 Registration System

The main purpose of taking security is to reduce credit risk by obtaining priority over competing secured or unsecured creditors, yet credit risk would very unlikely to be reduced without proper registration systems and rules. In Hong Kong and other common law jurisdictions, registration systems had been established for

---

28 Sealy and Hooley (n4) 1150.

specific charges created by companies and instrument affecting land. The main purpose of registration system is to provide information for the public to ascertain the ownership of asset or whether the assets are encumbered.[29] In Hong Kong, specified charges created by companies have to be registered within five weeks after the date of creation under section 80 of the Companies Ordinance. Registerable charges include a charge on land, book debts, and floating charge on the company's undertaking or property, non registration of registerable charges are void against other creditors.

The Land Registration Ordinance shared similar intention. It was enacted in order "to prevent secret and fraudulent conveyances in the Colony of Hong Kong and to provide means whereby the title to real and immovable property may be easily traced and ascertained."[30]

In commercial transactions, information as to the ownership and whether the property subject to prior encumbrances are of paramount importance, creditors would take into consideration of the quality of security before making loans. Registration systems are vitally important in determining the priorities of competing chargees or mortgagees, without a registration system, it would be very difficult, if not impossible, to ascertain the ownership of the property and the priority of competing charges. Without a proper registration system, charges created upon virtual items in virtual world may face the same difficulties as unregistered security interests in the real word. To facilitate commercial transactions in a virtual world, a registration system similar or equal to that in the real world should be established in the virtual world by the service providers.

---

29 Financial Services and the Treasury Bureau, "Second Consultation Paper in Companies Ordinance Rewrite" (2008).

30 SH Goo and Alice Lee, *Land Law in Hong Kong* (3 edn, LexisNexis 2010) 316.

5. Challenges of Applying the Law of Security to Virtual World Transactions

Though tangibility is not a prerequisite for the creation of all types of security interest, it does not imply that taking security over virtual assets is practicable in the virtual world and enforceable in the real world. There are two major challenges in applying real world law of security to virtual transactions. The first issue is how the rules are incorporated in the virtual world. The second concerns the enforceability of the rules in the real world. Both are discussed in detail below.

5.1 Incorporation

As discussed earlier, the principles of English security law is conceptually applicable in virtual world. The issue here is how to make the users bound all users. Jacob Rogers suggested that "transactions and behaviors that occur completely inside the virtual world should be regulated by a terms of service contract. Second, transactions that occur outside the virtual world but that involve virtual world goods or relationships should be treated no differently than real world transactions that involve similar in nature real world goods or relationships."[31] He also suggested that contracts are sufficient to govern virtual world transactions because the contract is binding.

In an American case *Mortgages Plus Inc v DocMagic Inc*,[32] it had shown that terms of services agreement is enforceable and binding. It is suggested that providers could incorporate third-party beneficiary clauses into the terms of services agreement so as to enable the user seeks relief against another user.[33]

---

31 Jacob Rogers, 'A Passive approach to Regulation of Virtual World' (2008) 76(2) *The George Washington Law Review* 405, 418.

32 No.,03-2582-GTV-DWJ, 2004 U.S. Dist.

33 Michael Risch, 'Virtual Rule of Law' (2008) 112 *West Virginia Law Review* 51.

Incorporation of the law of security into contractual terms would be technically possible since the terms of services agreement could regulate real world transactions as well as enable individual users to take action against another.

5.2 Interaction with the Real World

Identifying which transactions are completely within the virtual world that involves real world relationships could be chaotic. If avatar A owns two plot of lands, but running out of virtual currency to develop the land, and avatar A asks avatar B to finance the development and the loan is secured by a virtual land. At this point the transaction is still completely inside the virtual world. However, the transaction may be regarded outside the virtual world if user A controlling avatar A pays user B in return.

The abovementioned illustration has shown that the first part of the transaction was done in the virtual world whereas the latter part of it was outside the virtual world. Whether the terms of services agreement can sufficiently deal with these transactions remains doubtful. Whether the transactions fall outside the virtual world will also depends on the interpretation of the transactions, it could be argued that the money that user A agreed to pay user B is a honorarium, the virtual loan agreement was completely within virtual world, but it could also be argued that the sum was a consideration or price for the transfer of virtual currency (the license right). If the latter interpretation prevails, part of the transaction falls outside the virtual world, and the real world law of contract should apply. If this is the case, the question will be whether the real world court has jurisdiction to adjudicate the dispute.

5.3 Willingness for Incorporation

Governing virtual world transaction by way of contract is a good idea. The English law of security can be incorporated into the terms of services agreement but the rules governing real security and quasi-security are sophisticated rules. Incorporating those rules together with the registration systems into the virtual world by adapting the real world law of security into the terms of services agreement would not be a practical option for service providers and developers. Currently the terms of services contract governs only the relationship between the service providers and individual owners, the main purpose is to protect the service providers but not to outline the rights and obligations between individual users. Given the fact that the cost of adapting the principles into the terms of service agreement and maintaining the registration system could be exorbitant, it would not create any immediate monetary benefits to the service provider. The service provider would have no incentive to incorporate such complicated principles into the terms of service agreement.

5.4 Enforcement

Assuming the principles of security had been incorporated into the terms of services agreement, it doesn't means that the rules are enforceable in the virtual world or by the courts in real world. When it comes to enforcement, complicated issues such as the priority of creditors and the process of realization would arise. It would inevitably require the service provider to enforce and execute the terms of service contract on the aggrieved avatar's request.

Unlike the government in real world, the service providers are profit makers. They are very unlikely to be interested in policing and enforcing the term of services agreement for the benefit of the users in the virtual world. It is suggested that the service providers are unwilling to enforce contractual terms in real world courts, due to publicity reasons and costs.[34] James Grimmelmann suggested that the service provider deliberately not to enforce

---

34 Risch (n 33) 32.

the law in order to maximize profits.[35] Market-orientated service providers would be reluctant to allocate resources in policing and enforce the virtual transactions between two avatars if no income could be derived from enforcement.

5.5 Jurisdictional Issues

When it comes to remedies, the aggrieved party would have recourse to courts in real world to enforce the obligation or seek other remedies. This section will discuss the difficulties in enforcing transactions in real world courts.

Regarding transactions that involve real world relationships, enforcement would be far more complicated because virtual world is transnational. If an aggrieved users wish to take action in the real world court, the court may or may not have jurisdiction to hear the dispute. Georgios I. Zekos commented that "the Internet collapses traditional notions of location and the significance of geography for sovereignty and legal systems. The jurisdiction of national courts is based upon the domestic laws of individual countries and the legislative jurisdiction of a nation is limited to its territory. Nevertheless, border controls on the Internet are not impossible to develop and implement."[36]

Viktor Mayer-Schonberger suggested that "Real world lawmakers have a number of tools at their disposal to counter the danger of regulatory arbitrage on both the customer and provider level. One counter measure is to limit the ability of virtual world users to participate in virtual worlds provided in another jurisdiction... or they could interdict the sale of virtual goods for real money."[37]

---

35 James Grimmelmann, 'Virtual World as a Comparative Law' (2003) 49 *N.Y.L. Sch. L. Rev* 147.

36 Geirgios I Zekos, 'Cyber-territory and Jurisdiction of Nations' (2012) 15(12) *J. Int'l. Law* 3.

37 Viktor Mayer-Schonberger, 'Virtual Heisenberg: The Limits of Virtual World Regulability' (2009) 66 *Wash. & Lee L. Rev.*

That means enforcement in real world court is possible if all relevant parties are all within the jurisdiction of the forum court but that would hardly ever be the case. It would not be practical for the aggrieved party to take legal action in real world court, if the potential defendants are in another jurisdiction.

Further, the most intriguing question is whether the courts in real world has jurisdiction over an act done by avatar. If an avatar failed to repay the loan, the aggrieved party would be another avatar who lends virtual currency but not the user controlling that avatar. When the virtual world transaction concerns the relationship between two avatars, could the court step in a dispute between two avatars? This situation is not tested in court, there is no case from England or other common law jurisdictions that discussed this issue. Some suggested that avatars do not have any rights on their own to contest in court and it is argued that no real world court could bring avatar to justice.[38] If this position is adopted by the court, the users may not be able to enforce such lending agreement or security arrangement in court because the lending activities was done by avatars, even real world money may be paid in return, and the users are subjected to the jurisdiction of the court.

6.   Conclusion

Law of security reduces the credit risk of money lenders. It helps protect a creditor's interest and facilitates money lending business so that the virtual economy can be developed in a faster pace. In theory, the English law of security could be introduced into virtual world, save as pledge and lien, which is not applicable in virtual world because it requires physical possession. Other forms of non-possessory security such as charge and mortgage would work perfectly in the virtual world. However, incorporation,

---

38 Rogers (n 31).

enforcement and jurisdictional issue remain the major challenges. Services providers would be unwilling to incorporate the rules into terms of services agreement, given that the cost would be prohibitively high and it's not economically viable. The service providers would need additional resources in policing and enforcing the rules in cases of default. When the virtual economy gets in touch with real world, the court is also ill prepared to hear cases that involve virtual world relationships, whether the court has jurisdiction over the plaintiff and defendant and whether the plaintiff could enforce the judgment is uncertain.

The law governing real security and quasi-security is in theory applicable in virtual world provided that the transaction happens exclusively in virtual world and the service provider is willing to incorporate and enforce the rules. If the English law of security is incorporated into the virtual world, seeking relief in real world courts against the defaulting avatar or default events which took place in virtual world would not be a realistic option for the aggrieved parties. Taking security over virtual assets does not seem to be practical as the legal rules governing virtual transactions remain uncertain. When the enforceability of such transactions is in doubt, the benefit of bringing a test case in court would hardly ever justify the cost of doing so.

20

Securing Virtual World Debts via Real and Quasi Security: Challenges and Potential Solutions

Karolina LARSSON

1. Introduction

Since the formation of the Internet, the lives of millions of people have fundamentally changed. The spread of the Internet and related advances in technology are, perhaps, among the most significant happenings in the last decades. These technological advances include innovative improvements in video games with networked games and virtual worlds. Virtual worlds allow people and users to interact and "live" in a shared online environment as animated avatars that look like virtual humans. These avatars live their lives as real people and they consume goods and services, buy real estates, have careers and families, and even build and create virtual items.[1] Avatars buy and sell items with virtual currency that may, in some virtual worlds, be exchanged into real-world currency through a virtual world bank.[2] In fact, the virtual world is a million dollar business. For example, in 2008 over US$580 million was invested in 41 virtual worlds, a

---

1 Shannon L. Thompson, 'Securities Regulation in a Virtual World' (2009) 16 *UCLA Entertainment Law Review* 89, 92–93.

2 Michael H. Passman, 'Transactions of Virtual Items in Virtual Worlds' (2008) 18 *Alb. L.J. Sci. & Tech*, 261–262.

figure that has increased over the years.[3] A number of real people make their main income from creating, selling and buying items in virtual worlds and live off their virtual profits in the real world.[4] Thus, the virtual assets have real money value, which generates significant interest among users to use their assets to secure virtual debts when seeking financial support. Yet, whether virtual property rights are recognized in real world courts is not clear and therefore no safeguards for these kinds of properties or security interests are guaranteed.[5]

Lawyers as well as IT experts and users of the virtual worlds have highlighted the absence of a legal system within these parallel worlds.[6] The huge amounts of money invested in these worlds as well as the increasing number of virtually operating companies and commercial transactions create a need for legislation and a better framework to handle jurisdictional issues. It is not clear whether real world laws cover actions in virtual worlds or if virtual worlds instead are governed by the developers together with the users.

This chapter will examine the potential problems occurring in virtual worlds[7] due to the lack of real world remedies and laws covering the virtual commercial area. In the following

---

3 Benjamin Joffe, <www.slideshare.net/plus8star/virtual-worlds-in-asia-1144427> accessed December 3, 2013; See also 'How big is the RMT market anyway?' (Virtual Economy Research Network.com (VERN), March 2, 2007) <http://virtualeconomyresearchnetwork.wordpress.com/2007/03/02/how_big_is_the_rmt_market_anyw/> accessed December 3, 2013.

4 Garrett Ledgerwood, 'Virtually Liable' (2009) 66 *Washington & Lee Law Review* 818.

5 *ibid.* 813.

6 See Claude T. Aiken IV, 'Sources of Law and Modes of Governance: Ethnography and Theory of Second Life' (2009) *Journal of Technology Law and Policy* 16; See also Thompson (n 1) 93–94.

7 Most sources used in this article refer to facts and circumstances from Second Life, owned by the American company Linden Research Inc., d/b/a Linden Lab, <http://secondlife.com>.

sections, the issues of security interests in the virtual world and whether real or quasi security interests can be used in virtual transactions will be discussed. This also includes an examination of the viability of a virtual bank in fostering secured transactions. Finally, this chapter will discuss potential solutions.

2.   Entering the Virtual World

There is an abundance of different virtual worlds that come in different forms, but often with common elements. These worlds are shared and give access to numerous users. The users are able to navigate the world and allow user interface with other users. In addition, the worlds are real-time and allow users to intermingle instantaneously. Virtual worlds exist as parallel worlds to the real world and exist even when the users are offline. Finally and most importantly, virtual worlds allow users to interconnect with each other in the appearance of avatars, designed illustrations representing the users.[8]

When entering a virtual world and starting interact with other users as avatars, there are often general terms of service that have to be agreed to, by the entering user, in order to get access to an individual account. For example, in the virtual world of *Second Life*, the avatar has to approve to the conduct law, stipulated by the developing company Linden Lab (Linden Research Inc.), and accept a certain term of governance by and within the virtual world. Further, there is an implied consensus and compliance among the avatars that a failure to live up to the standards set by "the gods" will be punished by the "gods themselves." Linden Lab stresses their wish for socially constructed norms established among the members themselves and also express that there is a

---

8   Bobby Glushko, 'Tales of the (Virtual) City: Governing property disputes in virtual worlds' (2007) 22(507) *Berkley Technology Law Journal* 251, 253.

need for paternalism in some extent, in order for the world to be a "commercially viable endeavor."[9] Thus, the laws of this virtual world are, as understood by this and also by the members, rather arbitrary. This is the situation for the majority of the virtual worlds.

Thus, there are no clear rules regarding conduct for the members and avatars within the virtual worlds even considering the existence of end-user license agreements. In addition, there is nothing that infers a higher degree of responsibility upon the members but the mere virtual social codes developed by themselves. Frankly speaking, the virtual worlds govern themselves.

Further, there is often a requirement to agree to an End User License Agreement (EULA) before entering the virtual world. This contract removes the user's property rights within the virtual world, such as the right to virtual items, built or created by the user by using tools provided by the developer of the virtual world. Instead, such rights belong to the developer and company behind the virtual world. In some virtual worlds, trading of virtual items and money into real money is considered illegal and the risk for potential damage to the economies of the virtual worlds is thereby taken into consideration when making the rules.[10] Yet, this is not the case of all virtual worlds. Many of them allow exchange of virtual currency into real money.

3.   The Virtual Banking Crisis

The large extent of commercial transactions within the virtual worlds means that there is a demand for banks in the virtual worlds. There are platforms within the virtual worlds where

---

9   Aiken (n 6) 10–11.

10   Passman (n 2) 263–264.

users buy virtual currency with real currency.[11] The exchange and transfer of real money makes it possible for the avatars to withdraw virtual money from virtual ATM's to use in their daily lives.[12] Yet, there are main differences between virtual and real currencies. There is no virtual central bank that issues currency. Instead, the users or developers themselves govern this aspect of the virtual transaction. There is no banking system that grants loans for the users, or avatars. Thus, there is no organized monetary system or authorization within the virtual world and no means to control the money supply. The stability in goods and money is instead determined by collective consumption and joint decisions by the users themselves.[13]

The unregulated situation has led to moments of crisis within the virtual economy, causing effects in the real world. The development and implementation of virtual investment banks began stormily in *Second Life*. At first, the virtual bank business was entirely free and unregulated, since there is no monetary control or authority, which led to dramatic consequences. In 2007, a virtual investment bank, Ginko Financial, the biggest in *Second Life* so far, promised investors enormous amounts in return. However, this was a Ponzi scheme[14] where the owner was unidentifiable and about US$750,000 was gone and never to be repaid to the depositors. This led to chaos among the avatars and to the implementation of a new policy in the virtual world, enforced by Linden Lab as the owner and developer of *Second*

---

11 Dominik Schrank, Trustful Payment System for Virtual Worlds: Design and Implementation of a Payment System for Virtual Worlds (Master's Thesis, Graz University of Technology 2009) 28.

12 Earn2Life, <www.earn2life.com/wiki/Earn2Life.com_ATM> accessed December 3, 2013.

13 Hiroshi Yamaguchi, An Analysis of Virtual Currencies in Online Game (2004) available at Social Research Center <www.ssrn.com/abstract=544422> December 3, 2013.

14 A fraudulent investment operation.

Life, which allowed exclusively real world banks with licenses to operate within *Second Life*. Yet, this has not brought any greater clearness to the legal issues of banking, the commercial relations, or security interests in the virtual worlds.[15]

4.   Security Interests

What can be concluded so far is that the lack of adequate regulations within the virtual worlds can cause damage for people using these services. Another issue to be highlighted is the need for money lending services in the avatars' lives. As the life of an avatar to a great extent corresponds to a human life, it also includes issues of financial situations and need for capital sources in the form of, for example, house loans or credit, to buy a bigger car for a growing avatar family. The business of selling and buying virtual land assets is enormous. One of the most respected virtual real estate moguls has become a real world millionaire by purchasing and selling virtual land assets.[16] As the land assets increase in value, the demand for house and land mortgages grow, virtually that is. Further, the users are able to create new items and buy other virtual items with a high real money value. Consequently, this creates a demand for securing virtual loans via such items.

4.1   Real and Quasi Security Interests in the Real World

Initially, the definition of security interest in common law will be presented. Securities are instruments that provide protection for the creditor and at the same time encourage the creation of

---

15 Clare Chamber-Jones, *Virtual Economies and Financial Crime: Money Laundering in Cyberspace* (Eward Elgar Publishing Limited 2012) 51–52.

16 Aiken (n 6) 7, 27.

capital, reduce the cost of credit and are private sources of rescue for bankrupt businesses by offering a safety net for the lender. By providing security, the lender has a defensive form of control. A security interest is created when a person, the creditor, to whom an obligation is owed by another person, the debtor, by statue or contract, obtains rights exercisable against certain property or asset in which debtor has an interest. Such a right is obtained in order to enforce the promise of discharge of the debtor's obligation to the creditor.[17] The essence of a security is two folded: (1) the secured creditor can force a sale of the property and use the profits to pay the secured debt and have priority over unsecured creditors; and (2) the debtor, on the other hand, can assert a resale of the creditor's right of realization on payment of the secured debt and redemption.

There are different forms of security interests. A distinction can be made between real and quasi securities, or secured and unsecured, and depending of what kind is given, there will or will not be a transfer of the asset.

Real securities include mortgages, charges, pledges and lien. These kinds of securities give the creditor the right to a specific property that the debtor, or a third person, owns. Pledge is a transfer of possession between the debtor and the creditor. Under common law, the debtor, under certain circumstances, has the right to redemption of the secured property and the creditor has the right to sell the secured asset. Lien is a security of interest in a property that includes a transfer of possession. A lien cannot generally be enforced by sale, except permitted under contract, by trade usage or statute. Mortgage is a transfer of interest in a property and also shares, and thus, is a transfer of title of the asset where the debtor has the right to get it back when the loan

---

17 Roger LeRoy Miller, *Fundamental of Business Law: Summarized Cases* (Cengage Learning, 2013) 337–338.

is repaid. Charge means that some rights over the property are vested to the creditor and no complete transfer of title is made.[18]

There are several other types of arrangements, having the same effect as real securities, in a commercial sense, which the debtor and creditor can use instead. These quasi securities do not truly construct a security interest in a property or asset. A debtor can instead offer a personal security, where a third party provides financial support in favor to the creditor. These favors are divided into guarantees and indemnities. A guarantee is when a third person, the guarantor, will be liable to the creditor if the debtor cannot and does not repay his debt. Thus, there is no security in any asset given, merely a secondary obligation that relates to the primary obligation, i.e. the loan between creditor and debtor. An indemnity is comparable to a guarantee but is providing a greater extent of protection than a guarantee as it is a primary obligation, which will continue even if the underlying contract is cancelled, set aside or if the obligations of the debtor are discharged.[19]

4.2 Virtual Security Interests

We will now go back into the virtual world and examine what options that are available to the avatars in seeking financial support, capital and credit and what safeguards are offered, if any.

One example where a system of security interests was introduced was in the virtual world *Eve Online*. *Eve Online* was established and developed by an Icelandic game company,[20] set in a science fiction space setting.[21] With 300,000 players paying

---

18 Agasha Mugasha, *The Law of Letters of Credit and Bank Guarantees* (The Federation Press 2003) 108–109; Brian Coyle, *Bank Finance* (Financial World Publishing 2002) 59–66.

19 *ibid.* 65.

20 CCP hr or CCP Games (Crown Control Production).

21 <www.eveonline.com/> accessed December 3, 2013.

US$15 a month to use the platform, in 2009, this virtual world is a successful business. There are over 60 market places within the world and about 5,000 items purchased in over one million transactions every day with the virtual currency, interstellar credits (ISK). The huge amount of transactions led to a demand for credit for users with lack of ISK. This was recognized by a mogul who established a bank, within the world, granting loans for virtual depositors if pledging their virtual assets as collateral. The possessions of the virtual assets were transferred from the moneylenders to the bank, such as spacecrafts. The bank accumulated almost nine trillion ISK in deposits among 6,000 users and the new security interest system was a success. However, the bank's top executive stole about 8%[22] of the deposits, amounting to about US$4,700, from the bank and sold them for real world money on the black market exchange within the virtual world. It was revealed that the 27-year old financial shark used the money to put down his own deposit on his real world house and pay real world medical bills. There were 5.5 trillion ISK withdrawn from the bank by the depositors. Eve Online is trying to recapture the money but the legal situation is unclear. The only concrete measure taken so far was to exclude the fraudulent player from the virtual world, in accordance with the terms and conditions of *Eve Online*.[23]

The scandal was called the start of the "virtual version of the credit crunch."[24] Similar to the case of Ginko Financial, real world finances were affected by the unfair acts of virtual actors. People are in need of real world enforcement agencies to govern

---

22 Reports are still unclear.

23 Chamber-Jones (n 15), 52–53; Rob Cox, 'A Virtual Bank With Real Woes' (*New York Times*, 2009) <www.nytimes.com/2009/06/15/business/15views.html?_r=0> accessed December 3, 2013.

24 'Billions stolen in online robbery' (BBC News.com, July 3, 2009) <http://news.bbc.co.uk/2/hi/technology/8132547.stm> accessed December 3, 2013.

the virtual worlds. As described in media,[25] and even by a Court of Appeal judge,[26] the virtual customers are tempted to appeal to a higher authority when these kinds of scandals appear.

There is clearly a demand for a system of security interests within these virtual worlds since users invest real money in virtual assets, and not surprisingly want to access the value without selling them when buying new items or land assets. The nature of security interests and the transfer of possession in real securities relations surely invite fraudulent behavior, in the real world as well as in the virtual. The existence of a, maybe rather boldly expressed, complete legal system in the real world, including legislation with remedies of aggrieved persons and legal institutions striving for justice, is one of the most fundamental pillars of a successful and well-functioning society. This, of course, also includes the real and quasi security arrangements surrounded by safeguards. In the situation of *Eve Online*, the security arrangements were not secured in that there were no safeguards for the users who let the bank get possession of their assets, and the risk of getting into the hands of wrong people, as always exists in the real world as well, was realized. The arrangement was not optimal in this sense. On the other hand, the virtual pledge arrangement as such must be considered as a "secured debt" and "a real security" as the term is understood in the real world, since the bank's money was protected by the possession of assets and the user was granted the loan because of the protection provided by the asset.

As avatars in worlds like *Second Life* and *Eve Online* can have jobs, careers and earn virtual money, they can be seen as more or less creditworthy. An avatar with high creditworthiness should be able to provide quasi security to virtual banks when another

---

25 Cox (n 22).

26 See statement by Judge Richard Posner, Passman (n 2) 268.

avatar is seeking financial support from it. Yet, these kinds of secondary obligations means risks on the side of the creditor, since the debtor remains in possession of his or her assets and there is merely another users or avatars fortune and possibility to pay, to protect the creditor. If a personal security is arranged, what options are there for the creditor to do when the payment is absent and the guarantor all of a sudden closed his or her account? This surely hampers the willingness of virtual banks to engage in such quasi security arrangements.

5. Recognition of Virtual Property Rights

What is missing in the cases of *Eve Online* and Ginko Financial is the recognition of virtual property rights by the real world and real remedies through real world dispute resolution mechanism. There are transfers of assets with actual value which are transferred to the banks in exchange for loans (or returns in the case of Ginko). In the real world there are safeguards to protect people in their daily lives and businesses when engaging in transactions. Security interests are secured by law, which provides a right to remedies in the case of default of security arrangements.

It has been argued that agreements entered into within virtual world should be enforceable, as in the real world. The clauses of the EULA's excluding the user from ownership in favor of the developing company and not recognizing virtual world transactions as transfer of ownership have been claimed by scholars to be unenforceable. This is because the EULA's are seen as one-sided, lacking evidence of true negotiation, are complicated, and not subject to change.[27]

Moreover, the essence of contract law is that the contract

---

27 Passman (n 2) 266–269.

generally enforces the "reasonable expectations" of the parties. These expectations change with each transaction and contract. In virtual world transactions, when parties enter into electronic contracts, the expectations of users of the virtual worlds are to be considered. A study of this shows that, in large part, the expectations are based on the fact that virtual items or assets are parts of computer programs that easily can be copied when permissions are granted. Therefore, in short, the character of virtual items or assets are more like licenses, not true ownerships, as licenses are used for property with these characteristics.[28]

Further, another scholar has discussed the legal form of virtual items and concluded that the relationship between a user and a developer of an online world is similar to that of a landlord and tenant, where the user leases the online space and the developer can be held liable for losses under such lease contract.[29]

Virtual property rights have been recognized by the real world and liability has been vested on the developing company behind the virtual world. In *Li Hongchen v Beijing Arctic Ice Technology Development Company*[30] in 2003, also called the "first virtual property right dispute case," the question of liability of virtual theft was determined. A player created a virtual weapon that was stolen by a hacker who broke into the players account. The player contacted the gaming company and claimed the weapon was worth real money and that he wanted compensation since the company not provided a safe server. The company did not take any measures, did not compensate him and held that virtual assets

---

28   Passman (n 2) 269–273.

29   Ledgerwood (n 4) 821–822.

30   *Li Hongchen v Beijing Arctic Ice Technology Development Company*, Beijing Chaoyang District People's Court, no 02877 (19 December 2003); Jay Lyman, 'Gamer Wins Lawsuit in Chinese Court Over Stolen Virtual Winnings' (Technewsworld.com, December 19, 2003) <www.technewsworld.com/story/32441.html> accessed December 3, 2013)

merely were "piles of data" with no real value.[31] The court found that the company was negligent in securing its servers against attack, and the negligence was directly responsible for the loss of the player's property. Thus, the court recognized a property right in the virtual goods.[32]

Moreover, the court stressed the lack of security in the servers of Arctic Ice and held the company liable for the theft of the player's virtual items and also the player's ranking. It is hard to establish any further conclusions regarding the liability of the developer since the argument in the case was rather wide and open-ended. However, an indication of established ownership of virtual goods by the player appears to be confirmed by the decision since the developer had to compensate the player for the loss. On the other hand, it is not surely necessary to make a distinction of who really owned the item in this case since the person suffering the loss from lost or defective items is not always the owner of the item (e.g., a rental relationship).

Thus, what seems clear is that the case of Arctic Ice acknowledges the value of virtual assets and by this arguably also accepts virtual property rights to virtual assets. It is hard to say to what extent this case is applicable to other virtual situations due to the unclear situation of jurisdiction of virtual worlds. The question is whether a Chinese case applies in another jurisdiction or merely when there is a Chinese person aggrieved of their property rights and suing a real world company for omissions or acts online.

Arguments made by different developing companies behind the virtual worlds reject a wide extent of their own liability, for actions in the virtual world, since this would be overwhelming for them. This argument has been questioned and even if a

---

31 Hong Xue, *Cyber Law in China* (Kluwer Law International 2010) 81–82.

32 Glushko (n 8) 262.

vested liability on the developers would mean an overwhelming responsibility—and this claim is well founded—is this reason enough for courts to deny such liability?[33]

The situation of the pledges in *Eve Online* creates further questions concerning the liability. This case did not concern breaches of the duty in securing the servers. It concerned a fraudulent person seated on a high position within a virtual bank acting in a virtual world. Can a person, independent from the company behind the virtual world, be held liable for selling the pledged assets without authority?

6.   A Uniform Law for Virtual Transactions

Scholars have compared virtual stocks to real stocks and highlighted the need for protective legislation since virtual stocks carry the typical characteristics of real stocks.[34] Parallels to virtual securities can surely be drawn from this comparison because virtual security arrangements can mirror real security arrangements. Potential legislative solutions for transactions in the virtual world have been presented and brought up in the debate. One scholar suggests a narrow, flexible and fair uniform law for virtual transactions. Such law would cover virtual commerce and recognize virtual sellers as merchants.[35] Furthermore, such law could provide for the rights of the seller, such as an unpaid seller's lien. This brings security interests to the fore and would make security arrangements possible. It would allow a seller to exercise its right to enforce the lien when a payment by the virtual buyer is absent.[36] Yet, it is not clear whether the rights

---

33 Ledgerwood (n 4) 814.

34 Thompson (n 1) 117.

35 Passman (n 2) 285–289.

36 cf. Sales of Goods Ordinance (Cap 26) 1979, s 41.

of a virtual seller already exist by applying real world law in virtual world scenarios. Even if there are several grounds to form such arguments, the issue of jurisdiction still exists. Which real world law of the sale of goods will apply when a user in France sells virtual items to a buyer in Hong Kong within the same virtual world and the buyer does not pay? A uniform law could contribute to a more just and predictable system.

7.　Conclusion

Online worlds and games are a huge business, involving real money and real lives. The value of virtual items and avatars is recognized by several court decisions and frequently highlighted in debates and by scholars. Virtual world economies mirrors real world economies and the development of virtual economies is rapidly increasing. However, legal institutions and regulations have not caught up to real world trends.

There is a willingness to secure virtually granted loans and credits with virtual items or assets, as demonstrated in the case of *Eve Online*. This scenario along with Ginko Financial shows that a trust relationship can be built between users as well as between users and the developer. The absence of safeguards and lack of remedies for people trusting the system creates a gap in the regulation of the virtual economy.

Even though the EULA's of most virtual worlds precludes the transfer of possession and transfer of title of virtual goods, thus reinforcing the rights of ownership in developing company, the notion and concept of property rights are arguably too strong and rooted to be held back by these vague, complex and one-sided agreements. Therefore, the EULA's may not always be enforceable given the apparent trend in courts around the world that recognize the real value of virtual items. Once this is established it might arguably pave the way for the recognition of real and quasi security interests within the virtual world.

Moreover, the question of liability in online frauds must be solved by determining what legal relationships there are to be found within the virtual world, between users and between users and the developing company. It is suggested that the relationship between user and developer is to be seen as a license agreement, where the user has a license to create and use the virtual space. This surely invites the users to use such licensed space to create and buy items with which they secure loans, as we have seen in the case of *Eve Online*. In *Eve Online*, there was a virtual transfer of possession of virtual items. The question is to what extent the developer can be held liable for the theft done by the top executive of the virtual bank, under a lease contract. The Chinese case does not really answer this since there is no situation of hacking into the system but merely an abuse of trust within the virtual world. An opinion by a member of the crowd demonstrates the reckless risk taken by others in transferring possession virtually: "I guess if you're dumb enough to give real money to a virtual bank without knowing who owns it, what they will do with your money, and what the reserves there are, maybe you deserve to lose it?"[37] Of course measures of care have to be taken when engaging in online actions. However, such rash conclusions are too simple. Fraudulent behavior must be prevented everywhere when there is a possibility that real money and real life can be damaged.

The question remains as to who shall be held liable? A wide responsibility of developing companies would in some ways cave the whole idea and notion of the virtual world as "free zones," as the developers themselves argue. A uniform law which considers users, and thereby avatars, as subjects under law would instead vest responsibilities into the users and provide real world remedies and let users seek higher authorities is suggested. In the

---

37 Christine Hurt, 'Banking Crisis: Has Second Life become Pottersville?' (The Conglomerate.com, January 29, 2008) <www.theconglomerate.org/2008/01/index.html> accessed December 3, 2013.

case of *Eve Online*, the thief would have been held liable for the theft. The sub issue here is the anonymity provided online as it is abused to hide real identities' from their fraudulent behavior. This is met by only letting real world banks with real licenses open branches in the virtual worlds. This is already happening, and the Swedish Financial Supervisory Authority granted, in 2007, a license to a real bank to operate in a virtual world.[38] The problems induced from anonymity are here reduced and tackled since users who secure loans with assets will be provided the same services and safeguards as in the real world. If the CEO in a real bank would sell of pledges, the legal issue of liability will be solved by real world regulations. This is a step towards a safeguarded security system within the virtual arena and leaving behind a system where the only guaranteed sanction is excluding the criminal from the community by erasing his or her account.

Another aspect that could be highlighted is the practical consequences of making virtual security arrangements involving real world values and money more attractive, by surrounding them with safeguards. Virtual loans online are arguably very accessible, efficient and convenient for users. However, there is always a risk with providing this kind of financial support without real world verifications and due diligence of virtual world avatars. I think it can be argued that the use of credit to finance a luxury online life is not included in the real world policies behind the security interest and arrangements. There is also a risk of ordinary people with limited finances to be stuck in virtual debts with high virtual values where assets of real money value are secured. The two folded relationship between debtor and creditor is therefore not balanced, and the arrangement cannot be seen as equal to a real security arrangement.

---

38 MindArk, 'Virtual World Entropia Universe Issue First Ever Virtual Banking Licenses for $400,000' (MindArk Press Release, May 8, 2007) <www.mindark. com/press/press-releases/documents/EntropiaUniverse_Virtual_Bankin_Licenses. pdf> accessed December 3, 2013.

While virtual worlds continue to proliferate within the online world, there is little concrete legal knowledge and regulations governing virtual worlds, especially in the area of real and quasi security. Lawyers, legislators, and developers would benefit from recognizing the reality of commercial transactions within the virtual world and take measures in establishing a framework to ensure the availability of real solutions to virtual problems in the area of the law of security.

Part IX
Money Lending and Banking Virtual World

21

The Regulation of Banks and Money Lending Activities in the Virtual World

Joyce Yuk Han LIANG

1. Introduction

Banks and money lenders are usually strictly regulated, especially in developed countries. As such, people might have a false impression that virtual banks and money lending activities in the virtual world are also well regulated to protect their interest. In fact, the legal regime for the virtual world is not comprehensive and public interest may be violated as a result. This chapter discusses the operation of money lending activities by the money lenders and banks in the virtual world and analyzes whether the laws regulating money lenders and banks in the real world should apply to the virtual world for the public interest.[1]

Among various jurisdictions, Hong Kong's regulation of money lenders and banks will be used as the primary reference since Hong Kong has one of the highest concentrations of banking institutions in the world, with 70 out of the world's largest 100

---

1 "Real-world regulators around the world have been examining virtual world economies and contemplating whether real-world regulation should be applied to financial transactions conducted in-world, for example, applying securities and payments regulations with a view to providing greater consumer protection to virtual world users." Janet Lo, 'A Virtual Fortune: Consumer Protection for Banking and Consumer Fraud in Virtual Worlds' (January 2012) <www.piac.ca/consumers/consumers_should_be_wary_of_risks_in_virtual_worlds/> accessed December 3, 2013.

banks having an operation in Hong Kong. In addition, the Hong Kong banking industry is well regulated with no bank failure for the past 20 years.[2]

Following this brief introduction, section 2 discusses the licensing and deposit protection scheme whilst section 3 discusses the requirement on the financial standing of the bank. Then section 4, section 5 and section 6 depict the requirements of the shareholders of a bank, the due diligence requirements on customers, the restricted use of the name "bank" and excessive interest rate respectively. Finally, this chapter analyzes the legal charge on property for bank financing.

2.   Licensing and Deposit Protection Scheme

2.1 Virtual World

A Swedish video game developer, namely Mind Ark, claimed that it has been granted approval for a real banking license by the Swedish Finance Supervisory. It seemed that Mind Ark was going to be just like a bank in the real world. It was to be backed by a US$60,000 deposit insurance scheme, facilitating a way for customers to pay bills online, accepting deposits by offering interest-earning accounts and making loans to its customers.[3] The next few sections will look at the characteristics of Mind Ark's banking license as compared with real world banking.

---

2 Kelvin Wong and Theresa Tang, 'Hong Kong Calms Depositors After Bank East Asia Run' (Bloomberg, September 25, 2008) <www.bloomberg.com/apps/news?pi d=newsarchive&sid=aYRtj2VUKLZc > accessed December 3, 2013.

3 'Online game gets banking licence' (BBC News, March 20, 2009) <http://news. bbc.co.uk/2/hi/technology/7954629.stm> accessed December 3, 2013.

2.2 Real World

In Hong Kong, pursuant to Sections 15 and 16 of Banking Ordinance, the approval to operate a licensed bank is given by the Hong Kong Monetary Authority. The Hong Kong Monetary Authority grants authority to a restricted license bank or a deposit taking company which are sometimes referred to as authorized institutions.[4] In contrast, sections 11, 12 and 13 of Money Lenders Ordinance give the Licensing Court the authority to grant a license to authorized money lenders.[5]

2.3 Application to be a Bank

Hong Kong maintains a three-tier system of deposit-taking institutions, namely, licensed banks, restricted license banks, deposit-taking companies. They are collectively known as authorized institutions.

Per Section 11 (Banking business restricted to licensed banks) of the Banking Ordinance, a banking business cannot be carried out by anyone except by a bank. An individual as well as a director or manger of a company who contravenes this section commits an offence. Under the Section 2 of Banking Ordinance, banking business means the business of either or both of the following-

> "(a) receiving from the general public money on current, deposit, savings or other similar account repayable on demand;
>
> (b) paying or collecting cheques drawn by or paid in by customers."[6]

According to Section 15(1) (Application for authorization) of the Banking Ordinance, a company must obtain the authorization

---

4 Banking Ordinance (Cap 155) 1986, ss 15–16.

5 Money Lenders Ordinance (Cap 163) 1980, ss 11–13.

6 Banking Ordinance (Cap 155) 1986, s 2.

of the Monetary Authority in order to carry on businesses of banking, or deposit-taking as a deposit-taking company or a restricted license bank.[7] Even the Monetary Authority grants the authorization, it may impose some conditions for the authorization as it thinks fit as per Section 16 (Grant or refusal of authorization).[8]

2.4 Application to be a Money Lender

Pursuant to Section 11 (Determination of application for license) of Money Lenders Ordinance, the licensing court may grant a license upon the hearing of an application to be a money lender lodged under section 9(5) of Money Lenders Ordinance.[9]

Nevertheless, there is a valid period for the license. As per Section 12 (Effect and duration of license) of Money Lenders Ordinance, the money lender is authorized to engage in the business for a period of 12 months with the license, and as per section 13 (Renewal), "a licensee may apply for the renewal of his license within a period of 3 months prior to the expiration."[10]

2.5 Revocation and License to Operate as a Bank or Money Lender

Both banks and money lenders are subject to revocation of license and suspension of operation.

Banks are subject to the Banking Ordinance. In accordance with section 22 (Revocation of authorization) of Banking Ordinance, "the Monetary Authority may, after consultation with the Financial Secretary, propose to revoke the authorization of an authorized institution,"[11] and with section 24 (Temporary

---

7 Banking Ordinance (Cap 155) 1986, s. 15.
8 Banking Ordinance (Cap 155) 1986, s. 16.
9 Money Lenders Ordinance (Cap 163) 1980, s 11.
10 Money Lenders Ordinance (Cap 163) 1980, s 12.
11 Banking Ordinance (Cap 155) 1986, s. 22.

suspensions) of Banking Ordinance, in any case where the powers of the Monetary Authority become exercisable under section 22 with respect to an authorized institution and "the Monetary Authority considers that it is necessary in the interests of depositors or potential depositors of the institution; or it is advised by the Financial Secretary that he considers that it is in the public interest, that urgent action be taken, the Monetary Authority may, after consultation with the Financial Secretary by notice in writing served on the institution suspend its authorization for a period not exceeding 14 days; or if he thinks fit, by reason of the urgency of the matter or otherwise, so suspend such authorization without giving the institution an opportunity of being heard." [12]

Money lenders are subject to the Money Lenders Ordinance. By section 14 (Revocation and suspension) of Money Lenders Ordinance, a licensing court may revoke or suspend any license granted, based on the application of the Registrar or the Commissioner of Police. [13]

2.6 Deposit Protection Scheme Ordinance

The Ordinance, which was enacted on May 5, 2004, provides for the establishment of a deposit protection scheme in Hong Kong. The scheme was enhanced in 2010. The deposit protection limit was raised to HK$500,000 per depositor per bank since January 1, 2011. The scheme is managed by the Hong Kong Deposit Protection Board. All licensed banks in Hong Kong are members of the scheme unless otherwise exempted by the Board.

In summary, the regulation to the start-up of the bank by Mind Ark looks quite simulated to that in real world, with license granted by a government authority and depositors protected by deposit insurance scheme. However, the amount of protection

---

12 Banking Ordinance (Cap 155) 1986, s 24.
13 Money Lenders Ordinance (Cap 163) 1980, s. 14.

limit for the Mind Ark is not very adequate, in view of the increasing transaction amount in the virtual world.

3.   Requirement on the Financial Standing of a Bank

3.1   *Virtual World*

On May 8, 2007, after months of active bidding, the creator of the virtual world *Entropia Universe*, MindArk PE AB announced the results of the first virtual banking license auction.[14] The five licenses were sold for an astounding total of SEK404,000 (equivalent to about HK$480,760) to five parties. In order to get the virtual banks operational, each winner must add SEK100,000 (equivalent to about HK$119,000) as operational capital.[15]

3.2   *Real World*

When looked at from the perspective of real world regulations, specifically in Hong Kong, the virtual world companies may not have been able to obtain licenses as quickly. For example, pursuant to schedule 7 (Minimum Criteria for Authorization) of Table A of section 153 (Transitional provisions in relation to Banking (Amendment) Ordinance 1997) of Hong Kong's Banking Ordinance, the Monetary Authority requires that the company presently has, and will if it is authorized continue to have, adequate financial resources for the nature and scale of its operations as per the below sections:

> "(a) in the case of a company seeking authorization to carry on banking business in Hong Kong, the aggregate

---

14   Elina Heng, 'Virtual World Entropia Universe Issue First Ever Virtual Banking Licenses For $400,000' (EntropiaPlanets, May 8, 2007) <www.entropiaplanets. com/wiki/Virtual_World_Entropia_Universe_Issue_First_Ever_Virtual_Banking_ Licenses_For_$400,000 > accessed December 3, 2013.

15   *ibid.*

amount of its paid-up share capital and the balance of its share premium account is not less than HK$300 million or an equivalent amount in any other approved currency;

(b) in the case of a company seeking authorization to carry on a deposit-taking business as a deposit taking company, the aggregate amount of its paid-up share capital and the balance of its share premium account is not less than HK$25 million or an equivalent amount in any other approved currency;

(c) in the case of a company seeking authorization to carry on a deposit-taking business as a restricted license bank, the aggregate amount of its paid-up share capital and the balance of its share premium account is not less than HK$100 million or an equivalent amount in any other approved currency." [16]

The Monetary Authority, pursuant to Section 16(10) of the Banking Ordinance, has issued a "Guideline on Authorization of Virtual Banks" (the "Guide"), which sets out the principles which the Monetary Authority will take into account in deciding whether to authorize "virtual banks" applying to conduct banking business in Hong Kong. As per the Guide, virtual banks are required to maintain minimum levels of share capital of HK$300 million (including paid-up share capital and balance of share premium account). [17]

It is also stipulated in section 102 (Liquidity ratio) of Banking Ordinance that every authorized institution shall maintain a

---

16 Banking Ordinance (Cap 155) 1986, Schedule 7 (Minimum Criteria for Authorization)

17 Hong Kong Monetary Authority, 'Guideline on Authorization of Virtual Banks' (September 2012) <www.hkma.gov.hk/media/eng/doc/key-functions/banking-stability/guide-authorization/Chapter-9.pdf> accessed December 3, 2013.

minimum liquidity ratio of 25% in each calendar month.[18]

In summary, unlike the virtual world in which the license to operate a bank is sold by the operator of the virtual world, in the real world, both the Hong Kong Monetary Authority and the Licensing Court are the government authority for granting the license to operate a bank and the license of money lender respectively. In addition, in Hong Kong, the Hong Kong Monetary Authority has a much higher requirement on the financial standing of a "virtual bank" with minimum share capital of HK$300 million versus that of about HK$119,000 in the virtual world of Entropia Universe. Obviously, the more stringent requirement on the financial condition of the bank will protect the depositors more.

4.   Background of the Shareholders of the Bank

4.1 Virtual World

The winners for the auction to run a bank in the virtual world *Entropia Universe*, include Avatar Janus JD D'Arcwire, a Russian Internet Payment Provider MONETA.ru, a virtual night club owner Jon NEVERDIE Jacobs, a virtual celebrity and entrepreneur Anshe Chung, and an avatar "Jolana Kitty Brice" (a so called veteran *Entropia Universe* participant and entrepreneur who wishes to remain anonymous).[19]

4.2 Real World

As per the Guide, "a virtual bank incorporated in Hong Kong should be at least 50% owned by a well-established bank or

---

18 Banking Ordinance (Cap 155) 1986, s 102.

19 Heng (n 13).

other supervised financial institution in good standing in the financial community and with appropriate experience. This is in keeping with the long-standing general policy of the Hong Kong Monetary Authority that a person who intends to hold 50% or more of the share capital of an authorized institution incorporated in Hong Kong should be a well-established bank (or equivalent institution). Where a bank enters into a 50–50 joint venture with a non-bank, the bank (or equivalent institution) should have the right to appoint the chairman of the virtual bank and the chairman should have a casting vote.

According to the Guide, the ownership of virtual banks is particularly important because they are usually new ventures which could be subject to higher risks in the initial years of operation and it is essential that there should be a strong parent behind to provide guidance and financial support. In this regard, the parent bank (or equivalent institution) should undertake to provide additional capital and/or liquidity support when such a need arises. The Hong Kong Monetary Authority would also expect the parent bank (or equivalent institution) to play an active role in overseeing the business and affairs of the virtual bank through its participation in the board of directors."

Also, according to Section 71 (Chief executives and directors require the Hong Kong Monetary Authority's consent) of Banking Ordinance, a person must obtain consent in writing of the Hong Kong Monetary Authority in order to the chief executive or a director of an authorized institution incorporated in Hong Kong.[20]

In summary, in the virtual world, the identity of the shareholders of a virtual bank is not required to be disclosed. Some shareholders can maintain their anonymous identity.

---

20 Banking Ordinance (Cap 155) 1986, s 71 (Chief executives and directors require the Hong Kong Monetary Authority's consent).

However, even for those who disclose their identity, the disclosed identities are not the real names of the shareholders. In the real world, the Hong Kong Monetary Authority requires the shareholding of a virtual bank should be at least 50% owned by "a well-established bank or other supervised financial institution in good standing in the financial community and with appropriate experience" in order to ensure that the virtual bank should be run by experienced bankers.

5.   Due Diligence Requirements on Customers to Prevent Money Laundering

5.1   *Virtual World*

In the virtual world, the identities of the players can be concealed. The players are not obliged to disclose their real names and source of funds for deposit into the virtual bank. "Virtual world transactions involve payment methods and 44% of surveyed senior anti-money laundering compliance officers in North America and Europe cited virtual world payment systems as a great threat to banks."[21]

5.2   *Real World*

In the real world, Part 2 (Customer Due Diligence Requirements) of Schedule 2 (Requirements Relating to Customer Due Diligence and Record-keeping) of Section 91 of Hong Kong's Anti-Money Laundering and Counter-Terrorist Financing (Financial

---

21 Tony Savvas, 'New payment systems heighten fraud concerns at banks' (Computer Weekly, November 13, 2008), <www.computerweekly.com/news/2240087466/New-payment-systems-heighten-fraud-concerns-at-banks> accessed December 3, 2013.

Institutions) Ordinance requires that a financial institution must carry out the customer due diligence measures listed below before establishing a business relationship with the customer;

"(a) identifying the customer and verifying the customer's identity on the basis of documents, data or information provided by—

    (i)   a governmental body;

    (ii) the relevant authority or any other relevant authority;

    (iii) an authority in a place outside Hong Kong that performs functions similar to those of the relevant authority or any other relevant authority; or

    (iv) any other reliable and independent source that is recognized by the relevant authority;"[22]

In summary, knowledge on the real identity of the depositors and their source of fund is the minimum requirement for due diligence to prevent money laundering. Without such requirement on the banking industry in the virtual world, it will be very difficult to tackle the problem of money laundering in the virtual world. In fact, in May 2013, "law enforcement officials in the United States brought charges against a group of men who allegedly manufactured an Internet-based currency to launder about $6 billion in ill-gotten gains, a sign of authorities' rising concern with digital cash."[23]

---

22 Anti-Money Laundering and Counter-Terrorist Financing (Financial Institutions) Ordinance (Cap 615) 2012, s 91.

23 Reed Albergotti and Jeffrey Sparshott, 'U.S. Says Firm Laundered Billions' (*The Wall Street Journal*, May 28, 2013) <http://online.wsj.com/article/SB10001424127 887323855804578511121238052256.html> accessed December 3, 2013.

6.   Restricted Use of the Name "Bank" and Excessive Interest Rates

6.1 Virtual World

In the virtual world, no matter whether the entity obtains its license to operate a bank from a government authority or not, it can still name itself as a bank and usually there is no restriction on the interest rate charged by the "bank."

6.2 Real World

According to Section 97 (Restrictions on use of name "bank") of Banking Ordinance,

> "(1) Subject to this section, any person, other than a bank, or an institution which is recognized as the central bank of the place in which it is incorporated, who, without the written consent of the Hong Kong Monetary Authority given generally or in any particular case or class of case-
>
> (a) uses the word "bank" or any of its derivatives in English, or any translation thereof in any language or uses the Chinese expression "*ngan hong*," or uses the letters "b," "a," "n," "k" in that order, in the description or name under which such person is carrying on business in Hong Kong; or
>
> (b) makes any representation in any bill head, letter paper, notice, advertisement or in any other manner whatsoever that such person is a bank or is carrying on banking business in Hong Kong, commits an offence." [24]

Regarding the prohibited interest rate, Section 24 (Prohibition of excessive interest rates) of Money Lenders Ordinance stipulates

---

24 Banking Ordinance (Cap 155) 1986, s 97.

that "any person (whether a money lender or not) who lends or offers to lend money at an effective rate of interest which exceeds 60% per annum commits an offence."[25]

While authorized institutions ("AIs"), which are generally banks, are exempt from complying with the Money Lenders Ordinance ("MLO"), section 12.3 of the Code of Banking Practice sets out certain restrictions on the charging of interest rates by AIs. It stipulates that the annualized percentage rates charged by AIs should not exceed the level presumed to be extortionate under Section 25 of MLO, i.e., 60% per annum, unless the AI concerned can justify that such rate is not unreasonable or unfair.

In summary, in the virtual world, some people may be misled to believe that the entities using "bank" in their name are well regulated with good financial standing just like those in the real world. In addition, they may not be aware that the interest rate charged by these "banks" could be extremely high. Each of these potentially damaging aspects of virtual banks should be regulated as in the real world to protect the participants of the virtual world.

7. Legal Charge on Property for Bank Financing

7.1 *Virtual World*

To buy, sell and trade goods, services or land in the virtual economy of *Second Life*, users have to exchange real money into the official virtual currency, the Linden dollar.[26]

---

25 Banking Ordinance (Cap 155) 1986, s 24.

26 Grace Wong, 'How real money works in Second Life' (CNN Money, December 8, 2006) <http://money.cnn.com/2006/12/08/technology/sl_lindex/> accessed December 3, 2013.

The operator *Second Life* claims that almost all virtual land in "belongs" to users or residents of *Second Life*, and new users can "buy" land. [27]

Although it seems that users can "own" land in *Second Life*, the rights of users are unclear. On April 15, 2010, four users of Second Life filed a suit to seek damages of US$6 million against Linden Lab, the operator of *Second Life*, which was alleged to lure users to believe that they can "own" virtual land but subsequently claimed that land is a "service" that Linden Lab controls and can cancel. One comment from a legal expert is that "In these worlds, we are somewhere in like the 16th century" in terms of legal systems, said James Grimmelmann, an associate professor New York Law School who focuses on technology and the law.[28]

Theoretically, land in the virtual world has value and virtual banks can lend money to the landlord against the mortgage of the land.

7.2 Real World

According to Section 44 of Conveyancing and Property Ordinance ("CPO"), a mortgage can be effective at law only by a charge by deed expressed to be a legal charge.[29]

As per Section 3 (Priority of registered instruments; effect of non-registration) of Land Registration Ordinance, the registered deed and other instruments in writing, will have priority over the other according to the sequence of the respective dates or registration.[30]

---

27 'Second Life: Buy Land: Frequently Asked Questions' (Official Website of Second Life, June 11, 2013) < http://secondlife.com/land/faq/> accessed December 3m 2013.

28 John D. Sutter, 'Can people actually 'own' virtual land?' (CNN, May 10, 2010) < http://edition.cnn.com/2010/TECH/05/10/virtual.property.second.life/index.html> accessed December 3, 2013.

29 Conveyancing and Property Ordinance (Cap 219) 1984, s 44.

30 Land Registration Ordinance (Cap 128), s 3.

7.3 Rights and Remedies of Mortgagee

If the mortgagor defaults in payments to the mortgagee, the mortgagee can sue the mortgagor to pay the principal and interest. The mortgagee is also entitled to pursue other remedies such as foreclosure, sale, taking possession and appointing a receiver, among which sale is the most usual enforcement method.[31]

7.4 Power of Sale

The CPO implies a power of sale in mortgage by deed unless it is expressly excluded. The mortgagee is only able to sell without incurring liability to mortgagor when any one of the three conditions has been fulfilled:

> "(i) Some interest payable under the mortgage must be one month or more in arrears; or
>
> (ii) The mortgagee must have served notice (Section 62 of CPO) on the mortgagor requiring repayment of the loan, and the mortgagor must have failed to repay the mortgagee for one month or more after receipt of notice; or[32]
>
> (iii) The mortgagor must have been in breach of some other condition in the mortgage. (Paragraph 11 of the fourth schedule of the CPO) The assignment by the mortgagee shall assign to the purchaser all the mortgagee's interests in the mortgaged property subject to prior interests. It discharges the property from the mortgage and any subsequent mortgages and interests to which the mortgage in focus has priority (Section 53 and fourth schedule of CPO)."[33]

---

31 Halsbury's Laws of Hong Kong: Volume 5 (LexisNexis 2011) para 280.625.

32 Conveyancing and Property Ordinance (Cap 219) 1984, s 62.

33 Conveyancing and Property Ordinance (Cap 219) 1984, s 53 and Schedule 4.

The proceeds of sale shall be distributed in the order stated in Section 54 of the CPO.

> "Any money received by a mortgagee or a receiver from the sale or other dealing with the mortgaged land or any security comprised in the mortgage shall be applied according to the following priority —
>
> "(a) in discharge of all rent, taxes, rates and other outgoings due and affecting the mortgaged land;
>
> (b) unless the mortgaged land is sold subject to a prior encumbrance, in discharge of that prior encumbrance;
>
> (c) in payment of the receiver's lawful remuneration, costs, charges and expenses and all lawful costs and expenses properly incurred in the sale or other dealing;
>
> (d) in payment of mortgage money, interest and costs due under the mortgage, and any residue shall be paid to the person who, immediately before any sale or other dealing, was entitled to the mortgaged land or authorized to give a receipt for the proceeds of the sale of that land." [34]

In summary, in the virtual world such as in the *Second Life*, the land registration system is clearly not adequate enough to protect the rights of the players. As such, at this stage, the banks or money lenders in the virtual world cannot rely on land as a security for lending. For money lending based on security, such as land etc., to be possible in the virtual world, there should be rules and regulation resembling to those in the real world, such as the Land Registration Ordinance and the Conveyancing and Property Ordinance.

---

34 Conveyancing and Property Ordinance (Cap 219) 1984, s 54.

8. Conclusion

In July 2008, *Second Life* banned gambling, an event which caused a bank run that resulted in Ginko Financial being unable to repay US$750,000 that it had collected from its investors.[35] This was as a result of the loosely regulated operating environment of money lending in the virtual world. In order to better protect the interest of the participates in the virtual world and to ensure greater credibility and protection of the money lending or banking industries in the virtual world, a comprehensive legal framework similar to that in real world is necessary.

---

35 Musa Fubber, Ethics & virtual worlds Second Life as a Case Study (*Tabah Analytic Brief*, No. 9, June 2009).

PART X
CONSUMER PROTECTION IN VIRTUAL WORLD TRANSACTIONS

22

The Applicability of Real World Laws in Protecting Consumers of Virtual World Transactions: An Analysis of Hong Kong and the United States

Michael Ka Hei LAU

1. Introduction

With advanced technology today, everyone can have a second life. It is not that we can re-start our life after death but we may live in another universe, by creating and representing ourselves as avatars in online software platforms called virtual worlds. Virtual worlds are not exactly parallel to our familiar real world because players often spend real money in acquiring in-world items (e.g., virtual currency, lands, weapons etc).[1] Some virtual world platforms even allow avatars to exchange virtual currency for real money, making it possible for real world individuals to make a fortune through virtual activities.[2] As more online ventures are developing, virtual worlds are gaining economic power. Naturally, virtual world players will be more concerned with protections

---

1 'In-world' refers to 'in virtual worlds.'
2 Greg Lastowka, 'User Generated Content and Virtual Worlds' (2008) 10 *Vand. J. Ent. & Tech. L.* 893.

regarding the transactions of virtual properties.[3]

An important issue within virtual word commercial transactions is the protection of consumers such as virtual world players when they decide to enter into a contract to purchase virtual world property. The focus of this chapter is to examine the consumer protection in virtual world transactions and how it may or should be developed. Firstly, we review the basic mechanism of the transactions of virtual properties in the context of protection of virtual property. Next, we will evaluate the in-world consumer protection rules and mechanisms. In addition, we will analyze the consumer protection laws in Hong Kong and its applicability to virtual world transactions by comparing consumer protection laws in Hong Kong with those of the United States.

This chapter concludes by arguing that current law is barely developed and far from effective in protecting consumers in the virtual world. It is still a long way to a well-established consumer protection regime which makes people feel safe when they are purchasing in-world properties.

2.   The Virtual Landscape and In-world Items

In the virtual world, players are represented as avatars and interact with one another without necessarily revealing their real identities. By having personal access to and control over their accounts, a user can affect the way his avatar behaves and also the surrounding virtual items. Other players can see the avatar possess certain property in the virtual world. The market for selling non-replicable virtual items involving in-world currency, or even real money, grows from the persistent availability of

---

3   Viktor Mayer-Schonberger, 'Napster's Second Life?: The Regulatory Challenges of Virtual Worlds' (2006) 100 *Nw. U. L. Rev.* 1775.

virtual properties within the virtual landscape.[4] This important feature leads to in-world economic development in which virtual properties are transferred from one avatar to another. Virtual properties have certain economic value to a sector of the real world population. However, one underlying disputed issue is what the consumers actually purchase for their money in legal terms.

An undoubted aspect of virtual properties is that they only have values within the virtual world since it just has in-world usage. Hence, its value and the rights in owning it have to be interpreted within the terms which determine the rights of the players. These terms can primarily be found in the Terms of Service ("TOS") or End User License Agreements ("EULA") of the software platform.[5] TOS or EULA works as the source of governance over virtual properties, as well as over players' acts regarding virtual properties, because of the absence of real world law ruling the conducts of avatars and in-world transactions. Players must agree to the TOS or EULA to gain access to the virtual world. Often, the game developers take the intellectual property rights from the players with written clauses in the TOS or EULA. The clauses also give the developer a great power against the players, even taking away the virtual properties the players have.[6] It appears that players merely obtain virtual properties as licenses of using the software. Players' property rights in any in-world property are not addressed.[7]

---

4 Michael Meehan, 'Virtual Property: Protecting Bits in Context' (2006) 13 *Rich. J. L. & Tech.* 7.

5 Jordan Ludwig, 'Protections for Virtual Property: A Modern Restitutionary Approach' (2012) 32 *Loy. L. A. Ent. L. Rev.* 1.

6 Janet Lo, 'A Virtual Fortune: Consumer Protection for Banking and Consumer Fraud in Virtual Worlds' (2012) <www.worldcat.org/title/virtual-fortune-consumer-protection-for-banking-and-consumer-fraud-in-virtual-worlds/oclc/785802306> accessed December 3, 2013.

7 Michael Passman, 'Transactions of Virtual Items in Virtual Worlds' (2008) *ALB. L.J. SCI. & Tech.* 259

Virtual property transactions, nonetheless, have real world economic value like other property in the real world. At least, some game developers reckon some virtual property has rights to a limited extent and allows exchange of virtual properties for real money, although there is no acknowledgement of the legal nature of these rights.[8] This indicates that virtual game players have a sense of possession over their virtual properties and the developers are aware of it. The economic value or sense of possession is sometimes addressed by real world law enforcing departments. In Hong Kong, the police have a Technology Crime Division which has the duty to investigate virtual world property theft.[9] Although criminal prosecutions do not represent legal recognition of virtual property rights under the Hong Kong law, it shows that authorities recognize that transactions of virtual property hold some significance to the general public, which demands calls for protection.[10]

3. In-world Consumer Protection

Consumer protection can be conveniently found within virtual worlds. It appears that players have taken steps in protecting themselves in transactions and utilizing the Terms of Service (TOS) or End-User Licensing Agreements (EULA) to their benefits.

---

8 Jeff LeBlanc, 'The Pursuit of Virtual Life, Liberty, and Happiness and Its Economic and Legal Recognition in the Real World (2008) 9 *Fla. Coastal L. Rev.* 255.

9 Ludwig (n 5); citing Alisa B. Steinberg, "Note, For Sale—One Level 5 Barbarian for 94,800 Won: The International Effects of Virtual Property and the Legality of Its Ownership" [2009] 37 *Ga. J. Int'l & Comp. L.* 381, 385.

10 "Awareness campaign to curb illegal online gaming abuses—CHOICE # 331" (Consumer Council, May 14, 2004) <www.consumer.org.hk/website/ws_en/news/press_releases/p33101.html> accessed December 3, 2013; the relevant offence is "access to computer with criminal or dishonest intent," under Crimes Ordinance (Cap. 200), s 161.

In-world social norms formed by players truly represent how the players expect transactions to be conducted and how they view virtual properties. The social norms develop into community rules which cover a wide range of activities, including transactions.[11] Players may form their own codes to forbid certain behaviors, which differ on various game platforms. For example, in the popular game *World of Warcraft*, there is a rule against defrauding others to gain virtual properties, such as weapons and gold.[12] Breach of the community rules will result in sanctions, like expulsion from the community group carried out by the community of players, and occasionally by the virtual world operator when official complaints are made.[13] Players work as a watchdog of themselves. If a problematic transaction comes to the knowledge of the community, there is likely certain quick and summary sanction enforced by the community itself to protect the consumer who suffers loss in that transaction.

Players may further form an in-world justice system. The system may consist of virtual courts, lawyers and law enforcement departments, mimicking the system in the real world. Taking *Second Life* as an example, there is a police department, which even has attracted the Vancouver Police Department to take part in by putting up avatars.[14] When players bring disputes to the in-world court, it takes guides from laws in the real world but it mainly brings effect to in-world community rules and TOS or EULA. Sanctions can be fines or recommended banishment, where the main sanctions are conducted by the operators upon receiving

---

11 Lo (n 6).

12 Lo (n 6); see World of Warcraft, "Terms of Use" under "Code of Conduct" <http://us.blizzard.com/en-us/company/legal/wow_tou.html> accessed December 3, 2013.

13 Lo (n 6).

14 Lo (n 6); citing "VPD: Virtual Police Department: A Vancouver police officer stands in a virtual recruitment hall typing on an invisible keyboard" (*The Vancouver Sun*, May 29, 2007) <www.canada.com/vancouversun/news/story.html?id=0c37d98d-c54f-44d3-9e72-0c19cf828565> accessed December 3, 2013.

complaints. Some in-world lawyers even form associations to hold conference in order to develop better regulations.[15] Mere rules have evolved into a more sophisticated justice system, giving a more formal mechanism to consumer protection.

Apart from the above, in-world dispute resolution is another mechanism which provides protection to consumers. In-world dispute resolution starts with one player filing a complaint to the operator online or is detected by the software itself.[16] The operator will then judge the dispute in accordance with the TOS or EULA and give respective sanctions of varying degrees. For instance, in *Second Life*, if a violation is confirmed after investigation by the operator, the responsible player may face suspension or even termination of his player account.[17] Yet, the operator is often unwilling to provide personal information of one disputant to the other. Thus it is hard for the players to seek remedies outside the virtual world.[18] Unlike the other two types of consumer protection, in-world dispute resolution bypasses the community standards or rules, and goes directly to the application of terms in the TOS or EULA by the operator. It may not reflect the values of the players and is only concerned with TOS or EULA as the rule for consumer protection.

However, even if the abovementioned mechanisms may provide a medium for players to tackle issues arising from virtual property transactions and to lodge complaints, there is no precise

---

15 Lo (n 6).

16 Claude Aiken IV, 'Sources of Law and Modes of Governance: Ethography and Theory in Second Life' [2009] *University of Pittsburgh School of law Journal of Tech. Law and Policy* 1.

17 *ibid* (citing <http://secondlife.com/newsletter/2006_02_15/blotter.php> accessed December 3, 2013).

18 Janet Lo (n 6); citing Brendan James Gilbert, "Getting to Conscionable: Negotiating Virtual Worlds' End User License Agreements Without Getting Externally Regulated" (Buffalo Legal Studies Research Paper No. 1375408 (2009)) <http://papers.ssrn.com/sol3/papers.cfm?abstract_id=1375408> accessed December 3, 2013.

regulation for in-world transactions.[19] It is not surprising that all these in-world mechanisms of consumer protection are largely related to the TOS or EULA because the document provides the fundamental governing rules and rights. Yet, the document is an instrument designed to govern the virtual world activities to the extent that the developer's and player's rights are clearly provided. It is not for the purpose of governing in-world trades, let alone providing detailed consumer protections. Furthermore, the in-world mechanisms often in the end include some sanctions enforced by the virtual world operator. If a conflict involves a player and the operator/developer, is the operator/developer a trustable adjudicator? There is an apparent conflict of interest. What if the rules derived from the TOS or EULA are themselves in favor of the operator/developer?

4. Underlying Problem — Unconscionability

Players waive most of their property rights in virtual properties upon agreeing to the TOS or EULA. The terms therein are designed by the game platform developer and not subject to negotiations as players must agree to them to enter the game.[20] The developers often reserve the right to cease the virtual properties or terminating the player's account for any reason. The implication here is twofold: firstly, this works as an arbitrary restriction of players' freedom to deal with their virtual property rights; secondly, it gives the developer an unfair advantage when a disputed virtual property transaction involves the developer.

However, players should be entitled to gain property rights despite the stringent contractual terms for the time and effort they spend on acquiring virtual properties. It is generally against

---

19 Aiken IV (n 16).

20 Passman (n 7).

the public policy to restrict an owner's freedom to pass his property right by consensus.[21] It is not hard to see the high degree of unfairness in the terms because of the power imbalance. This suggests challenges against the contractual terms on the ground of unconscionability in the Common Law.

Traditionally, unconscionability can be divided into two categories: procedural unconscionability and substantive unconscionability. The former concerns the circumstances where a party agrees to a contract without noticing certain terms for some reason, such as terms in languages which are hard for consumers to understand and hence worsen the power imbalance between the parties.[22] TOS or EULAs usually are provided on a web page with a long list of terms and only require a player to click "I agree" to proceed into the game. This is commonly known as "clickwrap" agreement. Considering the terms are not negotiable and written by the stronger party, this quick agreeing process may be procedurally unconscionable for not taking a step to facilitate the understanding of the weaker party. The latter refers to terms which unduly enrich one party over the other and therefore inequitable and unconscionable.[23] This may include terms giving the developer the absolute power to confiscate a player's virtual properties in the game while barring the player to sue the developer in the real world.[24]

---

21 *ibid.* (citing Jankowich, 'Property & Democracy in Virtual Worlds' [2005] 11 *B.U.J. Sci. & Tech. L.* 173, 183; Glen O. Robinson, 'Personal Property Servitudes' [2004] 74 *U. Chi. L. Rev.* 1449, 1480).

22 Kriegshauser (n 3).

23 Kriegshauser (n 3); citing Earl of Chesterfield v Janssen (1751) 28 Eng Rep 82, 100.

24 This is the scenario of the notorious case, *Bragg v Linden Research, Inc.* 487 F. Supp. 2d 593 (E.D.Penn. 2007). The case will be discussed later in this chapter.

5. Hong Kong Consumer Protection in Virtual World Transactions

After seeing the potential that unconscionability doctrine may protect consumers in virtual property transactions against the developers, it is to see to what extent the doctrine can be applied in Hong Kong. Unconscionability doctrine was developed under the Common law and has been codified in Hong Kong's Unconscionable Contracts Ordinance (UCO).[25] The UCO provides assistance to consumers against harsh or oppressive terms in consumer contracts.[26]

Regarding the procedural unconscionability, the court can consider several matters in the circumstances when the contract is made. For example, among other things, the court can consider the bargaining positions of the consumer and the other party and whether the consumer is able to understand the terms.[27] As for the substantial unconscionability, the court may consider factors such as the reasonable necessity of the repressing conditions.[28]

Where a contract for sale of goods is found unconscionable, the court may refuse to enforce it, entirely or partly, or alter the unconscionable parts.[29] The term "goods" shares the same meaning under Sale of Goods Ordinance.[30] Accordingly, "goods" is defined to include all chattels personal other than things in action and money.[31]

---

25 Unconscionable Contracts Ordinance (Cap. 458) (UCO).

26 Mark Williams, 'End of the Line for Caveat Emptor?' (*Hong Kong Lawyers*, May 2008).

27 UCO, ss 6 (1) (a) and 6 (1) (c).

28 *ibid.*, s 6 (1) (b).

29 *ibid.*, s 5.

30 *ibid.*, s 2 (1).

31 Sale of Goods Ordinance (Cap. 26), s 2 (1).

A problem arises while applying the UCO to virtual property transactions because, strictly speaking, the players only acquire licenses for their money as explained above.[32] Even though stealing or defrauding in-world items is well-recognized as an offence of "access to computer with criminal or dishonest intent" in Hong Kong, there is no element in the criminal law that suggests the court is ready to articulate virtual properties as goods.[33] The offence is only classified as a type of illegal interception, but not theft or other illegal appropriation which contains an element of property rights.[34]

Apart from the legislations, there is yet to be a case in Hong Kong which invites the court to determine whether virtual properties are goods. In spite of the UCO providing consumer protection for sale of goods, it is unclear if it is applicable to virtual properties due to the lack of recognition in the legislation and uncertainty of the attitude of the court.

Unfortunately, since the applicability of the consumer protection law in Hong Kong does not seem readily applicable, in-world disputes over transactions may fall back to relying on the in-world mechanisms which cannot provide satisfactory consumer protection, especially when disputes are against the developers. It can be helpful to see how other common law jurisdiction in similar situation of Hong Kong deals with virtual property disputes.

---

32   Lo (n 6).

33   Crimes Ordinance (Cap. 200), s 161.

34   Kam Wong and Georgiana Wong, 'Law and Order in Cyberspace: A Case Study or Cyberspace Governance in Hong Kong' (2005) 23 *J. Marshall J. Computer & Info. L.* 249.

6. US Consumer Protection in Virtual World Transactions

The United States have a similar background of lacking a legal recognition of virtual properties as goods like Hong Kong. Nonetheless there have been cases inviting the court to decide on this issue. The very first relevant case that went to trial in the United States is *Bragg v Linden Research, Inc.*[35] The facts of the case illustrate how the in-world mechanisms failed to provide satisfactory protections and the reasoning of the court shows how unconscionability may be applied in a dispute over virtual properties.

The case started from a dispute over virtual properties between a player and the game developer. The claimant, Marc Bragg, was a player of the game *Second Life* and bought a plot of virtual land by exploiting a flaw of an in-world auction. The operator/developer of the game, Linden Lab, considered Bragg's purchase of virtual land from an unauthorized in-world auction to be a fraud and therefore suspended Bragg's account, erased his avatar and confiscated all his virtual properties, not just the piece of virtual land. Bragg sued the developer for violations of several consumer protection laws and filed other actions under the law of contract and tort. In particular, he argued that Linden's CEO had previously made representations suggesting *Second Life* recognizes players' virtual property rights were the same as property rights in the real world.[36] On top of that, it was alleged that the *Second Life* TOS, which provided Linden Lab the power to cease virtual properties and freezing players' accounts, was unconscionable.

---

35 *Bragg v Linden Research, Inc.* 487 F. Supp. 2d 593 (E.D.Penn. 2007).

36 Pennsylvania Unfair Trade Practices and Consumer Protection Law (73 Pa. Stat.) s 201–1; the California Unfair and Deceptive Practices Act (Cal. Bus. & Prof. Code), s 17200; the California Consumer Legal Remedies Act (Cal. Civ. Code), s 1750; and, Cal. Civ. Code, s 1812.600; c.f. "Case Comment: Bragg v Linden Research " [2007] 13(7) C.T.L.R. N172–173.

The defendant later moved the case to federal court and argued that the case should be dismissed. They relied on an arbitration clause provided in the *Second Life* TOS which compelled arbitration, among other diverse grounds. Ultimately, the court refused to send the case to arbitration by deciding that the arbitration clause was unconscionable. The clause was held both procedurally and substantially unconscionable. It was because the unilateral impositions by the stronger party, the players' huge expense on arbitration, legal forum selection clause and other features all pointed out that the clause was not seeking an effective way to solve disputes. Instead, it inclined unfairly towards Linden Lab's favor against the interests of the players.[37] Nonetheless, the case abruptly ended as the parties decided to settle the dispute confidentially.

Despite losing the opportunity to invite the court to acknowledge virtual property rights, the result has its importance in recognizing consumers' rights. Overruling the arbitration clause in the *Second Life* TOS on the ground of unconscionability implies the possibility of rejecting other clauses on the same ground.[38] This is critical as developers may lose their reservation of virtual property rights from players, which is normally accomplished by contractual terms in the TOS, if the terms are too prejudicial towards players.[39] It also appears there may be more protection for purchase of virtual properties beyond TOS or EULAs as the court is willing to address the issues about virtual property transactions. On top of that, the result of the case suggests that in-world consumer protection may not be the final resort for the players.

---

37 Paul Riley, 'Litigating Second Life and Disputes: A Consumer Protection Approach' (2009) 19 *Fordham Intell. Prop. Media & Ent. L. J.* 877.

38 Charles Wild and Stuart Weinstein, *Neil MacEwan and Neal Geach, Electronic and Mobile Commerce Law* (University of Hertfordshire Press 2011) 186–188.

39 Greg Lastowka, *Virtual Justice* (Yale University Press 2010) 94–96.

The facts of the case are also helpful in showing how in-world mechanisms dealing with virtual properties can be unsatisfactory in protecting consumer's rights. Although there the developer's strict sanctions were in response to Bragg's dishonest acts, the same could happen to a virtual property dispute between players. The sanctioned player may not agree with the decision of the developer, but they may not have any property rights under the TOS or EULA to file a law suit.

Players should be protected outside the virtual worlds regardless of the unfair terms. It is unjust to leave consumers of virtual properties having no rights and being unprotected. In support of this view, the court in *Eros LLC v Robert Leatherwood & John* agreed that certain types of proprietary interest must exist if income can be generated from creativity of a person.[40] The case involved a party claiming their intellectual property right was infringed by copying of virtual property requested tracking of the real identity behind an avatar.

Deriving from the rulings of the court in these two cases, some vague property right seemingly are attached to virtual goods. Although this right is yet to be directly addressed, it should exist because interest can be generated from the virtual world transactions and developer's seizure of this right from players may constitute unconscionability.

Nonetheless, two earlier cases seemingly cast doubts on the rightness of the decision in *Bragg*.[41] In *Davidson & Associates v Jung*, in spite of the EULA of a computer game being a "clickwrap" agreement, the court held that it was not procedurally or substantively unconscionable.[42] It was because the players had the

---

40 Charles Wild and Stuart Weinstein (n 38) 190–191; see *Eros LLC v Robert Leatherwood & John* 1–10 Does Florida Middle District Court No: 8 2207 Civ 01158.

41 Bragg (n 35).

42 *Davidson & Associates v Jung* 422 F.3d 630 (8th Cir. 2005); see Riley (n 37).

choice to purchase other computer games or return the game for refund, and the terms were not too shockingly unconscionable. Another case is *Comb v. Paypal, Inc.* The issue was also unconscionability of an arbitration clause.[43] Nevertheless, unlike Bragg, the arbitration clause was not contained in a "clickwrap" agreement, but was rather provided on a separate web page, also known as "browsewrap" agreement. The court in Bragg relied on the judgment in Comb when deciding on the ground of procedural unconscionability, neglecting the difference between two types of agreements. Presumably, a person pays less attention to clauses to a completely separate web page ("browsewrap") than clauses on the same page as the "I agree" button ("clickwrap"), resulting in the former type being more procedurally unconscionable.[44] It is also observed that a court rarely holds click-through contracts unconscionable purely for procedural reasons.[45] Thus, the court in Bragg may have failed to do a thorough consideration.

These flaws, however, do not damage the authority of the *Bragg case.*[46] First, even if it looks like players have a choice in picking the virtual world they indulge with, being able to choose a player-friendly TOS or EULA is just a mirage. As mentioned above, it is a common practice that developers put strict terms which restrict players' property rights greatly and reserve tremendous power to control virtual properties.[47] No matter which game players choose, it is very likely that there are terms repressing their virtual property rights. Players do not have real choices. Second, although it is undisputable that the court in Bragg neither considered the distinction a "clickwrap" agreement

---

43 *Comb v. Paypal, Inc.* 218 F. Supp. 2d 1165 (N.D. Cal. 2002); see Riley (n 37).

44 Riley (n 37).

45 Michael Meehan (n 4);citing Margaret Jane Radin, "Humans, Computers, and Binding Commitment" [2000] 75 *IND. L.J.* 1125, 1156.

46 Bragg (n 35).

47 Michael Meehan (n 4).

from a "browsewrap" agreement nor explained its deviation from the usual reluctance to reject click-through contracts on procedural grounds, it should be noted that the judgment based heavily also on the substantial unfairness of the arbitration clause itself. In the future when a TOS or EULA of a virtual world game is challenged, the Bragg decision still stands as a strong suggestion of applying unconscionability to look at the problem.

The legal recognition of virtual property rights in the United States is more or less at the beginning stage like Hong Kong. Yet, the court has demonstrated the viability of applying unconscionability doctrine to a dispute over virtual property without directly addressing the legal status of virtual properties. It is good start to alarm the virtual world developers and players that the court cares about the consumer's right in virtual property transactions. The court's approach should be supported as players should be entitled to some property rights, despite the rights is still vague in legal terms. Hong Kong courts should be encouraged to deal with similar problems before a clear legal determination on virtual property right is established.

7.   Other Possible Consumer Protections

Another possibility to protect consumers of virtual property transaction is using the misrepresentation doctrine. Part of the consumer protection laws are concerned with the impact of representations on consumers.[48] This was actually presented as an alternative to the unconscionability argument in the *Bragg* case. It was argued that the representations made by the CEO of the developer amounted to a modification of terms in the TOS.[49] Nonetheless, the court had no chance to deal with the

---

48   Riley (n 37).

49   Bragg (n 35).

issue of misrepresentation. Linden Lab has made numerous representations regarding the virtual land, conveying the message that consumers would obtain land ownership and property ownership over virtual lands by using terms of real property and suggesting Second Life is not just a game but an extension of the real life.[50] All these factors point to a high possibility that the players would actually believe they obtain property rights through virtual property transactions, while all they have are probably mere licenses under the TOS. If the case had been tried in Hong Kong, players who suffered loss from the misrepresentation could possibly have claimed damages for their loss under this doctrine.[51]

Unluckily the misrepresentation approach is not a perfect model. Developers usually reserve the right to modify the game and the mechanism within to upgrade the game. Devaluation or even a loss of virtual properties may happen during the modification process. Therefore, any change of this sort may change the underlying representations of virtual properties.[52] If the court takes the representations too strictly, this will not fit for the business reality.

Since the attitude of the court towards virtual property rights remains unclear and it is a good idea to look outside the box of litigation. Online alternative dispute resolution (ADR) is a developing mechanism which facilitates settlements among different in-world parties. Using ADR to solve consumer disputes in the real world is a familiar practice in Hong Kong. For example, the Consumer Council in Hong Kong encourages mediation between disputants and even tries to promote complaint settlement purely by mediation and without

---

50 Riley (n 37); citing Symposium, "Ownership in Online Worlds" [2005] 21 *Santa Clara Computer & High Tech. L.J.* 807, 821.

51 Misrepresentation Ordinance (Cap 284), s 3.

52 Michael Meehan (n 4).

adjudication.[53] Technologies allow mediation to be conducted online. The settlement agreements between the disputants are generally enforceable by the courts. It suits the international nature of the Internet.[54] Arbitration is another common ADR process. It starts with an agreement to arbitrate, allowing parties to decide what governing law to be applied and what procedures to be followed. The arbitration award is binding on the parties and enforceable in many countries.[55] As an example, after the *Bragg* case, Linden changed its arbitration clauses to allow non-appearance-based arbitration, where the process can be conducted online.[56] An obvious advantage of entailing ADR as a consumer protection is the flexibility in the governing law and process. Besides that, disputants may bypass the vexatious issue of virtual property rights and try to reach a solution satisfying both parties.

The question of fairness is the other side of the coin. Power imbalance in ADR can lead to unfair advantages enjoyed by the stronger party, which is the developer.[57] The more flexibility parties have, the more opportunities the stronger party is to exploit its position. This can come in many forms, such as monetary and legal resources. Taking arbitration as an example, if the adjudicating agency is chosen by the developer, perhaps the consumer will worry about the developer has more pull in

---

53 "Submission to the Chief Justice's Working Party on the Civil Justice Reform — Interim Report and Consultative Paper" (Consumer Council, April 23, 2002) <www.consumer.org.hk/website/ws_en/competition_issues/policy_position/20020423lawsreform.html> accessed December 3, 2013.

54 Elizabeth Longworth, 'The Possibilities for a Legal Framework for Cyberspace – including a New Zealand Perspective' in Bruno de Padirac (ed), *The International Dimensions of Cyberspace Law* (Ashgate Publishing Ltd 2000) 43–47.

55 ibid; see <www.iccwbo.org/products-and-services/arbitration-and-adr/arbitration/> accessed on March 31, 2013.

56 Riley (n 37).

57 D. Spencer and M. Brogan, *Mediation Law and Practice* (Cambridge University Press, Australia 2006) 223–237.

the agency's decision.[58] This problem may seem to be solved by the consumer appointing his own arbitrators, but it is doubtful whether the consumer has as much knowledge as the developer to make a considered choice.

8.   The Ultimate Goal

Consumer protection in virtual world transactions apparently has many ways to develop and can take various forms. No matter which way it goes, the ultimate goal is to provide players who take part in transactions as avatars with certain legal rights and mechanisms. The basic requirements of the law should aim to give players confidence in making in-world purchases and furnish players with clear information on the goods and their rights regarding the transactions.[59]

As the law stands at this moment, insofar as the case law has slowly developed, unconscionability doctrine, misrepresentation doctrine and online ADR mechanisms all show consumers that awareness of virtual property transactions has been raised. They are not entirely subject to in-world arbitrary controls of the developers. It is not only plausible but indeed possible for them to get redress in the real world, when they are not satisfied with the in-world rules or protections.

In spite of having some developments, there are gaps in current law. For example, the question of whether users are entitled to full property rights in virtual goods remains unclear and not consistent across jurisdictions. At the same time, the expanding recognition of the value of virtual properties calls for better consumer protection legislation to cover virtual property transactions. For

---

58 Aiken IV (n 16).

59 Andrew Sparrow, *The Law of Virtual Worlds and Internet Social Networks* (Gower Publishing Ltd. 2010) 178–182.

example, it can apply to developer's representations to consumers in light of business reality, cover transactions between players and even finally start a commodification over virtual properties.[60] A few countries, such as China, South Korea and the Netherlands, have acknowledged, or attempted to acknowledge, property rights in virtual properties.[61] Legislation is needed to build future consumer protection laws and mechanisms which echo the need of virtual world players in Hong Kong.

9.   Conclusion

There is an ever-growing economic power in virtual worlds and players require consumer protection for virtual property transactions. Regrettably, in-world consumer protections are all but unsatisfactory in many aspects. The problem is even more immense when a dispute involves the developer of the game. Consumers should enjoy property rights and be protected, but it is unclear whether or not they are under the stringent terms in TOS or EULAs.

The court in Hong Kong is hardly prepared to clearly address the property right in virtual properties by relying on current law whereas the *Bragg* case in the United States has shown a feasibility to bring redress to consumers of virtual properties under the unconscionability doctrine.[62] The case serves as a warning to developers who impose harsh terms against players and reminds players that the court, at least in the U.S., is able to provide certain protections even if the legal status of virtual property rights is unclear. Subsequent to the *Bragg* case, Linden

---

60   Riley (n 37).

61   Charles Wild and Stuart Weinstein (n 38); e.g., Dutch law recognizes 'virtual goods' as 'goods' which are hence possible to be stolen; see Riley (n 37).

62   Bragg (n 35).

Labs did amend their terms of service, taking into account the concerns of the court. There also seem to be other available consumer protection laws and mechanisms which may apply to virtual world transactions. Yet, none of those can answer the issue of virtual property rights as directly as legislation could possibly do.

Any law of consumer protection in virtual world transactions in Hong Kong is to be started from scratch. Legislation is a start but definitely not an end, as it gives new understandings to relevant laws and there are other difficult questions such as jurisdictional issues of the internet. It will take a long time before consumers of virtual property can be fully protected.

23

Consumer Protection in Virtual World Transactions: Are Players-Consumers Adequately Protected under the Current Regimes of Property Law and Contract Law?

Silvia Kin-man TANG

1. Introduction

Anshe Chung is a legendary real estate entrepreneur. Beginning with an initial investment of US$9.95, the business had made her a millionaire in just around two and a half years.[1] Today, her Anshe Chung Studios Ltd. employs more than 80 full-time staff, including designers and architects.[2] Custom designed landscape built by her Studios is available for rent and sale in Azure Islands. In 2006, Anshe Chung featured the cover of *Business Week*.[3]

---

1 Plush City @ Second Life and Wuhan, China @ Real Life, 'Anshe Chung Becomes First Virtual World Millionaire' (Anshe Chung Studios, November 26, 2006) <www.anshechung.com/include/press/press_release251106.html> accessed December 3, 2013.

2 Aaron Saenz, 'Entrepreneur Anshe Chung Makes a Fortune Selling Virtual Land, Banking and Fashion' (Singularity Hub, August 23, 2011) <http://singularityhub.com/2011/08/23/entrepreneur-anshe-chung-makes-millions-selling-virtual-land-banking-and-fashion/> accessed December 3, 2013.

3 Robert D. Hof, 'Cover Story Podcast—My Virtual Life' (*Bloomberg Businessweek*, April 30, 2006) <http://www.businessweek.com/stories/2006-04-30/my-virtual-life> accessed December 3, 2013.

However, neither Anshe Chung nor her company exists in real world. She is just a persona of Ailin Graef in a virtual world called *Second Life*.[4] Her fortune was accumulated entirely from the sale of virtual real estate. She began with "small-scale purchases of virtual real estate, which she then subdivided and developed with landscaping and themed architectural builds for rental and resale."[5]

In every minute, there are people migrating to different virtual worlds. Whilst some of them regard participating in virtual worlds as no more than playing a game, some users actually intend to earn real money in those unreal worlds. Regardless of their aims, the popularity of virtual worlds is growing at an explosive rate.[6] Strategy Analytics anticipated that, the overall population of virtual worlds will increase from 186 million in 2009 to 640 million in 2015.[7] There is also prediction that "one billion people will flock to virtual worlds by 2017."[8]

It goes without saying that, as more and more players become enmeshed in virtual worlds, an increasing number of disputes are bound to arise. Unprecedented problems are likely to happen as well. This catches the attention of legal scholars and practitioners as to the viability of applying the real world law to the

---

4 Plush City @ Second Life and Wuhan, China @ Real Life (n 1).

5 Robert D. Hof, 'Cover Story Podcast—My Virtual Life' (*Bloomberg Businessweek*, April 30, 2006) <www.businessweek.com/stories/2006-04-30/my-virtual-life> accessed December 3, 2013.

6 David Naylor and Andrew Jaworski, 'Virtual Worlds, Real Challenges' (2007) *Entertainment LR* 262, 262.

7 William Dobson, 'Market Research Firm Predicts Population Explosion for Virtual Worlds' (Joystiq, June 16, 2009) <http://massively.joystiq.com/2009/06/16/market-research-firm-predicts-population-explosion-for-virtual-w/> accessed December 3, 2013.

8 James Egan, 'One Billion People will Flock to Virtual Worlds by 2017' (Joystiq, June 6, 2008) <http://massively.joystiq.com/2008/06/06/one-billion-people-will-flock-to-virtual-worlds-by-2017/?utm_source=feedburner&utm_medium=feed&utm_campaign=Feed%3A+Massively+%28Massively%29> accessed December 3, 2013.

happenings in virtual worlds.[9] In particular, it is advocated that clear law should be laid down with regards to "virtual property," which has been the subject of heated debate over the past few years.

The major aim of this study is to examine whether the existing legal principles in property law and contract law afford adequate consumer protection to players-consumers. This chapter is presented in four parts. Part 1 provides an overview of virtual worlds, including some important terms and concepts. In Part 2, the relevance of the real world law to virtual worlds is analyzed. In the End-User License Agreements or Terms of Service to which the players must assent before they can get access to the virtual worlds, there is always a clause which expressly retains all ownership rights with the game developers. Accordingly, there are considerable difficulties in applying the property law and contract law to cases where the issue at dispute concerns "virtual property rights."

Part 3 suggests a practical way out to this problem. Having spent a substantial amount of time and money on acquiring the virtual property, players should be endowed with an additional identity—"consumers." This will then enable the consumer protection law to come into play, which is capable of addressing the inherent inequities of the property-based and contract-based approaches and is arguably the best area of law which protects the gamers' reasonable expectations of their rights in virtual property. With the consumer protection law in place, players-consumers will likely be entitled to the same level of protection as ordinary real world consumers. However, it must be noted that, for the smooth implementation of the consumer protection law, the legal status of "virtual property" must be properly recognized by incorporating "digital content" (which includes virtual

---

9 Juliet M. Moringiello, 'What Virtual Worlds can Do for Property Law' [2010] 62 *FLLR* 159, 160.

property) into the present regime of property law. The chapter is then summarized and concluded in Part 4.

2.   Virtual Worlds

Virtual worlds are online digital environments where users socialize and interact with each other, through the use of "avatars."[10] "Avatars are three-dimensional, custom designed characters that permit their creators to cultivate life in the virtual world."[11]

Virtual worlds can be divided into two categories, namely, game-oriented virtual worlds (e.g., *RuneScape*, *EverQuest*) and socially-oriented virtual worlds (e.g., *Second Life*, *Blue Mars*). In the game worlds, players are required to obtain certain game objects in order to achieve higher status and take on more challenging missions;[12] as for social worlds, there are no "levels" and thus no objective at all—its focus lies on the interaction with other players and the environments.[13]

Second Life, where Anshe Chung gained fame and fortune, is one of the most well-known virtual worlds, with its economy being described as "the most robust of all."[14] In 2009, the total size of its economy reached US$567 million, which accounted

---

10   Wayne Rumbles, 'Theft in the Digital: Can You Steal Virtual Property?' [2011] 2 *Canterbury LR* 354, 354.

11   Julie M. Pharr, 'A Research Agenda for Investigating the Effectiveness of Branding in Virtual Reality' *J Management & Marketing Research* <www.cbpp.uaa.alaska.edu/afef/virtual%20reality%20journal_mgt.htm> accessed December 3, 2013.

12   Cory Ondrejka, 'Escaping the Gilded Cage: User Created Content and Building the Metaverse' [2004] 49 *NYL Sch LR* 81, 89.

13   Moringiello (n 9) 170.

14   Linden Labs, '2009 End of Year Second Life Economy Wrap-up' (Second Life, January 19, 2010) <http://community.secondlife.com/t5/Features/2009-End-of-Year-Second-Life-Economy-Wrap-up-including-Q4/ba-p/653078> accessed December 3, 2013.

for almost a quarter of the entire US virtual property market.[15] *Second Life*'s economy is based on "Linden dollars," a currency which can be exchanged to US$ at approximately L$250 to US$1.[16]

Whilst focusing on social interaction among "residents," *Second Life* also involves consumption as one of its elements.[17] Since there is no requirement for the residents' "survival," the symbolic value of the property is believed to be the driving force behind consumption.[18]

As more and more players are willing to pay real capital for virtual goods, it is not surprising that virtual worlds actually have "the potential to be a promising online business model."[19] Indeed, virtual goods are fundamental to the functioning of all virtual worlds. Without their presence, players will lose their incentives to participate in the worlds. To many gamers, real world values are attached to virtual property. For instance, in 2004, an Australian gamer spent US$26,500 on acquiring a virtual island with an abandoned castle and beaches in Project Entropia.[20] Such transactions are not peculiar to virtual social worlds. In virtual game worlds, magic weapons and powerful armor can also be traded for real money.

15 Lucy Stevenson, 'Marketing Methods: Second Life Marketplace' (Illamasqua Research Blog, January 11, 2012) <http://illamasqua-research-blog.blogspot.hk/2012/01/marketing-methods-second-life.html> accessed December 3, 2013.

16 Digital Currency Wiki, 'Linden Dollars' (Digital Currency Wiki) <http://wiki.dgcmagazine.com/index.php?title=Linden_Dollars> accessed December 3, 2013.

17 Jennifer Martin, 'Virtual Worlds Research: Consumer Behaviour in Virtual Worlds' (2008) *J Virtual Worlds Research* 1, 3.

18 Martin (n 17) 6.

19 Yue Guo and Stuart Barnes, 'Why Do People Buy Virtual Items in Virtual Worlds? An Empirical Test of Conceptual Model' (2009) *ECIS* 49, 49.

20 BBC News, 'Gamer Buys $26,500 Virtual Land' (BBC News, December 17, 2004) <http://news.bbc.co.uk/2/hi/technology/4104731.stm> accessed December 3, 2013.

From the developers' perspective, virtual goods are the basis of their economic systems. The sale of virtual items usually makes up a substantial part of the developers' revenue, especially for those which charge no, or little, membership fees. This explains the phenomenon of vigorous commodification in virtual worlds. Take *Second Life* as an example, Linden Lab has actively commodified *Second Life* by selling land to its users and encouraging them to subdivide, rent or even resell it. Furthermore, to foster currency exchange, it runs the LindeX, a platform where Linden dollars can be bought from real money.[21]

Because of commodification, "players" are transformed into "consumers,"[22] who, by virtue of their financial investments, form a reasonable expectation that they should be entitled to the ownership rights over their virtual property. According to Professor Jack Balkin,

> "...if platform owners encourage real world commodification of virtual worlds, encourage people in these worlds to treat virtual items like real property, and allow the sale and purchase of these assets as if they were property, they should not be surprised if courts, legislatures, and administrative agencies begin to treat virtual items as property."[23]

It follows that, the issue of "consumer protection" inevitably ensues from commodification of virtual worlds.

However, it is not until recent years that the issues of "virtual property rights" and "consumer protection" receive much public concern and attention. It is gradually brought to light that virtual

---

21　Second Life Wikia, 'LindeX' (Second Life Wikia) <http://secondlife.wikia.com/wiki/LindeX> accessed December 3, 2013.

22　Paul Riley, 'Litigating Second Life Land Disputes: A Consumer Protection Approach' (2009) *Fordham Intell Prop Media & Ent LJ* 877, 910.

23　Jack M. Balkin and Beth Simone Noveck (eds), *The State of Play: Law, Games, and Virtual Worlds* (New York University Press 2006) 95.

world players are actually blindsided by the developers' decisions to shut the servers down and end the virtual worlds at any time. For instance, in late December 2011, just one month before the game *Baking Life* was taken offline, its developer ZipZapPlay announced that the game would be closed on January 31, 2012. Users were informed that '[a]ll virtual currency (Zip Cash) and virtual items will be lost after January 31. Any remaining Zip Cash (even if it was purchased and unused) is *not transferable* between or among different games or applications and is *not redeemable* for any sum of money or other monetary value.'[24] This means that, everything that players had invested money and effort in would vanish from then on.

This case is just a tip of the iceberg. Regrettably, in none of these shut-down situations are gamers refunded or compensated with the real world money that they have spent. Also, these players have no legal basis to claim against the developers unless the courts recognize their status as the "owners" of their virtual property. This gives rise to certain legal issues, which will be addressed in the following.

3. Relevance of Real World Laws to Virtual Commercial Transactions

3.1 Property Law

Although virtual goods are merely computer codes composed by a stream of ones and zeros,[25] there have been suggestions

---

24 Dan Crawley, 'Angry Bakers have Fingers Burned as Baking Life Facebook Game Gets the Chop' (Venture Beat, January 20, 2012) <http://venturebeat.com/2012/01/20/angry-bakers-have-fingers-burned-as-baking-life-facebook-game-gets-the-chop/> accessed December 3, 2013.

25 Andrew Sparrow, *The Law of Virtual Worlds and Internet Social Networks* (Gower Publishing Ltd 2010) 55.

that they should enjoy the same status as "real goods."[26] Some scholars viewed that, "an understanding of property theory suggests that property rights in virtual goods are bound to be recognized or created."[27] Professor Joshua Fairfield provided a justification for judicial recognition of virtual property, including three features exhibited by virtual property which render them more like physical property than mere computer codes. These three features are *rivalrousness, persistence and interconnectivity.* Fairfield interpreted *"rivalrousness"* as "the ability to invest in my property without fear that other people may take what I have built."[28] For example, a gamer who owns a piece of land can exclude everyone else in the same world from entering it. As for *"persistence,"* Fairfield defines this by stating that it "protects my investment by ensuring that it lasts."[29] Beyond dispute, a virtual property does not disappear when the player signs off and turns off his computer. Finally, *"'interconnectivity'* increases the value of my property due to network effects"[30]—this can be instanced by the lease of virtual land to other users.

It should be noted that, there is a global trend towards applying traditional property law to intangible objects.[31] In *Kremen v Cohen,*[32] the Ninth Circuit Court held that property rights exist in intangible domain names. The court laid down a three-prong test for the determination of the existence of property rights in intangible property: "First, there must be an interest capable

---

26 Joshua A. T. Fairfield, 'Anti-Social Contracts: The Contractual Governance of Virtual Worlds' [2008] 53 *McGill LJ* 427, 452.

27 Theodore J. Westbrook, 'Comment, Owned: Finding a Place for Virtual World Property Rights' (2008) *Mich St LR* 779, 781.

28 Joshua A. T. Fairfield, 'Virtual Property' [2005] 85 *BU LR* 1047, 1054–5.

29 *ibid.*

30 *ibid.*

31 Steve James and Sam Kempsey, 'Virtual Worlds and Online Theft After the RuneScape Saga' (2012) *E-Commerce Law & Policy* 8, 8.

32 337 F 3d 1024 (9th Cir 2003).

of precise definition; second, it must be capable of exclusive possession; and third, the putative owner must have established a legitimate claim to exclusivity."[33] The court noted that, as the domain name was registered under Cohen's name, all three requirements were satisfied. By the same token, as convincingly argued by Allen Chein, virtual property can also satisfy the test:[34] a virtual asset, once acquired by a gamer, will be possessed and controlled by him, who enjoys the right to dispose of the property as he wishes.

In fact, it seems that many courts are moving forward to recognize "virtual property," which may be a prelude to the recognition of "virtual property rights." In the U.K., an Ashley Mitchell, who stole 400 billion virtual poker chips, was convicted of theft because the judge recognized the legal status of those chips.[35] Similarly, in China, a guilty verdict was upheld against a man who had stolen and sold other players' virtual property, the appeal court said that "online game players had spent time, energy and money gaining the game's equipment and adding value to the virtual goods."[36] In 2012, the Dutch Supreme Court handed down a judgment, which was described as "a ground-breaking case."[37] In that case, two youths were convicted of theft because they had forced the victim to give up his password in

---

33 337 F 3d 1024 (9th Cir 2003) 1030.

34 Allen Chein, 'Note, A Practical Look at Virtual Property' [2006] 80 *St. John's LR* 1059, 1090.

35 The Guardian, 'British Hacker Jailed over £7m Virtual Gaming Chips Scam' (*The Guardian*, March 18, 2011) <www.guardian.co.uk/technology/2011/mar/18/hacker-jailed-gaming-chips-scam> accessed December 3, 2013.

36 The Sydney Morning Herald, 'Verdict on Virtual Property Thief Upheld' (*The Sydney Morning Herald*, April 4, 2006) <www.smh.com.au/news/breaking/verdict-on-virtual-property-thiefupheld/2006/04/04/1143916492279.html> accessed December 3, 2013.

37 The Virtual Policy Network, 'RuneScape Theft—Dutch Supreme Court Decision' (The Virtual Policy Network, February 1, 2012) <www.virtualpolicy.net/runescape-theft-dutch-supreme-court-decision.html> accessed December 3, 2013.

his *RuneScape's* account and transferred certain items from his account to theirs. The Supreme Court determined that virtual goods hold genuine value because of the time and effort gamers have invested in acquiring them, and thus, they are valuable "commodities" which can be bought and sold in the same way as physical goods. The court also compared virtual property to money and passports, which, although being the undisputed property of the Government, can still be rightfully possessed by those who hold the property under their "exclusive dominion."[38]

Unfortunately, the discussion does not stop here. Even if the legal status of virtual property is recognized, there comes another hurdle—who is the actual owner of the property?

3.2   Contract Law

In order to create an account in virtual worlds, gamers have to agree to the developers' End-User License Agreements ("EULAs"), or sometimes being referred to as the Terms of Service ("ToS"), which provide the foundation of the developer-user relationship and define the ownership rights of virtual property. The EULAs are usually "clickwrap" agreements, to which the prospective gamers must assent by clicking "I agree" or "I accept" before they can get access to the worlds. *Second Life's* ToS states clearly: "By using Second Life, you agree to and accept these Terms of Service. If you do not so agree, you should decline this Agreement, in which case you are prohibited from accessing or using Second Life."[39]

While the specific terms of EULAs vary, all of them contain a clause which "explicitly attacks the notion of virtual property

---

38 *ibid.*

39 Second Life, Terms of Service (Second Life, 7 May 2010) <http://secondlife.com/corporate/tos.php> accessed December 3, 2013.

rights"[40]—by stating that ownership of all rights remains with the game developers. For example, the EULA of *Entropia Universe* provides that, "all virtual items, including virtual currency, are part of the Entropia Universe System and/or features of the Entropia Universe, and MindArk and/or respective Mindark's Planet Partner(s) retains all rights, title, and interest in all parts."[41]

The effect of such terms is that, as against other gamers in the same virtual world, the players are entitled to all the property rights, such as the right to exclude others from their land, or in some circumstances, the right to transfer; however, their rights are actually subject to the developers' *ultimate* ownership rights. Therefore, strictly speaking, they are not the "owners" of their property, they are merely the licensees.

Notwithstanding the clear stipulation, there are still countless disputes between users and developers as regards the issue of "ownership" over virtual items. As the governing constitution over virtual property lies in the EULAs or ToS, contract law has a vital role to play in these disputes. Therefore, the gamers must launch contract-based attacks to knock out the EULAs or ToS in order to establish the property-based justification.

The aggrieved gamers are likely to initiate the attack by arguing that the EULAs are unenforceable: All EULAs and ToS are mostly "clickwrap" agreements, presented on a "take-it-or-leave-it" basis, where developers are allowed to lay down whatever terms they like.[42] Moreover, these documents are usually very long. *Second Life*'s ToS, when printed out, consists of 13 pages.[43] It is

---

40 Kurt Hunt, 'This Land is not Your Land: Second Life, CopyBot, and the Looming Question of Virtual Property Rights' (2007) *Texas R Entertainment & Sports L* 141, 150.

41 Entropia Universe, End-User Licence Agreement (Entropia Universe, May 5, 2011) <http://legal.entropiauniverse.com/legal/eula.xml> accessed December 3, 2013.

42 Hunt (n 40) 153.

43 Moringiello (n 9) 171.

hardly convincing that one would spend time reading through the whole document before assenting to it. In fact, many users simply accept the agreements without a cursory reading because "one must accept these terms of use or simply not engage with the [game]."[44] By clicking "I agree" or "I accept," a developer-user contract is formed. Developers can then take advantage of the power of contract law to enforce the terms against their users at any time they wish. Nevertheless, given the unequal bargaining power between the parties, strictly speaking, the contract is not "voluntarily" entered into.

Despite the inherent unfairness to the gamers, courts have generally upheld the validity of the "clickwrap" licenses. For example, in *ProCD v Zeidenberg*,[45] the Seventh Circuit Court held that the terms contained in "clickwrap" licenses, which explicitly required the users to read before clicking "OK," were enforceable. Similarly, the Ontario Superior Court of Justice upheld the "clickwrap" agreement in *Rudder v Microsoft Corp*,[46] where the terms and conditions were deemed to be agreed by the user with his act of clicking on the "I Agree" button.

Accordingly, the aggrieved players are likely to fail on grounds of "unenforceability." They may then seek to rely on the doctrine of "unconscionability" in order to avoid the EULAs.[47] In fact, some commentators take the view that the EULAs of all virtual worlds should be struck down as unconscionable "because of their complete one-sidedness."[48] Professors Gregory Lastowka and Dan Hunter also commented that, "we will likely see courts

---

44 Benjamin Tarsa, 'Licensing of Virtual Goods: Misconceptions of Ownership' (*Gnovis Journal*, April 26, 2012) <http://gnovisjournal.org/2012/04/26/licensing-of-virtual-goods-misconceptions-of-ownership/> accessed December 3, 2013.

45 86 F 3d 1447 (7th Cir 1996).

46 [1999] OJ No 3778.

47 Erez Reuveni, 'On Virtual Worlds: Copyright and Contract Law at the Dawn of the Virtual Age' (2007) *Indiana LJ* 261, 300.

48 Andrew Jankowich, 'The Complex Web of Corporate Rule-Making in Virtual Worlds' [2006] 8 *Tul J Tech & Intell Prop* 1, 52–3.

rejecting EULAs to the extent that they place excessive restrictions on the economic interests of users."[49]

As famously put by Judge Skelly Wright in *Williams v Walker-Thomas Furniture Co*,[50] "unconscionability has generally been recognized to include an absence of meaningful choice on the part of one of the parties together with contract terms that are unreasonably favorable to the other party."[51] The doctrine has two components: procedural unconscionability and substantive unconscionability.

Procedural unconscionability usually results from "defects in the bargaining process."[52] Factors include, *inter alia*, absence of meaningful choice, unequal bargaining power, lack of meaningful negotiation[53] and boilerplate language offered on a take-it-or-leave-it basis.[54]

While developers may allege that gamers are given meaningful choices, this argument is clearly flawed. Given the similarity of all the EULAs and ToS, it is a case of Hobson's choice for the gamers—they either give their assent or choose not to participate in any virtual worlds at all.[55] Thus, the procedural element is very likely to be satisfied. It follows that, a finding of substantive unconscionability becomes the key as to whether an EULA can be declared void.[56]

---

49 Gregory Lastowka and Dan Hunter, 'The Laws of the Virtual Worlds' [2004] 92 *Cali LR* 1, 50.

50 350 F 2d 445 (D C Cir 1965).

51 350 F 2d 445 (D C Cir 1965) 449.

52 Wayne R. Barnes, 'Social Media and the Rise in Consumer Bargaining Power' [2012] 14 *U Pennsylvania J B Law* 661, 661.

53 Hunt (n 40) 153.

54 David Horton, 'Unconscionability in the Law of Trusts' [2009] 84 *Notre Dame LR* 1675, 1694–5.

55 Erez Reuveni, 'On Virtual Worlds: Copyright and Contract Law at the Dawn of the Virtual Age' (2007) *Indiana LJ* 261, 301.

56 Hunt (n 40) 154.

Since substantive unconscionability concerns the existence of contractual terms which are so one-sided that unreasonably favor one party,[57] the actual terms in the EULAs must be examined. As one may expect, EULAs are constructed to bias towards the developers' interests. Many terms are drafted to offer great protection to the developers' rights. For instance, they are always provided with a wide range of one-sided remedies[58] and they retain discretion and control over in-world disputes. Take *Second Life* as an example, under its ToS, Linden Lab has the right to suspend or terminate the gamers' account if they *determine in their discretion* that it is necessary or advisable to protect their own interests.[59] Moreover, section 5.1 confers upon Linden Lab the power to "revoke the Linden Dollar License at any time without notice, refund or compensation" [60] if they *determine* that the concerned account is associated with fraud or other illegal conducts.

Developers are also empowered to alter the EULAs as they desire. This implies that the terms of the developer-user contracts are potentially subject to changes from time to time. In some cases, the terms may be changed secretly, without even notifying the users or asking for their assent to the modified EULAs. This can be instanced by a class action in 2010,[61] where a group of *Second Life*'s users filed an action against Linden Lab over a virtual land dispute, claiming that their contractual property ownership had been changed. "The lawsuit alleges

---

57 David Horton, 'Unconscionability Wars' (2011) *Northwestern U LR* 13, 32.

58 Andrew Sparrow, *The Law of Virtual Worlds and Internet Social Networks* (Gower Publishing Ltd 2010) 113.

59 Second Life, Terms of Service, s 11.4 (Second Life, May 7, 2010) <http://secondlife.com/corporate/tos.php> accessed December 3, 2013.

60 Second Life, Terms of Service, s 5.1 (Second Life, 7 May 2010) <http://secondlife.com/corporate/tos.php> accessed December 3, 2013.

61 *Evans, Spencer & Carter on behalf of all similarly situated individuals v Linden Research, Inc* No 10-1679 (E D Pa Feb 3, 2011).

that Linden Lab tried to differentiate *Second Life* from other virtual worlds by repeatedly emphasizing that users would have indefinite ownership of any property purchased online."[62] Back in 2003, the then CEO of Linden Lab, Philip Rosedale, announced that, "[w]hat you have in *Second Life* is real and it's yours...It doesn't belong to us. We have no claim to it."[63] This announcement had incentivized more than 50,000 *Second Life*'s users to invest approximately US$100 million for purchasing and developing virtual property.[64] However, the idea of ownership was subsequently quietly removed "at an unknown date,"[65] and Second Life's users were no longer entitled to the actual ownership of their virtual property, but a mere license. Worse still, "these customers had no choice but to click on the new ToS agreement or they could not have access to their property."[66]

Furthermore, it is common for developers to stipulate mandatory arbitration to solve any disputes relating to the use of service in their EULAs. Therefore, when a dispute arises, while developers are always entitled to exercise their self-help options (e.g., by suspending the gamers' accounts), the deprived players, after being forfeited with their property and interests in the virtual worlds, have no choice but to initiate arbitration if they

62 David Lazarus, 'A Real-World Battle over Virtual-Property Rights' (*Los Angeles Time*, April 30, 2010) <http://articles.latimes.com/2010/apr/30/business/la-fi-lazarus-20100430> accessed December 3, 2013.

63 Wahab & Medenica LLC, 'Art Imitating Life?—Property Lawsuits for Virtual Real Estate Gain Traction against Second Life' (*New York Business Lawyers*, August 10, 2010) <http://wrlawfirm.com/BlogWP/technology-social-media/real-property-lawsuits-virtual-real-estate-second-life/> accessed December 3, 2013.

64 Courtney Rubin, 'A Virtual World Spawns a Very Real Lawsuit' (Inc., May 3, 2010) <www.inc.com/news/articles/2010/05/second-life-virtual-land-dispute.html> accessed December 3, 2013.

65 *Complaint—Class Action for Damages and Injunctive Relief, Evans, Spencer & Carter on behalf of all similarly situated individuals v Linden Research, Inc* No. 10-1679 (E D Pa Feb 3, 2011) para 96.

66 Matt Osborne, 'Second Life Sued' (Osborne Ink, May 3, 2010) <www.osborneink.com/2010/05/second-life-sued.html> accessed December 3, 2013.

wish to resolve the disputes or object to the developers' decisions.

This can be reflected in *Bragg v Linden Research, Inc.*,[67] where the plaintiff was induced by Philip Rosedale's press announcements and signed up to participate in *Second Life* in 2005. "By taking advantage of an exploit in the *Second Life* system,"[68] he bought Taessot, a piece of virtual real estate, for US$300. However, this was actually in violation of the *Second Life*'s ToS. After learning of the exploit, Linden Lab froze Bragg's account, deleted his avatar, and confiscated all his virtual property, including those which had been purchased before the dubious transaction concerning Taessot. Linden Lab denied passing any title or ownership to its users. Furthermore, it filed motions to dismiss the lawsuit by claiming that Bragg had assented to its ToS which contained a mandatory arbitration clause, and accordingly, the dispute should be resolved by arbitration.

Judge Eduardo Robreno held that the ToS, being a "contract of adhesion,"[69] was procedurally unconscionable because "the weaker party is presented the clause and told to 'take it or leave it' without the opportunity for meaningful negotiation."[70] Supported by the following facts, there was also a finding of substantive unconscionability.

First, the out-of-pocket arbitration expenses can be very onerous. The court estimated "the costs of arbitration with the ICC to be $17,250"[71] or even higher. This would definitely be cost-prohibitive for many aggrieved gamers. In addition, the then ToS prescribed that the arbitration must be conducted in San Francisco, California. Therefore, it is possible that the cost

---

67 487 F Supp 2d 593 (E D Penn 2007).

68 Juliet M. Moringiello, 'What Virtual Worlds Can Do for Property Law' [2010] 62 *Fl. L.R.* 159, 164.

69 487 F Supp 2d 593 (E D Penn 2007) 27.

70 487 F Supp 2d 593 (E D Penn 2007) 28.

71 487 F Supp 2d 593 (E D Penn 2007) 36.

of travel and arbitration for settling the disputes may actually exceed the real world value of the virtual property at issue. The high costs, together with the selection of the seat of arbitration, were plainly oppressive to the gamers.

The issue of "confidentiality" also gives rise to another problem. In the area of dispute resolution, "confidentiality" is one of the most attractive features of arbitration as compared with litigation.[72] However, confidentiality in such situations is a blessing to the developers but a curse to the players-consumers. It places the developers in a superior position—whilst the gamers have no means of access to any previous arbitral decisions, the developers can accumulate knowledge and experience which can then be used to avail themselves of constructing the best arguments in their favor. In essence, "arbitration itself is fought on an uneven field…Linden becomes an expert in litigating the terms of the ToS, while plaintiffs remain novices without the benefit of learning from past precedent."[73]

The court refused to enforce the mandatory arbitration clause by noting that:

> "…[t]aken together, the lack of mutuality, the costs of arbitration, the forum selection clause, and the confidentiality provision that Linden unilaterally imposes through the ToS demonstrate that the arbitration clause is not designed to provide Second Life participants an effective means of resolving disputes with Linden. Rather, it is a one-sided means which tilts unfairly, in almost all situations, in Linden's favor."[74]

---

72 Gloria Miccioli, 'Features—A Selective Guide to Online International Arbitration Resources' (LLRX.com, June 21, 2004) <www.llrx.com/features/intarbitration. htm> accessed December 3, 2013.

73 487 F Supp 2d 593 (E D Penn 2007) 41.

74 487 F Supp 2d 593 (E D Penn 2007) 41.

While *Bragg v Linden Research, Inc.*[75] may appear to be good news for gamers, it should be noted that, it is just one of the very few cases where the EULA (or ToS) was struck down by virtue of unconscionability. In fact, "existing case law tends to weigh against parties attacking EULA on grounds of unconscionability."[76]

"Unconscionability" is a difficult hurdle for the aggrieved players-consumers as it is the courts' default position to enforce general contractual terms. Moreover, courts may even be more reluctant to rule a contractual term as substantively unconscionable "when all that is at stake is participation in what is considered a 'game'."[77]

Therefore, it can be concluded that, contract law is incapable of providing adequate protection to players-consumers. The EULAs are the most powerful "flak jacket" that can shield the developers from their gamers' claims or attacks. Unless the EULAs are held to be unenforceable or unconscionable, the developers can always rely on the terms, which are written mainly for protecting their interests.

4.   The Practical Way Out: Consumer Protection Law

All virtual worlds' EULAs (or ToS) intertwine property and contract law issues. From a doctrinal perspective, both the property-based and contract-based approaches to judicial recognition of virtual property are problematic. "Even the most practical and plausible of the property-based approaches first

---

75   487 F Supp 2d 593 (E D Penn 2007).

76   David P Sheldon, 'Claiming Ownership, but Getting Owned: Contractual Limitations on Asserting Property Interests in Virtual Goods' [2007] 54 *UCLA L.R.* 751, 777.

77   Erez Reuveni, 'On Virtual Worlds: Copyright and Contract Law at the Dawn of the Virtual Age' (2007) *Indiana L.J.* 261, 302.

requires a court to strike down [the EULA]."[78] However, with the likely continued enforceability of these agreements, any potential claims of property rights by the aggrieved players-consumers are destined to be ineffectual and impotent.

In such circumstances, consumer protection law is the last, yet the most powerful, resort. It is capable of addressing the inherent inequities of the property-based and contract-based approaches, and can thus provide the players-consumers with their deserved remedies where common law cannot.

As mentioned in Part 1, commodification endows players with an additional identity — "consumers." This distinction should be judicially recognized so as to afford legal protection to the players-consumers. As put by Professor Jack Balkin, "the more that the platform owner attempts to make the game space a new version of the shopping mall, the less likely the [law] will or should protect them when the state wants to vindicate the reliance and property interests of the players."[79] It means that, the more commodified a virtual world is, the more likely that the consumer protection law should be invoked.

When assenting to the EULAs (and subsequently purchasing virtual goods from the developers), the players-consumers are at a vulnerable and disadvantaged position because their counterparties are actually the drafters of the EULAs, which govern everything in the worlds. As one of the focuses of consumer protection law is to "redress this imbalance of power,"[80] this makes it a particularly useful tool to the deprived gamers. Moreover, it is arguably the best area of law which acknowledges and protects the gamers' reasonable expectations of their rights in

---

78 Riley (n 22) 906.

79 Jack M. Balkin, 'Virtual Liberty: Freedom to Design and Freedom to Play in Virtual Worlds' [2004] 90 *Virginia LR* 2043, 2073.

80 John Goldring, 'Consumer Law and Legal Theory: Reflections of a Common Lawyer' [1990] 13 *J Consumer Policy* 113, 116.

virtual property.[81] After devoting a substantial amount of time and money to acquiring virtual property, it is logical for the players-consumers to assume that they can have a claim of ownership to those assets. "No rational person, given the chance, would invest their time and money in a market where their goods can be seized at will by the company that owns the trading space."[82] It is hardly sensible that, having spent a certain amount of virtual currency (which has real world value), the purchasers actually do not gain any ownership interests over the property and are left with no proper cause of action in case any unpleasant events take place.

A well-drafted legislation can effectively plug the loophole left by common law. Among all, the European Union law is highly praised as having "a powerful consumer protection regime,"[83] which is a paradigm for drafting or amending the relevant legislation. The Council Directive 93/13/EEC of April 5, 1993 on Unfair Terms in Consumer Contracts has already come into force for two decades.

Despite being a short Directive with just 11 Articles, it is capable of offering concrete protection to consumers. Article 3(1) clearly states that "a contractual term which has not been individually negotiated shall be regarded as unfair if, contrary to the requirement of good faith, it causes a significant imbalance in the parties' rights and obligations arising under the contract, to the detriment of the consumer'[84] and Article 6(1) provides that

---

81 Balkin (n 79) 2081.

82 Benjamin Tarsa, 'Licensing of Virtual Goods: Misconceptions of Ownership' (*Gnovis Journal*, April 26, 2012) <http://gnovisjournal.org/2012/04/26/licensing-of-virtual-goods-misconceptions-of-ownership/> accessed December 3, 2013.

83 Jas Purewal, 'What Happens When a Game with Virtual Goods Closes?' (Gamer Law, January 23, 2012) <www.gamerlaw.co.uk/2012/what-happens-when-a-game-with-virtual-goods-closes/> accessed December 3, 2013.

84 Unfair Terms in Consumer Contracts, Council Directive 93/13/EEC of April 5, 1993, art 3(1).

such unfair terms are "not to be binding on the consumer."[85]

With the consumer protection law in place, players-consumers will likely be entitled to the same level of protection as ordinary real world consumers. At the very least, they can seek to void the unfair contractual terms.

However, before the consumer protection law can be applicable, the status of "virtual property" must be properly recognized by law. A useful reference can be drawn to a recent UK Government's move. In July 2012, the UK Department of Business Innovation and Skills proposed the Consumer Bill of Rights, which suggests changing the law on consumer rights with regards to "digital content." A paper titled "Consultation on Enhancing Consumer Confidence by Clarifying Consumer Law" was also issued.

Adopting the definition laid down in Article 2(11) of the EU Consumer Right Directive,[86] "digital content" in this context means "data which are produced and supplied in digital form."[87] Acknowledging that "digital content" is neither "goods" nor "service," the UK Government seeks to treat it as a separate category[88] and ensure proper application of consumer rights to "digital content" supplied under a contract.[89] According to paragraph 7.169, '[d]igital content can often be supplied without payment of money. This could be in exchange for something of value other than money such as ... virtual currency."[90] Moreover, it is expressly noted that, a player who "purchases in-world

---

85 Unfair Terms in Consumer Contracts, Council Directive 93/13/EEC of April 5, 1993, art 6(1).

86 2011/83/EU.

87 EU Consumer Right Directive 2011/83/EU, art 2(11).

88 Department for Business Innovation & Skills, Consultation on Enhancing Consumer Confidence by Clarifying Consumer Law (2012) para 2.7.

89 *ibid*, para 7.8.

90 *ibid.*, para 7.169.

credits to buy virtual items within the virtual world [will be covered by the proposal]."[91] In such circumstances, the "digital content" supplied is the virtual world, and the access to it is a "related service." Thus, when a gamer exchanges real world currency for in-world credits (which he later uses for acquiring virtual items), he is essentially paying for the "digital content."

The UK Government admitted that, the 1893 Sale of Goods Act fails to cater well for the concept of "digital content" and no legislation deals specifically with transactions involving "digital content," rendering the law unclear and uncertain.[92] Although nothing in the consultation paper has come into force yet, it is definitely a right move in the right direction.

4.1   The Situation in Hong Kong

Since the Sale of Goods Ordinance was designed to be Hong Kong's equivalent to the U.K.'s 1893 Sale of Goods Act, the Ordinance inevitably fails to overhaul the digitalization of the society as well. "Goods" is defined as "all chattels personal other than things in action and money."[93] Virtual property, with no physical existence, can hardly be qualified as "goods." In addition, "access to digital content" is unlikely to be treated as a "contract for the supply of a service,"[94] therefore, no protection can be sought from the Supply of Services (Implied Terms) Ordinance. The Unconscionable Contracts Ordinance has no applicability either—because it only applies to contracts which supply goods or services.[95]

Although the courts in Hong Kong have not dealt with any disputes concerning ownership of virtual property thus far, given

---

91 *ibid.*, 133.

92 *ibid.*, para 4.18.

93 Sale of Goods Ordinance (Cap 26), s 2.

94 Supply of Services (Implied Terms) Ordinance (Cap 457), s 3.

95 Unconscionable Contracts Ordinance (Cap 458), s 5(1).

the global trend to recognize "virtual property," the law should be amended accordingly. As such, it is a recommendable move to follow the U.K.'s lead—to incorporate "digital content" (which includes virtual property) into the present legal regime and entitle the players-consumers to their deserved rights.

5. Conclusion

With the vigorous commodification in virtual worlds, the virtual goods-based business models are prospering. It follows that, the issues of "virtual property rights" and "consumer protection" have generated heated discussion—What do the players actually acquire with their investment of money and effort? And will they be entitled to any remedies in case anything goes wrong?

Despite the similarities between virtual property and real goods, which gives rise to the viability of applying traditional property law to virtual items, it should be borne in mind that, this requires the EULAs to be void. However, given the courts' default position to uphold contractual terms, they can hardly be convinced to strike down the EULAs to which the aggrieved gamers have assented. It is also very difficult to attack an EULA on grounds of unconscionability.

Accordingly, it is an arduous task for gamers to avoid the EULAs, which usually contains a clause expressly retaining all ownership rights with the developers. Vested with no virtual property rights, the players-consumers are prone to exploitation. Developers can enforce their self-drafted contractual terms at their discretion—they are empowered to confiscate their users' property or terminate their accounts "for any reason at any time without compensation."[96] If the players wish to resolve the

---

96 Bobby Glushko, 'Tales of the (Virtual) City: Governing Property Disputes in Virtual Worlds' [2007] 22 *Berkley Tech LJ* 251, 270.

disputes or object to the developers' decisions, they are usually left with no choice but to initiate the costly arbitration proceedings.

With such an imbalance in the respective parties' remedies, consumer protection law should step in and provide a proper channel where the deprived players can seek redress for their grievances. Nevertheless, an important step must be taken in advance—conferring a legal status on "virtual property." This can easily be achieved by including an additional category—"digital content"—in the relevant legislation, so that true recognition can be given to "virtual property," and players-consumers can then be afforded concrete protection should any unpleasant events take place.

24

Virtual World EULAs and Transactions: Consumer Friendly or Void of Consumer Protection?

Vimal Deepak SADHWANI

1. Introduction

In the past decade, virtual worlds have come into limelight as human beings fantasize a life in a world which is simulated by avatars and objects, made possible by the advancement in technology. A virtual world is often described as an online community through which users can interact with each other in an environment of their choice and every user gets to choose an avatar of their liking and appear as a textual two-dimensional or three-dimensional character.[1] With the growing number of users interacting in this virtual world, a natural evolution occurred, allowing virtual world users to engage in trade among themselves and to establish businesses online.

In a virtual world like *Second Life*, there was a need to create a currency in order to facilitate business among users of the virtual world and to attract new users to this online simulation. Hence, the Linden Dollar, *Second life*'s in-game currency was introduced. Market entrants could trade real life money for Linden Dollars.

---

1 Dave Wieneke, 'The State of Business and Law in Virtual Worlds', Thomson Compu Mark, May 2008.

Like any other currency, the exchange rate for this currency is always changing but is generally traded at 270 to 300 Linden Dollars for 1 US Dollar.[2] The total size of *Second Life*'s economy grew to US$567 million; about 25% of the entire US virtual goods market was in *Second Life* and it was reported that gross resident' earnings in the simulation were about US$55 million. There is also an active real estate market where land is bought and sold for millions of dollars. To govern the trade between *Second Life* users in this simulated environment, Linden Labs has created a terms of service agreement between themselves and new users of *Second Life*. Similarly, the other virtual worlds like Entropia Universe also have an End User License Agreement to regulate in-game transactions. However, to what extent are these laws consumer friendly?

This chapter focuses on the protection of consumers in virtual world transactions such as those in *Second Life* and *Entropia Universe* by taking into account current practices in these simulations. This chapter is divided into three sections. Section 1 focuses on the unequal bargaining position which users face when they join these simulations and how they are deceived by misrepresentation. Section 2 shall compare how consumers are protected in the real world in the trade of goods and services in countries like Hong Kong and Singapore. The final section shall propose a framework of changes which have to be employed in the virtual world in order to make it more consumer friendly.

2.   Consumer Protection or the Lack of It?

Despite the success of the virtual world in the past decade, users often feel that they have been cheated because they invested their

---

2 Second Life, 'Exchange Rate' accessed at <http://compsimgames.about.com/od/secondlife/qt/exchangerate.htm> accessed December 3, 2013.

time and money on something which did not or rather cannot pay dividends due to the harsh agreements they entered into with the game developers.

To begin with, virtual property ownership is not regulated like property in the real world despite it having legal, economic and social importance as that of real property. After promoting its in-game economy and currency exchange rates, Linden Lab refused to recognize any regulation or protection for virtual property. This allowed them to profit from the sale of virtual property without protecting player interests.[3]

This section outlines some of the key contractual problems which users in the virtual world like *Second Life* and *Entropia Universe* face when considering the terms they enter into agreement. Some of these issues include unconscionability, misrepresentation and false promises made by the game owners.

2.1 Unconscionability

A contract is said to be unconscionable when it is so unfair to one party that no reasonable or informed person would agree to it. Consumers in *Second Life* come under the purview of Section 3 of the Unconscionable Contracts Ordinance and can be said to be dealing as consumers.[4] Unconscionability can be categorized as either procedural or substantive. Procedural unconscionability refers to defects in the bargaining process in an agreement and substantive unconscionability is when obligations are unreasonably favored to one of the parties.

In a virtual world like *Second Life*, the End User License Agreements (EULA) has consequences of a power imbalance between users and the developer as the users have no choice but

---

3 Kurt Hunt, 'His land is not your land: Second Life, Copybot, and the Looming Question of Virtual Property Rights' (2007) 9 T*ex. Rev. Ent. & Sports L.* 141–174.

4 Unconscionable Contracts Ordinance (Cap 458), Section 3.

to accept the terms and conditions unfavorable to them. Many EULA terms are one-sided in favor of developers. The Terms of Service agreement (TOS) in *Second Life* attack user's ownership of virtual property in that they stipulate that the players have no ownership rights in "any data Linden Lab stores on Linden Lab servers."[5] In another section, Linden Lab warns that "content, currency, objects, items, scripts, equipment, or other value or status indicators...may be deleted, altered, moved or transferred at any time."[6] Further, it is also stipulated that "notwithstanding any value attributed...by you or any third party, Linden Lab... expressly disclaims...any value, cash or otherwise, attributed to any data residing on Linden Lab's servers.[7]

These are only a few examples of how consumer protection is not adequately provided for in *Second Life* as players don't actually own property or goods, and thus would not be able to recover damages or any remedies if those items were devalued, taken or deleted. It is submitted that these are clauses of both substantial and procedural unconscionability as the agreements are operatively harsh to the users and are described as boilerplate agreements. The users are forced to enter into agreements on a take-it-or-leave-it basis.

Further, entering into these unconscionable contracts has the effect of nullifying any dispute resolution clauses as the contracts were void. The problems related to this can be seen in cases about virtual properties where arbitration clauses are held invalid. For example, in *Second Life*, in the case of *Bragg v Linden Lab*,[8] the plaintiff argued that the provisions requiring the parties to settle their disputes to arbitration under California's unfair competition law was "both procedurally and substantively unconscionable"

---

5 Terms of Service Agreement in Second Life's EULA, Section 7.3.

6 Terms of Service Agreement in Second Life's EULA, Section 7.5.

7 Terms of Service Agreement in Second Life's EULA, Section 10.2.

8 Bragg v Linden Lab, Inc 487 F. Supp. 2d 593 (E.D.Penn. 2007).

as he had no choice but to accept those terms of conditions. The court held that terms were indeed unconscionable and decided that they had jurisdiction to decide the matter instead of it being decided by arbitration. This only goes to show that the terms which require parties to settle their dispute by arbitration in *Second Life* are impracticable and the lack of finality in the Terms of Service Agreement in *Second Life* which means that should a dispute arise among consumers in the game, it would be hard for the consumers to rely on terms in *Second Life*'s EULA.

Virtual Worlds like *Entropia Universe* widely advertise its "Real Cash Economy" and even sells "virtual banking licenses" that grant "the right to exclusively operate banking services within the Entropia Universe," however, Section 6 of the *Entropia Universe* EULA[9] states that *Entropia Universe* has the right to terminate any account and Section 7 of the EULA provisions[10] state that the user will not gain any ownership interest whatsoever in any virtual item. This is another example of a boiler plate agreement, which might be termed as unconscionable by the courts should a dispute arise and it questions the effectiveness of the consumer protection laws in these virtual worlds.

2.2 Misrepresentation

Another pivotal problem which users in the virtual world face is the misrepresentation adduced by the operators about the ownership of goods and properties. At common law, Misrepresentation is defined as "an assertion that is not in accord with the facts" and can void a contract if it is likely to induce a reasonable man into believing that fraudulent statement. As an example of how such information induces a misrepresentation, let us consider the virtual world of *Second Life* again. A user in

---

9 Entropia Universe End User License Agreement (EULA), Section 6.

10 Entropia Universe End User License Agreement (EULA), Section 7.

Second Life upon creating an account, agrees that he will not gain any ownership whatsoever in any virtual item. When he enters the game, a user may enter into a contract with the developer of *Second Life* for the purchase of one or several properties. Upon doing some research, it is found that most properties in *Second Life* are initially sold by public auction and purchasers enter into an ownership deed and the sale is treated as any other sale of land in the real life world. Similarly, *Entropia Universe* promises its user of an in-game economy and the option to trade in-game currencies back for real life currencies.[11]

If such an issue arises, the question which the courts or arbitration tribunal would have to answer is whether the terms and conditions which state that the users will not gain any ownership override the representations made by the developers in the virtual world about the ownership of properties and goods in the virtual world.

It is argued that the language used in virtual world contracts amounts to a material or fraudulent misrepresentation as the contract which a user subsequently enters into in the virtual world is not in accord with reality and is likely to induce a reasonable person to give in and accept the terms. Once terms and conditions are unequally accepted by users, there is fraudulent misrepresentation when users are promised value for their purchases in the virtual world, but in reality, they don't have a right to anything. This is a grievous problem to virtual world users as they fail to realize that they are not in fact the owners of any virtual goods.

2.3 *Promissory Estoppel*

The doctrine of promissory estoppel prevents one party from withdrawing a promise made to a second party if the latter has

---

11 Hunt (n 3).

reasonably relied on that promise. In the case of virtual worlds, users join these simulations based on the promises that if they invest money and time into the virtual world, the presence of the "Real Cash Economy" would allow them to trade in game currencies into real life money at some point. However, this is merely a promise and as discussed earlier, the unequal terms and conditions fail to recognize the fact that users own any property or goods in the virtual world. The law fails to protect consumers and it is submitted that users can rely on the doctrine of promissory estoppel in order to enforce their assets in the virtual world. However, the present state of EULA's in these virtual worlds seems to defeat consumer claims and it is submitted that consumers are not adequately protected if they do not have access to litigation resources.

2.4 Problem of Enforceability

In addition the cumbersome and one-sided terms of service agreement has been questioned for its enforceability. Scholars like Jack Balkin opine that "it is not clear whether the courts will enforce EULA's terms and conditions and recognize the rights of the users in the virtual world."[12] Further Lastowka and Hunter have stated that "[t]hough property rights may exist in virtual assets, the courts may still reject any property rights vested in users in the virtual world."[13] The effect which the unenforceability of virtual assets would have could be disastrous to users. For example, Ailin Graef, a multi-millionaire in the virtual world who sells real estate would not have any more assets than a pauper in the virtual world as she does not own any assets under the current terms of service agreement. The game developers

---

12 Jack Balkin, 'Virtual Liberty: Freedom to Design and Freedom to Play in Virtual World' (2004) 90 *Virginia Law Review*.

13 F. Gregory Lastowka and Dan Hunter, 'The Laws of the Virtual Worlds' (2004) 92 *Cal. L. Rev.* 1.

also argue that the courts in the user's country of residence lack jurisdiction complicating matters further on enforceability. A case where a virtual world user had problems in enforcing his assets was that of Li Hongchen.[14] Li Hongchen had spent two years and about US$1,210 in developing weapons in the virtual world. His stock of bio-chemical weapons was stolen by hackers. He sued the company called Beijing Arctic Ice Technology Development Co. to get his virtual property back as it was this company who was in charge of running the game. The company defended itself and claimed that the items in the game had no value and were just piles of data in game servers and as such, Mr Li had no right or ownership in any of the assets and could not enforce his gains in the virtual world.

Thus, it is submitted that consumers in the virtual world are not adequately protected as they enter into boilerplate agreements in order to gain access to the virtual world. Furthermore, such agreements may contain misrepresentations and false promises which make it difficult for consumers to find and enforce their rights under the agreement.

3.   Consumer Protection in the Real World: A Comparison of Jurisdictions

In most common law jurisdictions like Hong Kong and Singapore, the trade of goods and services is well regulated by national legislations such as the *Sale of Goods Ordinance*[15] in Hong Kong and the Singapore's *Consumer Protection (Fair Trading) Act*[16] in Singapore. This section considers how consumers in these

---

14 *Li Hongchen v. Beijing Arctic Ice Technology Development Co. Ltd.*, <www. virtualpolicy.net/arcticice.html> accessed December 3, 2013.

15 Sale of Goods Ordinance (Cap 26).

16 Consumer Protection (Fair Trading) Act of Singapore (Chapter 52A).

jurisdictions are protected by breach of contract issues such as Unconscionability and Misrepresentation should the courts decide that they have jurisdiction on the matter.

3.1 Hong Kong

The *Unconscionable Contracts Ordinance (Cap. 458)*[17] applies to contracts in Hong Kong for the sale of goods or supply of services provided that one of the parties to the contract deals as a consumer. By virtue of this legislation, the courts can hold a contract void where the contract terms are very oppressive on one party. In the case of *Shum Kit Ching v Caesar Beauty*,[18] the court held a contract for the services of beauty products to be unconscionable and refused to enforce a contract and laid down the requirements of when a contract would be held to be unconscionable. The court described three requirements for it to give relief under the doctrine of unconscionable bargain. They are:

(1) The bargain must be oppressive to the complainant in overall terms.
(2) The complainant was suffering from a bargaining weakness.
(3) The wrongdoer knowingly took advantage of the complainant's weakness.

When considering consumer protection in the virtual world, it seems almost inevitable that if Hong Kong's domestic law is to apply, the court will hold the End User License Agreement in *Second Life* and *Entropia Universe* to be invalid as the clauses in the boilerplate agreements discussed earlier in the essay are unconscionable by virtue of section 6(1) of the *Unconscionable*

---

17 The Unconscionable Contracts Ordinance (Cap. 458).

18 *Shum Kit Ching v Caesar Beauty Centre Ltd* [2003] 3 HKLRD.

Contracts Ordinance.[19]

Further, the operation of the *Control of Exemption Clauses Ordinances (CECO)*[20] has the effect of protecting consumers from such harsh terms and conditions such as in the EULA's in *Second Life*. Section 3 of the CECO requires an exemption to satisfy the requirement of being fair and reasonable and prevents operators from exempting liability in terms of all agreements.[21]

The Misrepresentation Ordinance helps protect consumers on agreements where they have been induced either fraudulently or negligently. Section 4 of the *Misrepresentation Ordinance*[22] provides that service providers cannot exclude liability for fraudulent misrepresentation as cited in the case of *HIH Casualty & General v Chase Manhattan.*[23]

3.2 Singapore

Singapore has by far one of the most effective consumer protection policies in the world. Singapore's *Consumer Protection (Fair Trading) Act*[24] places special importance on the rights of consumers and enables them to bring an action where unfair practice is involved. Any sale of goods transaction in Singapore falls within the ambit of this statute and consumers rely on this statute for protection.

Under the statute, it would constitute unfair practice in a consumer transaction for a service provider to:

(1) To deceive or mislead a consumer.

---

19 Unconscionable Contracts Ordinance (Cap. 458), Section 6(1).

20 Control of Exemption Clauses Ordinances (Cap. 71).

21 *Oriental Pearl South Africa Project CC v Bank of Taiwan* [2006] HKCU 1670.

22 Misrepresentation Ordinance (Cap. 458).

23 *HIH Casualty and General Insurance Ltd v Chase Manhattan Bank* [2003] UKHL 6.

24 Consumer Protection (Fair Trading) Act of Singapore (Chapter 52A).

(2) To make a false claim.

(3) To take advantage of a consumer if he is in an unequal bargaining position.

This statute effectively deals with contractual problems such as unconscionability and misrepresentation as they effectively preclude service providers from attaining any unfair advantage.

Thus, it is submitted that the framework of consumer protection laws in jurisdictions like Hong Kong and Singapore effectively deal with problems in the virtual world where the owners of a simulation engage in fraudulent misrepresentation in inducing users to buy property and goods in the virtual world, however such law only comes into play if the service providers acknowledge them in the End User License Agreements and give these countries jurisdiction to decide the matter.

4. Consumer Friendly Proposals for Virtual Worlds

After analyzing the fallacies of the End User License Agreements in *Second Life* and *Entropia Universe*, the following are some suggestions that would make these interfaces more consumer friendly.

4.1 Right to Ownership

It is proposed that if these virtual worlds have to attract consumers and keep improving their economy, they must recognize the user's ownership of properties and goods in the simulation. The case of *Bragg v Linden Labs*, discussed earlier points out litigation problems which *Second Life* would have to face should they not recognize user's ownership. Although Bragg's case was settled, it is highly foreseeable that these virtual worlds might lose litigation battles should a similar case arise.

The Terms of Service Agreement should first be altered in stating that *Second Life* recognizes the ownership and subsequent sale of goods and properties by users.

4.2   Facilitating Currency Exchange

Another important proposal is for the virtual worlds to allow users to freely convert (i.e., without currency exchange penalties) their in-game currencies back to real life currencies in a virtual world like *Entropia Universe*. Unless this is practically affected, users might be wasting their time and money in the virtual would without any material gain.

4.3   Removing Disclaimers and Deletion Clauses

It is submitted that *Second Life*'s EULA which contains clauses allowing the developer to delete any virtual asset and disclaimers about resident's ownership of property are too unrealistic and should be amended giving the users the right to freely trade in the virtual world without fear of losing any of their assets.

4.4   Arbitration Friendly Clauses

It is further proposed that the End User License Agreements in *Second Life* and *Entropia Universe* contain arbitration clauses that are too unfair to consumers. It is proposed that the consumers should be able to rely on consumer protection acts of a particular jurisdiction and should be able to select a seat of arbitration near their country. At present, it seems highly improbable that aggrieved virtual world users who are situated outside *Second Life*'s jurisdiction can bring their claims under California's Unfair Competition law.[25] Greater consideration needs to be given to the practical implications of dispute resolution in virtual world transactions.

---

25 Unfair Competiton Law of California, ("UCL") §§ 17200 et seq.

5. Conclusion

Virtual worlds like *Second Life* and *Entropia Universe* are thriving markets and have a booming economy. However, it is important to protect the rights of consumers in these worlds as consumers face problems in contractual agreements between themselves and users. Most of these contracts are unconscionable as consumers are in unequal bargaining positions. It is hoped that these virtual worlds may adopt the changes discussed in this article and grant jurisdiction to courts which are more consumer protection friendly such as Hong Kong and Singapore. It is hoped that by incorporating changes such as recognizing the ownership of assets by users in the virtual world, more consumers would think it just to invest their time and money into the virtual world.

25

EULAs vs. Consumer Rights and Protections in Virtual World Commercial Transactions: Finding a Healthy Balance

Mitchell Kwun Yin LI

1. Introduction

The virtual world market has grown dramatically over the past five years. In the second quarter of 2011, the estimated registered virtual world accounts had already reached 1.39 billion.[1] Virtual worlds give users not only a new channel for social interactions but also provide entrepreneurs with a new platform to run their businesses.

There are many successful stories for virtual world businesses. An outstanding example is Anshe Chung, an avatar[2] of *Second Life*, who becomes the first virtual world billionaire.[3] She owns a business Anshe Chung Studios with more than 80 full-time employees and the property she has developed accommodates

---

1 'Q2 2011 VW cumulative registered accounts reaches 1.4 billion' (KZER Worldwide) <www.kzero.co.uk/blog/q2-2011-vw-cumulative-registered-accounts-reaches-1-4-billion/> accessed December 3, 2013.

2 Representational proxies in ... virtual spaces are known as "avatars," a word of Hindu religious origin. F. Gregory Lastowka & Dan Hunter, 'The Laws of the Virtual Worlds' (2004) 92 *Cal. L. Rev.* 1, 6.

3 Rob Hof, 'Second Life's First Millionaire', *Bloomberg Business Week* (United States November 26, 2006) <www.businessweek.com/the_thread/techbeat/archives/2006/11/second_lifes_fi.html> accessed December 3, 2013.

thousands of residents over 40 square kilometers of land.[4]

These virtual assets are no longer valueless because most virtual games and virtual worlds enable users to convert their virtual assets into real money. Many scholars suggest using real world legal rules to protect virtual world users. For example, Kane comments that "the commercialization of virtual environments will result in the online industry being subjected to real world laws and regulations as users seek to monetize the value in virtual property."[5] As more and more consumers gravitate to the virtual world, one of the key issues is whether virtual worlds offer sufficient consumer protection.

This chapter attempts to study consumer protection in virtual world transactions. Part I defines virtual worlds and describes how virtual economies develop in light of *Second Life*. Part II discusses the consumer rights and potential risks involved in virtual world commercial transactions. Part III evaluates how existing laws could potentially protect the consumers. Part IV suggests additional steps that can be taken to enlarge the scope of consumer protection.

2.   Introduction of Virtual Worlds

2.1 Defining Virtual Worlds

A virtual world is an online and interactive world in which players can create avatars to interact with each other.[6] Depending on the world, customers are able to experience a vast degree of complex commercial and social interactions that mimic the real

---

4 (Anshe Chung Studios) <http://anshechung.com/> accessed December 3, 2013.

5 Kane, S. F., 'Virtual Worlds: "Passporting" of avatars and property between virtual Works' (2007) 9 *E-Commerce Law & Policy* 12.

6 Mark W. Bell, "Toward a Definition of "Virtual Worlds" (2008) 1 *Journal of Virtual Worlds Research* 1.

world.[7] For instance, socializing with other users and trading virtual items for virtual currency.

Generally, virtual worlds share the following characteristics that distinguish themselves from single-player video games:

(1) a shared space with multi-user access;

(2) a 3-D graphical user interface;

(3) instant and simultaneous interactions;

(4) persistence i.e., the virtual world continues to exist and develop whether or not the user has logged in;

(5) interactivity i.e., allow users to change or create customized content;

(6) social interaction i.e., allow social in-world groups such as neighborhoods; and

(7) the use of avatar, a graphical representation of the user in the virtual world[8]

2.2 Virtual Economies

Massively multiplayer online role-playing games (MMORPGs) such as *EverQuest*, *Guild Wars*, and *World of Warcraft* have a market exchange system in which the virtual commodities can be traded, thereby establishing virtual world economies. For instance, a player in the virtual game, *Entropia Universe*, sold his virtual nightclub for US$635,000, setting the record for the most expensive virtual item purchased.[9]

---

7 Woodrow Barfield, 'Intellectual Property Rights in Virtual Environments: Considering the Rights of Owners, Programmers and Virtual Avatars'(2006) 39 *Akron L. Rev.* 649, 649-700.

8 OECD (2011), 'Virtual Worlds: Immersive Online Platforms for Collaboration, Creativity and Learning', (2011) OECD Digital Economy Papers, No. 184 <http://dx.doi.org/10.1787/5kg9qgnpjmjg-en> accessed December 3, 2013.

9 Daniel Bates, 'Internet estate agent sells virtual night club on an asteroid in online game for £400,000' Mail Online (UK November 18, 2010) <www.dailymail.co.uk/sciencetech/article-1330552/Jon-Jacobs-sells-virtual-nightclub-Club-Neverdie-online-Entropia-game-400k.html> accessed December 3, 2013.

Avatars often play the role of consumer as well as entrepreneur within virtual worlds. The type and amount of economic activity depends on the rules created by the operator.[10] For instance, *Second life* avatars can sell the goods in the marketplace for Linden dollars, which can be converted into real world currencies, such as US dollars and the euro.[11] Calculating from April 2007, the trading activity of Lindex, *Second Life*'s currency exchange, has reached approximately $250,000 a day on average.[12]

Broadly speaking, there are two types of MMORPGs: traditional and non-traditional. The traditional type requires users to increase the "level" of their avatars by accepting progressively more challenging tasks. For example, a *World of Warcraft* user must kill small animals at an early stage before progressing to slay the powerful beasts.[13] *Second Life* belongs to the non-traditional type. It has no objectives in and of itself.[14] Users socialize with each other in the virtual world by taking part in activities varying from running a business, staging a political rally for a real-world presidential candidate to attending lectures.[15]

Second Life is a glaring example of how the virtual economy runs. *Second life* has two essential features that distinguish it from other MMORPGs: ownership and creativity.[16] Account users can create the content of their virtual world with the aid of the tools

---

10 Kurt Hunt, 'His land is not your land: Second Life, Copybot, and the Looming Question of Virtual Property Rights' (2007) 9 *Tex. Rev. Ent. & Sports L.* 141.

11 David P. Sheldon, 'Claiming Ownership, but getting owned: Contractual limitations on asserting property interests in virtual goods' (2007) 54 *UCLA L. Rev.* 751.

12 Second Life's Official Website (Second Life), <http://secondlifegrid.net/spt/resources/factsheet/economics> accessed December 3, 2013.

13 Paul Riley, 'Litigating Second Life Land Disputes: A Consumer Protection Approach'(2009) 19 *Fordham Intell. Prop. Media & Ent. L.J.* 877.

14 'Second Life-FAQ' (Second Life), <http://secondlife.com/whatis/faq.php> accessed December 3, 2013.

15 *ibid.*

16 *ibid.* (Is Second Life a Game? Yes and no. While the Second Life interface and display are similar to most [MMORPGs], there are two key, unique differences: Creativity...Ownership.)

provided by Linden, the operator of *Second Life*. Cory Ondrejka, a former executive of Linden, has repeatedly said "all of the content of *Second Life* is built by its users inside the world."[17]

In *Second Life*, users would not be able to sell their virtual creations unless they have become the land owners.[18] To own land, a user must pay (1) a monthly membership fee, (2) a land use fee and (3) purchase the land from Linden or other avatars.[19] Accordingly, land ownership is important to both the *Second Life* users and Linden (i.e., the main source of revenue for Linden comes from land sale; users cannot operate a business without acquiring land.) Users who cannot own land are known as "basic users." They can still interact with other avatars using the construction tools, but cannot operate a business.[20]

3. Consumer Rights under Standard Form Contracts

Numerous commercial transactions take place in virtual worlds every day. In fact, similar to the real world, commercial activities in virtual worlds are full of hidden risks. Perhaps, the risks in virtual worlds are even higher and wider in scope. Since virtual assets can now be turned into real assets, it is essential to identify the rights consumers have and protect them through legal means.

Consumers are bound by the game rules to which they have agreed. There rules are set out in two documents: extensive end-user license agreements (EULAs) and Terms of Service (TOS) or Terms of Use (TOU).

---

17 Symposium, "Regulating Digital Environments: Ownership in Online Worlds", 21 *Santa Clara Computer Clara & High Tech. L.J.* 807, 820 (2006)

18 Second Life-Frequently Asked Questions from Beginning Landowners, <https://support.secondlife.com/ics/support/default.asp?deptID=4417&task=knowledge&questionID=5198> accessed December 3, 2013.

19 *ibid.*

20 *ibid.*

The EULAs and TOS allocate rights and responsibilities to the users with respect to virtual items. In general, customers are identified with three rights, namely the right to use, the right to exclude and the right to transfer.[21]

3.1 Right to Use

Each EULA explicitly and implicitly gives the users the right to use the avatars associated with their accounts and the right to use virtual items within the game.[22]

3.2 Right to Exclude

The right to exclude is understood as the right to prevent others from exerting control over the virtual goods.[23] However, most virtual-world providers do not give this right to consumers. In doing so, providers insert a clause in the TOU to retain all rights, title and interest in virtual objects and data.[24] For example, the *World of Warcraft*'s TOU states: "all rights and title in and to the Service... are owned by Blizzard [the operator] or its licensors."[25]

Interestingly, *Second Life* grants users the intellectual property rights over the virtual content they create, including the rights of copying, modifying and transferring their virtual content to others.[26] However, such rights are subordinate to the operator, and hence not absolute. In the U.S., users can enforce their rights

---

21 Sheldon (n 11).

22 *ibid.*

23 *Loretto v. Teleprompter Manhattan CATV Corp.*, 458 U.S. 419, 433 (1982).

24 Sheldon (n 11).

25 World of Warcraft TOS (World of Warcraft , August 22, 2012) <www.worldofwarcraft.com/legal/termsofuse.html> accessed December 3, 2013.

26 Clause 4.4, Second Life TOS (Second Life, December 15, 2010) < http://secondlife.com/corporate/tos.php> accessed 3 December 2013; Second Life-IP Rights, <http://secondlife.com/whatis/ip-rights.php> accessed 3 December 2013.

in accordance to the Digital Millennium Copyright Act.[27]

3.3   Right to Transfer

In *Second Life* and Entropia Universe, users can transfer virtual items among themselves for real cash. To engage in commercial transactions, they require users to pay cash directly to the operator as a means to obtain virtual currency. Further, the operator of *Entropia Universe* periodically creates new areas in their virtual world and sells the land to the users.[28]

However, it must be noted that the purchase of a virtual item is a license, not a sale. Consequently, there is a transfer of a license to use that item, not the ownership of it. One expert says: "[t]he industry uses terms such as 'purchase,' 'sell,' 'buy,' etc... because [those words] are convenient and familiar, but the industry is aware that all software... is distributed under license."[29] Indeed, it is often explicitly stated in the TOS; however, a few customers would pay attention to them. For instance, clause 5.2 of *Second Life* TOS states: "*Second Life* offers a Linden dollar exchange, called the LindeX exchange, for the trading of Linden dollars, which uses the terms 'Buy' and 'Sell' to indicate the transfer of Linden Dollar Licenses."[30]

---

27   Digital Millennium Copyright Act, Pub. L. No. 105-304, 112 Stat. 2860 (1998); Second Life-DMCA: Digital Millennium Copyright Act, <http://secondlife.com/corporate/dmca.php> accessed 3 December 2013.

28   Eutropia Universe's official website < http://www.entropiauniverse.com/> accessed 30 March 2013.

29   Adobe Sys., Inc., v. One Stop Micro, Inc., 84 F. Supp. 2d 1086, 1091 (N.D. Cal. 2000).

30   Clause 4.4, Second Life TOS (Second Life, December 15, 2010) <http://secondlife.com/corporate/tos.php> accessed March 30, 2013; Second Life-IP Rights, <http://secondlife.com/whatis/ip-rights.php> accessed December 3, 2013.

Licenses differ from sales of goods in that the licensed items "can be transferred and simultaneous maintained by the transferor."[31] Hence, when purchasing a virtual item, buyers should not expect an absolute ownership of it.

4.   Risks in Virtual World Commercial Transactions

Commercial transactions take in two forms: (1) customer-to-customer and (2) customer-to-operator. The first form broadly covers any commercial transactions between avatars within virtual worlds, such as exchange of virtual items. For the second form, *Second Life* residents, for instance, have to purchase land from Linden to run a business. Both types of transactions expose customers to numerous risks as the only regulation comes from the EULAs and TOS. The potential risks are discussed below.

4.1 Consumer-to-Consumer Conflicts

Fraudulent activities always happen within a virtual world. In most cases, however, customers are unlikely to be successful in seeking redress or compensation for their losses. It is explained with the example of EVE Online Bank Scandal.

In 2006, a player named "Cally" established a virtual bank called the EVE Investment Bank ("EIB") in EVE Online.[32] As Cally promised high investment returns, numerous users were

---

31 Station Exchange FAQ < http://stationexchange.station.sony.com/faq.vm> accessed December 3, 2013 (describing the rights granted by the EULA to use or sell EverQuest II goods as a "limited license right, not an ownership right"); Second Life TOS (defining the term "sell" in relation to Second Life's currency exchange as "to transfer for consideration to another user the licensed right to use Currency in accordance with the Terms of Service").

32 Tudor Stefanescu, 'EVE Online Economy Suffers 700 billion ISK Scam' (Softpedia, August 24, 2006) <http://news.softpedia.com/news/Eve-Online-Economy-Suffers-700-billion-ISK-Scam-33737.shtml> accessed December 3, 2013.

attracted to place deposits with EIB.[33] Some aggressive users had even converted real money into Inter Stellar Kredits (ISKs), the virtual world currency, for the investment.[34]

Unknown to the users, the returns to existing investors were paid by new investors, not from profit earned by the bank.[35] In other worlds, Cally had perpetuated a Ponzi scheme, which is a fraudulent investment plan.[36] In August 2006, Cally closed EIB without noticing the virtual investors. EIB held around 790 billion ISKs at the time the bank was closed, equivalent to around US$170,000 in the real world marketplace.[37]

As a result of the loss, the victims pressed Crowd Control Productions ("CCP") to take actions.[38] However, CCP denied any responsibility and refused to take any actions. CCP argued that before starting the game, users have agreed to a clause, which warns users that fraudulent behavior is expected, in the document "Reimbursement Policy."[39] Accordingly, CCP did not delete Cally's account but only promised to monitor the account closely to ensure that the virtual currencies therein would not be converted into real money.[40]

Within virtual worlds, users are deemed to be protected by the rules of the game, the TOS, in case any in-world dispute arises. However, as illustrated, virtual operators rarely take the initiative

---

33 *ibid.*

34 *ibid.*

35 *ibid.*

36 U.S. Securities and Exchange Commission, 'Ponzi Schemes' <www.sec.gov/answers/ponzi.htm> accessed December 3, 2013.

37 Thomas Paine, 'What at first was plunder assumed the softer name of revenue' <www.gamerswithjobs.com/node/26703> accessed December 3, 2013.

38 Caroline McCarthy, 'Cons in the Virtual Gaming World' CNET News (31 August 2006) <http://news.cnet.com/Cons-in-the-virtual-gaming-world/2100-1043_3-6111089.html> accessed December 3, 2013.

39 *ibid.*

40 *ibid.*

to do so and, as a result, EIB investors lost all their virtual assets. A reasonable explanation for CCP's passive approach is that doing nothing is the best way to secure their business interest, the sole interest they are concerned. If we look at the rules of the game, users are forced to assume unreasonable risks, such as expecting fraudulent activities to occur within the virtual world.[41]

It is also noteworthy to point out that CCP has not learnt a lesson and allows the same event happening again and again. With the growth of users using real money to make investments, more regulations are called.

In *Second Life*, for resident-to-operator dispute, it can be resolved by real world arbitration. However, when resident-to-resident dispute arises from commercial transactions, for instance, false description of the sold items or sale of defective items, Linden explicitly states in "Terms of Service Arbitration FAQ" that dispute resolution procedure does not apply.[42] This leaves all the risks to customers. The problem can be serious as virtual items can be sold at high price.

4.2 Consumer-to-Operator Conflicts

The relationship between consumers and operators is governed by the EULAs and TOS. However, the author notes that these documents always put the customers in a disadvantaged position.

Before proceeding to the virtual worlds, users are required to click on-screen "I agree" for the EULAs and agree to be bound by the TOS.[43] The provisions outline the basic rights and

---

41 *ibid.*

42 'Linden Lab Official: Terms of Service Arbitration FAQ' (Second Life) <http://wiki.secondlife.com/wiki/Linden_Lab_Official:Terms_of_Service_Arbitration_FAQ> accessed December 3, 2013.

43 Peter J. Quinn, 'A Click too far, The difficulty in using adhesive American Law License Agreements to govern global virtual worlds' (2010) 27 *Wis. Int'l L.J.* 757.

responsibilities of both the users and the operators.[44] However, the terms are usually unfavorable to the users in three senses: Firstly, there is no mutuality of obligations between the users and the operator (i.e., users have fewer rights than obligations). Secondly, operators often limit their liabilities to the greatest possible extent. Thirdly, as there is no option for negotiation, users must either accept the standard terms or leave no matter how objectionable the terms are.[45]

Second Life provides us a good example. The *Second Life* TOS attacks the owners' virtual property rights. Despite a demonstrated market value for the virtual items, Clause 4.5 states that "Linden Lab owns the bits and bytes of electronic data stored on its Servers, and accordingly will not be liable for any deletion, corruption or data loss that occurs in connection with the Service…"[46] Hence, from Clause 4.5, Linden Lab bears no liability even if it deletes the virtual items created by the users.

Under Clause 6, Linden Lab is given the power to revoke the Virtual Land License at any time without notice, refund or compensation in the event that (1) users violate any terms of the TOS or (2) users fail to comply with the Account's payment requirements.[47] By this clause, Linden Lab retains unilateral control over the virtual land purchased by its users. This clause upsets many users who have spent a considerate sum of money to obtain land and started their businesses. As mentioned in Part I, they have to pay for a monthly membership fee, land use fee as well as purchase land from Linden or other users.

More unfavorably, Clause 11.3 states "Linden Lab may

---

44 *ibid.*

45 *ibid.*

46 Clause 4.4, Second Life TOS (Second Life, December 15, 2010) <http://secondlife.com/corporate/tos.php> accessed December 3, 2013; Second Life-IP Rights, <http://secondlife.com/whatis/ip-rights.php> accessed December 3, 2013.

47 *ibid.*

suspend or terminate your Account if you violate this Agreement, along with any or all other Accounts held by you or otherwise related to you as determined by Linden Lab, and your violation of this Agreement shall be deemed to apply to all such Accounts." It further states that the sole remedy available to the user is "receive the stated current value of any credit balance held in your [the user] Account(s)."[48]

Thus, according to the TOS, Linden Lab can terminate the account and seize all the users' virtual assets of the users whenever it thinks the TOS is breached. What is important is that it solely depends on the decision of Linden. Indeed, Linden encourages users to makes investments as to secure its interest, but makes no attempts to protect them. Large investors, such as Anshe Chung are therefore subject to exceptionally high risks. It also appears that if the virtual world shut down, Anshe Chung's assets would all disappear.

Accordingly, some commentators begin to question the enforceability of the documents. Professor Balkin says: "It is not clear that courts will enforce EULAs that place complete discretion in the hands of game owners to destroy investments in virtual assets." Lastowka and Hunter agree by saying that "We will likely see courts rejecting EULAs to the extent that they place excessive restrictions on the economic interests of users."

5.   Legal Protection

As demonstrated in Part II, the virtual rules are designed to serve the operators' own interest, putting the customers' interests at stake. As virtual and real world converge, law rules must step in to restore justice and fairness. In the real world, consumers are protected by a variety of laws, which differ across jurisdictions.

---

48   *ibid.*

For instance, in the U.S., consumers are protected under contract law, tort law, property law, consumer protection law, etc. This section discusses that different legal approaches suggested by scholars to fill up the loopholes in virtual world transactions. Before discussing the legal approaches, an issue must be resolved; that is whether virtual property is recognized by the courts.

5.1 Judicial Recognition of Virtual Property

Most commentators agree that virtual properties should be recognized by the courts because of normative and practical reasons. Professor Joshua Fairfield provides a normative justification. He argues that three features of virtual property make it similar to physical property than something like computer code; they are rivalrousness, persistent and interconnectivity.[49]

The virtual properties in *Second Life* are rivalrous because once a user has purchased a virtual item, other users are excluded from using it. Second, they are persistent because the virtual items still exist even after the user has logged out his account. Third, it exhibits interconnectivity as users can exchange their virtual items.[50]

Another commentator, Allen Chein, justifies from a practical perspective. He looks at the court's decision in *Kremen v. Cohen*[51] for an answer.[52] In *Kremen*,[53] the Ninth Circuit determined the issue whether a property right existed in the intangible domain name, sex.com.[54] The court applied a three-fold test for the issue.

---

49 Joshua A.T. Fairfield, 'Virtual Property' (2005) 85 *B. U. L. Rev.* 1054–1055.

50 *ibid.*

51 337 F.3d 1024 (9th Cir. 2003).

52 Allen Chein, 'Practical Look at Virtual Property' (2006) 80 *St. John's L. Rev.* 1073–1075.

53 *Kremen v. Cohen* (n 51).

54 337 F.3d 1024 (9th Cir. 2003) at 1030.

First, there must be an interest capable of precise definition; second, it must be capable of exclusive possession; and third, the putative owner must have established a legitimate claim to exclusivity.[55] The court decided that the domain name in dispute satisfied the test. The case's decision demonstrated its recognition of the value of intangible properties and the registrants' efforts in the investment. Allen Chein relied on the case to argue that the assets in virtual worlds can satisfy the same requirements.[56]

In fact, a number of jurisdictions have already recognized the consumer rights over virtual properties. In the U.S., the Circuit Court in *Bragg v. Linden Research*[57] showed its recognition of virtual properties.

In China, the courts protected the users' interest in relation to the virtual property starting from 2003. In *Li Hongchen v. Beijing Artic Ice Technology Development Co*,[58] the Beijing No. 2 Intermediate Court returned the stolen virtual items to the users.

Taiwan is also another active jurisdiction recognizing the virtual properties. In 2001, the Taiwanese Criminal Code announced promulgated by the Ministry of Justice states that virtual objects are indeed property, and theft of virtual goods constitutes a crime.[59]

Like other Asian countries, South Korea takes the same approach. South Korea's view of virtual property is that there is "no fundamental difference between virtual property and money

---

55   *ibid.*

56   Chein (n 52).

57   487 F. Supp. 2d 593, 604.

58   Jay Lyman, 'Gamer Wins Lawsuits in Chinese Court Over Stolen Virtual Winnings' TechNewsWorld (December 19, 2003) <www.technewsworld.com/story/32441.html> accessed December 3, 2013.

59   Implementing Information Security to Protect Individuals' Privacy (Sci. & Tech. L. Center) <http://stlc.iii.org.tw/English/Article_2-01.html> accessed December 3, 2013.

deposited in the bank."[60] In 2010, the Supreme Court decided that virtual currency is equivalent to real-world money.[61]

5.2 The Contractual Approach to Legal Protection

It is suggested that the principles of contract, such as unconscionability and promissory estoppel can be applied to virtual worlds.

With respect to *unconscionability*, as discussed above, the terms of the EULAs and TOS are often biased towards the operators, and consequently most scholars attack the validity of these documents based on unconscionability. Clauses such as granting the operators the unilateral power to remove virtual items are likely to be struck down by the court.

In the U.S., the court in *Bragg v. Linden Research*[62] came across this issue. The court centered its discussion on whether the mandatory arbitration clause of *Second Life* TOS was enforceable. In April 2006, Bragg discovered a loophole in *Second Life*'s auction system, which enabled him to purchase a piece of land valued at US$1,000 for US$300. Subsequently, Linden unilaterally terminated Bragg's account and confiscated all his land, claiming that his action had violated the terms of the TOS. Bragg brought a lawsuit in Pennsylvania state court, alleging a number of causes of action such as breach of contract, fraud, conversion, etc. Linden relied on the mandatory arbitration clause to compel Bragg to participate in arbitration. Bragg, on the other hand, sought to prevent Linden from enforcing the clause, arguing

---

60 Alisa B. Steinberg, 'For Sale-one level 5 Barbarian For 94,800 Won: The International Effects of Virtual Property and the Legality of its ownership' (2009) 37 Ga. J. Int'l & Comp. L. 381.

61 Choe Sun-uk & Lee Min-yong, Joongang Daily (Korea January 11, 2010) 'Supreme Court acquits two in cyber money game case' <http://koreajoongangdaily.joinsmsn.com/news/article/article.aspx?aid=2915126> accessed December 3, 2013.

62 487 F. Supp. 2d 593, 604.

that it was both procedurally and substantively unconscionable. The court decided the issue in favor of Bragg and hence refused to enforce the TOS. The court said:

> ...the lack of mutuality, the cost of arbitration, the forum-selection clause, and the confidentiality provision that Linden unilaterally imposes through the TOS demonstrate that the arbitration clause to provide *Second Life* participants an effective means of resolving disputes with Linden. Rather, it is a one-sided means which tilts unfairly, in almost all situations, in Linden's favor.[63]

The dispute was finally resolved when Linden and Bragg agreed to a confidential settlement. As the case shows, the American court is willing to strike down the unconscionable terms of TOS. However, as Paul Riley noted, it becomes difficult to argue in the same way subsequent to the court's decision because Linden had altered its terms in TOS, in particular, the mandatory arbitration clause.[64] For example, to reduce the potentially high cost of arbitration for the aggrieved customers, Linden allows customers to choose to either have their claims heard by arbitrators on the phone or based on written submissions.[65]

It is also noteworthy to look at the court's decision in *Davidson v. Jung*.[66] Although the case is within the computer software licensing context, it is relevant because it relates to enforceability of computer game EULAs. The court is likely to

---

63   *ibid.*

64   Riley (n 13) 900–901.

65   Second Life TOS (Second Life, December 15, 2010) <http://secondlife.com/corporate/tos.php> accessed December 3, 2013 (Clause 12.1 which states "The ADR provider and the parties must comply with the following rules: (a) the arbitration shall be conducted, at the option of the party seeking relief, by telephone, online, or based solely on written submissions...").

66   422 F.3d 630 (8th Cir. 2005).

regard MMORPGs such as *EverQuest* and *EVE Online* as a game. Further, the EULA at dispute was a "clickwrap license," which is common in the virtual world industry including *Second Life*.[67] The appellant court upheld the District's Court decision and decided that the EULAs were neither procedurally nor substantively unconscionable.

On the ground of procedural unconscionability, the court gave out two reasons. First, even though there was unequal bargaining power, it did not give rise to procedural unconscionability because players were given a choice to leave the game if they disagreed with the terms of the EULAs. Also, the players were noticed of the terms and were given sufficient time to decide whether to join or leave the game. On the substantive ground, the court found that the terms were neither harsh nor oppressive.

In *Davidson & Associates, Inc. v. Internet Gateway*,[68] the Federal Court reached the same decision with similar reasoning. The court rejected the case on both the grounds of procedural and substantive unconscionability. On the first ground, the court said: "the parties in this case did have unequal bargaining power because Blizzard is the sole seller of its software licenses; however, the defendants had the choice to select a different video game..."[69] "On the second ground, the court simply said 'the terms of the EULA and TOU in this case do not impose harsh or oppressive terms'."[70]

Based on these cases, if a customer seeks to challenge the enforceability of "clickwrap license" in the future, the case is likely to be rejected on the ground of procedural unconscionability.

---

67 Mark A. Lemley, 'Terms of Use' (2006) 91 *Minn. L. Rev.* 459, 459 (Online user clicks "I agree" to contract terms of use for the online program or service she desires to use).

68 334 F.Supp.2d 1164 (E.D. Mo. 2004).

69 *ibid.*

70 *ibid.*

On the second ground, it depends on the terms of TOS. The author notes that the nature of the game is a relevant factor. For example, in EVE Online, the developer advertises that it is purely a role-playing game.[71] It is contrast with *Second Life* where Linden asserts that it is a non-typical role-play game, which offers users a platform for business investment.[72] The court maybe more willingly to strike down the oppressive terms of *Second Life* TOS because users expect that in-world investment can bring them real economic benefits.

Promissory estoppel is another avenue that can be used to protecting consumers under the contractual approach. To enforce a promise based on promissory estoppel, the customer must establish that there was (1) a definite promise is made, (2) an expectation of reliance on that promise, (3) an actual reliance on that promise, and (4) that injustice would result if the promise was not enforced.[73]

Promissory estoppel can take place in many forms in virtual worlds. For example, Entropia Universe, in their marketing materials, asserts that "Entropia Universe Case Card" enables users to withdraw virtual currencies from real world ATMs.[74] This may induce users to invest real money into the game based on the belief that their in-world investment can be converted into real cash. If one day the operator terminated users' account

---

71 Hannah Yee Fen LIM, 'Who Monitors the Monitor? Virtual World Governance and the Failure of Contract Law Remedies in Virtual Worlds' (2009) 37 *Ga. J. Int'l & Comp. L.* 381.

72 *ibid.*

73 *Ricketts v. Scothorn,* 77 N.W. 365 (Neb. 1898) (outlining the requirements for a claim of promissory estoppel).

74 'Entropia Universe Cash Card' (Entropia Universe) <www.entropiauniverse. com/en/rich/5676.html> accessed Second Life TOS (Second Life, December 15, 2010) < http://secondlife.com/corporate/tos.php> accessed December 3, 2013. The Entropia Universe Cash Card is a Reloadable Debit Card. Not associated with any bank, the Cash Card can be used to withdraw funds from your Entropia Universe PED account from over 1 Million ATM Machines Worldwide.

unreasonably or ceased to offer any money exchange service, customers may be capable of relying on this doctrine. It is because the marketing materials seem to have never warned customers of the operator's unilateral powers.

Similarly, *Second Life* TOS explicitly states that users own the virtual items they create, which can then be traded for real money through Lindex.[75] This may induce users to invest time and real money in building their businesses. Take Anshe Chung as an example. If Linden suddenly and wrongly terminated her account and confiscated all her assets that can be sold for real money, injustice would occur. She may be able to rely on the doctrine for relief. However, there is a difficulty in establishing the definiteness requirement. As the TOS allows Linden to change the terms of the agreement at any point, it is difficult to prove that a definite promise was made.[76]

5.3 The Consumer Protection Approach

Most scholars support the use of consumer protection law. Paul Riley summarized four policy reasons for supporting the use of consumer protection law. First, statutory consumer protection law can cover grey areas which are untouched by common law. Second, consumer protection law considers the impact of a company's representatives on customers in a more flexible way than other areas of law. Third, the commodification of virtual worlds has transformed game players into consumers, reinforcing the need for consumer protection laws. Fourth, the breadth and flexibility of consumer protection law can provide consumers with wider protection.[77]

---

75 Clause 4.4, Second Life TOS (Second Life, December 15, 2010) < http://secondlife. com/corporate/tos.php> accessed December 3, 2013; Second Life-IP Rights, <http://secondlife.com/whatis/ip-rights.php> accessed December 3, 2013.

76 *ibid.*

77 Riley (n 13) 907.

The California consumer protection law is considered in this article as a number of EULAs choose California law to resolve disputes.[78] The California Unfair Competition Law (UCL) defines unfair competition and prohibits it under five prongs, namely (1) unfair conduct, (2) unlawful conduct, (3) fraudulent conduct, (4) deceptive advertising, (5) violations of §17500, California's "false advertising" statute.[79]

Under the "unfair" prong, the court must determine whether the business practice is immoral, unethical, oppressive, unscrupulous, or substantially injurious to consumers.[80] However, as there is no case precedence for consumer actions, it is still yet uncertain how the court would apply the test.

Several writes suggest that the customers have a higher chance of success under the "fraudulent prong."[81] A business practice is deceptive when "members of the public are likely to be deceived." "Likely to deceive" occurs when it is "probable that a significant portion of targeted consumers, acting reasonably in the circumstances, could be misled."[82] This is different from the common law standard of fraud, which requires the element of "intent."

The application of it is illustrated with the example of *Second Life*. Linden and Philip Rosedale, the founders of *Second Life* have repeatedly used the term "sale of land" on the website even though the users' purchase is simply a license of server space. The website uses the term "land sale" in discussing the process of

---

78 Clause 1, Second Life TOS (Second Life, December 15, 2010) <http://secondlife.com/corporate/tos.php> accessed December 3, 2013.

79 Sharon J. Arkin, "The Unfair Competition Law After Proposition 64: Changing the Consumer Protection Landscape", (2005) 32 *W. St. U. L. Rev.* 155, 157.

80 *People v. Casa Blanca Convalescent Homes,* 206 Cal. Rptr. 164, 177 (Cal. Ct. App. 1984).

81 Sheldon (n 11); Riley (n 13).

82 *Lavie v. Procter & Gamble Co.,* 129 Cal. Rptr. 2d 486, 495 (Cal. Ct. App. 2003).

acquiring land from residents.[83] Also, they wrote to the public in a press release, stating that "…world users…should be able to both own the content they create and share in the value that is created. The preservation of users' property rights is a necessary step toward the emergence of genuinely real online worlds."[84] Apparently, "property rights" may mislead the public to believe that they have absolute ownership of the virtual items.

The misleading effect is manifest especially when Linden and his colleagues emphasize that *Second Life* is not a game at all, but an extension of real world. Cory Ondrejka said; "there are virtually no traditional game elements in *Second Life* other than if you look at the real world as a game, it looks a lot like that."[85] Based on what he said, users may expect that they have property rights similar to those in the real world. Also, they also expected to receive compensation when their land was being taken away.

Further, the requiring of proving "damages" would not pose a hurdle for the claims of the aggrieved customers. As there is a market to trade virtual items for real world currencies, seizure of virtual assets would amount to loss of money.

6.   Recommendations

Customers lack protection because the EULAs are one-sided agreements that favor the virtual world developers. The crux of the problem lies in the unbalance bargaining power between the customers and the developers. Hence, any suggestion must aim to restore the bargaining position between them.

---

83   'Second Life and the Virtual Property Boom' (Games Blog), <www.guardian.co.uk/ technology/gamesblog/2005/jun/14/secondlifeand > accessed April 3, 2013.

84   Press Release, Linden Lab, Second Life Residents to Own Digital Creations (November 14, 2003) <http://lindenlab.com/pressroom/releases/03 11_14> accessed December 3, 2013.

85   (n 17).

Up till now, there is no direct regulation governing commercial activities within virtual worlds. Lacking legislative control, the terms of the EULAs vary in the virtual world industry. Also, the terms are always vague, subject to the interpretation of the developers. For instance, the *Second Life* TOS simply states that Laden has the right to terminate users' account if the agreement is violated. There is no disclosure of the decision-making process or an appeal system. Further, as customer-to-operator conflicts can be handled via arbitration, there is no proper means to deal with customer-to-customer conflicts in *Second Life*. It is important because the total value of transactions between customers is getting higher.

Considering that the operators lack the motivation to revise its EULAs unless compelled to do so, it is suggested that the legislature must step in for regulation. Alternatively, clear and comprehensive guidelines must be written at least to establish an industrial standard. For instance, the guidelines may require the operators to set up a virtual world judicial system for resolving in-word disputes. On the other hand, customers must be fully informed of potential risks of commercial transactions. A non-statutory government body can be established to achieve this purpose.

7.   Conclusion

David Post and David Johnson argued that cyberspace should be governed by its own set of rules apart from the real world.[86] However, this no longer holds true due to increased commodification of virtual worlds. When the virtual assets are seized, customers, in fact, lose assets which have real economic

---

86 David R. Johnson and David Post, 'Law and Borders-The Rise of Law and Cyberspace' (1996) *48 Stan. L. Rev.* 1367, 1375.

values. As a result, customers must be protected against potential risks in commercial transactions. Since the sole and primary concern of operators is to entice customers into investment, real world laws should be amended to restore fairness in transactions.

Part XI
Dispute Resolution/ADR in the Virtual World

26

Operators vs. Users:
A Comparative Analysis of the Use of ADR
in Virtual World Disputes

Carol Yan Lin CHOW

1. Introduction

When cultures change, games change.[1] Virtual worlds are increasingly relevant to our realistic worlds in the 22nd century. It was reported that, by 2009, there were approximately 186 million virtual world users globally.[2] Strategy Analytics Inc has predicted that this number will rise to 638 million in 2015.[3] In fact, virtual worlds no longer provide mere entertainment but have become new commercial environments for humans, where growing conflicts are inevitable.[4] As such, the methods to solve virtual world disputes are highly significant to users as it precisely determines the extent of their virtual rights and interests.

---

1 Marshall Mcluhan, *Understanding Media: The Extensions of Man* (The MIT Press, 1994) 221.

2 Peter J. Quinn, 'A Click Too Far: The Difficulty In Using Adhesive American Law License Agreements To Govern Global Virtual Worlds' (2010) 27 *Wisconsin International Law Journal* 757, 758.

3 Strategy Analytics, Inc., 'Virtual Worlds Forecast to Grow 23% Through 2015' (June 15, 2009) <www.strategyanalytics.com/default.aspx?mod=PressReleaseViewer&a0 =4745> accessed December 3, 2013 .

4 Ethan Katsh, 'Bringing Online Dispute Resolution To Virtual Worlds: Creating Processes Through Code' (2004) 49 *New York Law School Law Review* 271, 291.

This chapter centers on conflicts between virtual world operators and users, a relationship predominantly governed by the respective end-user license agreements ("EULA") or terms of services. Part 1 discusses the nature of virtual worlds and their commercial significance, including how virtual worlds act as an important source of business opportunities in the modern world. Part 2 analyzes alternative dispute resolution provisions in virtual world EULAs. Specific dispute resolution provisions adopted by various virtual world developers will be identified and scrutinized. Part 3 examines virtual world disputes in the practical sense by comparing and contrasting how virtual disputes are managed in different real world jurisdictions and outside the virtual worlds. Part 4 explores the creation of an in-world dispute resolution system in virtual worlds. Focus will be on evaluating the emerging proposals on developing an entirely self-sufficient dispute resolution mechanism that utilizes virtual technologies.

2.   Virtual Worlds and Their Commercial Significance

In modern age, virtual worlds offer users business opportunities to earn profits in real worlds.[5] Virtual worlds can be defined as software that allow users creating their own digital identities that act in a three dimensional reality.[6] Their particular commercial significance can be seen in what we call "open worlds." Unlike "game worlds,"[7] they aim not to compete in quests but allows users to "create their own content, events, and stories."[8]

---

5 Jamie J. Kayser, 'The New New-World: Virtual Property and the End User License Agreement' (2006) 27 *Loyola of Los Angles Entertainment Law Review* 59, 60.

6 Viktor Mayer-Schnberger and John Crowley, 'Napster's Second Life?: The Regulatory Challenges of Virtual Worlds' (2006) 100 *Nw. U. L. Rev.* 1775, 1781.

7 Yen-Shyang Tseng, 'Governing Virtual Worlds: Interration at 2.0' (2011) 35 *Washington University Journal of Law and Policy* 547, 553.

8 Yen-Shyang Tseng (n 7) 554.

2.1 Why Virtual Assets in Virtual Worlds Matter?

A prime example is *Second Life*, a 3D virtual world created by Linden Research Inc.[9] Users, who are known as "avatars," can own land, run businesses, create new products and parade in their latest luxury cars.[10] Indeed, over 99% of the objects in *Second Life* are created by users,[11] and a significant feature is that users own intellectual property rights of these creations.[12] These virtual world innovations are by no means superficial as users can sell them via the virtual currency, the Linden Dollar called "LindeX," which can then be converted into real US dollars. A vivid example is the success of "Anshe Chung," a character in *Second Life*, who has established a real estate business in the virtual world worth a staggering $1 million US dollars in real life.[13] She can sell her vast land developments to numerous users in real life and her virtual content no doubt is a significant source of real-world income. Indeed, her virtual assets now are not only limited to *Second Life*, but also exist in other virtual worlds including *IMVU, Entropia Universe and Frenzoo*.[14] This demonstrates why users have an economic incentive to viciously protect their virtual assets from operators.

The ready exchange between virtual currency and real currency is also increasingly popular in game worlds, including *Ultima*

---

9 Second Life 3D World, <http://secondlife.com/whatis/?lang=en-US> accessed December 3, 2013.

10 Paul Riley, "Litigating Second Life Land Disputes: A Consumer Protection Approach" (2009) 19, 3 *Fordham Intellectual Property, Media and Entertainment Law Journal* 877, 886.

11 Cory Ondrejka, 'Escaping the Guilded Cage: User Created Content and Building the Metaverse' (2004) 49 *New York Law School Law Review* 81, 87–101.

12 Second Life 3D World Terms of Service, <http://secondlife.com/corporate/tos.php> accessed December 3, 2013.

13 Anshe Chung Studios, <http://acs.anshechung.com> accessed 3 December 2013; Second Life Grid: Economics, <http://secondlifegrid.net/spt/resources/factsheet/economics> accessed December 3, 2013.

14 Yen-Shyang Tseng (n 7) 552; <www.anshex.com> accessed December 3, 2013.

Online and Star War Galaxies. The *Gaming Open Market*[15] and *Sony Station Exchange*[16] are such online market places which allow players to trade their virtual assets and virtual currency into US dollars instantly. In fact, this has cultivated an industry known as "gold farming," where people are employed to acquire virtual assets to sell online to other players, for popular online games in particular, *World of Warcraft*[17] and *EverQuest*.[18] This trend it particularly prevalent in Asia, notably China, with around 400,000 people in the industry, earning on average a monthly wage of £77, as reported in 2008.[19]

2.2   Virtual World Assets: Operator vs User

Since virtual items are now profitable commercial commodities recognized in the real world, disputes over these land and assets in virtual worlds are no longer a gaming issue, but a real legal issue. This begs the question of what happens when users have disputes with virtual world operators over their in-world assets. What is the conflict resolution process and how is it solved in the real world? As such, we now turn to examine the end-user license agreements ("EULAs") which govern the relationship between virtual world operators and users.

---

15 Created by James Hale <www.gamingopenmarket.com/index.php> accessed December 3, 2013.

16 Sony Station Exchange <http://stationexchange.station.sony.com/livegamer.vm> accessed December 3, 2013.

17 World of Warcraft <https://us.battle.net/support/en/games/wow> accessed December 3, 2013.

18 Everquest <www.everquest2.com> accessed December 3, 2013.

19 BBC News, "Poor earning virtual gaming gold" (August 22, 2008) <http://news.bbc.co.uk/2/hi/technology/7575902.stm> accessed December 3, 2013.

3.   Alternate Dispute Resolution Provisions in Virtual World EULAs

EULAs are the dominant governing tool adopted by virtual world developers.[20] They are essentially contracts between a virtual world operator/developer and users that sets out the rights and responsibilities of parties, the boundaries of permissible conduct and, in particular, the enforcement and dispute resolution mechanism in the respective virtual worlds.[21] These agreements are often a condition upon gaining access to the 3D program by clicking "I agree" when so prompted during installation, users submit themselves to the particular virtual world governance.[22]

The source of disputes between the operator and the resident often stems from the termination provision in the EULAs, a commonly used term as adopted by Linden Research,[23] Funcom[24] and Sony Online Entertainment.[25] This term allows the operator to terminate the resident's account and expel him or her from the virtual world upon a breach of the EULA, basically wiping out all the virtual land and weapons of a resident. Recalling the earlier emphasis of the real-world economic value of these assets, it is only natural for users to strongly protest the operator's drastic actions and it is at this point when the dispute resolution

---

20 Lucille M. Ponte, 'Leveling Up to Immersive Dispute Resolution (IDR) in 3-D Virtual Worlds: Learning and Employing Key IDR Skills to Resolve In-World Developer-Participant Conflicts' (2012) 34 *University of Arkansas at Little Rock Law Review* 713, 728.

21 Angela Adrian, *Law and order in virtual worlds : exploring avatars, their ownership and rights* (Hershey, PA : Information Science Reference 2010) 153.

22 Angela (n 21).

23 Second Life 3D World, Terms of Service, para 5.1 <http://secondlife.com/corporate/tos.php> accessed December 3, 2013.

24 Funcom, Terms of Services <www.funcom.com/corporate/gmbh_terms_of_service> accessed December 3, 2013.

25 Sony Station Exchange, Terms of Service para 9 <www.soe.com/termsofservice.vm> accessed December 3, 2013.

provision kicks in. Interestingly, the majority of EULAs provide for in-world disputes to be solved outside the 3D virtual worlds, via court, arbitration or mediation using real world processes.

3.1 Real-World Dispute Resolution Provisions Adopted in Virtual Worlds

Each virtual world provides users a different conflict resolution mechanism in its EULA. On this point, Lucile M. Ponte has recently published a useful article which extracted developer–user dispute resolution provisions from 45 different virtual worlds.[26] Among these virtual worlds based in the U.S.,[27] South Korea,[28] China[29] and Europe,[30] all, except for one, provide real world dispute resolution methods wholly separate from virtual world technologies.

The top choice of dispute resolution selected by virtual world operators is litigation in state courts,[31] with the forum and choice of law mostly being that of the operator's home state. For example, *Free Realms*, based in the U.S. indicates San Diego courts as its forum and California law as its choice of law.[32] On the other hand, *Runescape*, based in U.K. adopts its own Courts and English law.[33] The traditional method of courts apparently provides most comfort to the operators.

---

26 Lucile (n 20).

27 For example, World of Warcraft.

28 For example, Aion.

29 For example, Dragon Oath.

30 For example, Runescape.

31 Lucile (n 20) Table 1.

32 Free Realms, EULA, para 7 <www.freerealms.com/publicEula.vm> accessed December 3, 2013.

33 Runescape, Terms of Services, para 20 <www.jagex.com/g=runescape/terms/terms. ws> accessed December 3, 2013.

Another increasingly popular method is arbitration, including real-person or online arbitration. For instance, *City of Heroes*, developed in South Korea, indicated mandatory arbitration using the American Arbitration Association Commercial rules. It allows for in-person, online or telephone arbitration.[34] *Sims 3*, based in the U.S. further allows arbitration in writing under the same rules but excludes the participation of Swiss, Russian and EU residents.[35] Indeed, the growing preference of using arbitration over litigation to solve virtual world disputes is endorsed in the Unites States Federal Arbitration Act.[36]

A smaller number of virtual world EULAs also indicate the option of negotiation before resorting to courts and arbitration. This includes *Everquest III*,[37] which allows for informal negotiation 30 days before litigation and *Aion*[38] and *World of Warcraft*[39] provides the same negotiation time period before arbitration. Yet, since the mode and supervision of this mediation process remains unknown, one doubts the practical value of the option to negotiate provided to users.[40] This explains why a

---

34 City of Heroes, Terms of Services para 22 <http://infinityit.info/dedicated-servers-terms-of-service> accessed December 3, 2013.

35 Sims 3, EULA, para 11, 15 <http://eacom.s3.amazonaws.com/EULA_%20 THE%20SIMS%203%20UNIVERSITY%20LIFE%20ROW.pdf> accessed December 3, 2013.

36 9 USCS Para 2; also see federal policy in *Shaffer v ACS Gov't Servs* 321 Supp 2d 682, 685(D. Md. 2004).

37 Everquest III, Terms of Services, para 9 <www.soe.com/termsofservice.vm> accessed December 3, 2013.

38 Aion, Terms of Services <http://us.ncsoft.com/en/legal/user-agreements/http:// us.ncsoft.com/en/legal/user-agreements/aion-user-agreement.html> accessed December 3, 2013.

39 World of Warcraft, Terms of Services,<http://us.blizzard.com/en-us/company/legal/ wow_tou.html> accessed December 3, 2013.

40 Fred Galves, 'Virtual Justice As Reality: Making The Resolution Of E-Commerce Disputes More Convenient, Legitimate, Efficient, And Secure' (2009) 1 *The University of Illinois Journal of Law, Technology and Policy*, 44-45; Amy Schmitz, 'Drive Thru" Arbitration in the Digital Age: Empowering Consumers Through Binding ODR' (2010) 62 *Baylor Law Review*178, 202–203.

formal process with a greater degree of certainty, such as litigation in court and arbitration may take priority.

Clearly, regardless of the comprehensive components that can be created in modern virtual worlds, operators still uniformly prefer real life legal mechanisms in solving their virtual conflicts. A notable exception is *Active Worlds*, an open world based in the U.S. which provides an option to arbitrate before an in-world tribunal: the *Active Worlds Tribunal*.[41] Yet, creative as it may be, the developer has not clarified how this virtual tribunal effectively functions and how it determines legal rights, rendering it a theoretical possibility.[42] Since real world dispute resolution remains the predominant governing tool, let us now examine its practical application in case law.

4. Practical Examination of Virtual World Disputes in the Real World

This section reviews the development of dispute resolution for virtual world disputes by comparing several jurisdictions, including the U.S., China, Hong Kong and South Korea.

4.1 United States

A landmark case in this area is *Bragg v. Linden Research Inc*,[43] involving the virtual world *Second Life*. Bragg was a resident who has collected virtual assets worth up to thousands of US dollars, where some he managed to acquire through abusing an auction system to obtain land at much lower prices, including a piece of

---

41 Active Worlds, Terms of Services <www.activeworlds.com/edu/awedu_download. asp> accessed December 3, 2013.

42 Lucile (n 20) 731.

43 *Bragg v. Linden Research Inc.* 487 F. Supp. 2d 593, 611 (E.D. Pa. 2007).

in-world land, "*Taessot*" for $300.[44] In response, Linden Research discontinued Bragg's account and seized all his virtual land and currency accumulated in *Second Life*. When Bragg made a claim in court, Linden initiated compulsory arbitration according to its arbitration clause in its then EULA terms.

On the question concerning dispute resolution, the court focused on whether the arbitration clause was an enforceable provision. In striking down the arbitration clause as an invalid one, the court found the contract term to be unconscionable.[45] It was held to be procedurally unconscionable as it was "hidden under the lengthy paragraph of General Provisions" in the EULA with no alternatives[46] and substantially unconscionable for a lack of mutual remedies and inequality in resources between Bragg and Linden Research.[47]

This decision had important consequences for virtual world dispute resolution provisions as it demonstrates that the court will scrutinize the dispute clause in the EULAs to determine its enforceability. Indeed shortly after the decision, Linden amended its *Second Life* arbitration provision, which is now under a separate section "Dispute Resolution" and is limited as an option to users for disputes at an amount of $10,000 with minimal costs.[48]

After these revisions, *Second life*'s new arbitration provision was unsurprisingly upheld to be not unconscionable and enforceable by the courts in the recent case of *Evans v. Linden Research, Inc*[49] in 2011. Relevantly, in that case, a class of sub-

---

44 Bragg (n 43) 597.

45 Bragg (n 43) 611.

46 Bragg (n 43) 606.

47 Bragg (n 43) 609–10.

48 Second Life Terms of Service paras 7.1–7.41, <http://secondlife.com/corporate/tos. php> accessed December 3, 2013.

49 No. 10-1679, at 6 (E. D. Pa. Feb. 3, 2011) 11–12.

users claimed against Linden after its unilateral suspension of their accounts and confiscation of their virtual assets. Ultimately, this was resolved in the Northern District of California Court in November 2012,[50] where the users were granted class certification for their loss of virtual items and land based on Linden's promise that users acquire ownership in those assets.

It is also notable that a substantial amount of virtual world disputes involving intellectual property rights are regularly determined in traditional courts. An example includes *Blacksnow Interactive v. Mythic Entertainment Inc.*,[51] where the gamers of *Dark Age of Camelot* had their accounts terminated when they were found to have been engaged in operating a gold farming organization in Mexico. Mythic Entertainment claimed intellectual property rights in the virtual items they were selling. Other cases include *Blizzard Entertainment Inc. vs. Reeves*[52] and *MDY Industrial LLC v. Blizzard Entertainment Inc*,[53] which involve the online gamers of *World of Warcraft* on the creation of illegal downloading software and copyright infringement respectively.

4.2 China

In Asia, *Li Hongchen v. Beijing Arctic Ice Technology Development Co*[54] is the first case on a dispute relating to virtual assets. Li Hongchen, an online user in the virtual game Red Moon (also known as Hongyue) unfortunately had his collection of virtual weapons in his account stolen by a hacker. After his

---

50 *Evans v. Linden Research, Inc.*, No. C 11–01078 DMR, 2012 WL 5877579 (N.D. Cal. Nov. 20, 2012).

51 U.S. Dist. C.D. Cal.

52 No. CV 09-7621 SVW (AJWx) 2009 U.S. Dist. Ct. Pleadings 7621.

53 2011 U.S. App. LEXIS 3428 (9th Cir. 2011).

54 Official Judgment (December 20, 2004) at <www.chinacourt.org/public/detail. php?id=143455> accessed December 3, 2013.

demand for the hacker's identity was rejected by the operator, Ice Technology, he made a claim to the Beijing Second Intermediate Court for his loss. It was a successful action for Li, as the court emphasized that Ice Technology had a duty to restore the virtual property to Li and provided him a remedy that protected his rights in the virtual world.[55] It is noteworthy how the court compelled an obligation upon the operator to act when the theft was conducted by a third party hacker.

Another interesting dispute is *Zhang v Shanda Interactive* first reported by Pacific Epoch in 2007.[56] Zhang, an online player in *World of Legends*, discovered that six virtual weapons worth $1,500 yuan were stolen from his account. He sued the developer Shanda after establishing that Shanda has failed to return the items following police investigations. Deciding in favor of Zhang, the Hunan Qiyang People's Court demand Shang pay $5,000 yuan and an apology to Zhang. Again, virtual rights were protected by means of real-life courts.

Although this decision makes it clear that Chinese courts will go to the lengths of awarding real world money for seized virtual assets, it also demonstrates the utter irrelevance of the *World of Legends* Chinese EULA on this issue. Indeed, it remains uncertain if a dispute resolution provision even existed as the EULA was not made generally accessible to the public alike other virtual world EULAs.

In fact, compared to the U.S., the development of conflict resolution mechanisms between operator and user in Chinese EULAs is relatively weak. This is consistent with the lack of dispute resolution provisions in the EULAs of Chinese-based

---

55 Joshua Fairfield 'Virtual Property' (2005) 85 *Boston Law Review* 1047,1084.

56 Pacific Epoch News, 'Shanda pays for stealing gamers toys' (December 21, 2007) <http://pacificepoch.com/china-investment-research/articles/shanda-pays-for-stealing-gamers-toys> accessed December 3, 2013.

virtual worlds. For instance, in *Dragon Oath*[57] and *HipiHi*,[58] no dispute resolution mechanism, i.e., forum or choice of law clause exist. Also in *Fantasy Westward Journey*, the relevant dispute resolution provision only states that users must observe all laws of China.[59] This explains the lack of operator-user case law involving Chinese virtual worlds. However, as China is the strongest emerging player in this market, with the gaming industry taking in a revenue of 4 billion US dollars in the first half of 2012,[60] it is high time Chinese operators developed effective dispute resolution systems for its users. Other developments on dispute resolution in China mainly focus on protecting users against virtual theft from third parties instead of the relationship between users and virtual world operators. For example, the Chinese Government has consistently prosecuted virtual theft offenders under criminal law and has a strong stance against the protection of virtual property.[61]

4.3 Hong Kong

Conflicts between virtual world operators and users have also not been determined in Hong Kong courts or under Hong Kong law in arbitration. On the other hand, disputes between users in third party theft are more regulated. For example, virtual theft between users and hacking of virtual accounts are governed under

---

57 Dragon Oath, Terms of Services <http://us.changyou.com/terms.shtml> accessed December 3, 2013.

58 HiPiHi, Techcrunch Page <http://techcrunch.com/tag/hipihi/> accessed December 3, 2013.

59 Fantasy Westward Journey, Homepage <http://www.onrpg.com/boards/showthread. php?100593-Fantasy-Westward-Journey-Online-II> accessed December 3, 2013.

60 Xinahua Net, "Study calls for online games rating system" (10 March 2013) <http:// news.xinhuanet.com/english/china/2013-03/10/c_132223070.htm> accessed December 3, 2013.

61 Beijing Evening News ,"Two teenagers prosecuted of online theft" (Chinanews. com, 13 October 2004) <www.chinanews.com.cn/news/2004/2004-10-13/26/493946.shtml> accessed December 3, 2013.

the *Telecommunications Ordinance*[62] and *Theft Ordinance*.[63] A recent case involving theft of virtual assets in the virtual game can also be seen in *Ninja Saga is Emagist Entertainment Ltd v Nether Games (Hong Kong) Ltd*.[64]

The absence of operator-user case law in Hong Kong may be attributed to the lack of Hong Kong based virtual worlds in the main stream market, which also explains why Hong Kong is not a popular choice of forum or a source of applicable law.[65]

4.4 South Korea

This is a region known as the "wired society,"[66] where people spent a significant time in virtual worlds. It is estimated that one in four teenagers play the popular Korean-based virtual games *Lineage* and *Aion*.[67] These 2 games also contain dispute resolution provisions, containing options of litigation and arbitration.

A recent landmark Supreme Court case precisely involves a dispute between two *Lineage* players, Kim and Lee and the leading Korean developer, NCSoft.[68] The underlying issue of the case is the long existing problem of real money exchange of virtual currency, a practice strictly banned by traditional game worlds, including *Lineage*.[69] The dispute was that Kim and Lee

---

62 Telecommunications Ordinance (Cap 106).

63 Theft Ordinance (Cap 210).

64 *Emagist Entertainment Ltd v Nether Games (Hong Kong) Ltd and Others* (2013) HKCFI 15 (CFI).

65 Lucile (n 20).

66 Joshua (n 55) 1087; James D. Ivory, *Virtual Lives: A Reference Handbook* (ABC-CLIIO, 2009) 40.

67 Angela Adrian (n 21) 13.

68 Choe Sun-uk and Lee Min-yong, 'Supreme Court acquits two in cyber money games' (*Korea JoongAng Daily*, January 11, 2010) <http://koreajoongangdaily.joins.com/news/article/article.aspx?aid=2915126> accessed 3 December 2013.

69 similar to World of Warcraft.

have been exchanging *"Aden,"* the *Lineage* currency at lower prices and earning profits via online markets. As the EULA clearly prohibits such conduct and states that the consequence will be termination of user accounts,[70] NCSoft relied on these terms in terminating the accounts of Kim and Lee.

Nevertheless, the Supreme Court declared the actions of market exchange by Kim and Lee to be lawful, emphasizing that Kim and Lee has earned their virtual currency through "skill, not luck"[71] and even deemed NCSoft's confiscation of virtual assets as an unlawful measure. In practice, this decision basically rendered NCSoft's enforcement mechanism in the EULA toothless because its right to terminate accounts is left in doubt.

Contrasting the courts in the U.S. and China, the Korean Court appears to disregard the rules in the EULA of a virtual world and adopts a completely contradictory set of rules to govern operator-user disputes. This has important consequences globally, as Korean-produced game worlds *Lineage* and *Guild Wars*[72] have a large group of followers, particularly in the U.S. Hence it remains uncertain how the decriminalization of the trading of virtual currency and the now unlawful provision of termination in the *Lineage* EULA will affect non-Korean users.

4.5 Summary

From the above analysis, it is evident that disputes in virtual worlds are almost uniformly solved via real-life dispute resolution methods without reference to the virtual context. Yet, different jurisdictions may have varying approaches.

---

70 NCSoft.com, 'Lineage II User Agreement' <http://ncsoft.com/en/legal/user-agreements/lineage-2-user-agreement.php> accessed December 3, 2013.

71 *Korea Joongang Daily* (n 68).

72 Guild Wars, Terms of Service <www.guildwars2.com/en/legal/guild-wars-2-user-agreement/> accessed December 3, 2013.

The U.S. provide the most comprehensive dispute resolution provisions and its courts mostly uphold operators' EULA provisions upon reasonable scrutiny. On the other hand, while China is at the stage of including such mechanisms in their EULAs, Chinese courts do not hesitate to compensate virtual assets with real world money even if the EULAs are silent. As for South Korea, virtual world operators do include dispute resolution provisions; however its courts appear to adopt an interpretation which trumps and contradicts EULA provisions.

Since users of these game worlds and open worlds are connected globally, it is difficult for an average user to understand which method of dispute resolution is suitable for him when it changes along with the jurisdiction he is subject to. This, however, may not pose a problem for virtual world operators who can support a legal team to conduct extensive research.

Bearing in mind this inconsistency and a difference in bargaining power between large-size developers and a regular user, one question whether operators should develop an effective virtual world dispute resolution system—one that utilizes the technologies and functions of virtual worlds without resorting to varying real-world mechanisms.

5. A Virtual World Dispute Resolution System

Back in 1996, scholars such as David Post and David Johnson have already argued that in order to effectively resolve conflicts, virtual worlds should be governed by its own distinct system apart from the real world."[73] It should be free from the complex and expensive jurisdictional restrictions[74] and have uniform rules

---

73 David R. Johnson and David Post, 'Law and Borders—The Rise of Law and Cyberspace' (1996) 48 *Stanford Law Review* 1367, 1379.

74 *ibid.*

with respect to the doctrine of comity under international law.[75] The creation of a distinct cyberspace regime was compared to the origin of *Lex Mercatoria* in the Middle Ages.[76] At that time, since local landlords were designed for land disputes, merchants had no clear venue or rules on how to resolve commercial disputes, As such, a separate legal system, which we now know as commercial law was created, this includes new means to solve commercial conflicts. It was suggested that a distinct legal system for virtual worlds can similarly share such a complimentary relationship with the existing territorial legal system.[77] This will include not only the law, but the dispute resolution mechanisms as well.

This position parallels recent views in establishing a virtual world conflict resolution system which makes use of virtual technologies, in-world regulations and legal support and focuses on the virtual role, hence the real-life anonymity of the parties. This aims to promote equal bargaining power, encourage more mutually beneficial outcomes and enhance active participation in the conflict resolution process.[78] Through a fair and effective dispute resolution programs, developers may also end up "improving overall customer satisfaction and maintain greater player loyalty to their virtual worlds."[79]

Indeed, there are similar projects on this idea. A development plan called *VirtualLife* conducted by the European Union aims to promote such an in-world online dispute resolution platform which is wholly separate from the real world. In *VirtualLife*, parties can resort to an online mediation mechanism facilitated by an online character as the medium, subject to the law of "Supreme Constitution," "Virtual Nation Constitution" and

---

75 David and Post (n 73) 1391–1392.

76 David and Post (n 73) 1389.

77 David and Post (n 73) 1389–1390.

78 Lucille (n 20) 733–734.

79 Lucille (n 20).

contracts.[80] Considering the limitations that real-world dispute resolution imposes, namely the inconsistency among different jurisdictions, the lack of comprehensive EULAs and the unequal legal positions between virtual world software giants and an average user, the above views have their merit. A virtual world dispute resolution mechanism may present an opportunity to solve all these problems from root. While the idea is still largely at an experimental stage, one should be open to more creative methods of conflict resolution. Besides, if virtual world developers are able to demonstrate the process of in-world dispute resolution via detailed video links and clips, it will provide practical value to this method.

6. Conclusion

"Conflict is a growth industry."[81] As the market for virtual worlds continues to expand, there will only be an ever increasing number of disputes involving in-world assets.[82] As such, dispute resolution in the virtual world will no doubt continue to take many forms in its development, and it is important that both virtual world developers and users be aware of their legal ramifications. At the same time, one must not forget that at the heart of virtual worlds is creativity. In the foreseeable future, the world should be prepared to explore more creative options for dispute resolution of virtual world disputes.

---

80 VirtualLife Website <www.ict-virtuallife.eu> accessed December 3, 2013; Cornell University Law School "On A Legal Framework In A Virtual World: Lessons From The VirtualLife Project" (March 1, 2011) <http://blog.law.cornell.edu/voxpop/category/online-dispute-resolution/> accessed December 3, 2013.

81 Ethan (n4) 271 (quoting Roger Fisher and Ury, *Getting to Yes: Negotiating Agreement without giving in* (2nd edn, Houghton Mifflin Harcourt 1992).

82 David R. Johnson and David Post, First Monday "The Great Debate—Law in the Virtual World" (February 6 2006) <http://firstmonday.org/htbin/cgiwrap/bin/ojs/index.php/fm/article/view/1311/1231> accessed December 3, 2013.

27

Resolving Disputes of the Virtual World: An Analysis of Jurisdiction and ADR

Timothy Lok Tim HO

1. Introduction

In online role-playing games, it is fairly common nowadays that hackers hack into the players' accounts and steal all their virtual property while the owners of the accounts have no remedies against the hackers to recover their loss and damage. This virtual world problem first begs the question of whether the court has jurisdiction over the disputes of the virtual world. The second question is if it is possible for the court to address these disputes, given the global nature of the virtual world, could alternative dispute resolution (ADR) be used in order to enforce the rights and remedies much more easily, effectively and efficiently in all the states. Therefore, the purpose of this chapter is to analyze the jurisdiction of the court over virtual world disputes and how ADR works to resolve these disputes with the example of *Second Life* and other virtual worlds.

For a better illustration, this chapter is divided into four parts. Part I will provide the background of a virtual world by explaining its nature, introducing the virtual world of *Second Life* and defining ADR. Part II will analyze whether the court has jurisdiction and whether arbitration can be used to resolve disputes of the virtual world with two *Second Life* cases. Part III will outline the problems of resolving disputes of the virtual world by ADR with two *Second Life* cases. Lastly, Part IV will provide more simple online ADR methods than real life arbitration to resolve virtual world disputes.

2.   Background and Definitions

2.1 Nature of the Virtual World

Virtual worlds are animated three-dimensional environments created by computer software that connect to the entire world by Internet.[1] Most virtual worlds "are classified as massively multiplayer online role-playing games (MMORPG)."[2] In these worlds, a virtual world participant interacts with others via an "avatar," which is "a computerized character that represents the user, who can interact with objects in the virtual world and other user avatars at the direction of the user at his computer."[3] This new creation "to support fantasy via role-play and anonymity raises issues for real-world dispute resolution."[4] The issue is whether an avatar can only cause harm to another avatar or it can even harm an individual in the real world, which allows the latter to have "sufficient ties to support bringing suit" against the other individual controlling the other avatar in a certain jurisdiction in real life.[5]

In answering this question, it is necessary to identify the laws that govern the virtual world. Now, "the laws governing conduct

---

1 Peter Quinn, 'A Click Too Far: The Difficulty in Using Adhesive American Law License Agreements to Govern Global Virtual Worlds' (2010) 27 *Wis Int'l LJ* 757, 760.

2 *ibid.* 761.

3 *ibid.* 760.

4 Andrew Cabasso, 'Piercing Pennoyer with the Sword of a Thousand Truths: Jurisdictional Issues in the Virtual World' (2012) 22 *Fordham Intell Prop Media & Ent LJ* 383, 385.

5 *ibid.*

in virtual worlds exist largely in contract and in code."[6] The virtual world operator stipulates in the contract with the players about what kinds of conduct are allowed or prohibited in the virtual world, when there is a breach of contract, it allows "suit in a forum favored by the virtual world operator."[7] For most virtual worlds, the contract "grants the virtual world operator sovereign authority over the users. Therefore, the virtual world operators have a right of unilateral actions against a user when there is a violation of the terms of the contract."[8]

2.2 Second Life

Second Life is slightly different from the majority of other virtual world operators. In addition to the abovementioned characteristics of a virtual world, the creator of *Second Life*, Linden Research (Linden) acknowledges the property rights of *Second Life* participants for the digital content they created or owned in *Second Life*.[9] Its CEO personally publicized and confirmed this by announcing that "We believe our new policy recognizes the fact that persistent world users…should be able to both own the content they create and share in the value that is created. The preservation of users' property rights is a necessary step toward the emergence of genuinely real online worlds."[10] Furthermore, he even created his own avatar and held virtual meetings in *Second Life* where he made similar representations.[11]

---

6 *ibid.* 393.

7 *ibid.*

8 *ibid.* 394.

9 'Second Life's Terms of Service' <http://secondlife.com/corporate/tos.php> accessed December 3, 2013.

10 Matt Haughey, 'Second Life Residents to Own Digital Creations' Creative Commons (New York City, November 14, 2003) <http://creativecommons.org/press-releases/entry/3906> December 3, 2013.

11 *Bragg v Linden Research* 487 F Supp 2d 593, 596.

Therefore, *Second Life* avatars can buy, own, and sell virtual property. It explains why among all virtual worlds, the most successful virtual world now is *Second Life*.

2.3 ADR and ODR

ADR is any other means of dispute resolution apart from litigation. It includes negotiation, mediation and arbitration. Arbitration is "a method of dispute resolution involving one or more neutral third parties who are usually agreed to by the disputing parties and whose decision is binding."[12] The other two are parties working together "with the aim of reaching an amicable settlement or other solution" and it is not binding.[13] With the advancement of technology, Online Dispute Resolution (ODR) arises and it is "any form of ADR that incorporates the use of the Internet or technological tools."[14] It "stems directly from traditional ADR techniques."[15] However, it has the distinct advantage of giving "disputing parties who live on different continents the ability to resolve a conflict without the jurisdictional and logistical problems that normally follow traditional ADR processes."[16]

---

12 Christopher Kee, Romesh Weeramantry and Simon Greenberg, *International Commercial Arbitration: An Asia-Pacific Perspective* (Cambridge University Press 2011) 2 [1.3].

13 *ibid.* 19 [1.61].

14 Philippe Gilliéron, 'From Face-to-Face to Screen-to-Screen: Real Hope or True Fallacy?' (2007-2008) 23 *Ohio St J on Disp Resol* 301, 302.

15 Melissa Ung, 'Comment: Trademark Law and the Repercussions of Virtual Property (IRL)' (2009) 17 *CommLaw Conspect* 679, 719.

16 *ibid.*; Roger Alford, 'The Virtual World and the Arbitration World' (2001) 18(4) *J Int'l Arb* 449, 449.

3. Application of Arbitration in the Virtual World

3.1 Jurisdiction

In a virtual world like *Second Life*, players also choose the avatars that will represent them in interactions with all other players in the virtual world. It shows that "virtual world interactions are anonymous" and have "no ties to physical geography."[17] As such, the sovereigns do not have jurisdiction over the virtual world.[18] Consequently, it is inconceivable how disputes of the virtual world can ever be litigated or even be resolved by ADR in the real world.

However, since "cyberspace is really interconnected lines and hardware based in fixed locations around the world, courts have the power to exercise personal jurisdiction over a cyberspace-based action in the same manner"[19] as having jurisdiction over telephone system. Furthermore, "while these users might be accessing the Internet remotely, the call still emanates from a fixed location and ends at a fixed location…the harm created by these Internet contacts must produce effects in some tangible place."[20] Therefore, "every user constantly interacts with the virtual world maintained by the sovereigns; any dispute happens on computer servers [is] in the sovereigns' possession."[21]

Assuming but not conceding that the cyberspace argument fails, the theory of worldwide availment also supports the court having jurisdiction over virtual world disputes. This theory is based on the assumption that an "individual automatically avails

---

17 Cabasso (n 4) 386.

18 *ibid.* 421.

19 Michael Rothman, 'Comment: It's a Small World after All: Personal Jurisdiction, the Internet and the Global Marketplace' (1999) 23 *Md J Int'l L & Trade* 127, 128.

20 *ibid.* 138.

21 Cabasso (n 4) 430–431.

himself of all jurisdictions" when he enters and conducts business in a virtual world because everyone has access to it.[22] Therefore, one should accept the consequences of their conduct, like potentially being sued in a foreign jurisdiction. If this theory fails, "it would encourage anarchy in the virtual world" that infringers are sheltered from liability under their avatars.[23] Accordingly, it is possible to resolve virtual world disputes in the real world and the court has already heard cases concerning disputes of the virtual world of *Second Life*. The judgment of the court also shows that arbitration can be used to resolve disputes of the virtual world.

3.2   Bragg v Linden Research

In *Bragg v Linden Research*,[24] the plaintiff, a participant in *Second Life*, sued in front of the US Federal Court in the Eastern District of Pennsylvania against Linden and its CEO for unlawfully confiscating his virtual property in *Second Life* and denying him access to *Second Life*.[25] The relevant issue of this case was whether the arbitration clause in the Terms of Service (TOS) was valid, so that this case should be submitted to arbitration instead of litigation. The TOS is a contract between the players and the game operator because in order to participate in *Second Life*, each player must accept the TOS by clicking a button indicating his or her acceptance of the TOS.[26] The TOS had an arbitration clause, which stated that "Any dispute or claim arising out of or in connection with this Agreement or the performance, breach or termination thereof, shall be finally settled by binding arbitration

---

22   *ibid.* 409.

23   *ibid.* 443.

24   Bragg (n 11).

25   *ibid.* 595.

26   *ibid.* 603; George Friedman, 'Alternative Dispute Resolution and Emerging Online Technologies: Challenges and Opportunities' (1996–1997) 19 *Hastings Comm & Ent LJ* 695, 708.

in San Francisco, California under the Rules of Arbitration of the International Chamber of Commerce (ICC) by three arbitrators appointed in accordance with said rules."[27] Although the court refused to enforce the arbitration clause, declined to rewrite the clause to save it and denied the motion to compel arbitration, it was all because the clause was held to be unconscionable and not because the subject matter was non-arbitrable.[28] This shows the problems that need to be addressed to make arbitration possible for the virtual world.

In *Bragg*, the arbitration clause was unconscionable because it tilted "unfairly, in almost all situations, in Linden's favor."[29] Firstly, Linden "is not obligated to initiate arbitration"[30] to resolve disputes in *Second Life* because it had various one-sided remedies at its sole discretion that was expressly authorized by the TOS, like unilaterally freezing participants' accounts and confiscating their virtual property.[31] However, the only remedy the players had was to "initiate arbitration in Linden's place of business,"[32] which "involves advancing fees to pay for no less than three arbitrators at a cost far greater than … litigation,"[33] regardless of the amount of the claim. Furthermore, Linden even had the sole discretion to determine whether a player has breached the TOS and had the right to amend the TOS "at any time in its sole discretion by posting the amended Agreement [on its website]."[34] Secondly, the arbitration clause was inserted in a lengthy paragraph in the TOS

27 Bragg (n 11) 604.
28 *ibid.* 611–613.
29 *ibid.* 611.
30 *ibid.*
31 *ibid.*
32 *ibid.*
33 *ibid.*
34 *ibid.* 608.

under the heading of "General Provisions."[35] It is unconscionable because "there [was] nothing in the Agreement that [brought] the reader's attention to the arbitration provision."[36] Lastly, the confidentiality of the arbitration proceedings favored Linden even more because "through the accumulation of experience, Linden becomes an expert in litigating the terms of the TOS, while plaintiffs remain novices without the benefit of learning from past precedent."[37] Therefore, the arbitration clause was "not designed to provide *Second Life* participants an effective means of resolving disputes with Linden"[38] but merely to benefit Linden. Pursuant to Section 2 of the Federal Arbitration Act of the US, the arbitration clause was held to be invalid.

With the benefit of hindsight, Linden revised its TOS after Bragg on the areas that the court found unconscionable, namely the potential cost of arbitration to an aggrieved player and the ease of use of ADR.[39] Firstly, the revised TOS gives an option to *Second Life* participants to have a "binding non-appearance-based arbitration" that allows participants to choose to have their claims being heard by only one arbitrator via "telephone, online, or based solely on written submissions."[40] Unless the parties agree otherwise, the arbitration shall not "involve any personal appearance by the parties or witnesses."[41] This amendment saves time and cost and is more appropriate for virtual world disputes because participants want any kinds of interactions to be anonymous. Secondly, the TOS caps the total amount in dispute

---

35   *ibid.* 606.

36   *Higgins v Superior Court* 140 Cal App 4th 1238, 1243.

37   Bragg (n 11) 611.

38   *ibid.*

39   Paul Riley, 'Litigating Second Life Land Disputes: A Consumer Protection Approach' (2008-2009) 19 *Fordham Intell Prop Media & Ent LJ* 877, 900–901.

40   (n 9).

41   *ibid.*

for the arbitration option at US$10,000,[42] so that it avoids the problem in the old TOS, which "the cost of travel and arbitration for disputes would in most cases exceed the dollar amount at issue."[43] Finally, the revised TOS now includes the arbitration provision under a separate "Dispute Resolution and Arbitration" section.[44] These amendments of the TOS allow arbitration to be possible and feasible for resolving virtual world disputes, which was later confirmed by the court in *Evans v Linden Research*.[45]

3.3 *Evans v Linden Research*

In *Evans v Linden Research*,[46] the same problem in *Bragg* happened as the operator of *Second Life* again unlawfully confiscated the virtual property of the plaintiffs in this case and denied them access to the virtual world.[47] The plaintiffs brought this class action against Linden and its CEO in front of the same court in *Bragg*. However, this case is different from *Bragg* because this case was decided under the revised version of the TOS of *Second Life*.[48] Firstly, the new TOS allows the aggrieved players not appearing in San Francisco for arbitration for claims under US$10,000.[49] Secondly, the aggrieved players are not compelled to arbitrate for claims of US$10,000 or more.[50] Finally, the aggrieved players are not compelled to arbitrate under ICC and can arbitrate "through an established ADR provider mutually agreed

---

42 *ibid.*

43 Riley (n 39) 901.

44 (n 9).

45 763 F Supp 2d 735.

46 *ibid.*

47 *ibid.* 738.

48 *ibid.* 741.

49 *ibid.*

50 *ibid.*

by the parties."[51] Accordingly, the court held that the arbitration clause was "not unfair or unconscionable," so it was enforceable to both parties.[52]

Based on the judgments of *Bragg and Evans*, it shows that the court has jurisdiction to rule over disputes of the virtual world and these disputes can even be resolved by arbitration provided that the arbitration clause was drafted properly and appropriately. It reduces the uncertainty of dispute resolution in the virtual world and it encourages business development in the virtual world.[53] Businessmen need assurance to protect their investments made in the virtual world, so a virtual world with an arbitration clause provides security that they do not have to litigate abroad for disputes.[54] Therefore, there is a strong economic incentive to have an arbitration clause in the TOS of a virtual world and it is now common for most virtual worlds to have such a clause.[55]

4.   Problems of ADR in the Virtual World

Although litigation and arbitration may offer a means of dispute resolution to an aggrieved party, since all avatars are anonymous and virtual world players do not want to reveal their identities, enforcement of order or award is very difficult and costly, so cases are often ended up being settled to save time, costs and trouble. The issue of enforcement hinders the usefulness and effectiveness of arbitration available to the aggrieved party. It is confirmed by two empirical US cases of copyright and trademark infringement in *Second Life*.

---

51   (n 9).

52   Evans (n 45) 741–742.

53   Cabasso (n 4) 436.

54   *ibid.* 438.

55   *ibid.*

4.1 *Eros v Linden Research*

In *Eros v Linden Research*,[56] the US District Court for the Northern District of California heard a case of copyright infringement. The plaintiff was a seller of virtual adult products in *Second Life* and he sued an avatar for copyright infringement as the latter unlawfully copied products owned by the plaintiff. In this regard, pursuant to Digital Millennium Copyright Act of the U.S. (DMCA), if copyright-holders need to have their pirated content removed from *Second Life*, the plaintiff's identity and the identities of the alleged copiers would have to be released to the public.[57] Since the plaintiff enjoyed his anonymity, the case was eventually settled and the case was closed without the court hearing the issues.

4.2 *Minsky v Linden Research*

In *Minsky v Linden Research*,[58] the US District Court for the Northern District of New York heard a case of trademark infringement. The plaintiff had a business in *Second Life* called "ArtWorld Market" and he trademarked the phrase "SLART" in the USA for his *Second Life* business.[59] In this case, he sued against an avatar named Victor Vezina and Linden for infringing his federally registered trademark and not removing the infringing virtual items respectively.[60] The court granted the plaintiff a temporary restraining order preventing Linden from allowing any other *Second Life* players to use the SLART trademark.[61] However, the plaintiff could not serve Victor Vezina a summons, so the lawsuit against this avatar was dropped and the case

---

56 Case No. 09-CV-4269.

57 Cabasso (n 4) 398.

58 Case No. 1:08-CV-819.

59 Cabasso (n 4) 398–399.

60 Minsky (n 58).

61 Cabasso (n 4) 399.

against Linden was eventually settled.[62]

In light of these cases, it highlights the deficiencies of dispute resolution available to aggrieved parties. Unless the problems of enforcement are effectively addressed, litigation and arbitration will be virtually ineffective to resolve disputes of the virtual world.

5.   Availability of ODR in the Virtual World

For the purpose of addressing the deficiencies of litigation and arbitration in resolving virtual world disputes, ODR can offer assistance in overcoming the issues on identities of avatars and enforcement by conducting ADR online or electronically.

5.1   *Player-Supported Virtual Arbitral Tribunal*

For virtual world trademark and copyright infringement and bullying, the game operators of a virtual world, *League of Legends* (LoL), provide an ODR solution by creating a "player-supported virtual tribunal" to settle these disputes.[63] The LoL Players can form part of the tribunal and they have the power to review and rule on cases against other players who use "offensive language, bully, or commit any other sort of... infraction."[64] "In virtual world tribunals, avatars can remain avatars," so that virtual world players can remain anonymous.[65]

Similarly, *Second Life* also has established a trademark-registering institution, namely the *Second Life* Patent and Trademark Office, in its own virtual world to establish and

---

62 Minsky (n 58).

63 Cabasso (n 4) 394.

64 *ibid.*

65 *ibid.* 440.

protect virtual property, which is owned and operated by *Second Life* players and content creators.[66] For any trademark infringement, an aggrieved party can file a complaint and have a virtual arbitration hearing, which the tribunal is composed of "other virtual world members, who would then issue a binding decision."[67] This ODR bypasses the necessity of revealing true identities to the public required by the DMCA,[68] so it may be more suitable than real life arbitration to resolve virtual world disputes.

While these virtual tribunals bind only avatars not third parties like Louis Vuitton or other real life businesses, it does not exclude third parties from utilizing its facilities in the virtual world to resolve disputes with avatars.[69] Therefore, if this internal ODR idealistically provides an efficient and equitable resolution for the parties involved, it may attract third parties to submit their disputes to these virtual tribunals instead of having costly and lengthy litigation or real life arbitration.[70] However, the drawback of this ODR now is that the decision of the virtual arbitral tribunal may be very arbitrary and not based on any law, so it may cause more harm than good in resolving disputes.

5.2 Automated Negotiation

In addition to arbitration in the real world or virtual world, monetary disputes in the virtual world can also be resolved by negotiation in the virtual world via "blind bidding."[71] Cybersettle. com now provides this service.[72] This ODR is operated by a

---

66 Ung (n 15) 726.

67 *ibid.* 725.

68 *ibid.* 726.

69 Cabasso (n 4) 440.

70 *ibid.*

71 Gilliéron (n 14) 305.

72 Cabasso (n 4) 423–424.

software system, which plays the role of a negotiator.[73] This mechanism starts off with the aggrieved party presenting its request to a chosen institution, which then contacts the other party.[74] The other party can decline the offer of negotiation or is bound to this procedure under contract.[75] If the negotiation procedure is accepted, each party, in turn, "offers or demands a certain amount of money" to the system while these information are never communicated to the other party.[76] The system has an algorithm formula that when the amount offered and the amount demanded are sufficiently close, i.e., within a range of 5% to 30% depending upon the institution, the case is settled and the monetary difference is split between the parties.[77] Otherwise, the case is over and the claimant can either try again or resort to other ODR.

Although this ODR is primarily designed to solve financial disputes for insurance claims,[78] this mechanism is simple, technically feasible and relatively more efficient for avatars to settle their disputes in their own virtual world without any assistance of the real world. It will be much cheaper, faster and more suitable for MMORPG players to resolve their monetary disputes compared to complex and lengthy arbitration unless the disputes are complicated and require legal analysis.

5.3 *Virtual Mediation*

Second Life also provides avatars with mediation and arbitration services in e-Justice Centre, which was established by Faculty of Law of the Lisbon New University and the Portuguese Ministry

---

73 Gilliéron (n 14) 305.
74 *ibid.*
75 *ibid.*
76 *ibid.*
77 *ibid.*
78 *ibid.*

of Justice.[79] This Centre has a building in *Second Life* and avatars "can meet to first attempt to mutually settle their disputes through mediation, and then arbitrate unresolved issues through a relatively quick and inexpensive process that ends disputes with an arbitrator's binding determination."[80]

In short, all these ODR provide innovative and simple dispute resolution mechanisms to avatars, so that any disputes can be resolved without any involvement of the real world. As such, it is reasonable to foresee that if these ODR become much more sophisticated, reliable and authoritative in the future, virtual world disputes can be completely resolved in their own virtual worlds.

6. Conclusion

In conclusion, the court has jurisdiction over virtual world disputes and it is possible and feasible to resolve these disputes by ADR, either in the real world or even in the virtual world. Among the forms of ADR, "arbitration is the best suited for the resolution of in-game disputes."[81] It is because the decision is binding and, like what is stated in the TOS of *Second Life*, "any judgment on the award rendered by the arbitrator may be entered in any court of competent jurisdiction"[82] by virtue of Convention on the Recognition and Enforcement of Foreign Arbitral Awards (New York Convention).

However, the anonymous interactions of the virtual world hinders the enforceability of awards, so ODR, in the form of, for

---

79 Amy Schmitz, '"Drive-Thru" Arbitration in the Digital Age: Empowering Consumers Through Binding ODR' (2010) 62 *Baylor L Rev* 178, 232.

80 *ibid.*

81 Ung (n 15) 725.

82 (n 9).

example, automated negotiation, virtual mediation and player-supported virtual arbitral tribunal may provide better solutions to address the virtual world disputes. Therefore, there are legal mechanisms to address the problems faced by MMORPG players and they are the future of ADR.

28

Avatar vs Avatar Disputes:
The Future for Arbitration
in the Virtual World

Elaine Yuet Ling YUEN

1. Introduction

Virtual World means more than just a form of computerized entertainment. To some, it serves as a livelihood.[1] As the virtual world has become a more popular platform for users to communicate and to "live"[2] in the form of an avatar, virtual disputes are inevitable. Two types of virtual world disputes could occur: Operator–Avatar disputes and Avatar–Avatar disputes.

This chapter aims to explore the demand for virtual arbitration institutions as a platform for Avatar–Avatar disputes. In particular, the impact of online dispute resolution on the development of virtual arbitration will be examined. This chapter also aims to explore the possibility of future developments of arbitration in the virtual world where the law is not well developed. Three aspects will be discussed: (1) The possibility of establishing a set of Virtual Arbitral Rules; (2) the enforcement issues regarding Arbitral

---

1 Farnaz Alemi, 'An Avatar's Day in Court: A Proposal for Obtaining Relief and Resolving Disputes in Virtual World Games' (2007) *UCLA J.L. & Tech.* <www.lawtechjournal.com/articles/2007/06_080 130_alemi.pdf > accessed December 3, 2013.

2 R. V. Kelly, *Massively Multiplayer Online Role-Playing Games: The People, the Addition and the Playing Experience* (McFarland & Company 2004).

Awards; and (3) the possibility of Arbitral Precedent. The addition of these elements to the current virtual arbitration system would undoubtedly enhance procedural effectiveness and certainty.

2.   The Virtual Worlds

2.1 *The Way Virtual Worlds Operate*

Virtual worlds, also known as Massive Multiplier Online Role-Playing Games (MMORGs), are generally referred to as a simulated three-dimensional environment which exists only in cyberspace and is accessible via the Internet by multiple players at the same time.[3] *Second Life* and *Active Worlds* are examples of virtual worlds though not necessarily considered as MMORGs. The virtual environment resembles the daily surroundings of human beings, and even surreal environments, through graphical representations of physical objects.[4] Once a user is registered as a member of the virtual world, users create their own identities, known as "avatars," in whatever form they wish. This includes defining the gender, appearance or personality traits of one's avatar.

Avatars are free to explore the virtual world and engage in a wide range of activities such as socializing with other avatars, purchasing virtual properties and much more. Similar to the real world, virtual worlds such as *Second Life* do not stop or turn off when a user switches off the computer. Rather, it remains active and keeps moving forward.

---

3 Ryan Kriegshauser, 'The Shot Heard Around Virtual Worlds: The Emerging and Future of Unconscionability in Agreements Relating to Property in Virtual Worlds' (2007–2008) 76 *UMKC L. Rev.* 1079.

4 *ibid.* 1082.

2.2 Commercial Value and Economic Impact on Players

The virtual world parallels real world business opportunities.[5] In fact, virtual worlds have already boasted massive impacts on the economy, as evident in the millions of people who have signed agreements to be engaged in the virtual worlds.[6] Each virtual world has its own currency, usually convertible into real-world currency: for instance, the Operator Linden Lab operates the Linden Exchange wherein users could cash out their Linden dollars, from the Virtual World or through sale of their virtual property as well as exchanging for real-world money.[7]

The virtual space has become an increasingly popular platform on the Internet, with some visited even more than popular browsers such as Google.[8] Many players in modern times invest considerable amount of time, capital and emotional attachment to virtual worlds. If one were to perceive virtual worlds as merely advanced computer games without having any real world effects, it would be considered a misconception.[9] Elizabeth M. Reid, a researcher on Internet culture, made a remark that virtual world users "become emotionally involved in the virtual actions of their characters, and the line between virtual actions and actual desires can become blurred."[10]

---

5 Laurence H. M. Holland & David M. Ewalt, 'Making Real Money in Virtual Worlds' (Forbes.com, August 7, 2006) <www.forbes.com/2006/08/07/virtual-world-jobs_cx_de_0807virtualjobs.html> accessed December 3, 2013.

6 Kriegshauser (n 3) 1084.

7 Second Life, 'Buying and selling Linden dollars' (Second Life, June 8, 2012) <http://community.secon dlife.com/t5/English-Knowledge-Base/Buying-and-selling-Linden-dollars/ta-p/700107> December 3, 2013.

8 Arno R. Lodder, 'Short Note on Virtual Law Classes: Second Life and Other Three Dimensional Visual Worlds Next Phase for Online Dispute Resolution?' (2007) 4th International Workshop on ODR, San Jose (USA) 59–62.

9 Kriegshauser (n 3) 1084.

10 Elizabeth M. Reid, Text-Based Virtual Realities: Identity and the Cyborg Body in Peter Ludlow, *High Noon on the Electronic Frontier: Conceptual Issues in Cyberspace* (A Bradford Book 1996) 327, 340.

3.   Avatar–Avatar Disputes in the Virtual World

3.1   Common Types of Avatar–Avatar Disputes

With the rapid rise of such a new and expressive medium of the virtual world, it is only a matter of time before conflicts amongst avatars begin to surface.[11]

Virtual property transactions are as common in occurrence and as varied in type as property transactions in the real world.[12] In virtual space, players often use real-world dollars to sell and purchase virtual goods and own virtual estates. These transactions have led to disputes among avatars, ranging from avatar assaults to breach of virtual estate sales and intellectual property issues.[13]

3.2   Current Behavioral Regulations of Avatars: The End User License Agreements (the "EULA")

Prior to entering into the Virtual World, users ought to enter into agreements with the virtual world operators (the "Operators"), the creator of virtual worlds. These agreements are known as Terms of Use Agreements and EULA. They are basically contracts between the Avatar and the Operator which sets out guidelines as to the rules and functions of the in-world games and it usually sets out the behavioral guidelines that users ought to comply with. Payment and personal contact information should also be provided to the Operator.

---

11 Alan Sipress, 'Where Real Money Meets Virtual Reality, the Jury is Still Out' *The Washington Post* (United States, December 26, 2006) and Bettina M. Chin, 'Regulating Your Second Life Defamation in Virtual Worlds' (2007) 72 *Brook L. Rev.* 1303, 1310.

12 Kriegshauser (n 3) 184.

13 Joshua A. T. Fairfield, 'Anti-social Contracts: The Contractual Governance of Virtual Worlds' (2008) 53 *McGill L. J.* 427, 435–36.

The EULA of virtual worlds is currently the main behavioral regulation of avatars. The regulations of avatars' behavior vary according to the type of Massively Multiplayer Online Games they are engaged in. In the EULA, there are normally clauses which regulate Avatars' behaviors. For instance, the community standards, also known as the "Big Six," prohibit the following conduct: (1) Intolerance; (2) harassment; (3) assault; (4) disclosure of another participant's personal information; (5) indecency; and (6) disturbing the peace.[14] The community standard also sets out a three stage punishment system: first a warning, followed by a suspension, which is approximately one to seven days, and, finally, banishment from the game.[15] Where an account of a player is suspended, the Operators might as well suspend or terminate accounts associated with the breach and any other accounts belonging to the player.[16]

3.3 Lacunae of the Current EULA Mechanism: No Personal Relief Available to Aggrieved Avatars

The Operator and its representatives serve as the sole punishment authority in the virtual world. When an aggrieved avatar reports a case, the Operator applies the "Big Six" to determine the sanctions to be imposed on the avatar perpetrator. Besides, In-World Representatives known as Liaisons would occasionally address disciplinary issues by a temporary removal from the virtual world.[17]

---

14 Second Life, 'Community Standards'<http://secondlife.com/corporate/cs.php> December 3, 2013.

15 *ibid.*

16 Second Life, 'Terms of Service' (Second life, December 15, 2012) <www.secondlife.com/corporate/tos.php> accessed December 3, 2013.

17 Second Life, 'Community Standards'<http://secondlife.com/corporate/cs.php> accessed December 3, 2013.

Aggrieved avatars are often overlooked by game developers and academics.[18] While arbitration clauses are normally incorporated into virtual worlds' EULA, the effect of such clauses is often confined to resolving Operator–Avatar disputes only. What about Avatar–Avatar disputes? Why should aggrieved avatars be left hanging in the air without any means available to them to seek personal relief from fellow Avatar Perpetrators?

Despite these EULA regulations in the virtual world, avatar perpetrators are still able to circumvent those rules in different ways thereby causing harms, unfairness and disadvantages to aggrieved avatars. The current behavioral regulatory system of EULA is designed only for regulating perpetrators. It leaves little or even no rooms for aggrieved avatars to voice out their needs for relief against their perpetrators in the context of making a civil claim. Perhaps Operators have not foreseen the severity and consequence of deviant behavior of avatars as against other avatars, and matters of justice and relief to the aggrieved avatars have not been seriously considered.[19]

4.　The Development of Virtual Arbitration

The virtual worlds often seek to outsource their adversarial conflict resolution mechanisms to entities out of the virtual communities.[20] There are only limited virtual worlds such as the active worlds, which enables dispute resolution through an

---

18　Farnaz Alemi, 'An Avatar's Day in Court: A Proposal for Obtaining Relief and Resolving Disputes in Virtual World Games' (2007) *UCLA J.L. & Tech.* <www.lawtechjournal.com/articles/2007/06_080 130_alemi.pdf > accessed December 3, 2013

19　*ibid.*

20　Lucille M. Ponte, 'Levelling Up to Immersive Dispute Resolution (IDR) in 3-D Virtual Worlds: Learning and Employing Key IDR Skills to Resolve In-World Developer-Participant Conflicts' (2011-2012) 34 *UALR L. Rev.* 713, 735.

in world adversarial process.[21] It has provision on mandatory arbitration which is to be conducted either in Boston, Massachusetts, the AAA offices or before the Active Worlds Tribunal.[22]

However, the Active Worlds offers no public information regarding the procedures adopted in this Virtual Arbitration platform.[23]

4.1 The Impact of Bragg v Linden

Despite the growing academic interest in this area, no court has decided on the validity of the contractual agreements governing virtual properties until *Bragg v. Linden Research, Inc.*[24] In 2006, Bragg acquired a parcel of virtual land named "Taessot," in which Linden subsequently advised Bragg that Taessot had been improperly purchased through an "exploit." Linden then took Taesot away and froze Bragg's account, confiscating all his virtual property and currency.[25] The District Court exercised personal jurisdiction over Linden and refused to uphold the arbitration clause contained in the Terms of Reference agreed by Bragg prior to his entering into the Virtual World. Prior to entering into the virtual world, Bragg has accepted the Terms of Reference which included a mandatory arbitration provision. It was held to be unconscionable in a sense that the clause was fixed and parties were not given any room for bargaining and hence unenforceable.

Arbitration clauses in the virtual context are currently in a state of uncertainty and changes. As virtual law goes to press, some Virtual World Operators are changing their arbitration

---

21 *ibid.*

22 *ibid.* 736.

23 *ibid.*

24 487 F.Supp.2d 593 (E.D. Pa. 2007)

25 *ibid.*

provisions in response to the *Bragg* decision.[26] The decision of Bragg is nevertheless a milestone for Operators to draft dispute resolution or arbitration agreement terms more meticulously in order to avoid disputes similar to those faced in Linden.[27] As the decision has left many areas open and uncertain,[28] enabling rooms for innovation, it leads to the question of whether a similar arbitration clause should be incorporated into the Terms of Agreement and be made binding on Avatar–Avatar disputes.

Linden Lab later clarified that arbitration could take place in the Virtual World itself, which created the path leading to arbitration proceedings with Avatar Lawyers and Avatar Arbitrators conducting arbitration hearings entirely within the Virtual World.[29]

4.2 The Development from Online Arbitration to Virtual Arbitration

Many have opted for Online Arbitration to resolve disputes. An example of an online Arbitration System is the Financial Industry Regulatory Authority Arbitration Online Claim Filing, wherein an aggrieved party can file an online claim, followed by signing an agreement and relevant documents and finally obtaining a printed receipt with a tracking number.[30] With eBay, a Resolution Center is available for aggrieved parties. The parties will be communicating with email through the eBay Center, and in case an agreement cannot be reached, the eBay Customer

---

26 Benjamin Tyson Duranske, *Virtual Law: Navigating the Legal Landscape of Virtual Worlds* (American Bar Association, ABA Publishing 2008) 31.

27 Roxanne E. Christ and Curtis A. Peele, 'Virtual World: Personal Jurisdiction and Click-Wrap Licenses' (2008) *Intellectual Property & Technology Law Journal* 1.

28 *ibid.*

29 Duranske (n 26) 32.

30 FINRA, 'Arbitration Online Claim Filing' (FINRA, 16 April 2011) <www.finra.org/ArbitrationMediation/Parties/ArbitrationProcess/ArbitrationOnlineClaimFiling/> accessed December 3, 2013.

Support will intervene as an arbitrator and make an award.[31] Just as online users would resort to Online Arbitration, in a virtual setting when Avatar–Avatar disputes arises, it is equally sensible for avatars to be able to resort to Virtual Arbitration to seek resolution and relief. The mechanism of Online Arbitration, involving mere typed statements, gives rise to a danger of the parties being misinterpreted as a result of an "absence of social cues."[32] There is also a risk of the process being delayed due to lack of patience or confidence therein. For instance, if email was used by the parties as a means to arbitrate, he could simply walk away from the computer in real-life and escape from the process.[33] However, a three-dimensional Virtual Arbitration is likely to enhance the willingness of parties to arbitrate. In contrast to Online Arbitration which involves only a two-dimensional communication platform enabling limited forms of expressions, in Virtual Arbitration "body language, facial expressionisms, sighs and moans which all play key role in transferring information" [34] can be conveyed through avatars. This enables players to be more visually and psychologically engaged throughout the process.

In order for justice to be done, aggrieved avatars should be provided with a platform which allows them to seek direct relief from Avatar Perpetrators: an In-World Arbitration Centre.

4.3 The Portuguese e-Justice Centre: The First Platform for Virtual Arbitration

In 2007, the Portuguese Ministry of Justice, together with the

---

31 eBay, 'Resolving Transaction Problems in the Resolution Center' <http://pages.ebay.com/help/buy/resolving-problems.html> accessed December 3, 2013.

32 Janice Nadler, 'Electronically-Mediated Dispute Resolution and E-Comnerce' (2001) 17 *NiEcYr. J.* 333.

33 *ibid.*

34 Colin Rule and Craig Villamor, 'The Importance of Language in Online Dispute Resolution' (2004) ICC International Court of Arbitration Bulletin.

University of Aveiro and the Faculty of Law of the Lisbon New University, has established an "e-Justice Centre" as a platform for mediation and arbitration in the Virtual World. It serves as a platform to resolve a broad range of conflicts including contract and consumer transaction disputes.[35] Being the first country in the world to launch a virtual arbitration center, Portugal had a vision to develop from the ODR to a whole new level of virtual dispute resolution.

The e-Justice Centre adopts the United Nations Commission on International Trade Law (the "UNCITRAL Model Law") on International Commercial Arbitration.[36] Avatars have the choice to apply Portuguese law and virtual arbitrators will be assigned from the Lisbon New University faculty of law.[37] Avatars of the Virtual World would first file a complaint to the e-Justice Centre and request for arbitration, from which the e-Justice Centre would contact the other Avatar asking whether they wish to consent to the commencement of an arbitration proceeding.[38] Once consented, both parties are to pay 1% of the value in dispute to the e-Justice Centre and deposit an escrow of up to 5% of the value of their dispute.[39] Avatars can attempt to mediate their dispute and then arbitrate unresolved issues through a rapid and inexpensive arbitration process.[40] The Avatar Parties

---

35 Nuno Hipólito, 'Portugal's Department of Justice Launches Arbitration Centre in Second Life,' (MultiLingual Search, August 6, 2007) <www.multilingual-search.com/portugals-department-of-justice-launches-arbitration-centre-in-second-life/06/08/2007> accessed December 3, 2013.

36 Nobody Fugazi, 'Arbitration within SecondLife: E-Justice Center' (YOUR2NDPLACE, 6 August 2007) <http://your2ndplace.com/node/352> accessed December 3, 2013.

37 *ibid.*

38 e-Justice Centre, 'e-Justice Centre, ODR in Second Life' (E-Arbitration- T Project Online Dispute Resolution, 28 February 2008) <www.e-arbitration-t.com/2008/02/28/e-justice-centre-odr-in-second-life/> accessed December 3, 2013.

39 *ibid.*

40 *ibid.*

shall attend a hearing at the e-Justice Centre with a panel of one to three Avatar Arbitrators who are to make an arbitral award after the hearing.[41] The question then follows: are Virtual Awards legally enforceable outside Portugal? Although there are still grey areas and uncertainty in relation to the current Virtual Arbitration mechanism, the initial steps in creating the Virtual Arbitration Centre strongly indicate the European's determination, commitment and engagement to further develop arbitration in the Virtual Worlds and it certainly paves the way for establishing further similar virtual arbitration institutions.[42]

5.   The Future of Arbitration in the Virtual World

With over millions of Virtual World avatars, there is a tremendous demand for virtual arbitration institutions. Much more is expected to be done in order to pave a way into a more wholesome and advanced virtual arbitration system. The original idea of the Virtual World was to create an open space for user-driven design and innovation.[43] This is no exception to the innovative path towards a better Virtual Arbitration System. Three aspects will be discussed in this section: (1) The establishment of a set of Virtual Arbitral Rules; (2) Enforcement issues regarding Arbitral Awards; and (3) The possibility of Arbitral Precedent.

---

41   *ibid.*

42   KrisAnn Norby-Jahner, Ken Fox and Jessica Kuchta Miller, 'ADR and the New Frontier: the Future for Virtual Arbitration and Dispute Resolution' (CAPStone Paper, 2010) <http://law.hamline.edu/uploadedFiles/Hamline_Law/Content/Departments/DRI/content/ADR_and_the_New_Frontier.pdf> accessed December 3, 2013

43   Sisse Siggaard Jense, 'Actors and Their Use of Avatars as Personal Mediators: An empirical study of avatar-based sense-makings and communication practices in the virtual worlds of EverQuest and Second Life' (2009) 25(47) *Journal of Media and Communication Research* 29, 30.

5.1   *Virtual Arbitral Rules*

In arbitration, after having selected the seat of arbitration, parties are automatically bound by the lex arbitri (Arbitral laws) of the Seat unless agreed otherwise. The Parties are then to choose an Arbitration Institution for the arbitral proceedings to take place. Common institutions are the International Chamber of Commerce ("ICC"), the London Court of International Arbitration and the Dubai International Arbitration Centre, and they all adopt their own regulatory mechanism throughout the arbitration process.

In the Virtual context, a set of Virtual Institutional Rules should be established so that Avatars in dispute can agree to adopt those Rules in their arbitral proceedings. There are certain fundamental elements which should be considered. First, the Virtual Institution should select an Avatar Secretariat which assists the Virtual Institution to administer the arbitration process. Just like the role played by the ICC Secretariat, the Virtual Institution's relations with the Avatars and the Avatar Arbitrator are to be conducted through the Avatar Secretariat of each Arbitration Centre.[44] Second, the Virtual Institution should adopt procedural rules which would ensure Avatars commence the arbitration proceedings and exchange documents in a just and effective manner. Third, a list of non-exhaustive qualified arbitrators should be provided under the rules for the Avatars to choose according to their wishes. As to the qualification of Avatar Arbitrators, they should at least have acquired eight years of real world or virtual world business or legal experience and have been living in the Virtual World for at least two years. A more specified list of Virtual Arbitrator qualifications should be established in order to guarantee the quality of Virtual Arbitration. Criteria for real-world arbitrators can be used as reference, such as those set

---

44 Erik Schäfer, Herman Verbist and Christophe Imhoos, *ICC Arbitration in Practice* (Kluwer Law International 2005) 19.

out in the American Arbitration Association.[45]

5.2   Enforcement of Arbitral Awards

According to the Federal Arbitration Act of the United States, for instance, Courts have been willing to enforce online arbitral awards, and it is very likely that they would be willing to enforce Virtual Arbitration as long as the arbitration has been by consent by the Parties and was not entered into unconscionably.[46] Avatars would not necessarily have to enter into contracts in order to take part in Virtual Arbitration: as with the arbitration clause which enable Avatars a freedom of choice for online arbitration, similarly Avatars could enter into Virtual Arbitration by consent.

Therefore as long as the arbitration cause has been arrived by the Avatars' consent, that it is not procedurally and substantively unconscionable, and that no Virtual Institutional Rules have been violated, Courts are likely to facilitate the enforcement of Virtual Awards.

5.3   Establishment of a Virtual Database: A Body of Virtual Arbitral Precedents

It is common knowledge that international arbitration lacks the doctrine of precedent.[47] However, whether arbitration should be subject to precedential rule is subject to scholarly debates. In an

---

45 American Arbitration Association, 'Qualification Criteria for Admittance to the AAA National Roster of Arbitrators' <www.adr.org/aaa/ShowPDF?doc=ADRSTG_003878> accessed December 3, 2013.

46 Lucille M. Ponte and Thomas D. Cavanaugh, *Cyberjustice: Online Dispute Resolution (ODR) for E-Commerce* (Prentice Hall 2004) 96–97.

47 Gabrielle Kauffmann-Kohler, 'Arbitral Precedent: Dream, Necessity or Excuse?' The 2006 Freshfields Lecture (2006) 357.

International Arbitration Survey conducted in 2010,[48] respondents were asked whether they considered arbitration should be made confidential even without specific clause to that effect in the arbitration rules adopted or the arbitration agreement: 50% answered in the affirmative and 30% in the negative. According to Professor Gabrielle Kauffmann-Kohler, whether the development of binding rules through arbitral decisions is desirable depends on *necessity*, meaning the need for certainty and predictability, as well as the need for consistency or equal treatment.[49] Such needs clearly exist in area where the law is not yet well developed."[50] It is also to be borne in mind that the credibility of the dispute resolution system depends on consistency, and therefore settlements which give rise to inconsistency and unpredictability of results will lead to users losing confidence, thereby defeating the purpose.[51]

In the context of Virtual World, it is argued that since the laws governing Avatar–Avatar disputes are yet to be developed and matured, the need for certainty and predictability of results is crucial in order to do justice. A Virtual arbitration database should be established under each Virtual Arbitration Institution, in which different categories of awards will be divided. It should be noted that the Virtual Awards shall not be confidential *per se*, as held by Courts in certain jurisdictions such as Australia.[52] If Avatars wish to protect their commercial interest and ensure confidentiality of their rewards, they should do so expressly in

---

48 Queen's Mary College, "2010 International Arbitration Survey: Choices in International Arbitration" <www.arbitrationonline.org/docs/2010_InternationalArbi trationSurveyReport.pdf> accessed December 3, 2013.

49 Gabrielle Kauffmann-Kohler (n 47) 378.

50 *ibid.*

51 *ibid.*

52 *Esso Australia Resources Limited v Plowman* (1995) 183 CLR 10 (Australian High Court).

their agreements. Otherwise, their final awards shall be stored in the Virtual arbitration database.

6. Conclusion

With the ever-increasing population of users in the Virtual World, the demand for Arbitral Institutions follows. This essay has examined the areas left open for the development of a more advanced Virtual Arbitration System. Two proposals have also been considered, namely to create a set of Virtual Arbitral Rules and to create an Arbitral Database for the storage of Arbitral Awards. With innovative yet cautious planning, the Virtual Arbitration System would certainly take a huge leap in the coming centuries.

29

Application of ADR and ODR to the Virtual World: The Quest for Best Practices and Solutions

Camilla VENANZI

1. Introduction

This chapter concerns the topic of ADR and ODR in the virtual and online worlds, an area of growing importance the increasing number of disputes occurring among online and virtual world users in our contemporary society. Section 2 provides a definition of virtual worlds and a brief overview of the reality of *Second Life*. It addresses the question of the importance of virtual disputes in today's society and describes some of the methods employed to address disputes in virtual worlds. Section 3 introduces the processes of alternative dispute resolution (ADR) and online dispute resolution (ODR) and explains their application to disputes both in the physical and in the virtual world. Section 4 focuses on a few ODR mechanisms, analyzes their advantages and shortcomings and concentrates on the efficacy of online mediation. Section 5 suggests other types of ODR that may apply in the context of virtual world as alternatives to the traditional forms of negotiation and mediation. In addition, it analyzes the potential role of the courts in the ODR processes. Finally, this section proposes possible methods to increase the popularity of ADR and ODR in relation to online and virtual disputes.

2.   Virtual Worlds and Definitions

2.1   Definition of Virtual Worlds

Virtual worlds can be defined as software that allow users to create their own digital identities in the form of avatars that act in a three dimensional reality.[1]

They can be divided in two sub-groups, Mass Multiplayer Online Role Playing Games (MMORPG) and Multi User Virtual Environments (MUVEs),[2] the main difference between the two categories being that in the first one players are meant to carry out special and pre-set tasks in order to advance in the game while in the second one participants simply interact with each other as they wish through their personalized avatars.[3]

The most popular virtual worlds nowadays are probably *The Sims Online*, *World of Warcraft* and *Second Life*.

2.2   Second Life

Second Life was designed by Linden Lab in 2003. *Second Life* is a three dimensional virtual reality environment which simulates real world settings, for this reason it may be considered more similar to a MUVE (or no-end game) than to a MMORPG. While in MMORPGs the players' general purpose is to dominate other characters, to achieve specific targets or to engage in a quest,[4] MUVEs aim at connecting players with each other in a normal

---

1 Viktor Mayer-Schnberger and John Crowley, 'Napster's Second Life?: The Regulatory Challenges of Virtual Worlds', (2006) 100 *Nw. U. L. Rev.* 1775, 1781.

2 Dominik Schrank, 'A Trustful Payment System for Virtual Worlds Design and Implementation of a Payment System for Virtual Worlds' (Master's Thesis, Graz University of Technology 2009) 10.

3 *ibid.*

4 'Virtual Online Worlds: Living a Second Life' *The Economist* (September 30, 2006) 77–79.

everyday life fashion, for example by allowing them to meet up or participate in virtual commercial activities.[5]

Second Life possesses its own currency, the Linden Dollar, which allows users to enter into transactions involving virtual property (e.g., clothes, jewelery or real estate)[6] and which is linked to real currency through a foreign exchange.[7] *Second Life* also hosts virtual legal entities such as an International Justice Center (similar to the actual International Criminal Court) and bar associations.[8]

The peculiar forms of regulation of virtual worlds give rise to a series of very interesting socio-legal observations. While most contemporaneous real civilizations have developed quite a sophisticated understanding about social and commercial conflicts and their resolution over the past millennia, newly developed virtual societies have not had the same opportunity.[9] *Second Life*'s society seems to be regulated by a similar social contract as the one conceived by Locke;[10] all avatars are admitted to the *Second Life*'s virtual world without distinctions and without the possibility of not accepting its terms of governance, as avatars necessarily have to agree to Linden Lab's laws in order to enter the game.[11]

---

5 Bettina M. Chin, 'Regulating Your Second Life. Defamation in Virtual World'(2007) 72 *Brook. L. Rev.* 1312.

6 Kenneth James, 'Real Benefits in Virtual Worlds', *Business Times* (Singapore, December 11, 2006).

7 Sivan, Y., '3D3C Real Virtual Worlds Defined: The Immense Potential of Merging 3D, Community, Creation, and Commerce', *Journal of Virtual Worlds Research: Past, Present & Future. USA.* 7 (2008).

8 Andrea M. Seielstad, 'Enhancing the Teaching of Lawyering Skills and Perspectives through Virtual World Engagement' (2011) 12.

9 Claude T. Aiken IV, 'Sources of Law and Modes of Governance: Ethnography and Theory in Second Life Fall' (2009) 10 *Pittsburgh Journal of Technology Law and Policy* 3.

10 *ibid.*

11 *ibid.*

Linden Lab holds the greatest form of power[12] within *Second Life*'s virtual reality, which consists of the ability to forcefully evict non-rule abiding resident avatars from its domain; however, the fact that Linden Lab does not intervene in the majority of the disputes among *Second Life* users[13] may create problems of adjudication of ordinary inter-residents disputes, since the residents' only legitimate form of peer governance consists of isolating fellow users from their community.[14] Despite its limited practical effect, including violators in blacklists may be a useful tool to pressure Linden Lab into submitting disputes to arbitration, mediation or other forms of adjudication.[15]

Interestingly the world of *Second Life* shares great similarities with the pre-legal Homeric concepts of *themis* ("the law of the heavens") and *dike* ("the law of the earth").[16] The administrators of virtual worlds, as Prof. Kerr wrote, "do not merely act like governments in virtual worlds: they act like gods."[17]

The written bodies of law which regulate *Second Life* are the Terms of Service ("TOS") and Community Standards ("CS"). The Community Standards protect users from six wide categories of conduct, namely intolerance, harassment, assault, unreasonable disclosure of communications, indecency, and disturbing the peace.[18]

Where a suspected violation occurs a *Second Life* user can make a report that will be examined by a selected Linden team chosen to carry out investigations on residents' compliance with

---

12 Max Weber, *The Vocation Lectures: Science as a Vocation, Politics as a Vocation* (Hackett Publishing Company 2004) 33.

13 Aiken (n 9) 14.

14 Aiken (n 9) 22.

15 Aiken (n 9) 19.

16 J. M. Kelly, *A Short History of Western Legal Theory* (Clarendon Press 1992) 6–8.

17 Orin S. Kerr, 'Criminal Law in Virtual Worlds', *U. Chi. Legal. F.* 14.

18 Second Life <http://secondlife.com/corporate/cs.php> accessed April 3, 2013.

the rules. If it is found that a violation has in fact occurred, the wrongdoer can be suspended or directly disqualified from the game.[19]

The question of jurisdiction of the courts is a particularly complicated one since the users and residents of *Second Life* come from all over the (real) world[20] and, as the Joint Economic Committee put it, "virtual economies represent an area where technology has outpaced the law."[21]

A very good example of jurisdictional issues can be found in Linden Lab's Terms of Service. While Linden Lab is a California-based company and Section 12.2 of its Terms of Service states that all non-arbitrated disputes should take place in California under California law,[22] in reality and practice, California does not automatically acquire jurisdiction.[23] I will later consider the possibility of creating a global jurisdiction in the specific context of ODR and explain why it fails.

2.3 Are Virtual Disputes Serious?

The debate even seems to extend to whether real laws should apply to virtual platforms with the same stringency as to the real world; those who claim that they should not consider virtual worlds as merely games for recreational purposes not to be taken

---

19 Second Life, 'Terms of Service' <http://secondlife.com/corporate/tos.php?lang=en-US#tos8> accessed December 3, 2013.

20 David Assalone, 'Law in The Virtual World: Should the Surreal World of Online Communities be Brought Back to Earth by Real World Laws? (2009) 16 *Vill. Sports & Ent. L.J.* 163 ,188

21 Press Release, Congress of the U.S., Joint Econ. Comm., n. 109–98, 'Virtual Economies Need Clarification, Not More Taxes' (October 17, 2006).

22 n19.

23 See *Bragg v. Linden Research, Inc.*case.487 F. Supp. 2d 593 (E.D.Penn. 2007).

too seriously,[24] while the majority perceives that some kind of regulation is as necessary in virtual universes as it is in their parallel real world.[25]

Games and virtual spaces may serve much broader purposes than simple entertainment, they may be employed as educational channels, as Tom Hall proved by creating the games *Commander Keen* and *Wolfenstein 3D*,[26] designed to help children with learning disabilities; the same idea has also been borrowed by researchers in the last decade in the attempt to integrate games into school curriculums.[27]

The argument that disputes relating to online gaming cannot be attributed the same importance as real life ones does not adequately take into consideration the value players ascribe to the virtual world they are involved in, in terms of money and time.

Residents of *Second Life* generally spend consistent amounts of real money to build and design their virtual homes just as if they actually inhabited them,[28] which is a fact that clearly indicates the users' desire of recognition of such property as a real one.[29] On these premises it is not surprising that most players actually seek

---

24 Richard Siklos, 'A Virtual World but Real Money' *New York Times* (October 19, 2006); Bettina M. Chin, 'Regulating Your Second Life. Defamation in Virtual Worlds' (2007) 72 *Brook. L. Rev.* 1303, 1310.

25 Mark Wallace, 'The Game Is Virtual. The Profit Is Real.' (NY Times.com, May 29, 2005) <www.nytimes.com/2005/05/29/business/yourmoney/29game.html?pagewanted=print&_r=0> accessed December 3, 2013

26 Charles Malette, ADR Online? An Analysis of Multiplayer Video Games and ADR Processes (2005) 15, Student Scholarship <http://digitalcommons.law.msu.edu/king/65> accessed December 3, 2013.

27 Lucy Ward, 'Computer Games "Can Help Children Learn"'(UK Guardian, 27 October 2004) <http://education.guardian.co.uk/schools/story/0,5500,1336802,00.html> accessed December 3, 2013.

28 F. Gregory Lastowka and Dan Hunter, 'The Laws of the Virtual Worlds' (2004) 92 *Cal. L. Rev.* 1, 73, 6.

29 *ibid.* 49.

some kind of social order in virtual environments, [30] despite their fictitious character. Furthermore, as players develop independent virtual identities in games, being expelled may have serious distressing consequences in a similar way as being ostracized from a community of people in the physical world.[31] The seriousness of the sociological impact of virtual activities in contemporary societies is evident from surveys that indicate that about half the number of users[32] who play online games state that their virtual friends are "equal or better than their real life friends,"[33] while more than 25% of participants perceive the period spent in the virtual world as the "emotional highlight of the week."[34]

2.4 The Evolution of Virtual Games and the Solution of Disputes

As the complexity of the game strategies increases, the communication among the players also has to intensify and as a result the likelihood of conflict escalates as well. To maintain order and ensure that players abide by the above mentioned User Agreements/Terms of Service and Community Standards, virtual worlds appoint "game masters" umpires that perform a similar role as arbitrators in the virtual world.[35]

Although the idea is good *per se*, in practice game masters are employees of the companies overloaded with work that cannot

---

30 Malette (n 26) 21.

31 Malette (n 26) 16.

32 The survey cited that almost 40% of men and 53% of women out of 30,000 individuals report a sociological impact.

33 Alexandra Alter, 'Is This Man Cheating on His Wife?' (*Wall Street Journal*, August 10, 2007) <http://online.wsj.com/news/articles/SB118670164592393622> accessed December 3, 2013.

34 *ibid.*

35 Malette (n 26) 11.

be available to aggrieved players at all times.[36] Furthermore, there is no systematic process to control and ensure the quality of their performances.[37] What makes the game master's role even more difficult is that they often lack objectively assessable evidence of what in fact happened. As a result, it is fair to conclude that the risk of abuse in virtual worlds remain quite high.[38]

In response to the (in)voluntary abuses by game-masters, some virtual players have established groups of vigilantes to ensure that justice is done where the game masters fail. These organizations may eventually evolve into virtual Mafia so that the boundaries between legal and illicit actions become even more blurred.

Given the seriousness attached to virtual property and related disputes by virtual players, it would be in the public interest to apply ADR to the solution and prevention of such conflicts and in terms of perceived justice official ADR providers would be much preferable to vigilantes and mafia organizations. Companies however may resist hiring professional ADR providers because, firstly, they may be expensive to hire on a permanent basis, secondly it may be time consuming for virtual world designers to adapt the game to such system, and finally companies may not want to include the rules of the ADR provider in their standardized user agreements.[39]

3. ADR and ODR

3.1 *Alternative Dispute Resolution—"ADR"*

As mentioned, the use of ADR and ODR in virtual dispute

---

36 *ibid.*
37 *ibid.*
38 Malette (n 26) 12.
39 Malette (n 26) 19.

resolutions will be the focus of this chapter. I will concentrate on dispute resolutions specifically in virtual world where possible, however, due to the novelty of the topic and the lack of a comprehensive academic literature specifically on virtual worlds and ODR[40] I will also refer to dispute resolution of online transactions in general, which includes transactions of real value regarding virtual property as well. Alternative Dispute Resolution (ADR) is so called because it is considered as an alternative or substitution to the traditional court process. The most recognized forms of ADR include arbitration, mediation, and negotiation.[41]

Negotiation involves only the parties with interests at stake in the dispute who attempt to reach a (potentially) mutually beneficial compromise without the help of a neutral facilitator.[42] The main risk of unfairness in negotiation derives from the possibility that the parties may have very different bargaining power (e.g., where a company like Linden Lab confronts an individual user of *Second Life*).

Mediation could be seen as a facilitated negotiation[43] process where a neutral third person assists the parties in reaching a settlement; the main job of the mediator is to paraphrase the language employed by the parties by adding a more cooperative flavor to it and tuning down the often extreme emotions.[44] Mediators are by no means judges or deliberators and they should not give personal opinion on any of the matters at

---

40 Amy J. Schmitz '"Drive-Thru" Arbitration in The Digital Age: Empowering Consumers Through Binding ODR' (2010) 62 *Baylor L. Rev.* 178, 182.

41 Ethan Katsh, Janet Rifkin and Alan Gaitenby, 'E-Commerce, E-Disputes, and E-Dispute Resolution: In the Shadow of "eBay Law"' (2000) 15 *Ohio St. J. Online Dispute Resolution* 705, 707–708.

42 Shelley Ross Saxer, 'Local Autonomy or Regionalism?: Sharing the Benefits and Burdens of Suburban Commercial Development' (1997) 30 *Ind. L. Rev.* 659, 688.

43 Christopher Moore, The Mediation Process (1996)

44 Ethan Katsh, 'Bringing Online Dispute Resolution to Virtual Worlds: Creating Processes Through Code' (2004) 49 *New York Law Review* 271, 282.

issue. Mediation is particularly successful because it aims at re-establishing some level of communication between conflicting parties to enable them to develop their own creative solutions.[45] It is fundamental to the job of the mediator to build trust with both parties[46] so that they will feel able to communicate their true interests in the dispute that may be very different from their positional claims.

In arbitration the parties refer their case to a neutral third person who has the power to make an authoritative and binding judgment on the matter;[47] this is the most formal ADR process. Although the need for dispute resolution and prevention was not a priority at the time MMORPGs were invented, ADR are becoming increasingly relevant as virtual worlds are expanding and posing increasingly complex moral and legal issues.[48]

3.2 Early Attempts to Apply ADR to Online Disputes and the Creation of ODR

In the 90's, virtual worlds were simply constituted by MOOs and MUD, which were elementary text-based systems connecting large number of users at the same time. MOOs and MUDs had no graphics, sound or video, but only instructions directed to the users.[49] Resolving these kinds of disputes did not require

---

45 *ibid.*

46 Richard Salem, 'Trust in Mediation' in Guy Burgess and Heidi Burgess (eds) Beyond Intractability (Conflict Information Consortium, University of Colorado, Boulder) <www.beyondintractability.org/bi-essay/trust-mediation> accessed December 3, 2013.

47 Victoria C. Crawford, 'A Proposal to Use Alternative Dispute Resolution as a Foundation to Build an Independent Global Cyberlaw Jurisdiction Using Business to Consumer Transactions as a Model' (2001–2002) 25 *Hastings Int'l & Comp. L. Rev.* 383, 390.

48 Paul E. Schwanz II, 'Morality in Massively Multi-Player Online Role-Playing Games' <www.mud.co.uk/dvw/moralityinmmorpgs.html> accessed December 3, 2013.

49 Katsh (n 45) 282.

sophisticated communication skills[50] because all the umpire had to do was to deliver its ruling in a short textual form.

Mediation is much harder to exercise in the same way because the role of mediators is to listen to both sides, organize and process the information provided, which was too sophisticated process to be undergone through the available software both at that time[51] and it so is until today.

3.3 *The Virtual Magistrate Project (VMAG)*

The VMAG was created in 1996; it was administered and funded through NCAIR, the Cyberspace Law Institute, the Villanova Center for Information Law and Policy, and the American Arbitration Association[52] and purported to offer parties an arbitration forum for their online disputes. Arbitrators were appointed and trained by the American Arbitration Association and had to decide, on the basis of the online complaint file, whether the alleged infringing activity was reasonable or objectionable conduct and whether the offended party should be entitled to any remedies.[53]

The VMAG program was intended as an online arbitration tool using a combination of e-mail and a listserv;[54] a decision was to be reached within three business days once the initial complaint was received.[55] The VMAG finally proved unsuccessful for three

---

50 *ibid.*

51 *ibid.*

52 Robert C. Bordone, 'Electronic Online Dispute Resolution: A Systems Approach-Potential, Problems, and a Proposal'(1998) 3 *Harv. Negotiation L. Rev.* 175, 187–188.

53 Alejandro E. Almaguer and Roland W. Baggott III, 'Shaping New Legal Frontiers: Dispute Resolution for the Internet' (1998) 13 *Ohio St. J. On Disp. Resol.*, 723.

54 *ibid.* 719.

55 Richard Michael Victorio, 'Internet Dispute Resolution (IDR): Bringing ADR into the 21st Century' (2001)1 Pepp. Disp. Resol. L. J. 279, 283–84.

main reasons: (1) most disputes fell outside its jurisdiction, (2) the project was insufficiently advertised[56] and (3) the VMAG lacked the ability to enforce its decision.[57]

3.4 Online Dispute Resolution—ODR

ODR was originally created in response to conflicts arising in the cyberspace in general, including those in e-commerce platforms, not just for disputes arising within MMPORGs. ODR is basically equivalent to ADR but uses Internet-based resources which allow high-speed communication at long distance.[58] An ODR system is applicable to a vast range of disputes, from those related to e-commerce transactions to those involving domain names.[59] It has also been used in offline conflicts,[60] where and ODR system may be employed to save costs, promote convenience, resolve disputes where there are serious issues of security and safety, or conflicts where there is a potential power imbalance between the parties.[61] Just like ADR, ODR includes arbitration, mediation (facilitative, evaluative, or transformative),[62] negotiation

---

56 Victoria C. Crawford, 'A Proposal to Use Alternative Dispute Resolution as a Foundation to Build an Independent Global Cyberlaw Jurisdiction Using Business to Consumer Transactions as a Model'(2002) 25 *Hastings JNYL & Comp. L. Rev.,* 391-92.

57 Lucille M. Ponte, 'Throwing Bad Money After Bad: Can Online Dispute Resolution (ODR) Really Help Deliver the Goods for the Unhappy Internet Shopper?'(2001) 3 *Tul. J. Tech. & Intell. Prop.* 64.

58 Katsh (n 45) 272.

59 Sarah Rudolph Cole, 'Online Mediation: Where We Have Been, Where We Are Now, and Where We Should Be' (2006) 38 *U. Tol. L. Rev.* 193, 197 (2006).

60 George H. Friedman, 'Alternative Dispute Resolution and Emerging Online Technologies: Challenges and Opportunities' (1997) 19 *Hastings Comm. & Ent. L.J.* 695.

61 Seielstad (n 8) 19.

62 Llewellyn Joseph Gibbons *et al.*, 'Cyber-Mediation: Computer-Mediated Communications Medium Massaging the Message' (2002) 32 *N.M. L. Rev.* 27, 32–35.

techniques and even formal judicial proceedings.[63]

ODR fell into disuse after the dot-com bust and regained popularity after the creation of virtual worlds such as *Second Life*,[64] given the need to address pressing virtual e-commerce disputes primarily within virtual worlds.[65] Because of the increasingly important role that technology plays in our lives it will soon be inevitable to employ web to resolve disputes.[66] Although it may surprise many, ODR is not as popular in the U.S. as it is for example in Kenya, Nigeria and Sri Lanka, where even politically opposed factions have submitted their disputes to ODR.[67]

The United Nations is actively supporting ODR. Recently, sponsored a conference in Liverpool aimed at laying down the protocols of communication in dispute resolution.[68] As the importance of ODR is increasingly recognized at international level, all countries that have resisted their adoption, including the U.S., may finally align to the international practice.[69]

Because of increased privatization,[70] the ODR system appears to have been shaped based on customary practice, similar to the way in which the Law of Merchants developed in the Middle

---

63 Rudolph (n 61).

64 Jason Krause, 'Settling It on the Web: New Technology, Lower Costs Enable Growth of Online Dispute Resolution'(2007) 93 *A.B.A.J.* 42, 43.

65 Brian A. Pappas, 'Online Court: Online Dispute Resolution and the Future of Small Claims'(2008) 12(2) *UCLA Journal of Law & Technology* 1, 16–17.

66 Krause (n 66) 46.

67 Krause (n 66) 43.

68 *ibid.*

69 *ibid.*

70 Ethan Katsh, 'Online Dispute Resolution: Designing New Legal Processes for Cyberspace' (Athens, March 18–20, 2009) in Proceedings of the WebSci'09: Society On-Line.

Ages.[71] The Law of Merchants constituted a body of law restricted to the regulation of mercantile activity and was independent from any national rule.[72] Although the idea of a uniform set of rules for ODR is enticing, this goal may not be achieved globally because national censorships, conflict of laws and differing cultural perceptions between nations (e.g., China and the U.S.)[73] may bar its realization. Even if the basis for such a system were laid down, it would not take long before nations would start proposing competing systems,[74] with the effect of rendering the efforts of unification useless.

4.   Evaluation of ODR

4.1   Advantages of ODR

Perhaps most significantly, ODR is always available irrespective of a mediator's or a judge's time schedule. Thanks to technological means like e-mails, and discussion channels, agreements can be written and changed whenever the parties feel is convenient,[75] in other words, ODR are flexible means of dispute resolution which can adapt to the circumstances of most conflicts. [76]

Asynchronous means (such as e-mails) of communication may be beneficial as they eliminate the pressure of providing an

---

71 David R. Johnson and David Post, 'Law and Borders-The Rise of Law in Cyberspace' (1996) 48 *Stan. L. Riv.* 1367, 1389–90.

72 *ibid.*

73 Jennifer Sackin, 'Online Dispute Resolution with China: Advantageous, But at What Cost?' (2010–2011) 12 *Cardozo J. Conflict Resol.* 245, 274.

74 Lan Q. Hang, 'Online Dispute Resolution Systems: The Future of Cyberspace Law' (2001) 41 *Santa Clara L. Rev.* 837, 865.

75 Krause (n 66) 43.

76 Anita Ramasastry, 'Government-To-Citizen Online Dispute Resolution: A Preliminary Inquiry' (2004) 79 *Wash. L. Rev.* 159, 173.

immediate response, leaving the parties free to consider offers and to reflect on their replies. Communicating through synchronous means may on the other hand increase the spontaneity[77] of the parties' behavior.

ODR programs are meant to be accessible[78] even to the least sophisticated users of virtual worlds, as it only needs an Internet connection, which they would already be able to rely on as residents of virtual world. This kind of dispute resolution is also fast and convenient for most non virtual world users in developed societies in a way that it saves legal costs and travelling expenses to reach courts or ADR locations.

The most probable reason why ODR has not yet become a substantive factor in off-line disputes is that the public and the lawyers in particular may not be familiar with their existence or mechanisms; legal practitioner have slowly grown used to ADR processes and given their notorious resistance to technological change[79] they may need longer time than the general public to accept new technological tools as part of their practice. Another possibility is that lawyers who are aware of the availability of ODR may refuse to use them as they may fear that by encouraging the public to access alternative channels of dispute resolution to the courts the exclusivity of their profession[80] may be weakened.

4.2 Criticisms of ODR

ODR may actually be more expensive than other face-to-face

---

77 National Alternative Dispute Resolution Advisory Council, 'Dispute Resolution and Information Technology; Principles for Good Practice (Draft)' (March 2002), 10.

78 Ramasastry (n 78).

79 Robert J. Howe, 'The Impact of the Internet on the Practice of Law: Death Spiral or Never-Ending Work?' (2013) 8 *Va. J.L.& Tech.* 5, 13.

80 *ibid* 20.

dispute resolution methods, despite the widespread belief that they are convenient, depending on the level of security of the service and the costs of hiring an IT staff where required.[81] Despite the potential veracity of such argument, ODR still remains the only option open to most of the virtual disputants as they often reside in different jurisdictions and it would not be possible to conduct a traditional face-to-face ADR in such circumstances. Thomas Schultz explains that in order to increase the credibility of ODR it will be necessary to create "an architecture of confidence" consisting of recognized features and a transparent predictable process[82] that could bring legitimacy to ODR by proving the reliability and quality of the system.

The most common and serious criticism of ODR is that online processes cannot achieve an equivalent effect as face-to-face interactions with the mediator, which are often considered fundamental for mediators to read the body language of the parties and get immediate feedback from them through separate sessions in the attempt of building a less hostile environment. This problem can be partly solved through the employment of web cameras and services like Skype and LiveOffice which are currently very cheap,[83] although the risk of occasional lagging may, for example, convey misperceptions of hesitance.[84]

The added value of ODR will be evident once new online tools will be available to process data rather than just to transmit it.[85] These changes are likely to be firstly introduced in virtual worlds, because of their inherently lower resistance to technological

---

81 Krause (n 66).

82 Thomas Schultz, 'Does Online Dispute Resolution Need Governmental Intervention? The Case for Architectures of Control and Trust' (2004) 6 *N.C. J.L. & Tech.* 79.

83 Krause (n 66) 44.

84 Principles for Good Practice (n 79).

85 Katsh (n 45) 285.

change than in the physical world[86]: as virtual environments already host avatars the use of a "fourth party" as a mediation facilitator would be easily accepted, while it could be perceived as unnatural and inappropriate in the real world. It is also foreseeable that the "fourth party" avatar will become more and more discerning over time so to be able to interact with a large number of human beings in complex multi-party disputes once the software will become sufficiently powerful;[87] this way ODR will provide a combination of human expertise and machine efficiency.[88]

The use of ODR by government agencies would also likely lead to an increasing popularity and perceived legitimacy of the system, while users may, at the same, take the chance to create new dispute resolution applications and tools themselves.[89] Professor Ethan Katsh, Director of the Center for Information Technology and Dispute Resolution at the University of Massachusetts, is confident that such "fourth party" technology is the key to the success of ODR.[90] Although it is predictable that the usage of more sophisticated tools will lead to an expansion of ODRs, no material steps have been taken to acquaint the public with the system.[91] In order to build social trust it seems necessary for providers to display "regular, honest, and cooperative behavior"[92] with the disputants.

At a basic level trust may be built by requiring the ADR provider to ensure that all communication, written and oral,

86 *ibid.*

87 *ibid.*

88 *ibid.*

89 Katsh (n 45) 286.

90 Ethan Katsh and Leah Wing, 'Ten Years of Online Dispute Resolution (ODR): Looking at the Past and Constructing the Future' (2006) 38 *U. Tol. L. Rev.* 19, 21.

91 *ibid* 27.

92 Schultz (n 84) 79.

should deliver unambiguous and concise messages. In terms of social context and reputation ODR providers must disclose their areas of expertise so that customers can make informed choices as to which service fits their needs the best;[93] to this end, marks indicating customer satisfaction and dissatisfaction with services provided should also be shown, as it is already done by eBay.[94]

Square Trade has readily understood the need to increase consumers' trust by proving the reliability of its service and has accordingly adopted ethical guidelines for conflict management modelled on those of the Society for Professionals in Dispute Resolution.[95]

Following is a list of the core abilities of a mediator as laid down by Professor Ethan Katsh in his previously cited paper "Bringing Online Dispute Resolution To Virtual Worlds: Creating Processes Through Code" (pp. 17–19). Let us see whether and to what extent they can be mimicked by a "fourth party" avatar in the ODR of virtual disputes according to Professor Katsh.

1. Computational Ability—this is in substance the capacity to administer a flow of information. A classic example of it is the process of "blind bidding" particularly used in negotiations regarding money or quantifiable elements. Although the skill to make the parties reach an agreement while maintaining confidentiality would be highly valued in a human mediator, this ability is not as impressive in a computerized system.

2. Building Trust—software can partially achieve this goal by guaranteeing to the parties that

---

93 *ibid* 83–84.

94 eBay, 'How it works' <http://pages.ebay.com/help/feedback/howitworks.html> accessed April 3, 2013.

95 Rudolph (n 61) 209.

communications will be kept confidential through online monitoring of the security of messages.

3. Identifying Interests—this is the core purpose of a mediator,[96] in which the mediator should help the parties identify their interests while abandoning claims that are too positional and that would bring no real benefit to either side. Unfortunately there still is no software that can duplicate this specific function of mediators, so, to this extent, human mediators are still necessary.

4. Ascertaining Facts—a software application performing systematic record keeping of virtual activities may, in most cases, efficiently substitute the mediator's job of examining parties' expression and behaviors to assess their honesty.

5. Designing Solutions—given the non-physical nature of virtual worlds, the remedies offered through technology may be more drastic and creative than those in real life, for example it may be possible for virtual users bothered by certain objects to render the source of discomfort literally invisible to them in the virtual environment. An open ended list of such solutions may be stored in the database of ODR providers.

6. Monitoring Agreements—the essential scope of contracts is to give rights and impose obligations and penalties to non-complying parties; electronic notifications (such as "red flags") of non-compliance or deadlines will be much more effective than just the written agreements[97] and will offer an all-rounded monitoring service.

---

96 See Roger Fisher and William Ury, *Getting to Yes: Negotiating Agreement Without Giving In* (New York: Penguin Books, 1983).

97 M. Ethan Katsh, *Law in A Digital World* (Oxford University Press 1995).

7. Building on Experience—data collection not only makes it possible to obtain feedback on the ODR service from users who have been involved in disputes, but it may also help for example game designers to understand why disputes occur and consider ways to prevent them in the future.

5.   Other ODR mechanisms, the Role of the Courts and Suggested Improvements to Current ODR Systems

5.1   *Other Methods of ODR that may Apply in the Context of Virtual Worlds*

One well-known form of online dispute resolution is the use of Square Trade. SquareTrade.com has become one of the main dispute resolution providers in the world after it was chosen as eBay's dispute resolution provider in 1999.

Before employing a human mediator SquareTrade offers a technologically supported negotiation process that happens on the Web, and not simply by emails, as experience has shown that most of the people who resort to SquareTrade have already gone through unsuccessful attempts to negotiate through electronic post.[98]

SquareTrade has developed forms to be filled in by the parties that clarify and highlight both the type of issue arising and the potentially available solutions.[99] This has proved to be an extremely efficient process because by allowing the parties only a limited space to expose their own complaints, the communication is much less positional as the level of hostility between the parties

---

98   Katsh (n 45).

99   *ibid.*

is noticeably reduced.[100] Negotiation in SquareTrade is done through a virtual presence. Because of the lack of algorithms that can analyze responses, this process cannot be considered equivalent to mediation yet. In cases where the negotiation fails, SquareTrade finally provides a human mediator that will facilitate the communication through a web interface.[101]

A second form of online dispute resolution is Cybersettle. This service uses the process of blind bid negotiations to settle disputes: the parties submit three online confidential settlement bids through e-mail, which the software automatically compares and ranks to determine if the parties have arrived at a settlement. The amount of the bids is never disclosed.[102]

Both SquareTrade and Cybersettle may theoretically apply to disputes in virtual worlds: while SquareTrade may be employed in any kind of conflict ranging from virtual property to breaches of contracts between avatars, Cybersettle can only be used in disputes regarding quantities identifiable numerically, such as the value of a virtual car in a contract for sale.

Arbitration and negotiation are not the only tools to resolve disputes in virtual worlds. There are an increasing number of non-profit organizations and grassroots movements that utilizes virtual worlds to promote ideas through powerful advocacy; these attempts represent valuable brainstorming and problem solving activities that may propose solutions to disputes while avoiding the processes of mediation and arbitration.[103]

---

100 *ibid.*

101 *ibid.*

102 Cybersettle, 'About Us' <www.cybersettle.com/about-us> accessed 3 April 2013.

103 'Virtual world offers new locale for problem solving' (Penn State News.com, September 29, 2008) <http://news.psu.edu/story/183262/2008/09/29/virtual-world-offers-new-locale-problem-solving> accessed April 3, 2013.

5.2 The Courts as the "Fifth Party"

There would be several advantages in tying an ODR process to an online court system. Firstly, courts would provide legitimacy to the ODR process because they represent a more traditional transparent and authoritative form of adjudication which can also create establish binding precedents.[104] In a court system, the remedies are predictable and decisions are appealable and enforceable.[105] Courts may give a better impression of independence and impartiality from business interests because governments that administer them, in general, have no stake in the outcome of most of the matters in dispute.[106]

Courts are also perceived as having superior effectiveness as they are able to ensure parties' compliance with ADR/ODR outcomes[107] and as they have a longer experience than ADR/ODR in dealing with issues of due process they can guarantee a higher standard of fairness and integrity.[108] Lawyers may readily accept a Court + ODR system rather than simply an ODR mechanism.

Despite these favorable elements, I believe it is preferable to not to include the courts as the fifth party to dispute resolutions until all other means have proved ineffective. The reasons for this are that, firstly, the courts would render the subject matters of disputes public[109] by denying the parties the right of confidentiality and secondly, court proceedings, even online, will remain rather slow and expensive so that the legal fees may eventually be higher than the amount which can be retrieved from a successful medium-small claim.

---

104 Schultz (n 84) 85.

105 *ibid.* 103–104.

106 *ibid.* 89–90.

107 Ramasastry (n 78) 173.

108 *ibid.*

109 *ibid.* 168.

Finally, the same old question of jurisdiction arises: despite their online characteristics, courts are administered by national governments, so who will determine which jurisdiction would prevail in an international online dispute in the absence of an independent international code of law? I would conclude that if an online court system is introduced, it can only operate in the context of domestic disputes.

5.3   Factors That May Facilitate the Use of ODR in Virtual World Disputes

The following factors, if included in an online dispute resolution system, may help establish an effective dispute resolution system for virtual world disputes:

(1) Increased Accessibility—ODR service providers should cooperate with local community facilities to provide technological infrastructures to disputants who lack them.[110] ODR service providers should also ensure they employ means with an accessible bandwidth and software, so that even the less privileged can use the service. In addition to this, service provider should also follow the guidelines to grant accessibility to disabled user.'[111] Costs should be kept as low as possible.[112]

(2) Building Trust/Clarity of Terms and Conditions[113]—Virtual World developers and other websites designers should specify the methods of dispute resolution available in case of an online dispute.[114] ODR service providers could collaborate

---

110 Principles of Good Practice (n 79) 8.

111 *ibid.*

112 Ponte (n 58) 89.

113 Aashit Shah, 'Using ADR To Resolve Online Disputes' (2003-2004) 10 *Rich J.L. & Tech.*1, 11.

114 *ibid.*

with relevant agencies and network groups to encourage consumers' and practitioners' trust in technology.[115] On-line service providers should undergo quality accreditation processes to enhance consumers' confidence in the reliability of the service.[116] One way to achieve this is for online service providers to display a Trustmark or a webseal by an accredited organization which proves that the e-business complies with widely recognized qualitative standards.[117]

(3) Enforcement of Online ADR Decisions[118]—this could be achieved by making the parties sign the agreements they may reach under ADR/ODR so that, in case of non-compliance, the aggrieved party can sue in court for breach of contract.[119] Another alternative is to have the court endorse the agreement.

(4) Promotion of public awareness of ODR[120]—adequate marketing is necessary so that experiences like the failure of the VMAG will not be repeated. This can best be accomplished through increased and sustained public awareness campaigns designed to educate users on the benefits of ODR.

(5) Adoption of Model Rules and Best Practices[121]—The American Bar Association Task Force on E-commerce

---

115 Principles of Good Practice (n 79) 7.

116 *ibid.* 8.

117 American Bar Association Task Force on E-Commerce and Alternative Dispute Resolution, Addressing Disputes in Electronic Commerce: Final Report and Recommendations of the American Bar Association Task Force on E-Commerce and Alternative Dispute Resolution (August 2002) at 19.

118 Shah (n 115) 12.

119 *ibid.*

120 Robert C. Bordone, 'Electronic Online Dispute Resolution: A Systems Approach Potential, Problems, and a Proposal' (1998) 3 *Harv. Negot. L. Rev.* 175, 196–197.

121 Shah (n 115) 13.

and ADR has laid down Recommended Best Practices that highlight the importance of impartiality and suggest that the ODR provider must disclose any contractual relationships that it may have with online businesses.[122] Confidentiality, privacy, and information security should be treated with the utmost importance.[123] Model Rules would similarly cover the procedures to file complaints, time limits, remedies, confidentiality, guarantees of independence of third party and his/her power, whether the decision is binding, the jurisdiction where the award is enforceable, treatment of delays and allotment of costs.

6. Conclusion

To date, the negotiation and arbitration processes relating to online and virtual disputes may be carried out through a fourth party avatar. However, the same is not true for mediation, where the face-to-face element cannot be replaced by software technology just yet.

ADR, and especially ODR, have enormous potential to become the major forms of resolving disputes arising in the virtual and online world because of their flexibility, low costs, and high accessibility as compared with a traditional court-based system.

However, in order to ensure successful development and deployment of such online dispute resolution systems, it will be necessary to build broader public trust in the use of ADR and ODR through advertising and compliance with best practice rules of implementation and use.

---

122 American Bar Association Task Force (n 119).
123 American Bar Association Task Force (n 119).

Once the public's confidence in the quality of the process is firmly established, legal professionals may also more actively suggest and engage in ODR in various kinds of dispute, thus paving the way for a future in which ODR may eventually become an integral part of the legal system in contemporary societies.